THE FIRST 100 DAYS

45TH PRESIDENT OF THE UNITED STATES OF AMERICA DONALD TRUMP

PART 2

Chronicled *by*
D Francis
and
Daniel Francis

ISBN-13: 978-0992854843 (DF Books Limited)
ISBN-10: 0992854849

DF Books Limited
www.13june2005.com

Purpose

The purpose of this book is to document the historic speeches of the 45th President of the United States of America, Donald Trump.

A selection of the Official Speeches and Remarks of President Trump, Vice President Pence and The First Lady are presented in two books.

Limited to the first one-hundred days of the Trump Presidency; from Inauguration Day on 20 January 2017 to 29 April 2017.

Chapters 1- 85 are housed in Part 1, and in this book - chapters 86 -170.

Due to print restrictions the entire selection of speeches and remarks could not be housed in one single book.

Disclaimer:
The transcripts might not be verbatim.

Some of these speeches, remarks or information have been sourced directly from the White House or US Government websites; and thus represent their transcription of the speeches and remarks made, or represent the speeches as written for delivery or their understanding.

The transcriptions might not be perfect and are subject to human error.

Some key words and phrases have been highlighted by the compliers.

English-American spelling, direct from White House press releases, errors included.

The version presented might not be the latest version or update, as posted on third party websites. The compilers are not responsible for the contents of third party websites. Such websites might not exist at the time and date of your receipt or reading of this book, or the contents might have changed. There is no warranty in respect of such websites.

A few speeches and remarks are no longer visible on the White House website. No explanation has been provided as to why a particular post has been removed.

Other speeches and remarks have been transcribed direct from internet footage, such as YouTube etc.

The compilers are not professional transcribers. Some allowance should be given for transcription difficulties due to the audio quality of the video posts, presentation by the speaker, inaudibility of the speaker, venue, human error, and mishearing.

There is no intention to misrepresent a speaker, and any and all suggestions otherwise will be denied and defended.

The comments, sentiments, opinions and allegations mentioned by the speakers are solely theirs.

The production of this book should not be construed as the views and opinions of the compliers.

The First 100 Days Part 1 and Part 2, have been produced for the purposes of education.

TABLE OF CONTENTS

Chapter 86

15 March 2017

8:20 P.M. EDT

THE VICE PRESIDENT: Thank you so much.

Taoiseach, Fionnuola, Ambassador Anne Anderson, John Fitzpatrick, Kieran, Senator Mitchell, members of Congress, and distinguished guests, it is hard to describe what a privilege it is for me and my family to join you here tonight for the American Ireland Fund's 25th Silver Anniversary National Gala. Thank you for having us tonight. (Applause.)

I bring greetings tonight from my friend, the leader of the free world, the 45th President of the United States, and to the Taoiseach I would say, as he'll find out, a guy who likes to play golf in Ireland, President Donald Trump. (Applause.)

The President asked me to give everyone his greetings and his best wishes tonight. And also our hope is that my presence here tonight is a visible sign of America's enduring friendship with Ireland and all her people.

You know, I actually received the invitation to be here tonight nearly two months before the President and I were sworn in for these offices of ours. It was one of the very first invitations I received after the election, and I'm humbled to say, it was the first one that I accepted. And I'm honored and privileged to be here tonight. (Applause.)

Tonight is really a family affair. It's been said before from this podium this evening. I can tell you it feels that way to our family, and it's a joy for me tonight to be joined by my wife of 31 years and our new Second Lady, Karen Pence. (Applause.)

Karen and I are also delighted to be joined tonight by our Irish daughter Charlotte Rose. (Applause.)

And my Irish sisters, Annie and Mary, traveled from far across the country to be with us tonight. And if there weren't all these inches of snow, Mr. Taoiseach, I can assure my mother, 83 years young, red hair, crystal blue eyes, would still be here. But I know she's smiling. (Applause.)

This really does feel more like a homecoming for us, too, to be honest with you. And I'll talk about that on a personal level a little bit later.

It is my privilege to be here tonight on behalf of the President of the United States to address the American Ireland Fund. Since its founding in 1976, the fund and its sister organizations have raised a remarkable $550 million dollars to support peace, prosperity, and cultural accomplishment on the Emerald Isle. That's a staggering amount of generosity, as we've already heard before. Ireland, and all who call it home, have benefited tremendously from the generosity of you who are gathered here tonight and all who have gone before.

And that's worth dwelling on. There's a reason why so many in this room -- and in this country -- have been so generous towards Ireland. We may be separated by an ocean, but the American people have always been bound by a kinship to the Irish people, and we always will. (Applause.)

The bond between the people of America and the people of Ireland stretches back into the mists of American history. Drawn by the **promise of this brave new world, the sons and daughters of Ireland began leaving their land for ours as far back as the 17th century**. They came here, one by one, or sometimes in small bands. But what they lacked in numbers, we already heard tonight, they more than made up in courage.

Irish immigrants and their descendants became proud patriots in America. Thousands fought for their adopted homeland -- and the timeless ideals we hold dear -- in our Revolutionary War. No fewer than nine, as you've already heard, signers of the Declaration of Independence, no fewer than four of the Founding Fathers at our Constitutional Convention could trace their roots to Ireland. And no less a man than George Washington himself, our First President, referred to Ireland as a "friend of my country." And so it will always be. (Applause.)

From the Revolutionary War to the Irish Brigades in our Civil War, Irish Americans have fought for **freedom** in every American conflict. And before I go one step further, would the men and women who are with us here tonight who have worn the uniform of the United States of America, please stand and give us the opportunity to thank you one more time for your service to this country? You make us proud. (Applause.)

But Ireland's contributions to America didn't end with the establishment of the shining city on a hill. Indeed, none saw that beacon more clearly, or with more excitement, than the Irish across the sea. Whereas once they had come to America slowly, in a trickle, suddenly the children of Ireland came here in a swell as history records.

They spread to every corner of this continent, settling in cities and towns, in places where none had settled before. And wherever they went, opportunity and prosperity soon followed. From the vantage point of the present, it's clear that the Irish have left an indelible mark on the history of this country for the betterment of the American people and the betterment of the world.

Our history books are filled with the names of Irish immigrants and their descendants. More than 32 million Americans can trace their heritage back to Ireland, a reminder that the Irish are one of the strongest and most vibrant threads of our national fabric.

And tonight, it's an honor to be here on behalf of President Trump to reaffirm the United States' enduring commitment to the Republic of Ireland and Northern Ireland, to the peace process, and above all else, to the timeless and enduring friendship between our people and yours. (Applause.)

Tonight, I'd like to express our friendship by letting you know that Americans of all backgrounds have been heartened to see Ireland's extraordinary accomplishments in recent years. The story of the Irish everywhere is one of facing hardship and emerging stronger for it, and there's perhaps no better recent example than Ireland's remarkable economic success story over the past decade.

It's amazing to think of Ireland's recovery after the global financial crisis. It was the first country to exit the IMF's Eurozone economic assistance program. And for the last two years, Ireland has been one of the fastest growing economies in the European Union. (Applause.)

I firmly believe one of the key reasons for this is the drive, the determination, the character, and the ingenuity of the Irish people wherever they may live. Taoiseach, Ireland's success is testament I can say on behalf of everyone here to your strong leadership these past six years. And many leaders around the world would surely do well to emulate your example in Ireland. (Applause.)

Another sign of our friendship with Ireland is America's robust economic partnership with you. We host many innovative and successful Irish companies here in the United States, and in 2015 I'm pleased to see that Irish direct investment in America totaled $13.5 billion, creating many good-paying American jobs.

Tonight I'm proud to say with great confidence that our bond is strong, and it will grow stronger still. (Applause.)

But I'm not just here to discuss the Republic of Ireland. On behalf of President Trump, I'd also like to congratulate the people of Northern Ireland on their election only two weeks ago, which had one of the highest turnouts in recent memory.

The advance of peace and prosperity in Northern Ireland is one of the great success stories of the past 20 years. Many in this room, and the Ireland Funds across the world, have played a leading role in fostering this progress. Senator Mitchell, you have been properly paid tribute tonight. Let me thank you personally. It's an honor to be with you tonight. I'm proud to be an American, the nation that you call home. And I'm proud of what Senator Mitchell and all of you have done to advance the peace and the prosperity of people all across the island. (Applause.)

And we thank those unsung heroes in Ireland and Northern Ireland who day-in and day-out, do the difficult and important work of strengthening communities, educating children, building that brighter future for Emerald Isle and all who call it home. Their heroic actions bring to mind someone else, a proud son of Ireland, a proud servant of America -- Thomas Francis Meagher.

On this side of the Atlantic, we remember Meagher for his bravery in our Civil War. He led the Irish Brigade I mentioned just a few moments ago, and he ultimately rose to the rank of brigadier general. He was originally from Ireland. In 1848, he famously designed the Irish tricolor that flies over the republic to this very day.

Upon presenting his design, he spoke words that resonate even today, and I quote: "The white in the center signifies a lasting truce between the orange and the green -- and I trust that beneath its folds, the hands of the Irish Protestant and the Irish Catholic may be clasped in generous and heroic brotherhood."

Tonight, let's all pray that those hands of brotherhood may never separate. (Applause.)

Let's also pray to strengthen the hands of friendship that reach across the Atlantic, between the people of Ireland and Northern Ireland and the people of United States. This bond was forged by our forebears, and it endures to

this day, and it's bequeathed to us to strengthen it.
Whether they left their homeland for another, or stayed
in the country of their birth, they shared a heritage -- and
more than that, they shared hope for a brighter future,
and they strived to find it with all their might.

So many millions of them found it here on these shores.
And we're proud that they call America home. The story of
the Irish in America is the story of America itself. And as I
close, let me just say it's hard for me to express the pride
that I feel on night like tonight because my little family is a
small part of that story, the story of Ireland and America.
Like so many of my fellow countrymen, I literally carry
Ireland with me everywhere I go. On one of my first trips
to Ireland when I was a young man, I was sitting -- what did
you call it? -- in a public house. (Laughter.)

Pat Morrissey's Pub -- it's still open in Doonbeg to this day.
Pat was around back then, and he let me help out behind
the bar. I'll never forget the little old lady who spoke to
me. And I told her very quickly that I was related to the
Morrissey's, distant cousins. And I said, actually I'm Irish
by heritage. And she looked at me and smile and said, you
don't have to tell me, son, you've got a face like the map of
Ireland. (Laughter.)

It does all go back to that day. It was Inauguration Day just
a few short weeks ago. People ask me what I was thinking
about surrounded by my wife and my children, our beautiful new daughter-in-law. My mother was just there, a few
seats behind the President. I just kept thinking of that day
in April in 1923. That was the day when Richard Michael
Cawley stepped off the boat on Ellis Island. He was in
his early 20s when he steamed into Upper New York Bay
aboard the Andania, the ship that carried him here.

I can't imagine what the sight of the Statue of Liberty meant to him that day, holding aloft the **torch of freedom**. My grandfather went home to be with the Lord when it was in about my 26th year. But we were very close. He said I was the only Irishman born among the four boys in our family. (Laughter.)

Not sure yet what that meant. But I was flattered by it. My grandpa had grown up in a little town called Tobercur-ry, in County Sligo. When I was young man I had a chance to visit that house before they tore it down. It was just a two-room house where his eight brothers and sisters grew up. And I literally walked up the hill that -- when Karen and I and the kids visited Ireland just a few years ago, we walked up that hill, as well. The legend in our family was my great grandmother had stood outside that little house and looked over at the Ox Mountains and looked off to the west, and told him that he needed to go because she said, there's a future there for you.

He wouldn't speak to his mother for 25 years. And when he said the old country, he said with a reverence that I could never adequately express. He talked about crossing the pond, talked about the heartbreak of that separation. But as I stood on that inaugural stage, I just kept think-ing of that Irishman. I kept thinking of what he would be thinking about looking down from glory. And I know two things for sure.

Number one, knowing me as well as he did, he would be extremely surprised. (Laughter.)

Number two, I have to think he just thought he was right. He was right about America. He was right to summon the courage as generations did before and since to come here and follow **their dreams**, and make the contributions that they did. He was right to drive that bus for 40 years in Chicago. He was right to raise that irascible redhead that would marry a fast-talking salesman and follow work down to a little, small farm town in southern Indiana and raise six kids with the same heritage and the same values that she had been raised with.

The truth is that whatever honors I will receive over the course of my service as Vice President, and to receive an honor in the name of the Irish people and my Irish heritage will count as chief among them. **Because all that I am and all that I will ever be and all the service that I will ever render is owing to my Irish heritage.** And I will summon what is the best of it as I serve the people of this country with the faith, with the determination, with the cheerfulness, the humility, and the humor that is characteristic of the great people of the Emerald Isle.

So here's to Ireland. Here's to the United States of America. Here's to our shared heritage, and here's to **the confident, confident hope** that the ties between our people and the Irish people will only grow and expand as the years go on to the betterment of our people and the world.

Thank you very much for this honor tonight. And God bless you all. (Applause.)

END
8:36 P.M. EDT

Chapter 87

**REMARKS BY PRESIDENT TRUMP AND
TAOISEACH ENDA KENNY OF IRELAND AT
FRIENDS OF IRELAND LUNCHEON
U.S. CAPITOL
WASHINGTON, D.C.**

16 March 2017

12:12 P.M. EDT

THE PRESIDENT: Thank you very much, Speaker Ryan, for that wonderful toast -- although I've heard better jokes. (Laughter.)

And thank you to all of our friends and distinguished members of Congress for joining us here today -- a great honor. And a really great honor to be with you, Vice President Pence. You have been terrific. (Applause.)

And all of our friends welcoming Taoiseach. That's my new friend; he's my new friend. Great guy. (Applause.)

And, Fionnuala, you know, you are something very special. We sat, we talked, and I think we're friends now too, right? And it's really an honor. Thank you. Thank you. (Applause.)

Thanks, Fionnuala. Appreciate it.

Also, the delegation members -- very, very special. Spent some time together, and we're going to have a very, very great long-term relationship, as we would with Ireland anyway. But this is a very special group, so I very much appreciate it.

We're here today to celebrate America's commitment to Ireland and the tremendous contributions -- and I know it well -- the Irish immigrants and their descendants have made right here in the United States and throughout the world. The very first St. Patrick's Day Parade -- I spent a lot of time at St. Patrick's Day Parades over the years, I will tell you that - was held in my hometown, New York City, on March 17th, 1762. With each subsequent year, the Irish people marched, passed another accomplishment, and celebrated another very hard-earned success. And they have had tremendous success all over the world, but in this country they have had tremendous success.

Over the years, they marched past the beautiful St. Patrick's Cathedral, now an immortal monument to the faith of Irish Catholics in America. **They celebrated their shared success in American society with the election of John F. Kennedy.** (Applause.)

They fought for America in war and combat. And their battlefield courage has earned admiration and acclaim throughout the world. They have **great courage**.

The **proud tradition** that started in 1762 has flourished and is now celebrated by Americans of all faiths and backgrounds all across our very beautiful and very special land. As we stand together with our Irish friends, I'm reminded of that proverb -- and this is a good one, this is one I like; I've heard it for many, many years and I love it -- "Always remember to forget the friends that proved untrue. But never forget to remember those that have stuck by you." We know that, politically speaking. A lot of us know that, we know it well. (Applause.)

It's a great phrase.

The people of Ireland and the people of the United States have stuck together through good times and bad times. Over many centuries we have built a bond that thrives, inspires and endures. And with us, it's going to be closer than ever before, I can tell you that. (Applause.)

So as we celebrate our shared history and our enduring friendship, let us commit ourselves to working together, as we will, to build on that bond for the benefit of our citizens for many more generations to come.

Thank you. God bless you. And may God always bless our deep and lasting friendship and relationship. We love Ireland and we love the people of Ireland. Thank you very much for being here. (Applause.)

SPEAKER RYAN: Thank you so much, Mr. President. It is now my pleasure to introduce An Taoiseach, our friend, Enda Kenny. (Applause.)

TAOISEACH KENNY: Thank you very much. Thank you. (Applause.)

Thank you.

Mr. Speaker, Mr. President, Mr. Vice President, members of Congress, ambassadors, friends of Ireland, distinguished guests.

(Speaks in Irish.)*

I didn't say anything disparaging about you there. (Laughter.)

What I said was, it's a pleasure for me to be here, along with my wife, Fionnuala, to be amongst this august gathering. And on behalf of the government of Ireland and the people of Ireland, I wish you all a very happy St. Patrick's festival for you all.

They say the Irish have the capacity to change everything. I just saw the President of the United States read from his script, entirely. (Laughter and applause.)

I was going to say "a change is coming." (Laughter.)

Paul, it's a pleasure. And thank you for your visit to Ireland when you called to see me in government buildings with your family and on your visit down to Kilkenny. When I had the privilege of speaking to the President on the telephone very shortly after his election, I said to him if it would be possible to continue this tradition, which began so many years ago, and he said, without hesitation, of course -- followed by the Vice President and U.S. Speaker.

This is a unique occasion for Ireland and for its people. To have the facility of being honored by the Speaker of the House, the access to the President of the United States, the Vice President, and most of the team is something that we really do cherish. It goes back a very long way from when Tip O'Neill and Ronald Reagan and all of the others put this together in the first place. So it's a really important day for us, and we're very grateful to stand between these two flags, united in history and so much.

I haven't had the opportunity to present you with a par-

ticular piece of sculpture which is entitled "Arrival," by
John Behan. It's a miniature -- but it's quite large -- of
what stands at the United Nations in New York of the tale
and the story and the history of Irish immigrants after the
famine years.

So let me congratulate you, President Trump, on your election. You beat them all. (Laughter and applause.)

Whatever they say, elections are tough-going. I know, I've
been through 20 of them myself. (Laughter.)

But the President and the Vice President and this administration now holds within its hands the responsibility of
dealing with so many global international issues in a world
that is changing so rapidly and that is so fragile in so many
respects. And I know that you will do your utmost to work
in the interests of our common humanity, and you will
have the prayers and the support of the Irish people. And
let me say to you, and the European Union -- and the work
that you have to do in the times -- in the challenging times
ahead.

We discussed the kind of driver that the President uses
-- Titleist, 9-degree loft, Doonbeg, wind off the Atlantic. You have to roll the wrist at the top to get that shot
straight. And during the course of this presidency,
President Trump will visit Ireland, and he said he would put
the sticks in the hold of Air Force One.

Anyway, let me just say a few words here about our country. We've come through a torrid time a number of years
ago. When I took over the government back in 2011, we
were blocked out of all the markets, the Troika were in
town, our sovereignty was gone, our hope was gone; hem-

orrhage of immigration, and a falloff in all business right across every sector.

Now, because of the sacrifices of the people and tough choices made, we're in a different spot. Unemployment, which was 15.2, is now down to 6.6 percent and falling. Employment is the highest in 10 years. A growth rate of 5.2 percent last year. Fourth year running. Ireland is the fastest-growing country in Europe. Deficit eliminated next year. Two million-plus working now. I was accused in Cork three weeks ago of blocking up the Irish roads with people going to work. (Laughter and applause.)

That's the challenge of success, I suppose.

It's fair to say, as you know, Mr. President, we've got 700 Irish firms, and 65 percent of the 700 firms working in America have a full-time presence in this market. And they now employ 100,000 people across 50 states. And that's because of our participation in the European Union and the confidence that our people have to expand now beyond their own shores. And this two-way conduit is to the mutual benefit of our people and of the United States. And let me say that Ireland and the European Union will never be anything but a friend to your country, to these United States here. (Applause.)

And I want you to understand that all administrations, over the last 40 years and beyond, have worked in the interests of the fragility of our country. We've had our troubles. We've had real difficulties. And George Mitchell spoke last night at the Ireland Funds about the contribution that both Europe, and particularly the United States, made towards putting that fragile peace together. We're glad to see Ian Paisley here and, indeed, Gerry Adams, who have had their difficulties. We have put it all together and have maintained a fragile peace. And that's why it's important that we recognize the contribution made by the United States to that peace, where we have no border and where people can live their lives as one would expect to contribute to their country and their economies. And all presidents and all administrations over the years have assisted us in that regard. (Applause.)

So we want to protect this peace process, and I know that you're going to work with us in that context also. We have agreed with the British government that there would be no return to the border, as it used to apply years ago, with customs, posts on major roads, and every other road blown up or impassable because of sectarian violence that that brought with it. We have banished that. We want to see it remain banished. And the political agreement is no return to that kind of border of the past, and the challenge is to implement that in a way that works in the interests of the people North and South.

And let me say to you that as a member of the European Council, what we want to do is to work with America. I believe genuinely, with Europe having created 4.5 million jobs in the last three years, that **we can work with the United States to create more employment here, create opportunities for so many millions of Americans**. And it may well be that in a revised trade agenda, that we can do that to the mutual benefit of 500 million people in the European Union and your population here across the United States. We will work with this administration, Paul and Mr. President, Mr. Vice President, in the interests of everybody.

Thank you, Peter King, and thank you, Richard Neal -- I know you're here somewhere -- for the work you've done over the years with the (inaudible). (Applause.)

It may well be that it might be appropriate for the government and the administration to have a desk here in Washington which will associate itself with Northern Ireland, so that in the event of contact having to be made, that there's a voice to answer that.

You had in the past envoys appointed to Northern Ireland on practically a full-time basis. I think we can work now as a priority to get this executive up and running in the next short period. But to have continued connection here with the administration would be very important, and I'm sure Peter and Rich will work at that.

I just want to say, I had a very good meeting this morning with the Vice President and with General John Kelly. Sitting at the table, we were hosted by the Vice President in the traditional breakfast in the Naval Observatory. Didn't get much chance to eat the breakfast, I have to say; it's one of the difficulties in politics -- it's in front of you but you can't get near it. (Laughter.)

We did discuss the question of immigration, which is so important to the fabric of our people. And I know that in this country, this is an issue that the administration and the President are reflecting upon. And that's something that, again, we will work with you diligently in this regard in the two sectors that we used to have a facility for E3 visas for young people who want to come to America and to work here. We discussed that very constructively this morning. And secondly, as a part of the overall immigration reform that the Irish have contributed so much, it would be part of that. And we look forward to the works that will take place at the time ahead.

You might say that when **Mike Pence's grandfather landed here in Ellis Island in 192**3, that the contribution had been made by so many Irish for so many years. It was in 1771 that the friendly Sons of St. Patrick were put together in Philadelphia, and one of their first honorary members was a young man called George Washington. And seven years later, he handed the first commission to a naval officer called John Barry, who was co-founder of the American Navy. And he was joined later by John Holland, who designed the first submarine. And he was followed by Louis Brennan, from my hometown, who had a major impact on the navigation systems for torpedoes.

And so many others, from Henry Ford, through music and culture, and so many other areas, that 22 members of the American Presidents who sat in the White House had either Scots or Irish blood in them. And you follow in that line, sir.

And I'd just like to say in finality, this is what I said to your predecessor on a number of occasions: We would like this to be sorted. It would remove a burden of so many people that they can stand out in the light and say, now I am free to contribute to America as I know I can. And that's what people want. (Applause.)

I know you'll reflect on this, but I'm always struck by the American National Anthem when it's sung before the great occasions. And I suppose being an emotional Irishman, the hairs tingle at the back of your neck when you hear your own national anthem. But for us, when Old Glory waves, and you put your hand on your heart and you say, **"The land of the free and the home of the brave," ours is still as brave as ever, but maybe not as free.** Because of the 4,000 Congressional Medals of Honor given out to the defense forces, over 2,000 go to the Irish Americans. So they fought in the Revolutionary War. They beat the daylights out of each other in Fredericksburg and Gettysburg and Yorktown, and other places, in Atlanta. **They fought every war for America and died for America -- and will continue to do so. All they want is the opportunity to be free.**

And this administration, working with Democrats and Republicans, I hope, can sort this out once and for all. And for future years, you determine what it is that you want to do. As George Mitchell said last evening, you can't return to open immigration, but for the people who are here -- who should be here, might be here -- that's an issue that I'm sure your administration will reflect on. And we in Ireland will give you every assistance in that regard. There are millions out there who want to play their part for America -- if you like, who want to **Make America Great**. (Laughter.)

Heard it before? Heard that before? (Applause.)

So I see Vicki here in front of me. We didn't get as far as the Kennedy Center the other evening. I was talking to young people the other day, they were on about all the different things that are happening in the world, and they reminded me of one of JFK's statements: "This is our planet. Together, we shall save or we shall perish in its flames." We have work to do. Let's eat. Thank you. (Applause.)

END
12:31 P.M. EDT

[*NOTE: Direct from the White House transcript. The predominant language spoken in Ireland is English and Irish (Gaelic).]

Chapter 88

16 March 2017

2:12 P.M. EDT

THE VICE PRESIDENT: Well, good afternoon.

On behalf of the President of the United States, today it will be my great privilege to administer the oath of office to Senator Dan Coats, who will become the fifth Director of National Intelligence for the United States of America. (Applause.)

This is a singular privilege for me as I have known Senator Coats now for more than 30 years and couldn't be more grateful for his willingness to continue his service to the United States of America in this vitally important role in the life of our nation.

We're joined this afternoon by his wife, Marsha, his son Andrew, his daughter Lisa. And we send greetings from afar to his daughter Laura, who is watching from Louisville, Kentucky, I know with great pride in her father and in her parents and their continuing service.

Also very honored to be joined today by a member of the intelligence committee in the Senate, Senator James Lankford, and the newest member of the United States

Senate, Senator Luther Strange. Thank you both for being here for this occasion. (Applause.)

Senator Coats, you come here today after a long career in public service. In our home state of Indiana, you served with great distinction -- first answering the call to serve our country in uniform in the United States Army. You would be elected to the United States Congress in 1980, serving four terms in the House of Representatives, and then decade in the Senate, followed by four very distinguished years as the United States Ambassador to Germany.

You arrived literally -- your second day on the job was September 11th, 2001. And in that moment of crisis for the United States and crisis in the world, you played a leading role in marshalling European support for our nation in that dark hour.

Although you tried to retire from public service in 2005, you failed -- just as you have again. (Laughter.)

And you ran for the United States Senate in 2010 and served another term, serving on the intelligence committee. You chaired the joint economic committee, adding to the more than a decade that you served on the armed services committee in the United States Senate.

Throughout all of your years, you represented not only the state of Indiana well, but you represented the interests of the United States with extraordinary integrity and commitment.

From one Hoosier to another, I'm grateful and proud for your service to date. And I know that President Trump is grateful and proud of your willingness to serve our nation at such a time as this.

The President has called you to serve this country as our Director of National Intelligence. As you know from your many conversations with him, President Trump has no higher goal than the **safety** and **security** of the American people, and from this day forward, as Director of National Intelligence, you will bring your background, your experience, your integrity, and the relationships that you have built around this nation and around the world in integrating and improving the best intelligence community in the world to be even better still.

The President and I have absolute faith in you. You've served our country with distinction for decades, and the President and I are confident that you will continue that record of leadership, integrity, and devotion to this country in the days ahead.

And so, on behalf of President Trump, it is my great privilege to administer to you the oath of office.
(The Oath is administered.) (Applause.)

THE VICE PRESIDENT: Ladies and gentlemen, the Director of National Intelligence for the United States, Dan Coats. (Applause.)

DIRECTOR COATS: Mr. Vice President, thank you for a more than generous introduction. But more importantly thank you for the many years of friendship with you and Karen, for your service in the House of Representatives, on the leadership in that House, for being an outstanding governor for our cherished Hoosier state, and now being awarded the great privilege of being Vice President of the United States.

To know you, to know who you are, to be so proud of our friendship, so proud of you in terms of your leadership, and being part of the team that's going to do everything we can to **keep America safe**, to **keep America prosperous**, to **keep America being the America that serves all Americans**, the kind of country that is recognized around the world. I'm deeply grateful for your leadership with that. These are clearly uncertain times. It's so wonderful to be supported by a wife of many, many years who is -- and at my right-hand side -- counselor, supporter, a faithful companion; by our daughter Lisa; by our son Andrew; and our daughter Laura, who is in Louisville, Kentucky watching hopefully this procedure.

These are clearly uncertain times, but I inherit an intelligence community made up of men and women who have dedicated their careers and their lives. It's a 24/7-365-day operation. And it is designed to protect Americans from threats from home and abroad. It is designed to be the best intelligence agency in the world. It is functioning well, but everyone that serves in that community say we can even do better. It's a great privilege to be able to be selected to lead that effort and to continue to be the best intelligence service in the world providing our President, Vice President, and policymakers with the needed information they need to inscribe **safe** policies, good policies, and lead our nation; and in fact, **always lead the world as America has done since its founding**.

Mr. Vice President, I thank you. (Applause.)

END
2:20 P.M. EDT

Chapter 89

**REMARKS BY PRESIDENT TRUMP AND VICE PRESIDENT PENCE
AT ST. PATRICK'S DAY RECEPTION
EAST ROOM**

16 March 2017

6:03 P.M. EDT

THE VICE PRESIDENT: Well, good evening to you all. Fellow Americans, Irish friends, distinguished guests. I'm Mike Pence and I'm the 48th Vice President of the United States of America. (Applause.)

It's my honor, along with my wife, Karen Pence, to welcome you on behalf of the First Family to the White House on this very special occasion.

It is such an honor for the two of us to be able to welcome you here and welcome a special guest to the White House, and of course, our host to this podium for this 55-year-old tradition. Since Irish Ambassador John Joseph Hearne left a box of Ireland's most famous symbol at the White House in 1952, the shamrock exchange has grown to become a festive sign of enduring friendship during this memorable week, and an eternal bond between the American people and the people of Ireland.

Now, **the Irish are one of the strongest and most beautiful threads in our national fabric here in the United States**. For centuries, the sons and daughters of Ireland have come here from across the Atlantic.

More than 32 million Americans now trace their heritage back to the Emerald Isle.

And I say with a grateful heart and deep humility, I'm one of them. (Applause.)

My grandfather, Richard Michael Cowley, stepped off a boat onto Ellis Island in 1023.*

And that's how Michael Richard Pence got to serve in the White House.

My grandfather, as the legend of our family says, was told by my great-grandmother that he needed to go to America. **She said, there's a future there for you**. He wouldn't see his mother for 25 years, and he often spoke of their separation with a heavy heart.

My grandfather came here, like so many generations of Irish-Americans did, **with a dream**, but with character and with work ethic and a determination to build a family, a good name. And so he did.

My mother, who is 83 years young, bright red hair and blue eyes, is still with us today, and his memory and her influence continues to define my life.

The truth is my grandfather was very typical of the millions that would come to these shores. **He embodied all that's best about the Irish -- sturdy work ethic, faith in God, love of family, patriotism.**

And those are the enduring contributions of people of Irish descent in the history of this country. It's extraordinary to think of the contributions that the Irish have made.

In every single American conflict since our Revolutionary War, the Irish people have enriched America in incalculable ways, and they always will.

When I speak of those character qualities I know that they apply to the two people that we have the privilege of introducing tonight.

First is our special guest -- it's my high honor to invite him to the podium, along with our host. So, ladies and gentlemen, please join me in welcoming the Taoiseach of the Republic of Ireland, Enda Kenny; his wife, Fionnuala; and my friend, the 45th President of the United States of America, Donald Trump. (Applause.)

THE PRESIDENT: Thank you very much. It's a great honor. Taoiseach, Mrs. Kenny, Ambassador Anderson, Dr. Lowe, Vice President Pence, and distinguished guests, we gather here today in the White House to take part in the traditional **Shamrock Ceremony** and to celebrate the strong ties between the United States and a truly great country, Ireland.

I also want to extend a special welcome to a group of distinguished local political and society leaders -- and they are real leaders -- who are with us from Northern Ireland -- great people -- including the Mayor of Belfast and the Head of Northern Ireland Civil Service -- that's a lot of power there. (Laughter.)

Lord Mayor Kingston and Sir Malcolm McKibbin -- and it's wonderful to have you. Where are you folks? Where are you? Where are you? (Applause.)

Thank you. They're going to be having a great open championship very soon -- you know that, right? (Laughter.)

At a great course. At a great, great course.

St. Patrick's Day has become a truly important occasion
in the United States -- one embraced by Americans of all
faiths and of all backgrounds. I've been to many of them
and we love it.

The Shamrock Ceremony is a tradition that symbolizes the
bond between our two countries. It dates back to 1952
when the Irish Ambassador to the United States, John
Joseph Hearne, sent a box of shamrocks to a President
who did a very good job -- Harry S. Truman.

Our strong ties go back throughout **American history.**
Irish-Americans played a vital role in preserving our Union
during its hour of greatest need. So true, played a very,
very big role.

Many distinguished themselves in the American Civil War
with their grit and their bravery and their courage, earning
the nickname, the "Fighting Irish." And I know a lot about
the Irish -- they fight. They're tough. (Laughter.)

I know a lot. I know more than I'm ever going to tell you.
(Laughter.)

And when American Armed Forces joined the fight in
Europe during World War II, 75 years ago, our heroic
troops first stepped off ships in Belfast Harbour in Northern Ireland.

Throughout the centuries, hard-working Irish-Americans
contributed mightily to **America's innovation** and to
America's prosperity. They often overcame great hardship
-- really, I mean, it's like the hardship they overcame for us,

for our people, is inspiring and really helped a relatively young nation beyond what anyone really understands or knows. So we want to thank you -- just an amazing, an amazing history.

President John F. Kennedy, in an address to the Irish Parliament, said that "It is that quality of the Irish -- that remarkable combination of hope, confidence, and imagination -- that is needed more than ever today."

Now, he said that a long time ago, but it's perhaps even more true today. The words of America's first Irish-Catholic President ring just as true.

We hope confidence -- and I tell you what we want now is a lot of things, but we need that great Irish confidence -- and they are confident people, aren't they, Mike? (Applause.)

And I tell you what, **we all want it together to grow in the 21st century**. And grow we will. As I say, **bigger and better and stronger than ever before**.

We must have the **hope to believe in a better future, the confidence to pursue it**, and the **imagination** to figure out how to get there. A **new optimism** is sweeping across our nation. You see that when you look at the numbers -- the **optimism** is at the highest level in many, many years.

And **as America gains renewed strength**, Ireland will find us to be an ever-faithful partner and an always loyal friend. We will be there for you, and we will be there for you. (Applause.)

So thank you for being here. I wish you a very, very happy

St. Patrick's Day. And God bless you and may God bless Ireland, and Northern Ireland, and may God bless America. Thank you very much. (Applause.)

Thank you. Thank you very much.

TAOISEACH KENNY: Mr. President, Mr. Vice President, ladies and gentlemen. It's a great honor to be back again in the most famous house in the world to celebrate St. Patrick's Day, the most special of days for Irish men and Irish women and those of Irish descent the world over.

Since I had the privilege of being elected as Taoiseach in 2011, I've had the pleasure of being here in the White House each March to mark the enduring connections between our country and the United States. Fionnuala and I would like sincerely to thank President Trump for so graciously continuing this great tradition of hospitality which means so much to Irish people everywhere.

I'm proud, sir, to have the opportunity to contribute to maintaining and developing relations between Ireland and the United States, particularly at the beginning of the new era in our country's relationship following your election, Mr. President. Let me congratulate you and wish you and your administration the very best as you begin your term of office. (Applause.)

This job, the job you hold, is exceptionally demanding and exceptionally difficult. The United States remains the most influential, as well as the most powerful country in the world. You hold the hopes and the future of America, and indeed, the world in your hands.

But let me thank you for giving so much of your time today

to this visit. We had an excellent meeting, a first-class meeting this morning in the Oval Office, not there very often, where we discussed a variety of important issues of mutual concern. And I want to assure you, Sir, of our commitment to working closely with you and your administration as you face the many challenges up ahead.

The ties that bind our two countries are deep and historic. And Ireland and the United States have a unique relationship that goes back to the earliest days of the original 14 colonies. Irish foreign military officers assisted George Washington to win that war of independence.

Indeed, they've fought in every war for America since then. And this very house was designed by James Hoban from Kilkenny, modeled in part after the Leinster House in Dublin, where the Irish Parliament has met on our own Independence since 1922.

It's fitting that we gather here each year to celebrate St. Patrick and his legacy. **He, too, of course, was an immigrant.** And though he is, of course, the Patron Saint of Ireland, for many people around the globe, he is also a symbol of, indeed, THE PATRON OF IMMIGRANTS.

Here in America, your great country, 35 million people claim Irish heritage, and the Irish have contributed to the economic, social, political and cultural life of this great country over the last 200 years.

Ireland came to America because, deprived of liberty, deprived of opportunity, of safety, of even food itself, the Irish believed, four decades before Lady Liberty lifted her lamp, we were the "wretched refuse on the teeming shore."

We believed in the shelter of America, and the compassion of America, and the opportunity of America. We came, and we became Americans.

We lived the words of John F. Kennedy long before we heard them: We asked not what America could do for us, but what we could do for America. And we still do. **We want to give, and not to take.** We know the Irish have built the bridges and the roads, protected the public as fire-fighters and police officers. We've cared for the sick in hospitals, entertained as poets, as singers and writers, as politicians, as judges and legislators. And as entrepreneurs, they provided hundreds of thousands of jobs for Americans, including most recently, in exciting technology companies.

Two-way trade in goods is approaching $100 billion a year at the moment. Irish firms employ 100,000 people across 50 states in the U.S. And we want to build on this for the future.

Mr. President, as a small island on the edge of Europe, a natural bridge between the United States and Europe, and as a committed member of the European Union and a close friend of the United States, we will work hard with you, Mr. President, and with your administration in pursuit of strong and open relations between the United States and the European Union, including the strong trade relationships for the mutual benefit of millions of people either side of the Atlantic.

I believe that the strong people-to-people links that Ireland and the United States have developed over the generations will help us in this endeavor. And I wish you and the American people every success and happiness in the future.

To Irish-Americans coast to coast, I say, these days especially, we hold you in our hearts. And tonight, I thank you
again for your warm hospitality.

Mr. President, Mr. Vice President, may I wish you and your
lovely families every good wish and blessing on this very
special day. Indeed, I'm reminded in many ways **of the
dream of another American President** -- which Ireland will
work with you for -- when he spoke the words and said,
"My dream is of a place and a time where America will
once again be seen as the last, best hope of Earth." Spoken by Abraham Lincoln.

Mr. President, **Ireland will help you build on that foundation to achieve the ultimate dream**. Thank you, sir. And
God bless you. (Applause.)

END
6:23 P.M. EDT

[*NOTE: Direct from the White House transcript.
From the White House video footage of the event, the Vice
President could be heard stating the year as, 1923.]

"My dream is of a place and
a time where America
will once again be seen as the last,
best hope of Earth."
Spoken by Abraham Lincoln.

[Photo: screengrab]

Chapter 90

17 March 2017

10:12 A.M. EDT

MR. SCALISE: We appreciate President Trump having us into the Oval Office to talk about healthcare and the improvements that are being made. The President has worked and said, bring us your best ideas. And there are members of the Republican Study Committee who have brought those good ideas and worked in a very diligent way to ultimately get to a "YES" on this bill with changes that the President has asked us to make that we're going to make in the bill.

And with that, I want to lead it off to the Chairman of the Republican Study Committee, Mark Walker.

MR. WALKER: Thank you. We're excited about today because it's historic knowing that we're getting a couple of very important things to the steering committee members -- work requirements through the country, and also something what we call "block grants," which allows the states to be empowered. We believe they should be able to hold the reins when it comes to managing their population.

We also think this would provide more coverage for the

indigent, for those sick, and for those disabled.

So we're excited about it today, and that's why we've come today to celebrate the American Health Care Act and moving forward with a "yes."

THE PRESIDENT: I just want to say that these are folks that were either a "no" or a "maybe." And we had a nice meeting, and we've been talking all during the night. This didn't just happen over the last 20 minutes. This has been going all night long.

And we are doing some incredible things. I want everyone to know I'm 100 percent behind this. I want everybody to know that the press has not been speaking properly about how great this is going to be. They have not been giving it a fair chance.

The press is -- as you know, I call it the "fake news." This is going to be great for people. I watch -- I say, that's not the bill we're passing. And I also want everybody to know that all of these "nos," or potential "nos," are all "yeses." Every single person sitting in this room is now a "yes."

And we made certain changes, and, frankly, little -- although the block grant is very important, because I want the states to get the money and to run their program, if they want to run it, because they can do it better than the federal government. They're better-equipped than the federal government.

They also want people to know that Obamacare is dead; it's a dead healthcare plan. It's not even a healthcare plan, frankly. And I watched the architect of the plan -- yesterday I watched the old clip where he said the American people are stupid to have voted for it. I watched Bill Clinton saying, this is the craziest thing I've ever seen. And only because everyone knows it's on its last dying feat, the fake news is trying to say good things about it -- the fake media.

And there is no good news about Obamacare. Obamacare is dead. And unless we gave it massive subsidies in a year from now or six months from now, it's not even going to be here. So when they say, "Oh, more people on the plan," there's not going to be any people on the plan.

I was in Tennessee -- I was just telling the folks -- and half of the state has no insurance company, and the other half is going to lose the insurance company. The people don't know what to do. It's a disaster.

Obamacare is dead. Nothing to do with these peo- ple. Nothing to do with me. It's on respirator and it's just about ready to implode.

Now, we could wait for six months or a year and let it hap- pen. It's not the right thing to do for the people. This is a great plan. This is going to be fantastic. You're going to have bidding at the one level by insurance companies.

And remember this -- remember this: Those lines are go- ing to come out, you're going to have bidding by insurance companies like you've never seen before.

Plans are going to come out like nobody has ever seen before. Plans that nobody has even thought of now are going to be devised by insurance companies to take care of people.

And we're going to take care of people at all levels. So I

just want to let the world know: I am 100 percent in favor. These folks -- and they are tough, and they love their
constituents, and they love this country -- these folks were
"Nos" -- mostly "Nos" -- yesterday. And now every single
one is a "yes." And I just want to thank you. We're going
to have a healthcare plan that's going to be second to
none. It's going to be great. And the people will see that.

And, by the way, it will take a little while -- because before it all kicks in and welds together, it takes a little
while. With Obamacare it got worse and worse. Premiums went up 116 percent. They went up 58 percent. The
Governor of Minnesota said that Affordable Care Act --
Obamacare -- no longer affordable.

That's what he said. The Affordable Care Act is no longer
affordable. And he's the guy that -- he's a good Democrat,
he wanted Obamacare.

He said it's no longer affordable. Obamacare is not an
alternative. It's not there. It's dead. It's dead.

So I just want to say thank you very much. I really appreciate it. One hundred percent of the "Nos" are "Yeses." And some of them were strong "Nos." Some were
just "Nos." And we have a couple that were mixed.

But I just want to thank you folks. And we're going to have
a great, great, healthcare plan. Thank you very much.

END
10:18 A.M. EDT

Chapter 91

17 March 2017

10:31 A.M. EDT

THE PRESIDENT: A special group of people. Very special to me, very important. And I want to thank you all for being here and for your work on behalf of our nation's veterans, our great, great people, our veterans.

We're all united by a very common mission: **We will protect those who protect us**. I've been saying that a lot over the last two years at rallies and speeches.

We will protect those who protect us, and that's just starting, because I think the veterans have not been treated fairly.

And David and a group of brilliant, brilliant doctors and businessmen are forming a board, and you've got the most talented people that I've ever seen working with you. This is -- no more games going to be played at the VA.

And I want to thank David, your Secretary -- your new Secretary, who's going to be so outstanding. I think he actually passed 100 to nothing. When I heard that vote I said, where did that come from? A hundred to nothing, right? Passed 100 to nothing -- for bringing your vision,

experience and determination to the crucial task of re-
forming the VA and ensuring care for our returning heroes
and warriors.

And tonight I'm having a major meeting with some of
the people that we put on a board. Ike Perlmutter is an
amazing man -- Marvel -- is one of the great, great businessmen of our time, and others -- we're having a meeting
tonight at what we call affectionately the **Southern White
House**. Seems to be the most convenient location. Everybody always wants to go to the **Southern White House**.

So are you going to be at that meeting? You heard about
it, right? It's going to be great -- all about the VA.

The VA's mission statement is engraved in the plaques
outside its headquarters. It reads: "To care for him who
shall have borne the battle, and for his widow and his or-
phan." And that was stated by Abraham Lincoln. That was
Lincoln's Pledge -- called Lincoln's Pledge.

But for too many veterans, this hasn't been their experience at all. We've been reading horrible stories over the
years, and already, David, I'm hearing it's getting much
better. A lot of improvements are being made and it's going to change. And under my administration, it will change
-- very important to me.

During my campaign, **I outlined a detailed plan to re-
forming veterans' care** throughout the country, and we're
working to put that plan into effect. And it's moving, I
think I can, honestly, ahead of schedule.

As Commander-in-Chief, I will not accept substandard service for our great veterans. Every member of our govern-

ment is expected to do their utmost to ensure our veterans have the care that they're so entitled to -- maybe more entitled to than anybody. And that hasn't been the way they were treated. But it is the way they're going to be treated.

So again, I want to thank you all for being here. It's a great honor. And maybe I'll ask David just to say a few words.

SECRETARY SHULKIN: Sure. Thank you, Mr. President.

THE PRESIDENT: Thank you.

SECRETARY SHULKIN: Mr. Vice President. I wanted to let you know the people in this room are some of the most dedicated, passionate people advocating for our veterans. And they are our partners in this quest to transform VA. And we really are so grateful that they're here with us standing as partners.

I also want to thank you, Mr. President, for the budget. I think that you've honored your commitment to showing that this country cares about the veterans, and you've given us the ability to make sure that we are able to care for them.

I also wanted to tell you that yesterday the House passed an accountability bill, and we're very, very grateful for Chairman Roe's leadership and for the House's leadership in doing that. We're looking forward to the Senate bringing a bill forward.

And so, I think, as you said, **we're committed to the plan that you outlined during your campaign** to making the VA the type of organization that Americans want it to be, and we're well on our way to do that. So thank you very much.

THE PRESIDENT: Well, that's great. And unrelated, we just had a meeting with probably 12 congressmen, and it was an amazing meeting because they were all "nos," would you say, Mike?

They were all "nos" or pretty much "no," and after 15 minutes -- now, in all fairness, not 15 minutes, it was really actually about four or five days, but after 15 minutes, they went from "no" to all "yeses."

So the healthcare looks like it's going to be in great shape. It's a great plan. The press doesn't give it a fair read but I've heard that before. What are you going to do -- the fake news.

But it's a great plan or I wouldn't be involved with it. I wouldn't be involved.

So you have 12 "nos," and we have re-jiggered it and we've done some great things, but the "nos" in every single case went to a "yes."

So that was a great honor, and healthcare looks like it's really happening, and it's going to great.

Obamacare is dead. Some of you folks have yourself -- you have family members that have suffered greatly under Obamacare. It's dying. It's just about on its last legs.

If we did nothing, if we did absolutely nothing, Obamacare is dead. It will fail.

In Tennessee, where I just left, half of the state has no insurance and --no carrier. It's gone. And they're going to leave the other half of the state very soon.

You have that in many cases. Many states are down to one and they'll end up with nothing.

So Obamacare is dead.

We're going to come up with a replacement that's going to be fantastic.

We have no support from the Democrats. That's why it's a little -- we have to go interesting little routes.

Instead of just approving it, it has to be approved in pieces, and that's working out really well.

But we just got 12 very, very great people that went from "no" or "maybe" -- but "maybe" leaning to "no" -- right, Mike?

And they all have given me a commitment that they're voting for our healthcare plan. So that was great.

I want to thank you all for being here, and let's talk. And the press will leave. Thank you very much.

END
10:38 P.M. EDT

Chapter 92

**REMARKS BY PRESIDENT TRUMP IN
ROUNDTABLE DISCUSSION ON
VOCATIONAL TRAINING WITH
U.S. AND GERMAN BUSINESS LEADERS
CABINET ROOM**

17 March 2017

12:58 P.M. EDT

PRESIDENT TRUMP: Chancellor, thank you very much. Such a great honor to get to know you, to be with you.

I want to thank all of the business leaders who have joined us to discuss a subject that's very important to me -- training our workforce for the 21st century, **especially with respect to manufacturing jobs**.

We're working every day to **bring back jobs** to our country, and thousands and thousands are already coming back. You're seeing it, you're reading about it in the papers every single day.

We want to make sure that we have the workforce development programs we need to ensure **these jobs are being filled by American workers**.

Germany and the United States have incredible opportunity to deepen our partnership as we continue to develop a strong workforce in both of our countries.

Both Germany and the United States are pioneering job-training programs. Here in the United States, companies have created revolutionary high-tech and online courses.

And, of course, for decades, Germany has been a model for highly successful apprenticeship -- that's a name I like, **"apprentice"** -- apprenticeship programs.

As a result, Germany's youth unemployment rate is much lower than many of the other countries, especially the EU countries.

I welcome collaboration between our two countries and our industry leaders. We have some of our great industry leaders here, as you know, Chancellor. Great people.

We must embrace new and effective job-training approaches, including online courses, high school curriculums, and private-sector investment that prepare people for trade, manufacturing, technology, and other really well-paying jobs and careers.

These kinds of options can be a positive alternative to a four-year degree. So many people go to college, four years, they don't like it, they're not necessarily good at it, but they're good at other things, like fixing engines and building things.

I see it all the time, and I've seen it -- when I went to school, I saw it.

I sat next to people that weren't necessarily good students but they could take an engine apart blindfolded.

Companies across the country have a chance to **develop vocational training programs** that will meet their growing needs and to help us achieve greater **prosperity**.

The **German apprenticeship model** is one of the proven programs to developing a highly skilled workforce.

Germany has been amazing at this, and I'm glad that the leaders of so many companies represented today have recently launched successful programs right here in the United States.

And we need that because we're training people as the **jobs are pouring back in** -- and they are coming back in big league.

I believe that both countries will be stronger if we continue to deepen our bilateral cooperation on vocational training as we build off the best ideas, create the greatest opportunity for growth, and improve the lives of so many workers. I want to thank everybody in the room.

I want to thank my daughter Ivanka, who's with us today.

And mostly -- and most of all, I want to thank -- Chancellor, I want to thank you very much. It's a great honor to have you in the White House.

It's a great honor to have you in the United States. And I look forward to spending time with you.

Thank you.

CHANCELLOR MERKEL: (Speaks German.) [Transcript not available from the White House website.]

PRESIDENT TRUMP: Maybe before the press leaves I'd like to ask some of the folks around -- **the great leaders of industry and business to introduce themselves, say a couple of words**. And then we'll get onto a little bit more private meeting, okay?

Ginni.

MS. ROMETTY: Okay. I'm Ginni Rometty with IBM. And we're going to talk about two programs. One is a certification program, which, Mr. President, today, we're going to announce 2,000 veterans that we're certifying in cyber-security to be employed.

And then the second is something called P-TECH, a public-private partnership. Think of it as a six-year high school, but the graduates come out with an associate degree and with a curriculum that **business will hire**.

And we will have 100 schools by the end of the year. And you'll meet one of our recent graduates. In a second, Janiel Richards will introduce herself and tell you about herself -- trained at the intersection of business and technology.

PRESIDENT TRUMP: Great job.

PARTICIPANT [JARED KUSHNER]*: We've found that a lot of the private-sector companies have done a great job trying to train the workforce for the jobs that they need, the jobs of the future.

In a lot of cases in America, we're finding that we don't have enough qualified applicants for the jobs that we have available, so in working with the private sector -- and Ginni has been a great leader of that -- the White House has been trying to get behind a lot of these programs that can help make sure we're training the American people for the jobs that we're hopefully going to be producing in the future.

SECRETARY ROSS: Our hope is that, today, we really come with a way forward, some specific programs where we can interact between the educational community, the business community, and the government. Because this is a monumental problem that needs a monumental solution.

MS. RICHARDS: Thank you for the introduction. Good afternoon, all. Thank you for the opportunity to share my story. It is both an honor and a pleasure to be here today.

As mentioned, my name is Janiel Richards. In am 19 years old, and I am from (inaudible) [East New York, Brooklyn.]. Enrolling in IBM's P-TECH school was the best decision for me personally and professionally. I did not fully realize the weight of the opportunity I was given; however, looking back, **it was a life chance**.

[Photo: screengrab.]

P-TECH strengthened my confidence and provided me with mentors who helped me strive. I learned the importance of understanding computers, and gained new skills in both coding and programming. I graduated the program in four and a half years -- relatively early -- and I graduated with my high school diploma and associate's degree in computer science, as well as intern-ship experience at IBM.

I learned that technology is omnipresent and opens endless doors. I am now a digital commerce design developer at IBM, where I use my skills to create website pages and checkout pages for the marketplace.

I'm also pursuing my bachelor's degree at Early College. Without the support of P-TECH and IBM, I would not be where I am today. I believe that every student should be offered this chance.

Thank you all.

PRESIDENT TRUMP: That's a great job. Thank you very much. Great job. Wow. Who wants to follow that? (Laughter.)

MR. KAESER: Mr. President, Chancellor, Vice President, my name is Joe Kaeser, and I work for Siemens. It's a company which has been in this great country for more than 160 years. We produce revenues and services worth $24 billion ever year, and 60 manufacturing sites in all 50 states in the country.

So thank you for what you're doing. (Inaudible) in that aspect we brought the apprenticeship to the country, which has, in the meantime, also (inaudible) Department of Labor, so we roll it out everywhere in the community.

And I feel very honored today to be part of an initiative that brings not only the apprenticeship and the training for the current manufacturing into play, but also the next generation of manufacturing going forward so we combine the present and the **future for our great America and great manufacturing**.

PRESIDENT TRUMP: Great job. Great company too, by the way. Great company.

Marc.

MR. BENIOFF: Well, thank you very much, Mr. President, I am delighted to be here, and great to see you and the Vice President as well. Salesforce, as you know, is the fastest-growing of the top five software companies in the world today, and we're on a path to create 2 million jobs and add 200 GDP to the world economy through our platform.

Our software, as you know, 90 percent is engineered here in the United States, and, as the Vice President knows, handmade in Indianapolis and in San Francisco, where I'm from.

And I'll tell you, as we have kind of created these jobs all over the world, I see a great opportunity right here in the United States to create apprenticeships. And we'd love to encourage you to take a moonshot goal to create 5 million apprenticeships in the next five years.

And I think the key is, is that we see all these great programs and all these great companies doing workforce development. But if we all came together, if we all unified and created a great program with your leadership, I think we could create this 5 million extra jobs in the U.S.

And you know, our companies are some of the greatest universities in the world. We shape these employees, we train them, we educate them, we bring them in, and I think we can do this. I think this is really exciting.

THE PRESIDENT: Well, congratulations, and you're going an incredible job. And nice to know you. And really, what you've done is just amazing. And let's do that, let's go for that 5 million. Okay? (Laughter.)

Very good.

Ivanka, go ahead. Say something.

MS. TRUMP: Thank you. And welcome, Chancellor, and to the many U.S. and German CEOs who are here today to discuss vocational education and workforce development.

I applaud my father's commitment to creating millions of jobs, and specifically making sure that all Americans have the skills required and necessary to fill the jobs both of today and of the future.

[Photo: screengrab.]

As many of us realize, ingenuity, creativity often comes from the determination of the private sector, so it's great to have such great private sector leaders here to share their thoughts and best practices with us today. And thank you for being here.

THE PRESIDENT: Klaus.

MR. ROSENFELD: Mr. President, Madam Chancellor, ladies and gentlemen, my name is Klaus Rosenfeld. I am the CEO of Schaeffler. Schaeffler is a global automotive and industrial supplier with more than $14 billion U.S. sales, around 87,000 people globally and 75 clients.

We manufacture bearings and other high-precision components and systems for a broad variety of applications and sectors. Our products are everywhere where things turn, be it in cars, machines, airplanes, trucks, or even in washing machines.

The company is family-owned, so we place great value on a culture where we think long-term and focus on quality, technology, and innovation.

For us, the employee has always been critical, and will always be critical. We have started business in 1969 in South Carolina. Since then, the Schaeffler family has invested more than a billion in the Palmetto State. We have grown through acquisitions. We're about to finish multimillion expansions in Ohio and South Carolina.

For us, the U.S. is critical. We have started our first program here in the '80s -- 1980 in Wooster, Ohio -- and since then we have spent a lot of money in vocational dual training. Thank you very much, Mr. President.

THE PRESIDENT: Thank you. Thank you, Klaus, very much.

MR. KRÜGER: Thank you, Mr. President and Mr. Vice President. From my side, thank you for inviting us. Yeah, it's a great pleasure for us, for me. I would like to explain why, at BMW, we call the United States of America our second home.

I'm proud to be here because we were -- nearly 25 years ago we were founding our biggest plant in the BMW Group network in South Carolina. We created 9,000 jobs, and we know that in the area around South Carolina, I know we created an additional 4 to 5 to 6, 7 jobs -- the 9,000 people we employ at BMW in South Carolina.

We have invested heavily in the further education and training and vocational training. It was around about $200 million in the last five years, and I can commit that we will invest another $200 million into training in the next five years.

We are proud, as we are the biggest net exporter of vehicles in the United States. We have an annual net (inaudible) of $10 billion -- exported from South Carolina. Seventy percent of our production is being exported.

And I'm proud to be here because we have one apprentice who's with us from -- we have two main programs at Spartanburg, a BMW Scholar Program, which was founded in 2011 and has around about 100 people in the program, and they graduate and create -- get a great job at BMW. We are very proud on the skill-set -- we need them for maintenance jobs.

And I would like to talk about as well employment of

skilled veterans, which we are setting up with our dealers
in the United States to have their highly qualified veterans
working for BMW dealers in the future.

THE PRESIDENT: Well, I've seen your plant in South
Carolina. It is incredible. And congratulations, that's really
great. Thank you.

MR. KRÜGER: Thank you. May I invite you for the 25th
anniversary in June? (Laughter.)

THE PRESIDENT: I know I shouldn't have said that. (Laughter.) You know what, if I can, I will do it.

MR.KRÜGER: Thank you very much.

THE PRESIDENT: I wish I could, but if I can I'll do it. Absolutely.

MS. DAVIS: Mr. President, Madam Chancellor, ladies and
gentlemen, my name is Marie Davis, and I work at Schaeffler's Automotive and Industrial Plant in Cheraw, South
Carolina.

Cheraw is a small town with a population of 5,800, and is
nicknamed "The Prettiest Town in Dixie."

It is a great honor for me to be here today along with my
peers -- apprentice Chad Robinson with Siemens Gas Turbine Plant of Charlotte, North Carolina, and Maria Puckett
with BMW, from BMW plant Spartanburg, South Carolina --
and to be able to share my experiences with you regarding
the Schaeffler apprenticeship program. BMW and Siemens
also have very similar programs.

I joined the Air Force after high school and served for four years. After returning home, I applied to and was accepted into the Schaeffler apprenticeship program.

This is a very unique three-year program of classroom and hands-on experience, completed in conjunction with North-eastern Technical College, which provided me with special skills for my career. As part of the program, I also received an associate's degree in machine tool technology and a Department of Labor certificate as a certified journeyman apprentice.

After completing my apprenticeship, I worked as a CNC operator, was then promoted to (inaudible) leader, and am now planned maintenance supervisor.

I am very glad that such an apprenticeship program existed in Cheraw, which allowed me to start and build my career with Schaeffler.

I hope that more companies will follow BMW, Siemens, and Schaeffler and offer apprenticeship programs to develop skills that will allow for more manufacturing in the United States. It is an incredible privilege to be invited here today. Thank you so much for listening to me.

THE PRESIDENT: Thank you very much. Great job. Thank you. Very nice.

I know this one. (Laughter.)

MR. LIVERIS: Mr. President and Madame Chancellor, what an honor it is for me to be here. I'm Andrew Liveris from Dow Chemical.

I feel like Germany is our home, to match my BMW colleague's point about the U.S. being home.

We have been in Germany, and in fact the Chancellor's backyard of former Eastern Germany for a long time. And the Chancellor graced us with a visit to our apprenticeship program there which -- Mr. President, the two things I want to talk about today is in fact apprenticeship, and -- there's a book here that I can show which has DOW and Siemens' name on it.

And just to let you know that we are working already together as two collaborators across the Atlantic to actually scale up programs like the one that was mentioned by the young lady to my right.

So I want to talk about that and how we can scale it up through this great leadership that you're showing. And I also want to talk about veterans and displaced workers, especially in places like Michigan, where we are based.

We have community college work called *Fast Start*, which is taking displaced workers and reskilling them. When new tech meets industrial tech, as Madame Chancellor says, opportunity is there. But we've got to create it by scaling right. So I want to also talk about that.

And my last comment is, a big thank you for lending us or giving us Ivanka and Jared. They've been a tremendous duo in making this program real in very short weeks. Thank you.

THE PRESIDENT: Thank you very much. Mr. Vice President.

VICE PRESIDENT PENCE: Thank you, Mr. President. Let me

just express my appreciation, along with the President, for the participants in this important conversation.

All the businesses that are gathered here from across the United States and across Germany are an **inspiration, and the innovation** that you're bringing to career and technical and vocational education and to apprenticeship.

I'm especially impressed, Mr. President, with Janiel, and I don't know that I've seen a more inspiring debut at the Cabinet table than anyone. (Laughter.)

Let me also express my appreciation to the Chancellor for suggesting that we bring together, across the Atlantic, business leaders who have really been breaking new ground in this area, for which Germany is so celebrated.

We're grateful for your leadership and look forward to sharing ideas about how we can strengthen the workforce in both of our countries.

And lastly, let me just thank the President. As a former Governor from a great manufacturing state, I can tell you that one of our very first conversations was about the innovation that Indiana was bringing to career and technical and vocational education.

I can assure you that the passion that you see at this table today by the President is authentic, and at his direction, we're going to work as an administration to **strengthen the opportunities** from secondary education on forward to open the doors for more vocational education, more technical education, and more apprenticeships across the United States to the betterment of the people of this country.

And we look forward to working with our international partners **to drive greater opportunities for Americans**.

So thank you, Mr. President.

THE PRESIDENT: Thank you very much, Mike. Appreciate it. Okay, thank you folks.

END
1:18 P.M. EDT

[Note: * It is not known why the White House transcript did not mention Jared Kushner by name, but instead stated him as a PARTICIPANT only.]

Chapter 93

18 March 2017

Transcript:

My fellow Americans,
This week, I traveled to Nashville, Tennessee to lay a
wreath at the grave of Andrew Jackson, on the 250th anniversary of his birth.

[Photo: screengrab.]

Jackson was an American hero.

First, as the brilliant General whose crushing defeat of the
British at New Orleans saved our Independence in the War
of 1812.

And later, as the seventh President of the United States—
when **he fought to defend the forgotten men and women
from the arrogant elite of his day**. Does it sound familiar?

The memory of his leadership lives on in our people, and
his spirit points us to a better future.

This week, I also traveled to the Willow Run plant in
Michigan. At that facility during the Second World War, the
Ford Motor Company built not cars, but entire airplanes. At
one point, workers there produced a complete B-24
Liberator every single hour – hard to believe.

Today on that site is a new facility, where the cutting edge
cars of the future will be tested. And this week, the old
plant was filled once again with thousands of workers
and engineers. I was there to share the good news for the
American auto industry.

We announced we'll be reversing an 11th hour executive
action from the previous Administration that was threatening thousands of auto jobs in Michigan and across America.

And I mean threatening – it was very, very sad to see.

In fact, we are setting up a task force in every federal agency to identify any unnecessary regulation that is hurting
American businesses and American jobs.

The first two job reports of my administration show that
we've already added nearly half a million new jobs.

The days of economic surrender for the United States are
over. For too long, special interests have made money shipping jobs overseas.

The First 100 Days   **749**

We need a new economic model – let's call it
The American Model. Under this model, we will lower the
burden on American Business but, in exchange, **they must
hire and grow America and American jobs**. This will be a
win-win for our companies and for our workers.

**Let's Buy American and Hire American. Let's create jobs
in America. Let's imagine new industries. And let's build a
beautiful future together.**

Among the workers building B-24 bombers at the Willow
Run plant during World War II was one tough lady. You
might have heard of her: they called her Rosie the Riveter.
And when Rosie's country called her, she answered the
call.

Rosie was famous for her toughness and her strength—and
for the words that were emblazoned above her famous
image. It said very simply: "We can do it."

If **Americans unite**, and find **Again** within our nation the
Soul of Rosie and the **Spirit** of Jackson—I have no doubt
that "*We can do it*", and do it like never before.

Thank you. Enjoy your week.

*"Let's Buy American and
Hire American."*

Chapter 94

**REMARKS BY VICE PRESIDENT MIKE PENCE ON
OBAMACARE
MAC PAPERS
JACKSONVILLE, FLORIDA**

18 March 2017

2:38 P.M. EDT

THE VICE PRESIDENT: Hello, Florida! I want to thank your governor for that kind introduction. He's been a friend for many years. And, ladies and gentleman, how about that governor, Rick Scott? (Applause.)

Florida is incredibly fortunate to have a leader like Rick Scott. Since he took office, he's signed over 50 tax cuts, he balanced the budget year after year, and he helped create more than 1.3 million jobs -- one of the fastest-growing state economies in America. (Applause.)

The sun is definitely shining on Florida State with Governor Rick Scott. Give him another round of applause, would you please? (Applause.)

Governor, I have to tell you, President Trump and I are proud -- proud to partner with you to **Make America Great Again**. (Applause.)

The same goes with all the other dedicated public servants who are here with us today. And I'm honored to be in their presence. Congressman John Rutherford, Mayor Lenny Curry -- thank you for joining us.

And, Seema Verma, it is such a privilege to have you here. Folks, I had the honor of swearing her in this past Tuesday as the 15th Administrator of America's Center for Medicare & Medicaid Services. She happens to be a Hoosier, and she's one of the leading healthcare experts in the country, and she's going to do an incredible job for people all across this country. (Applause.)

Thank all these public servants. (Applause.)

I can say with confidence Seema Verma is going to help us **Make American healthcare Great Again**. And I want to thank you so much for your service, Seema. More than I can tell you, I'm incredibly proud.

Now, it is a great privilege to be with all of you today, back in this great Sunshine State. Last fall, thanks to all of you -- thanks to your hard work, your support, and your prayers -- the people of Florida voted to make Donald Trump the 45th President of the United States of America. (Applause.)

Florida made a difference. And the President asked me to stop by just to give his personal thanks to each and every one of you. Hard-working Americans like all of you were our biggest supporters.

And on behalf of the President and his family, and on behalf of my little family: Thank you, Florida. Your votes have set us on a path to **Make America Great Again**. And we're here to say thanks. (Applause.)

It was quite a campaign, wasn't it? And it's already been quite an administration. (Laughter.)

It's the greatest honor of my life to serve as Vice President to President Donald Trump. He's my friend. He's a man who loves his family, he loves this country -- boundless energy and optimism, broad shoulders and a big heart. And thanks I want to express on his behalf, as well.

To all the great business owners who are with us today, we enjoyed a great conversation today about the issue that I'll talk more about in just a moment. And join me in thanking these great job-creators in Jacksonville. Thank you for sharing your candid feedback about what we can do to help you grow jobs right here in Jacksonville. Give them all a word of thanks. (Applause.)

Last but not least, I want to thank Mac McGehee and the whole Mac Paper team for hosting us here today. Mac, your family now for three generations have been a pillar in the Jacksonville community for over 50 years, and today you have over 600 employees spread across nine states. You only get that way when you're doing something right and you're doing it for a long time. The President and I thank you for all that you do.

And let's give the whole Mac Paper team a big round of applause for their great, great success and the jobs they've created here. (Applause.)

Thank you.

And let me assure you, let me assure all the job-creators, all the people that work for businesses large and small: President Trump, I can assure you -- President Trump is going to be the best friend American small business will ever have. (Applause.)

You know, I grew up in a small business -- a small business family -- actually in a small town in southern Indiana. It was a gas station business. I was a -- I started working as a gas station attendant in one of my father's gas stations when I was only 14 years of age. And for you young people in the room, we'll explain later what a gas station attendant actually used to do. (Laughter.)

As the whole world knows, the President also grew up in a family business, too.

We actually both know, because of our life experiences in our families, we know the sacrifices that are required to make a business work. And more importantly, we know that when small business is strong, **America is strong**. (Applause.)

And **President Trump is going to fight for small business America**, just as he's done from day one.

We want to create jobs and prosperity and growth in America like never before. And small business is going to be the lion's share of that. Just look at what the President has already done.

On day one, President Trump went straight to work rolling back reams of red tape. He's instructed literally every agency in Washington, D.C. to find two regulations to get rid of before they issue any new federal red tape on job-creators in America. (Applause.)

He's taken decisive action already to **protect American jobs and American workers** by ending illegal immigration once and for all. (Applause.)

He also took action recently when he authorized the Keystone and Dakota pipelines that will create thousands of jobs and **protect** America's energy future. (Applause.)

And businesses are already responding to President Trump's **"Buy American, Hire American" vision** with **optimism and investment**.

From coast to coast -- Governor Scott will back me up on this -- companies are announcing that they're keeping jobs here, they're creating new jobs -- tens of thousands of them. Just last month, the American economy added 235,000 new jobs, and we are just getting started. (Applause.)

Under President Trump's leadership and working with great congressmen like your congressman, John Rutherford, we're going to cut taxes across the board for working families, small businesses, and family farms.

We're going to keep slashing through red tape, we're going to rein in unelected bureaucrats so they can't cripple the economy from the comfort of their taxpayer-funded metal desks in Washington, D.C. (Applause.)

And because **you hired a builder** to be President of the United States, we're going to **rebuild this country** so that Florida and every other state has the resources to have the best roads, the best bridges, the best highways, the best airports, and the best future we could ever imagine, with the infrastructure that we need. (Applause.)

But **Making America Great Again** doesn't just mean our economy. President Trump has no higher priority, I can assure you, than the **safety** and **security** of the American people.

Over the past year, the American people watched in horror as terror struck Orlando and Ft. Lauderdale. Our support and our prayers have been with you ever since. And so, for that matter, I can assure you, is our resolve.

Rest assured, President Trump will continue to take steps every single day to **protect** our nation, **protect** our way of life, and **protect** and prevent attacks by radical Islamic terrorism in this country **Again**. (Applause.)

Your former sheriff knows in his heart what people also know: President Donald Trump is standing with the men and women who serve in law enforcement in this country as never before. (Applause.)

Some of you are sitting, a lot of you are standing, but would you all mind getting on your feet and thanking all the men and women in law enforcement who are here with us today? (Applause.)

I promise you, under President Trump's leadership, we're going to make sure that the men and women who serve in law enforcement have the resources and the training and the tools that they need to **protect** our families and go home **safe** to theirs.

The President has also taken steps to **secure** our nation, to secure our borders -- which means building a wall, enforcing our laws, beginning with ensuring, as the President said before Congress, that gang members, drug dealers, and criminals that threaten our communities are off the streets of Florida and out of this country. (Applause.)

And while we talk about security, this last Thursday President Trump unveiled his budget. It's a budget that, at its very heart, will end the era of budget cuts for our armed forces. We will **rebuild** our military. We will **restore** the **arsenal of democracy**. (Applause.)

We will give our Soldiers, Sailors, Airmen, Marines, and Coast Guard the resources that they need to accomplish their mission and come home safe. That **I promise you**. (Applause.)

And, lastly, by nominating Judge Neil Gorsuch, who will go before the Congress this coming week, President Trump has kept his word to appoint a justice to the Supreme Court of the United States who will keep faith with the Constitution and uphold the God-given liberties that have been enshrined there for now more than two centuries. (Applause.)

So we've been busy. We've been busy. My friends, **President Trump is a man of his word**, and he's a man of action. And I believe he will **Make America Great Again**.

And make no mistake, about it: The Obamacare nightmare is about to end. (Applause.)

It's amazing -- really amazing to think about it. Virtually every promise they made about Obamacare, when it was passed into law, has been broken. We all remember what they were. Remember?

They told us the cost of health insurance would go down. Not true. They told us if you liked your doctors, you could keep them. Not true. They told us if you liked your health plan, you could keep it. Not true.

Just the other day, I joined President Trump to listen to
hard-working Americans who have suffered from these
broken promises. They told us in visceral and in emotional
terms the stories that I heard from business leaders today: sky-rocketing premiums, unaffordable deductibles,
fewer choices, higher taxes. They told us, just like these
employers did today, about the hard choices that they've
had to make, about how Obamacare is standing in the way
of not only their companies' aspirations, but the hopes and
dreams of the people that work there and desire to work
there. It was a heartbreaking conversation, then and now.
And they're not alone.

Think about it: Just last year, premiums, following Obamacare, spiked by 25 percent on average across America.
Millions have lost their plans. In one-third of the nation's
counties, Americans only have one insurance company
to choose from -- which essentially means they have no
choice at all.   Given all the failings, it's no wonder that
400,000 fewer people enrolled in Obamacare this year.

Now, your governor, I can tell you, has been remarkable on
this. He mentioned just a few moments ago -- we actually met when, as a private citizen, Rick Scott was fighting
against Obamacare before it ever became law. (Applause.)

And, Rick, let me thank you for that, and thank you for
your ongoing leadership.

As Governor Rick Scott said recently -- and he knew this
from the fight we fought then and the fight you fought
every day since -- that Obamacare was, in his words, "sold
on a lie." And then, in his typical plain-spoken way, Governor Scott said, it just plain "doesn't work." And he was
right.

Florida is actually a textbook example of everything that's wrong with Obamacare. Here in the Sunshine State, Obamacare premiums rose by 19 percent last year -- with some increasing by nearly 40 percent. Over 400,000 Floridians were scheduled to lose their plans at the start of this year. And nearly three-quarters -- 75 percent -- of the state has no choice at all when it comes to health insurance.

The truth is, Florida can't afford Obamacare anymore. And job-creators in Florida can't afford it either. (Applause.)

I heard it. I heard it earlier today. The small businesses represented here, they told me that Obamacare hits them with mandates, with regulations, with higher taxes and higher costs.

Mac Paper is actually a great case in point. Since Obamacare went into effect, Mac was telling me that they've been forced to spend more than $300,000 not on jobs, not on investments that will create more jobs, but on just trying to comply with this failed law.

That's just not right. That money would have been better invested in your workers, Mac. And I know that's where you would have liked to invest it -- in payroll and in benefits, in your future, instead of being wasted on the failed policies of Obamacare.

Men and women, this can't continue. Every day that Obamacare survives is another day the American people and American businesses are struggling. Obamacare has failed and Obamacare must go. (Applause.)

Since the day Florida helped send President Trump to the

White House, I can promise you he has been focused on repealing and replacing Obamacare with something that actually works.

We know that the core flaw of Obamacare was this notion that you could order every American to buy health insurance whether they wanted it or needed it or not. That was never the answer.

Just a few days ago in Nashville, President Trump actually called that Obamacare's "fatal flaw." The President couldn't be more right. That's why we're going to end this flaw. We're going to replace it with real solutions built on freedom, personal responsibility, and state flexibility and reform. That's what works, and that's what President Trump's plan for healthcare reform will do for the American people. (Applause.)

We're going to begin, though, by repealing Obamacare's taxes. We're going to end its mandates by eliminating the penalties. We're going to give Americans more choices. We're going to expand health savings accounts for every American. We're going to give Americans a tax credit that'll help them buy the coverage they need at a price they can afford. And we're also going to do it with what the President likes to call "big heart." We're going to make sure that Americans with pre-existing conditions still have access to the coverage that they need. And to you fellow parents out there with kids under the age of 26 -- I have three -- (laughter) -- we'll make sure you can keep your kids on your insurance until they're 26 years of age. (Applause.)

Now, folks, what I just laid out is only a small glimpse of everything our plan will do. The bill moving through the

Congress, the American Health Care Act, is an important step in the right direction. We're working around the clock with Congressman Rutherford and other members of the Republican majority in the House and the Senate; and with leaders here in Florida to make this bill even better.

President Trump laid out a few key elements just yesterday with members of Congress in the Oval Office, and we're going to continue to work with members of Congress to improve this bill. It's what the legislative process is all about.

And we're not going to -- we're going to do a couple of different things with a few recent amendments that are worth mentioning and are owing in part to the engagement that we had with Congress.

First off, we're going to stop any more states from expanding Medicaid and adding a burden to future generations. We're going to give states the option of block grants of Medicaid to the states so states like Florida can innovate and design Medicaid around the unique needs of the people in this community.

And we're going to allow states like Florida to include a work requirement for able-bodied adults ensuring that Medicaid's benefits are available for those who need it the most. (Applause.)

These are all common-sense solutions added to this legislation in a vigorous debate on Capitol Hill, and under the President's leadership, we'll continue to listen intently for ways to make this even better.

Just yesterday, President Trump made it clear he supports

the bill 100 percent, and we all do. Every day, more and more members of Congress are getting on board. And as we work to pass this first bill, rest assured our administration is also working with Dr. Tom Price over at Health and Human Services and with Seema Verma at the Center for Medicaid Services to give states like Florida the freedom and flexibility to help your most vulnerable in the ways that are going to be best for you.

Just this past week, they sent a letter to Governor Scott and other state leaders around the country saying that "a new era for the federal and state Medicaid partnership" has begun -- and so it is. (Applause.)

The fact is, and I say this as a governor of the state of Indiana, that the fact is Florida is a unique state with unique needs -- and this administration knows that state-based solutions, designed by your governor, your state legislature are the best way to give better coverage, and get better healthcare outcomes, particularly for the most vulnerable citizens across the state of Florida.

And under President Trump's leadership lastly just know this, we're going to give the American people the freedom to buy health insurance across state lines -- the way you buy life insurance, the way you buy car insurance. (Applause.)

That's the combination. President Trump and I know that the way to lower costs is to increase choices to create a dynamic national marketplace, and that's what our plan will do. Probably won't be too long before you see Flo and some little lizard on television -- (laughter) -- selling health insurance. **And that's the American way**.

And let me say a couple of things to you before I slip off and get on that plane and head back south with your governor. I want to assure the people of Florida: We're going to have an orderly transition to a better healthcare system in America that makes affordable, high-quality health insurance accessible for every American. (Applause.)

But be assured about this, be clear on this, though, folks, this is going to be a battle in Washington, D.C. All right?

Obamacare's defenders are working hard, so we have to work harder. And we're counting on Florida. We need every Republican in Florida to support this bill and support the President's plan to repeal and replace Obamacare.

AUDIENCE MEMBER: That's why we voted.

THE VICE PRESIDENT: And President Trump and I -- President Trump and I are confident -- we're confident that with your support, Florida will be there, and we will repeal and replace Obamacare once and for all. (Applause.)

It really is remarkable this time we find ourselves in, **a time of renewed hope and boundless opportunity for the American people.**   I think **we're at a pivotal moment in our nation's history that started last November the 8th.**

In this moment, though, I want to leave you with a challenge, we need every freedom-loving American who knew we could be stronger, who knew we could be better, who knew we could stand tall Again to yourselves stand up and speak out. It's time that we demanded government as good as our people.

We need you to tell the world that we can do better, that

we're **renewing and restoring** this country, that we're putting it back on **a path to a brighter future.** Tell your neighbors and your friends. Stop people outside the drug store. Just let them know how strongly you support the President's **vision** for this country, particularly when it comes to healthcare.

One of my favorite verses in the Old Book is from the Book of Jeremiah. It's hung over the mantle of our home since I first ran for Congress successfully in the year 2000, and now it hangs over the mantle in the Vice President's Residence in Washington, D.C.

It simply reads: "For I know the plans I have for you, plans to prosper you, and not to harm you, plans to give you a hope, and a future."

In November, I believe with all of my heart that the people of Florida and the people of this country voted to give America a President with the strength, the courage, and the vision, to **Make America Safe Again.**

You voted to give us a new leader who will **Make America Prosperous Again**. And I know in my heart with your continued faith and support, together we will **Make America Great Again.**

Thank you very much. Thank you for being here.

God bless you and God bless America. (Applause.)

END
3:03 P.M. EDT

Chapter 95

**REMARKS BY THE VICE PRESIDENT AT
CLUB FOR GROWTH
THE BREAKERS
WEST PALM BEACH, FLORIDA**

19 March 2017

THE VICE PRESIDENT: Thank you, to my friend David McIntosh, for that kind introduction.

You know, as you could tell from our history together, Dave McIntosh has always been a tough act to follow, and that's especially true today. (Applause.)

It's as true today as it was 17 years ago when I took your place representing the good people of Indiana's Second District, and I'm really honored to call you a friend. Thank you so much.

To David, to Chairman Jackson Stephens, to Senator Shelby, Senator Toomey, Senator Lee, Congressman Amash, Congressman Biggs, Congressman Blum, Congressman DeSantis, Meadows, Labrador, distinguished guests, it is great to be back to Club for Growth. (Applause.)

I am proud to say that in my first successful campaign for Congress in the year 2000, Club for Growth was there bringing pro-growth, conservative support to our campaign, and making it possible for us to serve in Washington DC. And let me say from my heart I will always be grateful to the men and women of Club for Growth for the support for my little family. (Applause.)

My years in the Congress, my years serving as the 50th Governor of Indiana. And today, it is -- it's almost hard for me to express how humbled I feel among so many old friends as stand before you as the 48th Vice President of the United States of America. Thank you, thank you all. (Applause.)

And let me say it's the greatest privilege of my life to serve alongside my friend, the 45th President of the United States of America, President Donald Trump. (Applause.)

The President sends his greetings tonight; he's actually just down the road at **Mar-A-Lago**, the **Winter White House** as it's come to be known.

But he asked me to be here tonight to let you know that whatever differences he's had in the past, that Club for Growth's motto -- **"Prosperity and Opportunity through Economic Freedom"** -- will be **a hallmark** of the Trump administration throughout our service to the people of the United States. (Applause.)

Let me assure you, serving alongside our President every day that we all believe in the same things. **You say prosperity and opportunity**. He says: **"Make America Great Again."**

With your help and with your support, and with the support of men and women who have been involved with the Club for Growth since its early days, its help for people like me and others, I know we will do just that and lead a **renewal and revival** for this country as never before. (Applause.)

You know, I've been in the trenches with most of you in

this room for years, so believe me when I say: **This is the moment** that we have worked so hard for and worked so long to see.

For the first time in a decade, thanks to your hard work, we have a pro-growth House, we have a pro-growth Senate, and we have a pro-growth President of the United States of America. (Applause.)

And President Donald Trump I believe has laid out an agenda that is **renewing** the **American Spirit** in ways that we haven't seen since the days of Ronald Reagan.

This is our moment. This is the time. And my friends, **this is our chance to prove that our answers are still the right answers for America.** (Applause.)

More **freedom.** Lower taxes. Less regulation and smaller government. **History will attest** that when **America builds on this foundation**, we reach heights that once seemed unreachable.

And **that is the foundation** of this administration. **President Trump's vision** is to **unleash growth in America** like never before, and the good news is: It's already happening.

On Day-One, President Trump went straight to work rolling back the reams of red tape. He instructed every bureaucracy in Washington, D.C. to find two regulations to get rid of before imposing any new red tape on the American people and on American free enterprise. (Applause.)

He's already taken action to put the Keystone and Dakota pipelines on the path to approval, **creating** tens of thousands of **American jobs** and **protecting** our American energy future. (Applause.)

And just this past Monday, President Trump set into motion a plan to reorganize the executive branch -- and that includes identifying and eliminating federal agencies that, frankly, we just plain don't need anymore.

It's leadership like that -- you can applaud that if you like. (Applause.)

It's leadership like this that's getting government out of the way of the American people and of American job creators. Businesses are already reacting to **President Trump's vision** and his **renewed optimism and investment**. And they're investing in America in ways that are lifting and creating jobs.

Last month alone the economy added 235,000 jobs. **Construction and manufacturing are booming once Again**. Business leaders and American consumers haven't been this confident in years -- and by some measures, in more than a decade.

Folks, the era of slow growth is over; **a new era of American growth has begun**. (Applause.)

You know and I know that economic growth begins with fiscal responsibility. I see my friend Senator Pat Toomey over there. We fought together in the House, shoulder to shoulder for fiscal restraint. And I know how enthusiastic he and the other great conservatives like Senator Mike Lee and others in the room are that just two days ago, President Donald Trump released the most conservative budget since Ronald Reagan sat in the Oval Office. (Ap-

plause.)

Our **vision** is simple. We want a government that will
keep Americans safe and that **leaves us free** to do what
the American people do best. That's why our budget first
and foremost gives our Soldiers, Sailors, Airmen, Marines,
and Coast Guard the resources they need to complete
their mission, protect our families, and come home safe to
theirs. We're **rebuilding** the American military under this
Trump budget. (Applause.)

But also at the President's direction, our budget offsets
$54 billion in military spending with government spending
cuts --a 31 percent cut at the E.P.A. (Applause.)

Double-digit reductions in no fewer than 10 federal depart-
ments. (Applause.)

And, folks, The Washington Post actually ran a headline
this week saying, they quote, "historic contraction of the
federal workforce." (Laughter.)

They meant it as a warning, we took it as a compli-
ment. (Applause.)

We're going to end the waste, the fraud, the abuse in D.C
and make sure that the American taxpayer gets the best
bang for their buck. I got to tell you this businessman
who has become President of the United States believes
in sharpened pencils. And he's been sharpening his pencils ever since the morning after Election Day. But beyond
the budget, we're going to keep slashing all the job-killing
regulations and rein in unelected bureaucrats in Washington, D.C. I want to commend the members of Congress
for sending those congressional review act bills. We're

going to keep rolling back regulation every chance we get so that this economy can't be crippled by bureaucrats in Washington, D.C. sitting behind the comfort of their metal desks. (Applause.)

We've heard from businesses large and small, all across America that red tape is strangling their ability to create jobs, and to grow and thrive. That's why we're working to get government off their back.

We're going to keep working with the Congress to repeal the last-minute mandates rushed through by the last administration. And, frankly, we're taking a hard look at every regulation on the books -- including, as President Trump said on Wednesday, the CAFE rule that is holding back the American automotive industry will now no longer stand in the way of economic prosperity and growth. (Applause.)

We're making sure federal agencies fast-track projects and permits and don't slow-walk them. And **we're going to roll back Dodd-Frank** so that American businesses have access to the best financial system in the world. (Applause.)

And with this Cabinet -- and how about this Cabinet? (Applause.)

With this Cabinet, President Trump has picked men and women who know that bureaucrats don't create jobs, businesses do.

The bottom line is that our agenda of more freedom and less regulation is going to usher in growth and opportunity and prosperity in this country like never before. And it's the vision that the Club for Growth has been about advancing since the very beginning of this organization. If you still have any doubt, there's also something else I want you to know. We're going to have the biggest tax reform and reduction in a generation in America before this year is out. (Applause.)

Under President Trump's leadership, we're going to cut taxes across the board for working families, small businesses, and family farms. It's going to be pro-growth, pro-savings, and pro-hardworking Americans keeping more of their hard-earned dollar.

We're going to simplify the tax code working with members of the House and Senate who are gathered here, and we're going to have lower rates across the board.

We're going to **make American businesses competitive again** by slashing one of the highest corporate rates in the developed world and **letting American companies bring the money back from overseas so they can invest in American and create American jobs with a lower business rate**. (Applause.)

And not only that, and I promise to you working with members of Congress, we're going to repeal hundreds of billions of dollars in taxes when we repeal and replace Obamacare. (Applause.)

My friends, the Obamacare nightmare is about to end. Now, I don't have to remind people here at the Club for Growth why this failed law has to go. You all have seen the headlines, and you know the facts. You've lived them in many places all over the country -- sky-rocketing premiums, unaffordable deductibles, mandates, higher taxes. The truth is the American people can't afford

Obamacare, and it's time we no longer ask them to put up with it. (Applause.)

In his joint address to Congress two weeks ago, the President outlined his plan to repeal and replace Obamacare once and for all. And we're working with members of Congress to advance that plan.

Make no mistake about it: Our plan is pro-growth and pro-freedom. It ends Obamacare's individual and employer mandates by eliminating their penalties by the time the whole plan is unfurled. It repeals the taxes I just mentioned right out of the gate. It expands health savings accounts. It enacts the biggest reform in Medicaid since the creation of that program in 1965.

These are the kind of solutions that conservatives like us have been talking about for years. And they're now within our reach. And let me be blunt: We need your help to get this plan passed. The House is set to vote next week on the beginning of this process. It's called the American Health Care Act, and it is a crucial step towards fulfilling our promise to repeal and replace Obamacare with something that actually works.

Now I know that there have been concerns expressed with the bill as it currently stands. And just know that the President and I are and our entire administration are listening. We're working with members of Congress to improve the bill and to make this bill even better than it already is.

And we're working with every single member of Congress -- the Republican Study Committee, the Freedom Caucus, the Senate Steering Committee, and all the lawmakers here tonight, just to name a few. Thanks to their input, we've actually added a number of great amendments just in the last 24 hours.

Beginning with, we're going to stop more states from expanding Medicaid by ceasing the expansion for states that did not expand Medicaid under Obamacare immediately. (Applause.)

Because of the voices of conservatives in Congress, we're going to be amending the Ho bill to give states the option for a Medicaid in a block grant in its entirety so states can reform Medicaid in the way that they see fit. (Applause.)

And thanks to the leadership and the collaboration of many of the great conservatives in this room, we're going to have an amendment to allow states to include a work requirement for able-bodied adults on Medicaid so we can ensure the program is there for people who actually need it. (Applause.)

Folks, I meant it when I said we're listening. And the President is going to continue to engage members of Congress in ways that we can improve this legislation. We had a meeting just yesterday in the Oval Office, and I was pleased that the leadership of the Republican Study Committee endorsed the bill that's moving through the House, and we're grateful for their support.

And while we're having a vigorous debate, the good news is that Republicans are in complete agreement, and we have complete consensus that Obamacare must go. (Applause.)

We'll continue to advance the President's agenda, and how we work that out is going to be the result of the legislative process and administrative action. But **President Trump's vision** is very simple: a national health-care marketplace and state-based Medicaid reform; allowing the American people to purchase health insurance across state lines the way you buy life insurance, the way you buy car insurance, and allowing states the **freedom** and flexibility to redesign Medicaid around the unique needs of their own people is a pathway toward a more prosperous future and better healthcare for the American people. (Applause.)

And it's important to remember that our healthcare plan doesn't begin and end with the bill that's moving through the Congress today. I wanted to make it clear to all of you this is only one part of the President's three-part strategy. The other two tracks are just as important in restoring free-market principles to American health care.

At this very moment, our administration is evaluating every possible administrative action to get government out of the way and allow for state-based innovation and reform. The name of the game is to seize the opportunity to change the regulations, and we've got a great team with Dr. Tom Price and Seema Verma heading up HHS and the Center for Medicaid & Medicare Services to do it.

Just this past week, they both sent a letter to every single one of America's governors saying, "a new era for federal and state Medicaid partnership" has begun -- and so it has. (Applause.)

Under Dr. Tom Price's leadership with Seema Verma at his side running Medicaid, we're going to give our states the freedom and flexibility they need with Medicaid to implement the kind of reforms that will do the most good for the most vulnerable -- state-based solutions, not one-size-fits-all federal solutions. And remember that truthfully it is about improving Medicaid.

When I was governor of the great state of Indiana, we brought about transformational change in Medicaid. For the first time in the history of Medicaid, we actually gained the approval to have people have to make a monthly contribution to a health savings account to receive full benefits. And tens of thousands of Hoosiers benefitted by that. We saw people already when I was governor moving from emergency room care to primary care, people taking advantage of preventive medicine.

Men and women I say from my heart as a former governor, now as your Vice President, the President's vision for state-based flexibility and reform is about improving the healthcare and improving the lives of our most vulnerable because states know how to do it in ways that will benefit their citizens. (Applause.)

And we're going to continue to partner with the Congress to pass other important healthcare reforms, including we're going to pass medical malpractice reform at last. (Applause.)

We're going to allow businesses around America to participate in association health plans, and as I mentioned before, we're going to give Americans the freedom to buy health insurance across state lines -- an idea whose time has come.

Not before too long I expect we're going to see that little lizard and Flo on television selling health insurance just the way they sell car insurance and sell life insurance. (Laughter and applause.)

Our three-part strategy, once enacted, we truly believe will create a dynamic national health-insurance marketplace, which is the key to making affordable, high-quality coverage accessible for every American.

Now we can't lose sight of what's at stake in the coming weeks. This is a momentous time. We literally have an opportunity to begin to accomplish what everyone in this room has fought so hard to achieve for so long. And President Trump and I look forward to continuing to work with all of you -- the men and women in public life who are here, and those of you who are patrons and supporters that are present.

And know this: When we repeal and replace Obamacare, we will also make room for even more tax relief for working families, small businesses, and family farms when we take up tax reform this spring. (Applause.)

But health care isn't the only place where we need your partnership. The same goes for the rest of our pro-growth, pro-freedom agenda.

Quite frankly, we're counting on you. And we know you'll be there. You've already demonstrated -- many of you for many years here at Club for Growth -- your dedication to the principles that we all share.

I look around this room and I see true patriots -- men and women who love this country and have been willing to devote your time and your talent and your treasure to the country's future without any regard to whether you'd ever be acknowledged or ever get credit for it. Those great candidates that you've supported over the years, and that now people the hallways of the House and the Senate serving the American people. The debt this country owes to the men and women in this organization and throughout the CONSERVATIVE MOVEMENT can only be repaid by keeping faith with the ideals and the principles that you have sought to advance.

You believe what I believe, you know what I know. This is an extraordinary country, that despite all the unparalleled achievements in our nation's history, **we have only just begun**. And President Trump believes we can and that we will astound the world with **our freedom**, with **our strength** and **our prosperity** because **the best days for America are yet to come**. (Applause.)

I truly do count myself blessed to stand shoulder to shoulder with my friend, the 45th President of the United States and to have stood for so long in this cause with so many of you in this room.

You know, we've been on this journey together for a long time. As David mentioned, when I ran for Congress, he was nice enough to mention that I'd lost the first two times. (Laughter.)

And then the Club for Growth helped me. The Club for Growth was there, supporting me and my little family in our desire to serve our country. We stood together then, and we've stood together ever since.

The reason that we're here with a pro-growth President and a pro-growth Congress on the cusp of repealing the failed policies of Obamacare is because, on the cusp of transformational tax reform, on the cusp of a whole range of reforms that will enliven this country's economy and open doors of opportunities for millions of Americans is

that year after year, **all of you in this room and conservatives around America never gave up**. And I'm just here to
say thanks, and to tell you to press on.

MY FRIENDS, THIS IS OUR MOMENT. **Now is the
time. This is our rendezvous with destiny**. And I know
we'll meet the challenge. It will come together. We'll
give all of our energy, our enthusiasm, our courage, and
our conviction, our passion, and our prayers. And in that,
I'm confident -- I'm confident we'll make the most of the
opportunity before us.

And under President Trump's leadership, I know we'll get
this economy moving **Again**. Under his leadership, I know
**we'll restore opportunity and prosperity for all our peo-
ple**. We'll make the best healthcare system in the world
even better with free-market principles, more jobs, higher
incomes, better healthcare in a **safer** and more **prosperous
America**.

In a word, my friends, with your help, and with God's help,
we'll **Make America Great Again**.

Thank you very much. Thanks for having me back and
God bless you and God bless the United State of America.
(Applause.)

END

"...A new era of
American growth has begun."

Chapter 96

**REMARKS BY PRESIDENT TRUMP IN A BILATERAL MEETING
WITH PRIME MINISTER AL-ABADI OF IRAQ
CABINET ROOM**

20 March 2017

3:28 P.M. EDT

PRESIDENT TRUMP: Mr. Prime Minister, it's an honor to have you here before our Cabinet, which I hope in years to come will be thought of one the great Cabinets in the history of the United States. We just spent a few minutes speaking in the Oval Office and learning and giving each other ideas. One of the things I did ask is why did President Obama sign that agreement with Iran, because nobody has been able to figure that one out. But maybe someday we'll be able to figure it out.

I want to thank you very much for being here, great respect for you. I know you're working very hard, and General Mattis and General McMaster and Rex Tillerson have all been telling me that you're doing a job -- it's not an easy job, it's a very tough job. Your soldiers are fighting hard. I know Mosul is moving along, but Mosul was ours until we left. So perhaps we shouldn't have gone in, and certainly we shouldn't have left. We should never ever have left, and the vacuum was created, and we discussed what happened.

But we'll spend a lot of time with you, with your group. And thank you all very much for being here. We appreciate it. And we will figure something out. Our main

thrust is we have to get rid of ISIS. We're going to get rid
of ISIS. It will happen. It's happening right now.

General Mattis and his team have done an incredible
job. A lot of things are different than they were even five
or six weeks ago. We've been here a short while and people have said they'd never seen such a difference.

So we are with you. And again, thank you very much for
being with us.

PRIME MINISTER AL-ABADI: Excuse me a second.

PRESIDENT TRUMP: Yes, please.

PRIME MINISTER AL-ABADI: (Speaks Arabic.) [The White
House did not provide a transcription.]

PRESIDENT TRUMP: Thank you very much, Mr. Prime
Minister. We very much appreciate your words, and we
will start discussing certain things right now.

Thank you very much, everybody.

END
3:33 P.M. EDT

Chapter 97

**REMARKS BY THE PRESIDENT AT SIGNING OF S.442,
NATIONAL AERONAUTICS AND SPACE ADMINISTRATION
TRANSITION AUTHORIZATION ACT OF 2017
OVAL OFFICE**

21 March 2017

11:07 A.M. EDT

THE PRESIDENT: Thank you very much. For almost six decades, NASA's work has inspired millions and millions of Americans to imagine distant worlds and a better future right here on Earth. I'm delighted to sign this bill -- it's been a long time since a bill like this has been signed -- reaffirming our national commitment to the core mission of NASA: human space exploration, space science and technology.

With this legislation, we support NASA's scientists, engineers, astronauts and **their pursuit of discovery**. **We support jobs -- it's about jobs also**. This bill calls for ongoing medical monitoring and treatment of our heroic astronauts for health conditions that result from their service. It's a pretty tough -- I don't know, Ted, would you like to do it? I don't think I would. (Laughter.)

I'm not sure we want to do it.

SENATOR CRUZ: You could send Congress to space. (Laughter.)

THE PRESIDENT: What a great idea. That could be. (Laugh-

ter.)

This bill will make sure that NASA's most important and effective programs are sustained. It orders NASA to continue -- and it does, it orders just that -- to continue transitioning activities to **the commercial sector** where we have seen great progress. It's amazing what's going on -- so many people and so many companies are so into exactly what NASA stands for. So the commercial and the private sector will get to use these facilities. And **I hope they're going to be paying us a lot of money**. But they're going to make great progress.

It continues support for the commercial crew program, which will **carry American astronauts into space from American soil once Again** -- been a long time. It supports NASA's deep space exploration, including the Space Launch System and the ORION spacecraft. It advances space science by maintaining a balanced set of mission and activities to explore our solar system and the entire universe. And it ensures that through NASA's astronauts and aeronautics research, the United States will remain a total leader in aviation.

Now, the astronauts are amazing. I've met some of them -- they are very brave people and their right at the forefront. So we salute them with this legislation. And we salute the ones that have lost their lives doing what they love to do.

America's space program has been a blessing to our people and to the entire world. Almost half a century ago, our brave astronauts first planted the American flag on the moon. That was a big moment in our history. Now this is [sic] nation is ready to be the **first in space once Again**. Today **we're taking the initial steps toward a bold and brave new future** for American space flight.

I am honored to sign this new bill -- the folks behind me have been so involved in it. They love NASA. They love everything it stands for, and they love the people in their areas. You have a couple of areas that are going to be very much benefitted by this.

So I just want to thank all of the people standing behind me. They've done a great service for the country and for their community. **A lot of jobs** -- and these are great jobs. So thank you very much. And we'll sign this.

(The Bill is signed.)

So we'll hold that up. A lot of pages. Look at the pages in there. That's a lot of (Laughter.)

We don't want to let that slip. (Applause.)

[Picture: screengrab.]

Who else should get these, Mr. Vice President?

ACTING NASA ADMINISTRATOR LIGHTFOOT: Mr. President, on behalf of NASA, I would like to present you with this astronaut flight jacket. Thank you very much for your support. (Applause.)

THE PRESIDENT: Thank you very much. Does anybody have anything to say? Ted, do you want to say something?

SENATOR CRUZ: Well, this is terrific. The first time in seven years we've had a NASA authorization bill. Thank you, Mr. President, for signing it. This means a great deal to the nation's space exploration, it means a great deal to the state of Texas, and it continues America's leadership in space. So thank you for your leadership.

THE PRESIDENT: Thank you, Ted. Marco?

SENATOR RUBIO: I just think I'm happy to see that Florida is going to continue to more than Texas is with NASA, Mr. President. (Laughter.)

THE PRESIDENT: Going to be a good competition.
Mr. Vice President.

Okay, Senator. Well, he's a Democrat. I wasn't going to let him speak. (Laughter.)

You guys love me.

SENATOR NELSON: It puts us on the dual track. We have the commercial companies going to and from the International Space Station, and we have NASA going out and exploring the heavens. And we're going to Mars.

THE PRESIDENT: I love that. I love that.

REPRESENTATIVE: Mr. President, if I may. Just as Americans remember that President Eisenhower was the father of the Interstate Highway System, with you[r] bill signing today and you[r] **vision** and leadership, **future generations will remember that President Donald Trump was the father of the interplanetary highway system.**

THE PRESIDENT: Well, that sounds exciting. (Laughter and applause.)

First, we want to fix our highways. We're going to fix our highways.

REPRESENTATIVE SMITH: Mr. President, as House Subcommittee chair, I'd like to -- and actually part of the author of the new crew act for our astronauts, that started in a meeting with astronaut Scott Kelly after he got back from nearly a year in space. And I said, what can we do for you in the House of Representatives? He said, take care of us. Make sure we're hanging on to this data so that future astronauts will be treated right and they'll know what to do, and make the proper adjustments for folks when they're up there in the ISS and on beyond. So I want to thank everybody here. I thank these astronauts who have put their lives on the line.

THE PRESIDENT: Thank you very much.

THE VICE PRESIDENT: I want to, on behalf of the President and all of us, I want to thank all these members of Congress, these courageous astronauts for their work on this, but to assure you that, in very short order, the President will be taking action to **relaunch the National Space Coun-**

cil. He's asked me to chair that, as Vice Presidents have in the past. And we're going to be bringing together the best and brightest in NASA and also in the private sector.

We have elected a builder for President. And as he said, America once **Again** has to start building and leading to the stars. So thank you, Mr. President.

THE PRESIDENT: Thank you. Thank you, everybody.

END
11:14 A.M. EDT

Chapter 98

**REMARKS BY PRESIDENT TRUMP AND
ADMINISTRATOR SEEMA VERMA
IN WOMEN IN HEALTHCARE PANEL MEETING
ROOSEVELT ROOM**

22 March 2017

11:24 A.M. EDT

THE PRESIDENT: Well, thank you very much for being here. It's a great honor, very great honor. I want to thank Vice President Pence, Secretary Tom Price, and Administrator Seema Verma -- who's done an incredible job, by the way -- for all of the time and energy they've put into repairing and replacing Obamacare ahead of tomorrow's crucial vote. Big vote tomorrow in the House.

I want to especially thank Seema, the Administrator of the Centers for Medicare and Medicaid Services --a wonderful job she's doing, and definitely a complex job, but you have it under control, right -- for hosting this very important meeting to discuss the vital role women play in healthcare and the hardships inflicted on them by the Obamacare catastrophe. It's been bad.

Administrator Seema Verma is playing the leading role for us in helping us to repeal and replace Obamacare. The doctors, nurses and healthcare professionals here today represent the millions of women -- millions and millions -- who play a vital and indispensable role in Americans' healthcare. Unfortunately, Obamacare is making their lives so much more difficult, as we all know, and putting enormous barriers in the way of helping patients who we are going to help. We're going to get this thing done. We're going to get it figured out. It's a tough situation our country has been put in. It's not easy.

Women doctors and healthcare leaders have changed the face of healthcare in America, saving and improving countless American lives. In 1965, only 9 percent of accepted medical school applicants were women -- 9 percent. Last year, nearly 50 percent of newly accepted applicants were women. Congratulations. Good job. It's a good job. Thirty-eight percent of physicians and surgeons are women, and that number will continue to grow. That's a big victory for our society, big victory for America.

I want to also thank all of the women nurses and healthcare aides for their incredible service and dedication to our country. What you do is remarkable. Unfortunately, Obamacare is making it much harder for all of the doctors, nurses and healthcare professionals, men and women alike, to do their job. As insurers flee Obamacare's broken marketplace -- and it is broken, it's broken badly; the insurance companies are fleeing -- millions of patients can no longer access the healthcare professionals the know and trust. In other words, "keep your doctor, keep your plan" didn't work out that way. You don't get your doctor, you don't get your plan.

So that is one of the more vital reasons why we must repeal Obamacare. It's one of the reasons why we're here today.

So with that, I want to turn it over to Administrator Verma, and we'll start a meeting.

ADMINISTRATOR VERMA: Thank you.

THE PRESIDENT: Thank you very much. You could probably do -- stay for this little while, and then we'll clear out
the room and talk, okay? Go ahead.

ADMINISTRATOR VERMA: Well, thank you, Mr.
President. Appreciate it. This gentleman has been very
supportive as I started my position at CMS, and I am very
appreciative to be a part of this great healthcare team.

THE PRESIDENT: Thank you.

ADMINISTRATOR VERMA: And thanks to all the women
that came today. It's great to see so many strong, professional women that are on the front lines of healthcare. So
thanks again for coming today.

Obamacare has just been a broken promise. Instead of
meaningful healthcare, we have higher costs, less choices,
and more mandates. Right now, we have the government
that's making decisions about our healthcare, not patients
and not doctors. As a mother and as a woman, the most
important thing about my healthcare is being able to pick
out the doctor that I feel comfortable with, but unfortunately, with Obamacare, we have less choices.

One-third of counties and five states only have one choice
of health plan. And so that tells us we are not getting
the choices that Americans deserve. And the problem is
getting worse. We have even more insurers that are saying
that they're going to leave the marketplace.

And I think the other thing that concerns me is hearing
from providers. Many providers are faced with deal-

ing with regulations and mandates instead of focusing on high-quality care and spending time with their patients. They are forced to deal with regulations.

And I came to D.C. because I was so concerned about the direction our healthcare was going in because of Obamacare. I want to be a part of the solution. I'm very excited about the American Health Care Act. There's a vote on that tomorrow.

I think this is an opportunity for us to finally get rid of Obamacare and move towards a system that's going to drive costs down, give Americans more choices, and put patients and doctors in control of their healthcare.

So once again, thank you for coming today. And I look forward to hearing all the stories.

THE PRESIDENT: Thank you very much.

END
11:30 A.M. EDT

Chapter 99

REMARKS BY PRESIDENT TRUMP BEFORE MEETING WITH MEMBERS OF THE CONGRESSIONAL BLACK CAUCUS CABINET ROOM

22 March 2017

3:10 P.M. EDT

THE PRESIDENT: Well, I'm deeply honored to welcome the members of the Congressional Black Caucus to the White House. We're going to have a lot of meetings over the years, and I very much appreciate you being here.

Throughout my campaign, I pledged to focus on improving conditions for African American citizens. This means more to me than anybody would understand or know. **Every American child has a right to grow up in a safe community, to attend great schools, to graduate with access to high-paying jobs.**

America has spent trillions and trillions of dollars overseas. I guess -- I heard just recently in the Middle East we've spent as of about two months ago $6 trillion -- $6 trillion, and you know where we are over there -- while neglecting the fate of American children in cities like Baltimore and Chicago and Detroit.

African American citizens have given so much to this country. They've fought in every war since the Revolution, and they've fought hard. They've lifted up the conscience of our nation in the march toward civil rights, enriched the soul of America -- and their faith and cour-

age. And they've advanced our country in the fields of science, arts and medicine.

Elijah Cummings, who was here about two weeks ago, who I happen to think is a terrific man -- I don't know if he'll say that about me, but I will tell you, I really liked him a lot. And we were talking about drugs and prescription drugs and the costs. And you go to Europe, you go to Canada, you go to other countries and you buy them for a fraction of what you pay in this country. And that's been a very big subject for him, and it's a subject for me that is very important. And we're going to either do it in health-care -- which I think we're going to do it in healthcare -- or we're going to do it separately.

But **we're going to bid on drug prices**, and we're going to try and have the lowest prices anywhere in the world, from really the highest. And that's not only the drugs, it's pre-scription drugs. But you go out to stores and you go even -- in any community, rich or poor community, and you look at the kind of drug prices that we're paying and it's really unfair what's happened in our country.

So we're going to be instituting a very, very strong bidding process. We'll probably need some legislation, but we're going to do it regardless. We have to do it. **And we're going to get drug prices way down, way down.**

Some people think it's as important as the healthcare measure, because people are being ripped off when they need their -- they need drugs, they need prescription drugs. And we're going to take care of that situation.

So again, I very much appreciate you being here. It's a tremendous honor for me. And we're going to work on different things, and we're going to see if we can get a lot accomplished.

And with that, let's get going. And thank you all very much.

END
3:13 P.M. EDT

*"African American citizens
have given so much to this country.
They've fought in every war
since the Revolution, and
they've fought hard.
They've lifted up the conscience of our
nation in the march
toward civil rights,
enriched the soul of America --
and their faith and courage.
And they've advanced
our country in the fields of science,
arts and medicine."*

Chapter 100

**REMARKS BY THE PRESIDENT IN MEETING WITH
TRUCKERS AND CEOS ON HEALTHCARE
CABINET ROOM**

23 March 2017

3:20 P.M. EDT

THE PRESIDENT: First of all, I want to thank you for your support on healthcare. That's been great.

I know you had a big problem with Obamacare, and everybody [does], so welcome to the crowd. But I very much appreciate you being here and I very much appreciate your support.

I'm honored to welcome all of the many truckers and the trucking industry leaders to the White House.

And I must say, really, you are the leaders. You are the big ones. I'm very impressed I was able to get you -- I think it WAS the White House that was able to get you. (Laughter.)

No one knows America like truckers know America. You see it every day, and you see every hill and you see every valley and you see every pothole in our roads that have to be redone. [Right?]

Every town, every forest, from border to border, to ocean to ocean -- it's true. It's true. And you love America, and you love the **Spirit**, and we love your **Spirit**. And we want to thank you very much, because -- very special people.

Through day and night in all kinds of weather, truckers course the arteries of our nation's highways. You carry anything and everything -- the food that stocks our shelves, the fuel that runs our cars, and the steel that builds our cities. You think I wrote that? (Laughter.)

Not bad, is it? (Laughter.)

Save that -- I want to save that paragraph. [Laughter.]

But America depends on you. And you work very hard for America. Many of you spend weeks away from your families doing what can sometimes be a very difficult and dangerous job, to put it mildly.

But you take care of yourselves, you look out for your friends, and you don't stop until the job is done. That's true.

Obamacare has inflicted great pain on American truckers. Many of you were forced to buy health insurance on the Obamacare exchanges.

You experienced a crippling rise in premiums and a dramatic loss in options. And you just take a look at what's happened to the costs, and it's incredible. You look at what's going on with deductibles where they're through the roof, so essentially you don't have it because hopefully you'll never have to use it because you won't have that kind of injury or sickness.

So you know the problems, and it's put a lot of the trucking businesses out of business, which is pretty tough.

In addition, many union drivers are slated to have their plans taxed to pay Obamacare, and they've been against it for a long period of time. And trucking companies that are considered large employers have to offer government-mandated health insurance.

You have the mandate that just doesn't work for them. You're forced to do things that you don't want to do.

Today, the House is voting to repeal and replace the disaster known as Obamacare. We'll see what happens, going to be a very close vote.

After we repeal and replace Obamacare -- and by the way, it's close not because Obamacare is good, it's close -- politics. They know it's no good. Everybody knows it's no good. It's ONLY politics, because we have a great bill, and I think we have a very good chance. But it's ONLY politics.

After we repeal and replace Obamacare, we're going to do everything we can to make sure truckers stay busy moving American goods made by American companies and workers.

Big difference out there now, don't you think? Big difference.

We will rewrite our broken tax code and fix our terrible trade deals. We will also eliminate job-killing regulations where -- you guys are so subject to regulations, and we're going to free it up. It's going to be freed up. You're going to be back to business.

And **we'll make sure America's infrastructure is the best**

in the world. Right now it's probably the worst it's been in 40 years. I have friends in your business, they say trucking from Los Angeles to New York and back, it's very tough on the trucks -- never used to be that way -- with the condition of the roads and the highways.

So I look forward to hearing from you. We're going to have a long talk -- although I'm not going to make it too long because I have to get votes. I don't want to spend too much time with you and then lose by one vote. (Laughter.)

Then I'm going to blame the truckers. (Laughter.)

But we're going to talk for a little while and then I'm going to go back to business. And I appreciate you all being here.

And maybe we'll go around the table, just introduce yourself and your company real fast, and we'll leave the press stay because I'm sure they'll be very excited by that.

And let's go.

MR. CONGDON: Okay. I'm David Congdon, I'm the CEO of Old Dominion Freight Lines. We're a truckload carrier based in North Carolina, and we operate 8,000 tractors, 25,000 trailers, and do about $3 billion in sales, 19,500 employees.

THE PRESIDENT: Wow, that's fantastic, David. How do you compare size-wise with the other big ones?

MR. CONGDON: We're the third-largest in the list of the truckload sector.

THE PRESIDENT: Who is the largest?

MR. CONGDON: The largest is Fed Ex Freight.

THE PRESIDENT: I see, and they're here, too.

MR. CONGDON: We have -- freighters at the table.

THE PRESIDENT: Where's Fed Ex Freight?

MR. DUCKER: Here, sir.

THE PRESIDENT: Very impressive. Oh, you're central casting, look at that. (Laughter.)

Great company.

MR. BURG: Good afternoon, Mr. President. Jim Burg, JBTC Trucking from Macomb County, Michigan -- a county you carried well.

THE PRESIDENT: I did.

MR. BURG: First time since 2004 [2011].

THE PRESIDENT: Love that state. (Laughter.)

Bringing back a lot of jobs, you see what's happening.

MR. BURG: Started the company with one truck in 1984, built it up to a 90-truck operation. We're a flat-bed carrier that hauls steel and construction materials within Michigan and the Midwest.

THE PRESIDENT: Fantastic. Say hello to Michigan for me.

MR. BURG: I certainly will.

THE PRESIDENT: We like that sound: Breaking news,
Donald trump has won Michigan. (Laughter.)

You know what, we're doing even better now because
we've brought back -- Ford is moving back in and
General Motors, they're going to be doing a lot of new
plants and thousands and thousands of people coming
back into Michigan.

MR. BURG: We'll be hauling the steel for those plants.

THE PRESIDENT: I know you will, I know you
will. Good. Thank you very much.

MR. BURCH: Mr. President, it's an honor to be here. My
name is Kevin Burch. I'm President of Jet Express Trucking
out of Dayton, Ohio, a truckload carrier. I'm also this year's
Chairman of the Board of American Trucking Association.

Originally from Flint, Michigan, we were involved with
handling a lot of the water, and appreciate all your support
in helping us...

THE PRESIDENT: They [We] just gave a check for $100
million [dollars] to Flint. Think of that whole horrible
deal. That's great political leadership. What a disaster. In
order to save a fee, they went to bad water and spent a
fortune on pipes and infrastructure. ***

[NOTE: The above three asterisks were left-in the official
transcript; the missing comments would seem to be "*Anyway we are helping out Flint*".]

[MR. BURCH: We are primarily a truck load company for
General Motors, around 300 loads a day just in time - right

The First 100 Days   799

in the summer. (Inaudible.)]

THE PRESIDENT: Yup, they are expanding as your know in [THIS COUNTRY. The rest of their expansion I don't care too much about, it doesn't matter, but I don't think they are doing too much.]

[Okay, that's my guy. Go ahead.]

[MR BURCH: Yes.]

[NEAL KEDZIE:] Mr. President it's and honor to be here.

I'm the President of the Wisconsin Motor Carriers Association. We represent the trucking industry in Wisconsin. There are 50 associations across the entire country ** the umbrella under the American Trucking Association.

[NOTE: The above two asterisks were left-in the official transcript; the commentary at this point was inaudible.]

We have over 1,100 members in our association. There are over 15,000 trucking companies in Wisconsin. And prior to that time, I spent 18 years in the Wisconsin state legislature.

And also, Reince Priebus and I are graduates from UW-Whitewater, and have been buddies for about 20 years ourselves. So it's an honor to be here, sir.

THE PRESIDENT: Thank you. He's doing a good job.

MR. NASH: Mr. President, Dennis Nash. I'm the Founder and CEO of The Kenan Advantage Group, based in Canton,

Ohio.

We're in the tank truck hauling business, primarily fuels and chemicals. We have about 10,000 drivers located in 38 states.

THE PRESIDENT: Great job.

MR. NASH: And I think they have a mutual friend, or had a mutual friend in Charlie Eichholtz (sp).

THE PRESIDENT: Absolutely.

MR. NASH: Yeah, his daughter is still running the company.

THE PRESIDENT: Great guy.

MR. FULLER: Eric Fuller, CEO of U.S. Xpress Enterprises, out of Chattanooga, Tennessee. We're the second-largest privately-held truckload carrier. We have about 7,000 tractor, 10,000 employees.

THE PRESIDENT: All right. Good job.

MR. SMITH: John Smith, from CRST in Cedar Rapids. Second generation -- my dad started the business. Third generation is coming in, so we hope to keep it going. Would like to invite you to Cedar Rapids. We also do a lot of training and bringing in the new blood to the industry, and I think it's quite unique and would love to get you out there.

THE PRESIDENT: Well, Cedar Rapids was very good to me. You know that, right? So I like Cedar Rapids. Say hello to the people.

MR. SMITH: I will.

MR. SPEAR: Mr. President, I'm Chris Spear. I'm President and CEO of the American Trucking Association. Thanks to you and Mr. Vice President for hosting us here today.

We have one in 16 jobs in this country. And in 29 states, truck drivers are the number one job. So for the 7.3 million employees in the industry, 3.5 million drivers, we have 12 of them here today that have 29.4 million accident-free miles. **Safety** is our number one priority. And obviously we are here to help you get the job done.

We would love to see Obamacare replaced. We love the bill. We want to bring costs down. We want to make our lives and our families better. And we believe this is the proposal to get the job done.

THE PRESIDENT: It's a great, great proposal. And you're going to have competitive bidding. You're going to have those insurance companies going wild for your companies. And you'll be able to pick the right plan and the right doctor -- which as you know, was a big lie. But you're going to have the plan and the doctor, yeah.

And I think we're doing well. We'll find out in about three hours.

MR. SPEAR: Absolutely.

THE PRESIDENT: I don't know why I'm with you. (Laughter.)

That's all right. Thanks, Chris.

MR. OSTERGARD: Mr. President, it's an honor to be here. I'm Tonn Ostergaard, President and CEO of Crete Carrier Corporation, a family-owned trucking company in Lincoln, Nebraska. We run a little over 5,000 trucks. And we're just proud to help you **Make America Great**. Thank you.

THE PRESIDENT: Thank you. Thank you very much. It's great. Thank you. Great place -- Nebraska.

MR. MCARDLE: Mr. President, Rick McArdle with UPS. I'm the President of UPS Freight, based out of Atlanta. It is the home of 350,000-plus employees here in the United States. We're just glad to be here.

We're also proud to be a member of the Truckers Against Trafficking. It's a tremendous organization that does a great job to help law enforcement try to stop and put an end to human trafficking.

THE PRESIDENT: Great. That's a big deal. It's a much bigger problem than people understand. Thank you very much, Richard.

MR. LANGER: Mr. President, Jerry Langer. I'm a Chief Commercial Officer for Langer Transport Corporation -- a family business in our 83rd year.

My two brothers and I are third generation. We are a liquid tank truck carrier, and work with raw materials and for the largest producers in the country for manufacturing.

And my grandfather came over from Russia, turn of the century, and started his business by being a handyman and carrying things around -- bought a horse and buggy, and one truck.

And today we have 1,200 trucks on the road. And love what we do -- 18 states -- and we want to be a partner with you, and keep growing your plan and your goals here. So thank you very much.

THE PRESIDENT: You're going to be loving it. Thank you very much.

MR. DUCKER: Mr. President, Mike Ducker, with Fed Ex Freight. I represent Fed Ex -- about 350,000-plus American employees. And we have 150,000 trucks. We're the largest LTL provider. And we thank you very much for having us here today.

We thank you for including the people that actually do the work, and that make the money for the company. And we thank you for tackling tough issues.

THE PRESIDENT: Thank you. And your Founder is a great gentleman, and a great friend of mine. You know that, right?

MR. DUCKER: Yes, sir. He sends his very, very best to you.

THE PRESIDENT: He is a great one. Thank you. Say hello to him.

MR. LEX: Thank you, Mr. President, for having us. I'm John Lex. I'm an American road Team Captain. Also a share-the-road professional.

I'm also a truck driver for WalMart transportation -- been driving for over 30 years, have 2.9 million accident-free miles.

And it's just an honor to be here today. Drive for a small little company out of company named WalMart. (Laughter.)

THE PRESIDENT: Great job.

MR. LEX: Thank you.

MR. PAUL: How you doing, Mr. President. Glad to be here. I'm Charlton Paul -- UPS Freight, America's road Team Captain, and Driving Trainer for UPS Freight.

This is my 21st year with UPS, and 2.1 million safe miles.

THE PRESIDENT: Fantastic.

MR. PAUL: And I'm depending on you to do great things. I appreciate you.

THE PRESIDENT: Be careful when you leave here now -- no accidents. (Laughter.)

MR. PAUL: Knock on wood.

THE PRESIDENT: It's a fantastic job.

MR. LOGAN: Mr. President, I'm Don Logan. I work for Fed Ex Freight. I'm from Topeka, Kansas. I've been a truck driver for 31 years, have 2.6 million safe driving miles.

THE PRESIDENT: Fantastic. Boy, that's a lot of miles.

MS. HARTMAN: Rhonda Hartman, Old Dominion Freight

Lines -- 34 years in the business, 2.7 million miles driving without an accident.

THE PRESIDENT: Fantastic.

MS. HARTMAN: And I say -- and a ticket. No tickets either. (Laughter and applause.)

THE PRESIDENT: That's pretty impressive.

MR. GARCIA: Mr. President, it's an honor to be here. Ralph Garcia, with ABF Brake Systems -- 38 years in the businesses -- and I am a proud *Hispanic for Trump*. You did it. (Applause.)

[The President and Mr. Ralph Garcia shake hands.]

MR. SIMPSON: Mr. President, Russel Simpson.

I reside in Springfield, Ohio where you held a large rally I attended.

I've been 31 years as a professional driver, and when you get ready to build the wall, I want to haul the first load of concrete. (Laughter and applause.)

[The President and Mr. Russel Simpson shake hands.]

[THE PRESIDENT: Thank you.]

THE PRESIDENT: What a group. (Laughter.)

[Mr. Earl Taylor stands up behind the President, and the President notices - turns round on his seat and shakes Mr. Earl Taylor's hand.]

MR. TAYLOR: How you doing? Mr. President, thank you for having us here. I'm really proud to be here.

My name is Earl Taylor -- been in the business 19 years. And unlike some of these guys who are over-the-road drivers, I drive in the cities around the state.

And I have 19 years in the business, and 1.2 million miles -- in the city. (Applause.)

THE PRESIDENT: They don't know, that may be tougher.

MR. TAYLOR: That's much tougher, Sir. Much tougher.

THE PRESIDENT: We know about the city. (Laughter.)

MR. FIELDS: I'm Steve Fields. It's an honor, by the way.

I work for Marcy Freight out of Kansas City, Missouri. I've been driving 32 years, and I have 3.1 million.

It's an honor to be here.

[The President and Mr Steve Field shake hands.]

THE PRESIDENT: Fantastic job.

MR. FIELDS: Thank you. I appreciate you.

THE PRESIDENT: Fantastic job. Boy, that's a great group of people.

I'm more impressed by them than I am with the executives. (Laughter and applause.)

Thank you very much, everybody. Thank you very much.

END
3:30 P.M. EDT

[NOTE: White House transcript included *** and ** without any additional data.

It is not known if the White House transcribers had intended to return to these gaps, to insert the previously missing commentary.

The compilers have transcribed the balance of the discussion direct from video footage.]

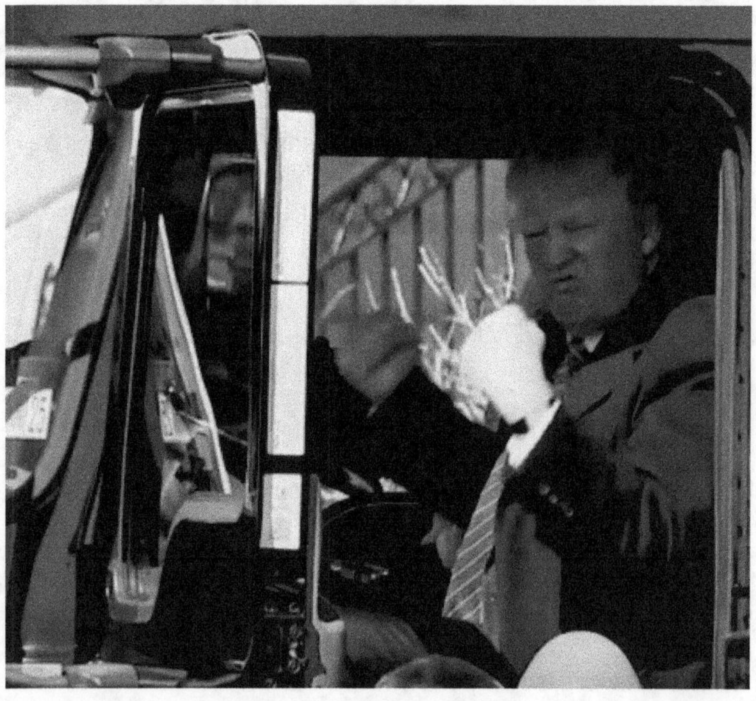

[Photo: screengrab - Outside the White House prior to the meeting.]

[Photo: screengrab. Outside the White House, prior to the meeting.]

Chapter 101

24 March 2017

THE PRESIDENT: Thank you very much for being here this morning. Today, I'm pleased to announce the official approval of the presidential permit for the Keystone XL Pipeline.

TransCanada will finally be allowed to complete this long overdue project with efficiency and with speed.

We're working out the final details as we speak. It's going to be an incredible pipeline, greatest technology known to man or woman. And frankly, we're very proud of it.

Russ Girling, President of TransCanada, is right behind me, and I'm going to have him say a few words. I know, Russ, you've been waiting for a long, long time.

And I hope you don't pay your consultants anything because they had nothing to do with the approval. (Laughter.)

You should ask for the hundreds of millions of dollars back that you paid them because they didn't do a damn thing except get a no vote, right?

It's a great day for American jobs and a historic moment for North American and energy independence. This an-

nouncement is part of a **new era** of American energy policy that will lower costs for American families -- and very
significantly -- reduce our dependence on foreign oil, and
create thousands of jobs right here in America.

And I also would like to add I think it's a lot safer to have
pipelines than to use other forms of transportation for
your product.

When completed, the Keystone XL Pipeline will span 900
miles -- wow -- and have the capacity to deliver more than
800,000 barrels of oil per day to the Gulf Coast refiner-
ies. That's some big pipeline.

The fact is that this $8 billion investment in American
energy was delayed for so long -- it demonstrates how our
government has too often failed its citizens and companies
over the past long period of time.

Today, we begin to make things right and to do things right.

Today we take one more step in putting the jobs, wages,
and economic security of **American citizens First.**

Put America First.

As the Keystone XL Pipeline now moves forward, this is
just the first of many energy and infrastructure projects
that my administration will approve -- and we've already
approved a couple of other big ones, very, very big ones,
which we'll be announcing soon -- in order to help **put
Americans back to work**, grow our economy, and **rebuild**
our nation.

And with that, I'd like to invite Russ to say a few

words. Russ is a very highly respected man in the energy world. He's President of TransCanada.

And I know you'll do a fantastic job, Russ, and get it up and hire plenty of American people.

Thank you.

MR. GIRLING: Thank you, Mr. President. And this is a very, very important day for us -- for our company.

So on behalf of thousands of people that have worked very hard to get here -- as you've pointed out, very long time to get here -- but we're very relieved, and very much just want to get to work.

Some of those folks I have with me today -- the building trades with Sean McGarvey; some of our -- construction contractor, Quanta; our pipe suppliers from Welspun.

There's thousands of people that are just ready and itching to get to work. We got a lot of work to do in the field, but as you pointed out, this is the safest and most reliable way to move our products to market. We're going to use the best technology and be able to create thousands of jobs and important tax revenues in local communities.

That's something often that's overlooked in new projects like this, is local communities benefit greatly from these projects. It gives them tax revenues in which they can invest in schools, hospitals, roads, teachers, nurses -- all of those things -- build the fabric of communities and make those places better for those folks to live.

So, again, thank you very much for this opportunity, and we're not going to let you down, sir.

THE PRESIDENT: Well, thank you, Russ. And I know the voters appreciate this. Some of them expressed it very, very strongly. The workers definitely appreciate it.

The building trades' heads didn't, but now maybe they're going to start to. Where are my building trades guys? I think they're going to start to, because other people were not going to be signing this bill. That I can tell you. And if it ever did get done, it would be years. But I don't think it would have ever gotten done.

So we put a lot of people to work, a lot of great workers to work, and they did appreciate it. And they appreciated it, Russ, very much at the polls, as you probably noticed. And so we're very happy about it.

So the bottom line -- Keystone finished. They're going to start construction when?

MR. GIRLING: Well, we've got some work to do in Nebraska to get our permits there --

THE PRESIDENT: Nebraska.

MR. GIRLING: -- so we're looking forward to working through that local --

THE PRESIDENT: I'll call Nebraska. (Laughter.)

You know why?

Nebraska has a great Governor. They have a great Governor.

MR. GIRLING: We've been working there for some time, and I do believe that we'll get through that process.

But obviously have to engage with local landowners, communities. So we'll be reaching out to those over the coming months to get the other necessary permits that we need, and then we'd look forward to start construction.

THE PRESIDENT: Okay. I'm sure Nebraska will be good. Peter is a fantastic Governor who's done a great job, and I'll call him today. So thank you all very much. Appreciate it. Thank you.

END
10:32 A.M. EDT

Chapter 102

**REMARKS BY PRESIDENT TRUMP AT JOBS ANNOUNCEMENT
WITH CHARTER COMMUNICATIONS
OVAL OFFICE**

24 March 2017

11:03 A.M. EDT

THE PRESIDENT: Thank you very much. We greatly appreciate you being here. I'm delighted to welcome Tom Rutledge, Chairman and CEO of Charter Communications -- a great company -- to the White House.

I'm also very honored that my friend, Texas Governor Greg Abbott -- my good friend and supporter -- we love you -- is here with us today. Very appropriate. He's done a fantastic job in Texas, and we had a previous Governor who did a very good job, right?

GOVERNOR ABBOTT: Right. (Laughter.)

THE PRESIDENT: Right. He's around here someplace. Standing right over there.

I'm very excited about the announcement we are about to make. First, some background.

Five years ago Charter Communications was a struggling company that had slowly emerged from bankruptcy.

Today, thanks to hard work and unbelievable leadership, truly great leadership, it's the fastest-growing television,

Internet, and voice company in the nation. I would say
that's a good job. Not bad.

Tom Rutledge and his team turned the company around,
and they did it very quickly. They created a culture of customer service and excellence. And, most importantly, they
brought back many jobs that had been shipped overseas
-- something that's happening far too often, but we're
changing that. That is very good for certain businesses but
not good for the United States, not good for America, not
good for our people.

When **American workers win**, America as a **country
wins. We want to have companies that thrive and hire
and grow right here in America. And we want them to
use American workers and American citizens.**

Today I am thrilled to announce that Charter Communications has just committed to investing $25 billion -- with a B,
$25 billion -- you're sure that's right, right? (Laughter.)

With a B, right -- $25 billion here in the United States, and
has committed further to hiring 20,000 American workers
over the next four years.

**Charter has also committed to completely end its off-
shore call centers -- that is such a big deal -- and to base
100 percent of its call centers here in the United States --
all American jobs.** This is **great** for their workers, it's **great**
for the customers, and it's certainly **great** for the United
States. And you watch, it will be one of your really fantastic decisions.

Tom will be opening a brand new beautiful call center in
McAllen, Texas -- you know McAllen, right, good place?

GOVERNOR ABBOTT: Great place.

THE PRESIDENT: I knew you would say that -- (laughter) -- where **they will create 600 new American jobs**. Charter's announcement follows a number of American business-es -- from Exxon to Intel to Lockheed to Boeing to many others -- that have recently announced billions of dollars in investment and thousands of jobs coming into the United States following my election victory.

And by the way, thank you for your support. The Governor was a great supporter -- a great supporter. I want to thank you for -- you've done a fantastic job.

We're embracing a new economic model -- The American Model.

We're going to massively eliminate job-killing regulations -- that has started already, big league -- reduce govern-ment burdens, and lower taxes that are crushing American businesses and American workers all over this country.

And we are really in the process of announcements and you're going to see thousands and thousands and thou-sands of jobs, of companies, and everything coming back into our country. And they're coming in far faster than even I had projected.

So we're honored. I'd like to have Tom Rutledge say a few words about what he's doing and about his great company. And after that, you guys can go back to health-care. (Laughter.)

MR. RUTLEDGE: Thank you, Mr. President. You know, it's a great pleasure to announce these jobs. And Charter has been in-sourcing jobs for the last five years, and as a result of that, our company has performed tremendously. Using high-skilled, high-quality workers actually saves money. It saves money.

As you know **as a builder**, if you do the job right the first time, it's a lot less expensive than redoing it.

And we found that in the service business, and we found that **we can actually do better with high-quality, high-skilled American workers**.

And so we've been doing that, and our company was so successful that we were able to recently do a huge transaction with Time Warner Cable and Bright House Networks, and put together this tremendous company.

And as part of that, we're going to in-source all the calls that Time Warner Cable outsourced -- 50 percent of their calls were leaving the country. So we're going to bring all that back, and create 20,000 new jobs. And we're very excited about that.

And **we're also excited about the opportunity**, in the right regulatory climate and right tax climate, to make major infrastructure investments. And we're going to spend $25 billion. We're committed to spending that predicated on the kind of regulatory consistency and efficiency that we expect as a country. And so **we're looking forward to the opportunity to create these jobs and to build this infra-structure**.

And Kip Mayo, who manages our call centers, would like to tell you what we're going to do in the McAllen specifically.

MS. MAYO: So with the opening of the McAllen center,
it gives us the capacity to be able to create over 600
good-paying jobs. That **allows us to in-source work that is
currently performed through third parties**.

The McAllen center will be our first fully bilingual call
center. It will allow customers who prefer to communicate
with us in Spanish to do so, and we will provide them with
service and technical support. We have already hired a
General Manager -- very qualified woman who is bilingual,
and is also, coincidentally, a native McAllen.

We expect to open the call center next month, and **we've
hired over 100 employees already**, and they will be
trained and they will be ready to assist our customers in
just a few short weeks.

So this is a very big step for us in our strategy and our plans
over the course of the next few years **to create jobs and
to bring work in from overseas and back to the United
States**.

MR. RUTLEDGE: And they're good jobs, too. And they're
high-paid jobs. They have pensions. They have healthcare.

They're the kind of jobs people want -- **they're good, solid
middle-class jobs, and we're proud to make** them available.

THE PRESIDENT: That's great. Thank you very much,
Tom. Fantastic job with the company. Unbelievable job.

I'd like to just close it out by asking my friend, Governor
Greg Abbott to say a few words, and he'll talk about the
company. But he's very proud of what they've been doing

in Texas. So am I. So, Greg.

GOVERNOR ABBOTT: Sure. Well, first, I'm proud of
you. **We have a President who's living up to his campaign
promise**, and that is to create more jobs, but also to create
more jobs by returning jobs from overseas back to the
United States.

I want to thank Charter Communications for the great job
you're doing, but also for expanding, in the great state of
Texas. We're happy that this first tranche of your expansion is in the Rio Grande Valley, in McAllen, Texas.

You talked about the tax environment, the regulatory
environment. Texas is number one in the nation for job
creation because of the pro-business climate that we have
because we have the right workforce to take care of the
needs of companies like Charter Communications.

**So this is a win-win. It's a win for the President. It's a win
for Charter. It's a win for the great state of Texas. The
country is better today because of the jobs that will be
created tomorrow in McAllen, Texas**.

THE PRESIDENT: Thank you very much. Thank
you. Thanks, Greg.

GOVERNOR ABBOTT: Thank you, President.

THE PRESIDENT: Thank you. Congratulations. Congratulations. Thank you.

END
11:12 A.M. EDT

Chapter 103

REMARKS BY PRESIDENT TRUMP AT
GREEK INDEPENDENCE DAY CELEBRATION
EAST ROOM

24 March 2017

2:37 P.M. EDT

[WHITE HOUSE CHIEF OF STAFF, R PRIEBUS: All right, thank you everyone very much. (Inaudible.) I'm honored to be with you today as we celebrate the 196th anniversary of Greek Independence. This day marks the 31st celebration of Greek independence here at the White House. A tradition started by the great President Ronald Reagan.

As a proud Greek American, I've had my eye on this event for weeks, and I'm grateful to welcome his Eminence Archbishop Demetrios, Father Alex, and all of our distinguished guests. I'd also like to extend my sincere gratitude to the Greek Orthodox Archdiocese of America and our local parishioners.

Greek Independence Day means so much to all of us. As we gather here in the President's house we are reminded of the values and ideals that inspired our democracy. The belief that we are all created equal; and government should be by the people for the people, was a revolutionary concept that has since paved the way to our prosperous and free nation.

Today, as we celebrate our shared desires for freedom sovereignty and self-governance. I can tell you that nobody

will work harder to preserve these standards then
President Donald Trump.

In working with this President every day, I see a President
working each and every day to follow through on his promises. I am awed by his energy and his tenacity; throughout
my career I have always been able to out-work any people
around me, its always been my secret weapon. But I must
say I have totally found my match in President Trump.
(Speaks in Greek.)

In just a few short months, I think you have seen President
Trump keep his word on many fronts. The first two jobs reports released since President Trump's Inauguration show
that we've already created nearly a half a million new jobs,
consumers and small business owners alike are showing
confidence in our economy in levels not seen in many
many years. And it's because of President Trump.

The President's commitment to cutting regulations, cutting
taxes, investing in priorities like infrastructure and education, and repealing and replacing the failed Obamacare is
getting America moving again.

As we find new, renewed strength at home, our friends
abroad will find us to be an even stronger ally. The
President knows just how important our enduring allies
are, and Greece is no exception.

That is truly why it is such an incredible honor, on this day
as a Greek American, to introduce to you, the 45th
President of the United States. Ladies and gentleman,
President Donald J. Trump.]

THE PRESIDENT: I love the Greeks. Oh, do I love the

Greeks. (Laughter and applause.)

Don't forget, I come from New York. That's all I see, is Greeks. They are all over the place. (Laughter.)

Thank you very much, Reince. Very much appreciated. Reince was the most successful leader the RNC -- that's called the Republican National Committee -- has ever had.

And now, as my really terrific and hard-working Chief of Staff, he has really one of the number-one -- and I guess you'd have to say, he's one of the top Greeks in the country.

And I know a lot of them right in the audience -- they're my friends. (Applause.)

And the list also includes, as you know, George Gigicos -- (applause) -- George. George is great. I said, make sure that microphone is absolutely perfect, George. He never lets me -- the Director of White House Advance.

And George Sifakis -- (applause) -- where's George? And these guys are with me right from the beginning -- the Director of the Office of Public Liaison. It's a great team.

It's a great, great team. Can't do any better.

They helped organize this wonderful event with the Greek Archdiocese of America and so many local parishioners. And I want to thank you all. You're here, you're all over the audience. I want to thank you all.

Your Eminence and Father Alex, it is a true privilege to host you at the White House. I was deeply honored to have you both at my Inauguration -- it was a great day -- and I am grateful for your presence here today.

I also want to thank you for awarding Reince and George the highest honor of the Greek Orthodox Archdiocese of America -- the *Medal of Saint Paul.*

To everyone in the youth choir who just performed -- they were beautiful. (Applause.)

I heard that music. I heard that music. With such elegance and grace, you're amazing -- you really are. Beautiful, beautiful sounds. I know you made your parents very proud. And you make all of us proud, right?

Today we commemorate an event that we have marked with a National Day of celebration for 30 years: Greek Independence Day. Very important.

President Ronald Reagan started this wonderful tradition, and we are thrilled to continue it, and always will.

Greek Independence Day celebrates the rebirth of liberty for the Greek people. It commemorates the fight for the Greek Independence that began on March 25th, 1821. After nearly 400 years of outside rule, the Greeks longed to regain their sovereignty.

This love of **freedom and democracy** has formed a lasting bond between our two countries. It is a bond that has its origins in Ancient Greece -- "the Birthplace of Democracy."

American President James Monroe and the great American statesman Daniel Webster both supported Greece's struggle for independence. And it was a tough, tough struggle, you know that. Then-Representative Webster honored the role of Greece in forming civilization, and said that "We, like the rest of mankind, are greatly her debtors."

In years to come, we don't know what will be required to defend our freedom, but we do know that it will demand great, great courage -- a courage from all of us -- and we will show it, and I have no doubt about that.

Drawing inspiration from our history and those who come before, we will rise to any occasion. We have a country that, as you know, has certain difficulties, has certain problems. We will solve those problems and we will quickly solve those difficulties. Just watch. (Applause.)

I want to thank you all for coming to the White House today. We celebrate Greek history, and we applaud the tremendous contributions of your people to our beloved country.

May God bless you all. And with that, I would like to recognize His Eminence. Thank you very much. Thank you. (Applause.)

[EMINENCE ARCHBISHOP DEMETRIOS: A transcription was not provided by the White House.]

END
2:42 P.M. EDT

Chapter 104

**REMARKS BY THE PRESIDENT IN A MEETING WITH
MEDAL OF HONOR RECIPIENTS
OVAL OFFICE**

24 March 2017

4:11 P.M. EDT

THE PRESIDENT: Thank you very much. This is a great honor for me. These are very, very brave people standing behind me. And we're here today to mark *Medal of Honor Day*, and it is my great privilege and high honor to welcome 25 *Medal of Honor* recipients to our White House. Very special honor, thank you all very much. (Applause.)

I can say officially they are much braver than I am, okay? (Laughter.)

Do you agree with that, General?

GENERAL MATTIS: I do, Mr. President. (Laughter.)

A MEDAL OF HONOR RECIPIENT: That's the right answer. (Laughter.)

THE PRESIDENT: It is the right answer.

One-third of the nation's 75 living *Medal of Honor* recipients are with us. So it's really -- that's a great tribute to all of us, a great tribute to our nation. Each of you has risen above and beyond the call of duty in defense of our country, our people, and our flag. You have poured out your hearts, your sweat, and your tears like few others, and your blood -- most importantly your blood for the United States of America. We thank you, very much thank you.

You are the soul of our nation, and a grateful republic salutes you. Constantly we're saluting you. We have great admiration and respect, believe me. I know what you've been through.

We write your names and deeds in our national memory, and we will forever remember -- forever, forever and ever -- those who did not come home, but who died for the cause of freedom.

I want to thank the *Congressional Medal of Honor Foundation* for preserving the incredible stories of our *Medal of Honor* heroes for future generations. Done a great job.

In this room hangs the portrait of our 26th President, Theodore Roosevelt. He was awarded the *Medal of Honor* for his courage alongside his band of Rough Riders at the Battle of San Juan Hill. You know about the Rough Riders, right? Right? Absolutely. His medal, which is also displayed here, is a reminder of how blessed we truly are to live in the land of heroes. And you are our greatest heroes.

To all of those gathered here today, and to all of those warriors who could not be with us, we thank you. Your acts of valor inspire us -- and they show us that there is always someone on the night watch to ensure a bright sun rises on America each and every morning.

God bless you. God bless our military and God bless the United States of America.

I want to just thank you very much for being here. It's my great honor. (Applause.)

And as you know, we have David who is doing a great job at the VA. Already tremendous signs are happening, positive signs. And we have General Mattis who is doing a great job out there on the field, and you see a big difference. A lot of difference taking place over the last six weeks. So I want to thank General Mattis, too. And thank you all, and it's great to have met you.

Oh, look at this.

A MEDAL OF HONOR RECIPIENT: Mr. President, on behalf of the *Medal of Honor Society*, I'd like to present a book "Portraits of Valor," which contains all the signatures of the men in the room here, plus about 200 *Medal of Honor* recipients.

THE PRESIDENT: That is very nice. That is very nice. (Applause.)

I know these folks would like to stand behind me when I do this, but I don't want to put them in a political situation, so we're going to talk a little politics. And I think it might be unfair to them, so I'll ask them to -- they're going to go over to the Roosevelt Room, and we'll see you a little bit later. We're going to do -- unless the press doesn't want to talk politics? (Laughter.)

No? Okay, well, they do. But I want to thank you all very much.

END
4:15 P.M. EDT

      Chapter 104

Chapter 105

**REMARKS BY PRESIDENT TRUMP ON
THE HEALTH CARE BILL
OVAL OFFICE**

24 March 2017

4:26 P.M. EDT

THE PRESIDENT: Thank you very much. We were very close, and it was a very, very tight margin. We had no Democrat support. We had no votes from the Democrats. They weren't going to give us a single vote, so it's a very difficult thing to do.

I've been saying for the last year and a half that the best thing we can do politically speaking is let Obamacare explode. It is exploding right now. Many states have big problems -- almost all states have big problems. I was in Tennessee the other day, and they've lost half of their state in terms of an insurer; they have no insurer. And that's happened to many other places. I was in Kentucky the other day, and similar things are happening.

So Obamacare is exploding. With no Democrat support, we couldn't quite get there. We were just a very small number of votes short in terms of getting our bill passed. A lot of people don't realize how good our bill was because they were viewing phase one. But when you add phase two -- which was mostly the signings of Secretary Price, who's behind me -- and you add phase three, which I think we would have gotten -- it became a great bill. Premiums would have gone down and it would have been very stable, it would have been very strong. But that's okay.

But we're very, very close. And again, I think what will happen is Obamacare, unfortunately, will explode. It's going to have a very bad year. Last year you had over a 100 percent increases in various places. In Arizona, I understand it's going up very rapidly again, like it did last year; last year it was 116 percent. Many places, 50, 60, 70 percent, I guess it averaged -- whatever the average was -- very, very high. And this year should be much worse for Obamacare.

So what would be really good, with no Democrat support, is if the Democrats, when it explodes -- which it will soon -- if they got together with us and got a real healthcare bill. I would be totally up to do it. And I think that's going to happen. I think the losers are Nancy Pelosi and Chuck Schumer, because now they own Obamacare. They own it -- 100 percent own it.

And this is not a Republican healthcare, this is not anything but a Democrat healthcare. And they have Obamacare for a little while longer, until it ceases to exist, which it will at some point in the near future. And just remember this is not our bill, this is their bill.

Now, when they all become civilized and get together, and try and work out a great healthcare bill for the people of this country, we're open to it. We're totally open to it. I want to thank the Republican Party. I want to thank Paul Ryan -- he worked very, very hard, I will tell you that. He worked very, very hard. Tom Price and Mike Pence -- who's right here -- our Vice President, our great Vice President. Everybody worked hard. I worked as a team player and would have loved to have seen it passed. But again, I think you know I was very clear, I think there wasn't a speech I made, or very few where I didn't mention that perhaps the best thing that can happen is exactly what happened today, because we'll end up with a truly great healthcare bill in the future, after this mess known as Obamacare explodes.

So I want to thank everybody for being here. It will go very smoothly, I really believe. I think this is something -- it certainly was an interesting period of time. We all learned a lot. We learned a lot about loyalty. We learned a lot about the vote-getting process. We learned a lot about some very arcane rules in, obviously, both the Senate and in the House. So it's been -- certainly for me, it's been a very interesting experience. But in the end, I think it's going to be an experience that leads to an even better healthcare plan. So thank you all very much. And I'll see you soon.

Q   Mr. President, is it now your intention to go for tax reform? Or what's next on your priority list?

THE PRESIDENT: We'll be going right now for tax reform, which we could have done earlier, but this really would have worked out better if we could have had some Democrat support. Remember this: We had no Democrat support. So now we're going to go for tax reform, which I've always liked.

Q   And you're confident in Speaker Ryan's leadership and his ability to get things done?

THE PRESIDENT: Yes, I am. I like Speaker Ryan. He worked very, very hard. A lot of different groups, he's got a lot of factions. And there's been a long history of liking and disliking, even within the Republican Party, long before I got here. But I've had a great relationship with the Republican Party. It seems that both sides like Trump, and that's good. And you see that, I guess, more clearly than anybody.

But we've had a -- I'm not going to speak badly about any-body within the party. But certainly there's a big history. I think Paul really worked hard. And I would say that we will probably start going very, very strong for the big tax cuts and tax reform. That will be next.

Q   Sir, **is it fair to Americans to let Obamacare explode**?

THE PRESIDENT: Well, it's going to happen. There's not much you can do about it. It's going to -- bad things are going to happen to Obamacare. There's not much you can do to help it. I've been saying that for a year and a half. I said, look, eventually it's not sustainable. The insurance companies are leaving -- you know that. They're leav-ing one by one, as quick as you can leave. And you have states, in some cases, who will not be covered. So there's no way out of that.

But the one thing that was happening, as we got closer and closer, everybody was talking about how wonderful it was, and now we'll go back to real life and people will see how bad it is. And it's getting much worse.

You know, I said the other day, when President Obama left -- '17, he knew he wasn't going to be here; **'17 is going to be a very, very bad year for Obamacare. Very, very bad**. You're going to have explosive premium increas-es. And the deductibles are so high people don't even get to use it.

So they'll go with that for a little while. And I honestly believe -- I know some of the Democrats, and they're good people -- I honestly believe the Democrats will come to us and say, look, let's get together and get a great healthcare bill or plan that's really great for the people of our country. And I think that's going to happen.

Q   If you could have passed the bill in the House without any Democratic support, why do you think you weren't able to craft a deal among the Republican Party?

THE PRESIDENT: Well, we were very close. We were just probably anywhere from 10 to 15 votes short. Could have even been closer than that. You'll never know because you'll never know how they vote. But in the end, I think we would have been 10 votes, maybe closer. And it was very hard to get almost 100 percent. You're talking about a very, very large number of votes -- among any group. And we were very close to doing it. But when you get no votes from the other side -- meaning the Democrats -- it's really a difficult situation.

Q   Will you reach out to the Democrats now?

THE PRESIDENT: No, I think we have to let Obamacare go its way for a little while, and we'll see how things go. I'd love to see it do well, but it can't. I mean, it can't. It's not a question of, gee -- I hope it does well. I would love it to do well. I want great healthcare for the people of this nation. But it can't do well. It's imploding, and soon will explode, and it's not going to be pretty.

So the Democrats don't want to see that, so they're going to reach out when they're ready. And whenever they're ready, we're ready.

Q   **Do you feel betrayed** by the House Freedom Caucus at all? They seemed to be the most difficult to get.

THE PRESIDENT: No, I'm not betrayed. They're friends of mine. **I'm disappointed** because we could have had it. So I'm disappointed. I'm a little surprised, to be honest with you. We really had it. It was pretty much there within grasp. But I'll tell you what's going to come out of it is a better bill -- I really believe a better bill. Because there were things in this bill I didn't particularly love. And I think it's a better bill.

You know, both parties can get together and do real healthcare. That's the best thing. Obamacare was rammed down everyone's throat -- 100 percent Democrat. And I think having bipartisan would be a big, big improvement.

So, no, I think that this is going to end up being a very good thing. I'm disappointed, but they're friends of mine, and they got -- this is a very hard time for them and a very hard vote. But they're very good people.

Q   You mentioned that there were things in this bill that you didn't necessarily love. What specifically are those?

THE PRESIDENT: Well, I think we could have things that I would have liked more. And if we had bipartisan, I really think we could have a healthcare bill that would be the ultimate. And I think the Democrats know that also. And some day, in the not--too-distant future, that will happen.

And I never said -- I guess I'm here, what, 64 days?

I never said repeal and replace Obamacare -- you've all

heard my speeches -- **I never said repeal it and replace it within 64 days**.

I have a long time.

But I want to have a great healthcare bill and plan -- and we will. It will happen. And it won't be in the very distant future. I really believe there will be some Democrat support, and that will happen, and it will be an even better bill. I think this was a very good bill. I think it will be even better the next time around. I don't think that's going to be in too long a period of time.

Q   Anything specifically you want to see changed going from this bill to the next bill?

THE PRESIDENT: No, I mean, I don't want to speak about specifics, but there are things I could have -- I would have liked even more. But I feel overall this was a very, very good bill. And I thought Tom Price -- Dr. Tom Price -- who really is amazing on healthcare, his knowledge -- I thought he did a fantastic job. Same with Mike Pence. I think these two guys -- they worked so hard and really did a fantastic job.

Thank you very much. Thank you.

END
4:36 P.M. EDT

Chapter 106

**PRESIDENT DONALD J. TRUMP'S WEEKLY ADDRESS
THE PRESIDENT'S WEEKLY ADDRESS IS NOW AVAILABLE TO
WATCH ON YOUTUBE.**

25 March 2017

Transcript:

My fellow Americans,
This week, in the company of astronauts, I was honored to
sign the NASA Transition Authorization Act right into law.

With this legislation, we renew our national commitment
to NASA's mission of exploration and discovery. And we
continue a tradition that is as old as mankind. We look to
the heavens with wonder and curiosity.

More than two decades ago, one scientist followed his
curiosity and dramatically changed our understanding of
the universe. The year was 1995. Taxpayers were spending billions and billions of dollars on NASA's Hubble Space
Telescope. The astronomer in charge had a novel idea. He
wanted to use the expensive telescope in a totally uncon-
ventional way.

Instead of pointing Hubble's eye at nearby stars or distant
formations, Robert Williams wanted to peer into the void.

He aimed the massive telescope at one of the emptiest
regions of the night sky. For ten days during Christmas of
1995, Hubble stared into the abyss—seeking whatever
light it could glean from the darkness. And it was total

darkness.

Fellow astronomers didn't know if he'd see much of anything. But Williams was rewarded—and the entire world was struck by the awesome images our satellite returned. In that tiny patch of sky, the Hubble Deep Field showed thousands of lights. Each brilliant spot represented not a single star but an entire galaxy.

The discovery was absolutely incredible. But the unforgettable image did not satisfy our deep hunger for knowledge. It increased evermore and even more and reminded us how much we do not know about space; frankly, how much we do not know about life.

With this week's NASA reauthorization, we continue progress on Hubble's successor, the James Webb Space Telescope. It is amazing.

The Webb Telescope is set to launch next year. It will gaze back through time and space to the very first stars and the earliest galaxies in the universe. We can only imagine what incredible visions it will bring.

At a time when Washington is consumed with the daily debates of our Nation, I was proud that Congress came together overwhelmingly to reaffirm our Nation's commitment to expanding the frontiers of knowledge.

NASA's greatest discoveries teach us many, many things. One lesson is the need to view old questions with fresh eyes. To have the courage to look for answers in places we have never looked before.

To think in new ways because we have new information.

Most of all, new discoveries remind us that, in America, **anything is possible if we have the courage and wisdom to learn.**

In the span of one lifetime, our Nation went from black and white pictures of the first airplanes, to beautiful images of the oldest galaxies, captured by a camera in outer space.

I am confident that if Americans can achieve these things, there is no problem we cannot solve.

There is no challenge we cannot meet.

There is no aim that is too high.

Whatever it takes and however long it will be, we are a Nation of problem solvers —and the future belongs to us.

We are truly a great place to be.

I love America.

Chapter 107

**REMARKS BY THE VICE PRESIDENT IN WEST VIRGINIA
CHARLESTON, WEST VIRGINIA**

25 March 2017

2:18 P.M. EDT

THE VICE PRESIDENT: Hello, West Virginia! It is great to be back, if only just to say thanks. Thanks to your hard work, your support, and your prayers -- West Virginia voted over-whelmingly to make Donald Trump the 45th President of the United States -- and we will never forget it. (Applause.)

Let me thank our host today -- Ronald Reagan Foster and Nancy Reagan Foster. I just said a little bit ago they're my second favorite Ron and Nancys I've ever met. (Applause.)

I want to thank them. I want to thank the whole Foster's Supply team and all the great employees who came out today. You've been building this state and building the **American Dream** since 1981.

In fact, Ron, I just heard that you have a **wall division** here at Foster's. Maybe we need to talk. (Applause.)

What you do and what you've done here since 1981 is what makes this country great. And the President and I are truly grateful for you and for all the good people who are part of the Foster Supply team and all the neighbors and friends who've gathered here today to stand with us. Give yourselves a round of applause for coming out on a Satur-day afternoon. (Applause.)

We couldn't be more grateful. And Congressman Evan Jenkins, thank you for being with us. We're so grateful for your support. And to Congressman Alex Mooney, thank you for your service to this country. It is great to be in your district. (Applause.)

It truly is.

You know, it is so humbling for me to stand before you today in this role. I'm just a small-town guy from southern Indiana. **My grandfather immigrated to this country, and to think that I had the privilege to raise my right hand on January 20th and accept the oath of office to serve as the 48th Vice President of the United States is the greatest privilege of my life.** And let me just say, on behalf of my whole family, thank you, West Virginia, for giving us the opportunity to serve. (Applause.)

I'll tell you, it is the greatest privilege of my life to be Vice President to President Donald Trump. President Trump is my friend. He loves his family and he loves this country, with boundless energy, optimism, courage and determination. And let me be clear on one thing -- President Donald Trump is going to be the best friend American small business will ever have. (Applause.)

That's why he picked Linda McMahon to lead the Small Business Administration. Isn't she amazing? (Applause.)

Linda McMahon knows an awful lot about small business. Linda and her husband started their company as a small business back in the 1970s, as Titan Sports, and they built it into an international entertainment enterprise -- the WWE. Any fans in the house? (Applause.)

I'm one. Now she's bringing that great business experience to building a business to help small businesses across America grow and thrive.

You know, Linda, we're grateful for your leadership. But maybe we could have used a few of your WWE superstars on Capitol Hill yesterday. (Applause.)

Give her another round of applause for leading the Small Business Administration with such great qualities. (Applause.)

With Linda McMahon at the SBA, we're listening to small business owners -- and that hadn't been happening for a while in Washington, D.C. -- been listening to people just like many who are with us today. Would you join me in thanking all the great small business owners who are gathered here today -- people that make West Virginia such a great place to live, to work and to raise their family. (Applause.)

Thank you all.

We just had a great conversation. We talked with these job-creators here in West Virginia about the President's pro-business agenda of less regulations, lower taxes, fair trade, better infrastructure, and a renewed focus on American energy. And I heard again from these West Virginia small business owners about the need to repeal and replace Obamacare. (Applause.)

They told me how Obamacare stands in the way and stifles growth. It's a burden not just to job creators, it's also a burden to the American people.

Folks, I wasn't surprised to hear it because every promise of Obamacare has been broken. You all remember what they were. Seven years ago, after Obamacare was signed into law, they told us if you like your doctor, you can keep them -- not true. They said if you like your health plan, you can keep it -- not true. We were all told that the cost of health insurance would go down. Well, that one wasn't true either. And West Virginia knows this better than most. It's heartbreaking to say that last year alone, Obamacare premiums here in West Virginia spiked by a stunning 32 percent. Over 40 percent of the state doesn't have any choice of an insurance provider on the Obamacare exchange.

West Virginians, and President Trump, we all know the truth about this failed law – that every day Obamacare survives is another day that America suffers. That's why the President worked tirelessly over the last several weeks to get Congress to repeal and replace Obamacare. You saw his resolve to work with whoever he needed to work with, to call whoever he needed to call to get our plan across the finish line this week on Capitol Hill.

I got to tell you, I was inspired by President Trump's determination and commitment to keep his **promise** to the American people. (Applause.)

And the President and I are grateful for Speaker Paul Ryan and all the House Republicans who stood with us in this effort to begin the end of Obamacare. But as we all learned yesterday, Congress just wasn't ready. You saw it -- with 100 percent of House Democrats -- every single one -- and a handful of Republicans actually standing in the way of President Trump's plans to repeal and replace Obamacare. We're back to the drawing board.

You know, Nancy Pelosi, the leader of the Democrats in Congress, actually said yesterday was a victory for the American people. But West Virginia knows better. Yesterday wasn't a victory for the American people. It was a victory for the status quo in Washington, D.C. And it was a victory for the disaster of Obamacare.

But **I promise you that victory won't last very long**. (Applause.)

The American people want Obamacare gone. And as the President said today, don't worry, America. He just tweeted this morning. Obamacare is going to continue to explode. And when Republicans and Democrats finally decide to come together and to repeal and replace Obamacare, we'll be ready to get the job done. (Applause.)

And as the President **promised** just this morning, "we'll all get together and piece together a great healthcare plan for the people." We will end the Obamacare nightmare and give the American people the world-class healthcare that they deserve. (Applause.)

Until then, I can **promise** you, President Trump is never going to stop fighting to keep his **promises** to the American people -- and we will **Make America Great Again**. (Applause.)

And we're moving forward. Next up, we're going to get back to the **President's three-part agenda** -- jobs, jobs, and jobs -- for every American, in West Virginia and across this country. (Applause.)

And the great news is we've actually been on that agenda from the very day President Trump was elected. It's been amazing to see jobs coming back to this country -- even since the day after the election. Last month the economy added 235,000 jobs. Construction and manufacturing are booming again. Companies are canceling plans to move jobs and factories overseas -- and **they're building them right here in America once Again**. (Applause.)

It's true. **Businesses and consumers haven't been this confident in years** -- and by some measures, for more than a decade.

Folks, the era of slow growth is over -- and a new era of American growth and jobs has already begun. (Applause.)

And it's all because the American people know President Donald Trump is a man of his word and he's a man of action. In fact, on day one, President Trump went straight to work rolling back reams of red tape that have been killing jobs and small business America across this country. He instructed every bureaucracy in Washington, D.C. to find two regulations to get rid of before issuing any new regulations out of our nation's capital. (Applause.)

He's already taken decisive action to **protect American jobs and American workers** -- and we will not stop until we end illegal immigration once and for all. (Applause.)

Just this week, the President authorized the Keystone Pipeline, creating tens of thousands of jobs and protecting our energy future. (Applause.)

And, folks, we're just getting started. Next up, as the President said yesterday, we're going to roll our sleeves up and we're going to cut taxes across the board for working families, small businesses, and family farms. (Applause.)

Working with this Congress, President Trump is going to pass the largest tax cut since the days of Ronald Reagan. And **we're going to get this American economy moving Again**. (Applause.)

We're going to reform the tax code and make it flatter and simpler and fairer.

I guarantee you there isn't anyone here, including the Fosters, who can make sense of the tax code. You know, there's an old joke -- there's an old joke about how the tax code in this country is 10 times the size of the Bible with none of the good news. (Applause.)

Right? The truth is our taxes makes it far too difficult for job-creators and hard-working people all across this country get ahead and to achieve the **American Dream**.

That's why **our tax plan will make American businesses and American opportunities more competitive all over this country**. We're going to also cut the corporate tax rate in America. We have one of the highest business taxes in America -- we're going to cut it to 15 percent so American companies will invest in American operations to create American jobs. (Applause.)

So we're going to cut taxes for every American, and we're going to cut taxes for free enterprise. But we're going to get this economy moving with less regulation, and more American energy. Let me make you a **promise** -- right after we dropped our right hands on January 20th, it was official: The war on coal is over. (Applause.)

And a new era of American energy has begun. (Applause.)

For far too long, politicians and bureaucrats in Washington, D.C. have crippled our nation's economy and crippled West Virginia's economy, without regard to the impact that it has on people's utility bills, and the impact it has on jobs of hard-working Americans. Right here in West Virginia, they've pushed mining companies to the breaking point. They jeopardized thousands of good-paying jobs, and cut off a brighter future for countless West Virginia families. It's heartbreaking to think that West Virginia has lost more than a third of its mining jobs over the last few years alone , and that over 130 mines have been shut down since 2009.

Folks, that's not right. The hard-working men and women of this state have been forgotten for too long -- and **they will be forgotten no more under President Donald Trump**. (Applause.)

From the first day of this administration, President Donald Trump has been fighting for West Virginia and fighting for American energy. We're working with leaders in Congress and we're working with the new director over at the EPA Scott Pruitt, to slash through red tape to make sure that unelected bureaucrats can't kill your jobs and cripple your economy from the comfort of their taxpayer-funded metal desks in Washington, D.C. (Applause.)

We're going to bring back jobs. We're going to get Washington out of the way of energy producers and coal miners -- because energy means growth for America, and President Trump digs coal. (Applause.)

Our country is going to be stronger, and West Virginia will be **stronger and more prosperous because of the President's leadership**.

When you get right down to it, **President Trump is going to create jobs and opportunity and prosperity in this country like never before.** But **Making America Great Again** isn't just about our economy. It also means **protecting our nation and defending our way of life**.

And let me tell you, I'm with him every day -- President Trump has no higher priority than the **safety and security** of the American people. And that will always be true. (Applause.)

That's why, from the first day of this administration, President Donald Trump has been standing with the men and women in law enforcement all across America. And we always will. (Applause.)

We'll work with the Congress to make sure those who protect our families and our communities have the resources and training they need to do their jobs and to come home safe to their families.

You know, there's a fair number of law enforcement personnel that are with us today. I know most of you are standing, but would all of you just take a minute to show the men and women in law enforcement here in West Virginia just how much we all truly appreciate the job that they do protecting our families. (Applause.)

President Trump is putting our **Security First** and our **Safety First**. That's why **he's strengthening our borders. This President is going to build a wall**, enforce our laws, and as he told the Congress, we're acting right now to take "gang members, drug dealers, and criminals that threaten our communities and prey on our citizens" off the streets of West Virginia and off the streets of America. (Applause.)

And as the father of a United States Marine, let me say this, from my heart ... (Applause.)

... I couldn't be more proud and grateful to say that **we have a President who will rebuild our military, restore the arsenal of democracy**, give our Soldiers, Sailors, Airmen, Marines, and Coast Guard the resources and training they need to accomplish their mission and come home **safe** at last. (Applause.)

He's going to do it.

So it's about jobs; it's about energy; it's about our national defense. And President Trump is also keeping one more **promise** I want to mention, and that's the **promise** that he made to nominate to the Supreme Court someone who will be faithful to our Constitution.

By nominating Judge Neil Gorsuch, President Trump has kept his word to appoint a justice to the Supreme Court who will keep faith with the Constitution and who will up-hold the God-given liberties that are enshrined there. (Applause.)

You saw it this week. My daughter was off work -- she got to watch CSPAN. She told me she watched a lot of Judge Gorsuch's testimony before the Senate. Three days of powerful testimony before the Senate, Judge Neil Gorsuch made it clear why President Trump nominated him to the highest court in the land, didn't he?

He demonstrated temperament and intellect -- explains why the bipartisan praise is rolling in. The truth is Amer-ica saw this week what President Trump saw when he made that decision. Judge Neil Gorsuch is one of the most respected, qualified, and mainstream nominees to the Supreme Court in American history. (Applause.)

But, remarkably, this week Senator Chuck Schumer and the obstructionists in his party in the Senate actually announced that the Democrats plan to filibuster Judge Gorsuch's nomination to be an associate justice. That's something that's never been done successfully in American history.

So let me say this to you, West Virginia. If we can get the help of Senator Joe Manchin, and with the help of Senator Shelley Moore Capito, Judge Neil Gorsuch will soon become Justice Neil Gorsuch -- and America and the rule of law will be better for it. (Applause.)

So let me be clear. President Trump and I are confident, the United States Senate will confirm Judge Neil Gorsuch, one way or the other. (Applause.)

It is great to be in West Virginia. (Applause.)

My friends, we've come to **a pivotal moment in our nation's history.** In this moment, I think we need every **freedom-loving American** -- we need all of you -- to stand up, speak out, and take time, as you've done today to come and be engaged and be involved.

We need you to keep telling your neighbors here in West Virginia we can do better, that we're **renewing and restoring this country, that we can put America back on a path to a brighter future.** And this I know we will do because I have faith.

You know, over the mantel of our home since my first run

for office back in the year 2000 there's been a framed copy of a verse from the Good Book. It was in our home in Indiana and it was in the Governor's Residence in Indiana when I served there. And now it hangs above the mantel in the home of the Vice President of the United States. And it simply reads these words: "For I know the plans I have for you, plans to prosper you, and not to harm you, plans to give you a hope, and a future."

In November, the people of West Virginia voted to give America a President -- a President with **the strength** and **the courage** and the **vision** to **Make America Great Again**. You voted to give us a new leader who would **Make America Prosperous Again**.

And I believe with all my heart, that with your continued support and faith, and with God's help, together **we will restore this country**, that our best days are ahead, and that, together, we will **Make America Great Again**. (Applause.)

Thank you, West Virginia. God bless you, and God bless the United States of America. (Applause.)

END
3:31 P.M. EDT

> *"President Donald Trump is going to be the best friend American small business will ever have."*

Chapter 108

REMARKS BY PRESIDENT TRUMP AND VICE PRESIDENT PENCE IN ROUNDTABLE WITH WOMEN SMALL BUSINESS OWNERS ROOSEVELT ROOM

27 March 2017

11:10 A.M. EDT

THE PRESIDENT: Good morning, everybody. Thank you very much. **It's my pleasure to welcome such incredible women, including my daughter --** (Laughter)

[Photo: screengrab.]

PARTICIPANTS: Yeah!

THE PRESIDENT: -- and unbelievable entrepreneurs and

small business leaders to the White House. And also,
Linda, thank you very much. You've been doing an amazing job -- I hear working 24 hours a day is what the word
is. (Laughter.)

Good. I'm not surprised.

ADMINISTRATOR McMAHON: Trying to keep up with you.
(Laughter.)

THE PRESIDENT: I'm not surprised. And I want to
thank Linda for joining us today. She's doing a fantastic job
leading the Small Business Administration, and she herself,
as you know, is a great, great success story and a woman entrepreneur at the highest level. So thank you very
much, Linda.

Empowering and promoting women in business is an absolute priority in the Trump administration because I know
how crucial women are as job creators, role models, and
leaders all throughout our communities.

As we conclude *Women's History Month*, I am thrilled
that we can meet to discuss how we can continue this
important mission. You all have incredible stories. Many
of you started businesses from scratch, with very, very
limited resources -- sounds like I'm right about you, Lisa,
right? (Laughter.)

But you had the grit and determination **to make your
dreams** become a reality, right?

ADMINISTRATOR McMAHON: Yes.

THE PRESIDENT: It's fantastic. Now you're providing hundreds of jobs across our country -- thousands of jobs. And you're really an inspiration to everybody -- and that's men and women, believe me. A lot of men out there, they're not doing what you're able to do.

Today, women are the primary source of income in 40 percent of American households with children under the age of 15. We also know that companies that promote women to senior leadership roles realize significantly better profits, according to statistics, than their competitors. I wouldn't have known that. Dina, how does that work? Tell me. That's pretty impressive.

We must ensure that our economy is a place where women can work and thrive. We will continue to address the barriers faced by women professionals and entrepreneurs, including access to capital, access to markets, and access to networks. We will make it very easy. It's going to be a lot easier. You do an amazing job. And for a while it was a very, very tough -- almost impossible -- job.

My administration will also continue to advocate for policies that support working families, including making childcare more affordable and accessible. That's something that **Ivanka Trump -- now Ivanka Trump Kushner** -- that you really have been working on and feel so strongly about -- **my daughter**.

I actually talked about it a lot during the campaign, and **Ivanka** was right up front. **I also want to recognize Ivanka for helping to lead a national initiative to promote women business leaders and entrepreneurs.**

And the **Chancellor of Germany is going to -- has asked Ivanka to go to Germany, and she'll be working on similar**

issues with Chancellor Merkel. So that will be very exciting for you. That's going to happen very soon. It's a very
great honor.

I look forward to hearing your stories and discussing how
we can work together **to help all of your dreams come
true and make it easier for those dreams to come true**.

And with that, I'm going to turn it over to our great Vice
President, Mike Pence. And thank you, Mike, for being
here.

THE VICE PRESIDENT: Thank you, Mr. President. And I
want to thank all these business leaders for taking the time
for a conversation with a President who I think is going
to be the best friend that small business in America will
ever have. And I believe that President Donald Trump is
the best friend that women in business in this country will
ever have. It is remarkable to think, here at the close of
Women's History Month, of the impact that women-owned
businesses have on our economy, Mr. President -- more
than 9.4 million firms, employing 8 million Americans, and
annual revenues of $1.5 trillion.

Women business owners and women-owned enterprises
are an enormous force in the American economy, and I
know this President is committed to continuing to promote
the kinds of policies that will make it possible for your
firms to grow, and for more women-led businesses to be
born and to thrive all across America.

The President is advancing an agenda of less regulation,
less taxes, and investments in infrastructure, fair trade, and
addressing healthcare costs to make healthcare affordable, not only for small business owners but for employees

across the country.

Mr. President, I'm particularly pleased to be able to wel-come a fellow Hoosier -- (laughter) -- to this conversation, Ms. Shirley Ann Perry. The owner of HydroTech is with us today, and she herself has a remarkable success story.

With that said, it's a privilege for me to be alongside the President today to listen in and to learn how we might bet-ter partner with each one of you and with women-owned businesses across the country to grow and thrive in this economy. **And one of the great women business leaders in the country is helping the administration accomplish that, and so let me turn it over to Ivanka Trump.**

[Photo: screengrab.]

MS. [IVANKA] TRUMP: Thank you, Vice President. And thank you all so much for being here. It's the perfect culmination of *Women's History Month* to have all of you around the table sharing with us both your successes and

also the unique challenges that you face as women entrepreneurs and small business owners.

I feel very blessed to have met so many of you over the
course of the past couple months -- Lisa in Baltimore; right
here in D.C., Claudia -- and hearing your personal stories
and your journeys of how you became job creators. And
you truly exemplify women's economic empowerment.

So we're grateful to have you join us today. And maybe
we'll launch right in -- Claudia, if you want to start us off
and tell us a little bit about your personal experience.

MS. MIRZA: My personal experience. Thank you very
much for taking the time to listen to us. It means a lot
as small business owners. Akorbi is a company with 930
employees. I started it after I lost my job. We provide
multilingual business communications around the world to
empower global corporations to do business abroad.

THE PRESIDENT: Great. And you've done a great job.

MS. MIRZA: Thank you.

THE PRESIDENT: Thank you very much. Lisa.

MS. NICHOLS: I'm Lisa Nichols. I'm the CEO and co-founder of Technology Partners. We're an information technology staffing and solutions company working across
the nation. We will celebrate our 23rd birthday May the
4th. And just very, very blessed to be a part of this roundtable. Thank you so much. I'm very thankful.

THE PRESIDENT: Thank you very much. And I hear that
Lisa Phillips has an amazing story to tell. (Laughter.)

Can you tell it in front of all these cameras? (Laughter.)

I hear that you have one of the really amazing stories
to tell. So you want me to ask the press to leave? I
will. (Laughter.)

Go ahead.

MS. PHILLIPS: I just hope I don't cry. So thank you, Ivanka,
Dina, Mr. President, Mr. Vice President. Thank you for this
platform. I'm Lisa Phillips. I'm the owner of *Celeebrate Us*
-- gift baskets and parties. I celebrate families.

I provide working families with very elaborate events that
they otherwise wouldn't be able to afford. And my own
personal story -- **I manage and help train homeless youth
because I was once homeless myself**. And I really, really,
really was almost to the point of hopelessness. And so
-- but what a great country we live in. **This is a country of
chances**. And I've been given chances, and so I employ
people that need a chance. And so, in May, I'll be receiving
my MBA, and you're all invited to my graduation. (Applause.)

But one of the things that is required for this country is
hard work. **And if you are willing to work hard, you'll get
that chance. And so I'm a product of hard work, and so
that's what this country was built on**. And thank you, Mr.
President. Thank you for giving us a seat at the table, because what we do is we're going to take this back to people
that couldn't be here, and give them the information and
empower them.

There's a dress owner at the store next to me, and I'm
wearing one of his outfits. So I'm going to take pictures,

and he's going to send these pictures back to India, to his family. And so that's how we help one another as business owners. We give someone else a platform. So thank you.

THE PRESIDENT: Thank you. Great job. You've done a fantastic job. Thank you, Lisa.

MS. TRUMP: One of the things that I was so amazed in your story -- and everyone around this table -- is not only the incredible job that you've done in building your businesses, but also the impact you're having within your communities in terms of the work you're doing to empower other men and women and children. So it's really remarkable.

MS. PHILLIPS: Thank you so much. Because the worst thing you can feel is hopeless. And so the youth that I train, the homeless, when they're dealing with breast cancer, I'll do a workshop and empower them that, hey, that no matter where you are, that you can be elevated.

Just look around, you're going to find someone that's willing to cheer you on. And so we just graduated a group of youth from our homeless unit in Baltimore -- our homeless program -- and now they're working at one of the local hospitals. And one of the hospital officials actually called me and said, can you send us some more. So kudos to those young people --

THE PRESIDENT: That's great.

MS. PHILLIPS: -- that they really want to be able to advocate.

THE PRESIDENT: Thank you, Lisa. Thank you very much.

MS. POPE-WELLS: That's a great story. My name is Amy Pope-Wells. I'm the owner of Link Staffing, but I also own another company called Tire Diva. There's not too many females in the tire business -- (inaudible).

THE PRESIDENT: Great name, actually. (Laughter.)

MS. POPE-WELLS: Thank you, Mr. President. You know, coming here today, I was thinking about what I would say, and my businesses are my passion, but we would never have a place at this table if it wasn't for you. Opening up your new administration is doing so much, and I need you to know that we're taking that to our communities.

One of the things that happened for me was -- part of my story is, I was a nurse by graduation, and I spent years -- and that was the status quo in the community that I lived in, but something inside of me wanted to do more.

And I'll never forget, my first job was an executive job, flying across the United States, going hospital to hospital, looking at the challenges and the problems, and I did that for 15 years, and it just felt like I was banging my head up against a wall, but I knew there was so much more opportunity.

So I went and started my own company. I said, you know what, I'll just be a boutique firm, but you can't keep that inside. So I started my business and grew it.

Started partnering with companies like Walmart and Starbucks, and just working myself to the bone to service them. And everybody was like, why are you doing that? And it's like, because it's the right thing to do. I'm giving hundreds of people jobs.

The First 100 Days   859

And that led those relationships over to starting Tire Diva.

What I did was I took that, and I started the Women's Empowerment Foundation three years ago, and I would bring
-- I bring 75 to 100, give or take, women that come, and
I want them to have that inspiration. And sometimes it's
difficult. But being here at this table gives me the inspiration to keep going, because I want to share that and make
people feel empowered. You always have to work hard, so
there's no quick, easy way to do it. But if you can provide a
guide, that's where it's at, you know?

THE PRESIDENT: Good job.

MS. POPE-WELLS: Thank you.

THE PRESIDENT: Great enthusiasm. Good. Thank you.

Yes, Lili.

MS. GIL VALLETTA: Yes, first of all, thank you so much,
Ivanka. You've been a facilitator for us. I know that you, at
the Hispanic Chamber of Commerce, have been instrumental in getting four of us Latinas around the table.

So I'm proud to be one of them, and grateful for the issues
and challenges that we face. **I'm an immigrant from
Colombia, and I came to this country with a suitcase, and
a student visa, and a pocket translator -- without speaking a word of a English -- at the age of 17.**

And then fast-forward, and after a successful corporate
career -- I was at *Johnson & Johnson* for 10 years -- passion
drove me to quit my corporate job, which was very comfortable. But what drove me was the shifting demograph-

ics of this country. If we are quickly becoming a majority minority nation, we have the advantage -- economic advantage -- of diversity. So what I do for a living with CIEN+, a culture (inaudible) big data analytics company, is helping the corporate leaders and Fortune 500 companies understand how to turn shifting demographics into money, into our lives, into growth.

And that's why I'm here. **I'm so delighted to share more about my journey as an immigrant**. We are there, working hard, and the **American Dream is real**.

So thank you for the opportunity to share with you, with Mr. Vice President as well, the SBA Administrator. I can't wait to find solutions for us to work together positively forward.

THE PRESIDENT: Thank you, Lili, very much. Thank you.

MS. PERRY: Hi, I'm Shirley Perry. I'm from Anderson, Indiana. I'm a very small environmental group engaged in environmental clean-ups and environmental consulting.

I have seven employees, so I'm little. We started it 30 years ago, and then I became sole owner in 2013. And we just do what we can for the environment. We clean up around gas stations, dry cleaners. We do testing of asbestos and mold. And it's just a good business to have, and it's a great day to be here.

THE PRESIDENT: You've done a great job. Thank you very much.

MS. PERRY: Thank you.

THE PRESIDENT: Linda, would you like to say something?

ADMINISTRATOR McMAHON: Well, I'm just delighted to be here this morning. And I know what it's like for women who are often working in a male environment. Goodness knows, I can recognize that. (Laughter.)

But it's just great to hear all of the stories from all of you, and I'm really excited to be at SBA because we do have our Women's Business Centers. We do have those centers to help guide, to help and advise, to help them do business plans. And we have them all over the country.

So we welcome you to come in, or for people who would like to (inaudible) to our centers, who would like to be helpful in any way we can -- helping to provide more access to capital. And I think we were talking about, Amy, just sometimes you just need a little wind beneath your wings. So we're going to help provide hard information, but also a little wind beneath your wings.

So thank you, Mr. President.

THE PRESIDENT: Thank you, Linda. Great job.

ADMINISTRATOR McMAHON: Thank you, Ivanka, Dina for setting this up. I'm really pleased to be here.

THE PRESIDENT: Thank you. Thanks so very much.

MS. FUNEGRA: Thank you, Mr. President. Thank you, Ivanka. That feels like a second date, right? (Laughter.)

MS. TRUMP: I feel very fortunate.

MS. FUNEGRA: We got together a little more than 10 days ago through the United States Hispanic Chamber of Commerce, and **I'm proud to represent immigrants and Hispanics today. I'm also an immigrant**. I moved from Peru 10 years ago to work in international development for a multilateral organization here. And I also quit my job and used my savings to start La Cocina VA, which is "the kitchen." It's an organization that provides vocational and technical education and jobs to unemployed and under-employed immigrant women, in partnership with local governments, with higher education institutions, with private sector, and help this population to start businesses.

So when Lisa mentioned how important it is to make our **dreams** come true, I have a unique position: I help others make their **dreams** come true with vocational education, empowering women to believe in the possibility of success and open businesses.

So the model that we are ready to replicate now in other cities and in other communities integrates governments, integrates private sector, and all the power and resources that that represents in order to really make impactful results in our communities. And we're growing as communities. Thank you.

THE PRESIDENT: Thank you very much. Thank you very much.

MS. SCANLON RABINOWITZ: Hello. My name is Suzie Scanlon Rabinowitz. I am Co-founder and Managing Director of an alternative legal model. We have a national network of more than 20,000 well-credentialed attorneys who are immediately available to support any legal department on a full-time or part-time engagement basis.

And how we're making a difference is the legal industry has historically really been challenged in working with women on a more flexible basis and also the diversity and inclusion issues. And so my businesses are helping to allow women who are returning to the profession after leaving to raise a family or take care of an aging parent come back and work on a more flexible basis.

And also what we're doing is we provide lawyers on an engagement basis to help Fortune 500 companies. And we're able to address some of the unconscious biases that exist by promoting women and minorities in roles that typically wouldn't go to women and minorities. And when our clients see how terrific our lawyers are, we give them permission to hire them directly. And it's really making an impact on promoting women and minorities at the highest level.

THE PRESIDENT: That's great. Great.

MS. SCANLON RABINOWITZ: Thank you.

THE PRESIDENT: Where are you based?

MS. SCANLON RABINOWITZ: So we're a virtual platform, but based in New York and Connecticut.

THE PRESIDENT: That's wonderful. Great job, thank you. Thanks, Suzie.

MS. SCANLON RABINOWITZ: Thank you.

MS. GIBBENS: Mr. President, Mr. Vice President, Dina, Ivanka, Administrator McMahon, it is an honor and pleasure to be here as part of this process.

I am Dyan Gibbens; I lead Trumbell Unmanned. We're a Houston-based, a Forbes Top 25, veteran-founded company, and we provide critical data to the energy sector. And we fly drones in challenging and austere environments.

Now, we primarily support oil and gas in environmental efforts, and we're all engineers, UV operators, and pilots. You know how you know if someone is a pilot? They'll tell you. (Laughter.)

They'll tell you that a personal passion is promoting STEM for the next generation. And we've partnered with BP for drone camps at Rice University. We've partnered with Intel for a global STEM initiative. We hope to reach thousands -- tens of thousands with that. We've also partnered with Microsoft for an online drone academy that we hope to reach millions of people.

So my goal today is to help change this meeting and create a movement. And thank you for your time.

THE PRESIDENT: Thank you very much. That sounds fantastic. Thank you.

Okay, folks, thank you. (Laughter.)

THE PRESIDENT: Oh, the most important --

MS. JOHNSON: Good morning, Mr. President, Vice President, Ivanka --

THE PRESIDENT: Stay for Jessica.

MS. JOHNSON: Administrator McMahon, my name is Jessica Johnson-Cope. I'm the president and CEO of

Johnson Security Bureau.

This week, Johnson Security will celebrate its 55th anniversary. We are a third-generation, family-owned and operated security services firm based in the South Bronx of New York.

And we provide security guard services, as well as armored car services to protect people, places, and valuable property across the New York metropolitan area.

And I really relate to your story. I relate to your working closely with Ivanka and working side by side because I took over my family's business once my father was diagnosed with terminal cancer. And we worked in the trenches until he passed away. And so I really respect what you two do together and hope to be able to continue our family legacy, and to help other family-owned businesses as a result of our conversation today.

THE PRESIDENT: Great job. Great job, Jessica. Thank you. Thank you very much, everybody.

END
11:31 A.M. EDT

Chapter 109

REMARKS BY THE PRESIDENT ON SIGNING HOUSE JOINT RESOLUTIONS 37, 44, 57, AND 58 UNDER THE CONGRESSIONAL REVIEW ACT

THE ROOSEVELT ROOM

27 March 2017

3:08 P.M. EDT

THE PRESIDENT: Thank you, everybody, for being here. I want to welcome many state and local leaders; and we've had them all over the White House today, and it's a great honor -- including Governor Eric Greitens of Missouri; Governor Gary Herbert of Utah; Lieutenant Governor Jenean Hampton of Kentucky -- who are all at the White House and who are all doing something very, very important today.

I'm signing four bills under the Congressional Review Act. Before this administration only one time in our history had a President signed a bill that used the CRA to cancel a federal regulation. So we're doing a lot of them, and they deserve to be done.

First House Joint Resolution 37 rolls back the so-called blacklisting rule. When I met with manufacturers earlier this year -- and they were having a hard time, believe me -- **they said this blacklisting rule was one of the greatest threats to growing American business and hiring more American workers**. It was a disaster they said. This rule made it too easy for trial lawyers to get rich by going after American companies and American workers who contract with the federal government -- making it very difficult. You all know what I'm talking about, right?

PARTICIPANTS: Yes, sir.

THE PRESIDENT: Does everybody agree? (Laughter.)

Next three bills I'm signing cancel three federal power grabs that centralize decision-making in Washington away from states and local governments, another big disaster.

House Joint Resolution 44 removes a Bureau of Land Management rule that took control of land-use decisions away from states and local decision makers and gave it to Washington, and that's not good. That's never good. (Laughter.)

It's proven, is that right?

A PARTICIPANT: Right.

THE PRESIDENT: Even though you're from Washington. (Laughter.)

You are --

A PARTICIPANT: No, we're not. We work in Washington.

THE PRESIDENT: Definitely from Wisconsin. You have your choice.

The other two bills -- House Joint Resolutions 57 and 58 -- eliminate harmful burdens on state and local taxes on school systems that could have cost states hundreds of millions of dollars. So it's the states and local-tax school systems, and that was very important. Parents, teachers, communities, and state leaders know the needs of their students better than anyone in Washington by far. So we're removing these additional layers of bureaucracy to encourage more freedom and innovation in our schools.

I will keep working with Congress, with every agency, and most importantly with the American people until we eliminate every unnecessary, harmful, and job-killing regulation that we can find. We have a lot more coming. (Applause.)

Thank you. This one you all know -- joint resolution.

(The Resolution is signed.)

THE PRESIDENT: That's going to save a lot of jobs. (Laughter and applause.)

THE PRESIDENT: Who gets this pen?

A PARTICIPANT: I do. (Laughter.)

Now, thank you, Mr. President.

THE PRESIDENT: That's okay.

(The Resolution is signed.)

THE PRESIDENT: Okay? (Applause.) (Laughter.)

I met your father once. He's been around a long time your father. He's doing great. He's doing great. He's a great guy. He endorses me out of nowhere. I said that was a great investment. (Laughter.)

(The Resolution is signed.) (Applause.)

THE PRESIDENT: Tom, I'm going to give you the -- right here because you've been so great, been my friend through thick and thin, right? Even if it doesn't apply to you, I think I can give you the pen. (Laughter.)

(The Resolution is signed.)

THE PRESIDENT: So I just want to thank everybody. It's an honor. This was a lot of work for a lot of people to get this done, but it's going to lead to a lot of good jobs and a lot less regulation.

And it's good for many, many, many people. So thank you all very much. (Applause.)

END

3:14 P.M. EDT

Further Research:
Congressional Review Act
The Obama Administration's "Fair Pay and Safe Workplaces" Order 2014, also known as the Blacklist Rule, required companies bidding for federal contracts valued in excess of $500,000, to report any violations of the labour laws (that had occurred in the previous three years).

Chapter 110

28 March 2017

7:26 P.M. EDT

THE VICE PRESIDENT: Thanks so very much. You may be seated. Well, on behalf of the First Family, it is a great, great privilege for Karen and I to welcome you to the White House for what I know will be a very special evening tonight.

And as the President of the Senate, it's particularly meaningful for me to welcome Republican and Democrat members of the Senate to this very special evening.

I want to give special appreciation to Leader McConnell and Leader Schumer. Thank you so much for both being here tonight. (Applause.)

Thank you for your service to the nation. And also, the President Pro Tem of the Senate, Orrin Hatch -- I think the longest-serving member of the United States Senate -- is with us. (Applause.)

And lastly, a rousing round of applause for the spouses that are with us tonight -- (applause) -- that make the sacrifices so that the members who are here can serve. (Applause.)

The First Family is particularly moved that so many family

members could be here this evening. So I thank you all for making time to be with us.

This will be an inspiring night, and hopefully the will be an encouraging night. I know the President and the First Lady and Karen and I are well familiar with the sacrifices of public life. And tonight is just, from the First Family to each one of you, a small token of their appreciation for your service to your state and your service to the people of the United States of America.

So, with that said, it is my high honor and distinct privilege to introduce our host and hostess for this evening -- the President of the United States of America and Mrs. Melania Trump. (Applause.)

THE PRESIDENT: Thank you, Mike. Thank you very much. (Applause.)

Thank you very much. Nobody ever told me that politics was going to be so much fun. (Laughter.)

But we're doing well. It's going very well.

We just had a call -- long call from General Mattis. And, John, I know, is very happy to hear that, but he knows better than anybody, we're doing very well in Iraq.

Our soldiers are fighting and fighting like never before, and the results are very, very good. So I just wanted to let everyone know.

I have some very special friends in this room, especially -- I must tell you, we have the Republicans, but I even have a couple of Democrats. I said -- we had a dinner here about three weeks ago, and it was so beautiful. We had these incredible musicians from the Marine Corps and from the Army -- incredible, actually. And I said, you know, I'd like to do something special -- I'd like to ask the United States Senate, with spouses, to come and hear how good it was. It was just a beautiful evening.

And so here we are. And shockingly, it's semi-bipartisan. A lot of people showed up that people weren't expecting, which is a very good thing. (Applause.)

Which is a very, very good thing.

And I know that we're all going to make a deal on health-care -- that's such an easy one. (Laughter.)

So I have no doubt that that's going to happen very quick-ly. I think it will, actually. I think it's going to happen -- be-cause we've all been **promising** -- Democrat, Republican -- we've all been **promising** that to the American people. So I think a lot of good things are going to happen there.

We're going to talk about infrastructure. We're go-ing to talk about fixing up our military, which we really need. There has been a depletion, and we're going to make it so good and so strong. And there's, I think, never been a time where we needed it so much.

And we're going to be doing a great job. But hopefully it will start being bipartisan, because everybody really wants the same thing. We want **greatness** for this country that we love. So I think we're going to have some very good relationships.

Right, Chuck? I see Chuck. Hello, Chuck. (Laughter.)

And I really think that will happen.

So, again, enjoy these incredible musicians. They are really something special. And I hope we're going to do this many, many times together as a unit. Thank you all for being here.

Melania, thank you very much.

Our Vice President. Did we make the right decision with Pence? (Applause.)

Right?

And, Karen, thank you very much. So nice. Thank you.

Thank you, everybody. Have a good time.

END
7:31 P.M. EDT

*"We want greatness
for this country
that we love."*

Chapter 111

28 March 2017

11:09 A.M. EDT

THE PRESIDENT: The press must like you people. Look at all the press. Well, you're the greatest people. You keep us safe, right?

PARTICIPANT: Yes, sir.

THE PRESIDENT: You keep us safe. It's a tremendous honor to welcome the *Fraternal Order of Police* to the White House. So many of you I know for so long, and you've been friends of mine, and you do a great job. Nobody braver.

I want to thank your entire leadership team, including your National President, Chuck Canterbury. I also want to thank you for your support during the election. I guess you probably know, the numbers were extremely lopsided, right? I'm just trying to figure out who were the few people that voted the other way. Who are they? (Laughter.)

Find out who they are, please, and let us know?

As I traveled the country during my campaign, I had the great privilege to spend time with our amazing police officers who risk their lives every day to keep us **safe**. And

I made a crucial pledge: We will always support -- and you people know that better than anybody, you know me -- the incredible men and women of law enforcement. I will always have your back -- 100 percent, like you've always had mine, and you showed that on November 8th.

I'm also pleased to have with us our great Attorney General, Jeff Sessions. Thank you, Jeff, for being here. That was a big day you had yesterday too, on sanctuary cities.

ATTORNEY GENERAL SESSIONS: Thank you.

THE PRESIDENT: That was a very, very important thing you did, and, frankly, a very popular thing. So congratulations. And Jeff is with us -- a strong supporter of law enforcement -- you know that. He was in Alabama. He was the attorney general. He was a U.S. attorney -- and a lot of people don't know that. They know him as the senator, but the law enforcement people knew him more even as the other. So here to do a great job. Good, Jeff. Great to have you with us.

Sadly, our police are often prevented from doing their jobs. When policing is reduced, the main victims are the most vulnerable citizens of our society -- and you see that all over. In too many of our communities, violent crime is on the rise, and in too many places, our citizens have not been **safe** for a very, very long time.

These are the painful realities many in Washington do not want to talk about. They just don't want to hear about it. And we have seen that -- we've seen it all over.

By the way, who is from the standpoint of New York?

Where are my New York guys here?

PARTICIPANT: No New York.

THE PRESIDENT: That's terrible. (Laughter.)

I have one sitting in my office. He's the greatest. He's coming right in.

Last year, in Chicago, 4,368 people were shot. Nearly 700 more have already been shot since January of this year alone. I ask, what's going on in Chicago, right?

What is going on there? There's no excuse for it. There's no excuse for it. I'm sure you're asking the same question: What's going on in Chicago?

I also want to thank our Vice President for being with us. Mike Pence has been amazing -- an amazing Vice President, and very much a believer in law enforcement and the job you people do.

All of our citizens have the right to live in **safety and peace**. We will work every day to remove the gang members, drug dealers, and violent criminals from your communities -- and we already are. They're being moved very quickly.

In fact, General Kelly, as you know, has done a fantastic job on the border. Down 61 percent since inauguration. People coming in down 61 percent, which is a tremendous number.

My highest duty as President is the **security** of our people, the **security** of our nation. That is why I've already taken numerous actions to enhance domestic security, including the creation of Task Force on Reducing Violent Crime, an inter-agency task force to dismantle criminal cartels, along with historic actions to secure our borders and remove criminals from our country. We're removing MS-13. We're removing criminals all over the country. They're getting out. We're taking them out. And for that, I thank you folks. I know you're in strict coordination with General Kelly and the border patrol and ICE, and you've been doing a fantastic job.

As President, I will work night and day to **Make America Safe Again**. And we've already done a big part of it. You'll see the numbers come out very soon. I just want to thank all of you for your leadership. I want to thank all of you for your expertise, the job you've done. And it's a great honor to be with you today.

And we'll now go around and just introduce yourselves. Introduce yourself in front of all this live television. It's always live for me. You know, unfortunately, the other guys -- they make a speech and don't -- with me, everything is live. One mistake and it's no good. But we just can't make mistakes, right? So we don't make mistakes.

Go ahead.

MR. CANTERBURY: I'm Chuck Canterbury, the National President of Fraternal Order of Police, from South Carolina.

MR. McDONALD: I'm Jay McDonald. I'm the Vice President of the *National Fraternal Order of Police*, and I'm from Ohio.

MR. PENOZA: I'm Tom Penoza. I'm the Treasurer of the

National Fraternal Order of Police, and I'm from Delaware.

MR. YOES: I'm Patrick Yoes. I'm the National Secretary, and I'm from Louisiana.

MR. MAYBERRY: Roger Mayberry, National Sergeant at Arms, from California.

MR. MCNESBY: John McNesby, President in Philadelphia.

MR. PERKINS: Joe Perkins. I'm the Chairman of the National Trustees, and I'm from Oklahoma.

MR. ANGELO: I'm Dean Angelo. I'm the President of Chicago Lodge 7.

MR. PASCO: Jim Pasco -- I'm the Executive Director of the National FOP, and I reside in Maryland.

THE PRESIDENT: Good. Okay, thank you very much.

END
11:16 A.M. EDT

"Last year, in Chicago,
4,368 people were shot.
Nearly 700 more have already been shot
since January of this year alone.
I ask, what's going on in Chicago, right?"

Chapter 112

**REMARKS BY PRESIDENT TRUMP AT SIGNING OF
EXECUTIVE ORDER TO CREATE ENERGY INDEPENDENCE
ENVIRONMENTAL PROTECTION AGENCY HEADQUARTERS
WASHINGTON, D.C.**

28 March 2017

2:14 P.M. EDT

THE PRESIDENT: Thank you. (Applause.)

Thank you very much. I guess they like what we're about
to sign. I knew they were going to like this one. Well,
thank you very much. I very much appreciate it. And
thank you to our great Vice President, Mike Pence.

I'm thrilled that everybody could be here with us today. I
want to give special thanks to Administrator Scott Pruitt,
Secretary Ryan Zinke, and Secretary Rick Perry for your
remarks. I told Rick, I said, run it the way you ran Texas
-- because this is going to be a great operation. And he did
a great job, and we're honored to have all three. And I'm
really honored to have our Vice President, because Mike
Pence has been outstanding. Hasn't he been outstanding? (Applause.)

Together, this group is going to do a truly great job for our
country. We have a very, very impressive group here to
celebrate the start of a NEW ERA in American energy and
production and job creation. The action I'm taking today
will eliminate federal overreach, restore economic freedom, and allow our companies and our workers to thrive,

compete, and succeed on a level playing field for the first time in a long time, fellas. It's been a long time. I'm not just talking about eight years; we're talking about a lot longer than eight years. You people know it maybe better than anybody.

Thanks, as well, to the many distinguished members of Congress who have taken the time to be here. I want to thank all of our industry leaders who are with us and who share our determination to create jobs in America, for Americans. And, Shelley, thank you very much also. I spotted you in the audience. Thank you.

That is what this is all about: **bringing back our jobs, bringing back our dreams** -- and **Making America Wealthy Again**.

I also want to thank the dedicated public servants who are with us this afternoon. **You're doing important work to protect our health and public resources**. So important.

Finally, I want to acknowledge the truly amazing people behind me on this stage: our incredible coal miners. (Applause.)

We love our coal miners. Great people. Over the past two years, I've spent time with the miners all over America. They told me about the struggles they've endured.

I actually, in one case, I went to a group of miners in West Virginia -- you remember, Shelley -- and I said, how about this: Why don't we get together, we'll go to another place, and you'll get another job; you won't mine anymore. Do you like that idea? They said, no, we don't like that idea -- **we love to mine, that's what we want to do**. I said, if that's what you want to do, that's what you're going to do. And I was very impressed. **They love the job.** That's what their job is. I fully understand that. I grew up in a real estate family, and until this recent little excursion into the world of politics, I could never understand anybody who would not want to be in the world of real estate. (Laughter.)

Believe me. So I understand it. And we're with you 100 percent, and that's what you're going to do. Okay? (Applause.)

The miners told me about the attacks on their jobs and their livelihoods. They told me about the efforts to shut down their mines, their communities, and their very way of life. **I made them this promise: We will put our miners back to work.** (Applause.)

We've already eliminated a devastating anti-coal regulation -- but that was just the beginning.

Today, I'm taking bold action to follow through on that promise.

My administration is putting an END TO THE WAR ON COAL. We're going to have clean coal -- really clean coal. With today's executive action, I am taking historic steps to lift the restrictions on American energy, **to reverse government intrusion, and to cancel job-killing regulations.** (Applause.)

And, by the way, regulations not only in this industry, but in every industry. **We're doing them by the thousands, every industry.** And **we're going to have safety, we're going to have clean water, we're going to have clear**

air. But so many are unnecessary, and so many are job killing. We're getting rid of the bad ones.

One after another, we're keeping our promises and putting power back into the hands of the people. First, today's energy independence action calls for an immediate re-evaluation of the so-called Clean Power Plan. (Applause.)

Perhaps no single regulation threatens our miners, energy workers, and companies more than this crushing attack on American industry.

Second, we are **lifting the ban on federal leasing for coal production**.

Third, we are **lifting job-killing restrictions on the production of oil, natural gas, clean coal, and shale energy**.

And finally, **we are returning power to the states** -- where that power belongs. States and local communities know what is best for them. They understand it. They get it. They've been doing it for a long time. It was taken away from them, and not handled well -- and they are the ones that we should now, and will now, empower to decide.

My action today is **the latest in a series of steps to create American jobs and to grow American wealth**. We're **ending the theft of American prosperity, and rebuilding our beloved country**.

We approved the permit to finally build the Keystone XL Pipeline, and cleared the way to completion of the Dakota Access Pipeline -- thousands and thousands of jobs. (Applause.)

We've already created a half a million new jobs in the first two jobs reports of my administration. And if you noticed today, Ford -- great company -- announced massive new spending on three big plants in the state of Michigan -- a state which I love very much. Do you remember what happened in Michigan? Remember, November 8th. Oh, that was an exciting Michigan evening.

And Ford just made that announcement. That's a great announcement. It's a very important announcement. It means jobs, jobs, jobs.

We are going to continue to expand energy production, and we will also create more jobs in infrastructure, trucking, and manufacturing. This will allow the EPA to focus on its primary mission of protecting our air and protecting our water. Together, we are going to start a new energy revolution -- one that celebrates American production on American soil.

We want to make our goods here instead of shipping them in from other countries. All over the world, they ship in, ship in -- take the Americans' money, take the money, go home; take our jobs, take our companies.

No longer, folks. No longer. We believe in those really magnificent words: **Made in the USA**. (Applause.)

Right, fellas?

We will unlock job-producing natural gas, oil, and shale energy. We will produce American coal to power American industry.

We will transport American energy through American pipelines, made with American steel. **Made with American steel**. Can you believe somebody would actually say that? (Applause.)

This came up a little bit coincidentally when I was signing the pipelines deals. I'm all signing, I've got them done. And I said, folks, where do we get the steel? And they said, I think it's from foreign lands. And I said, no good. Who makes it? Who makes those beautiful pipes for the pipeline? Sir, they're made outside of this country. I said, no more, no more. **So we added a little clause** -- didn't take much -- that you want to build pipelines in this country? You're going to buy your steel, and you're going to have it fabricated here. Makes sense, right? Doesn't it make sense, Bob? Think so. He knows. (Applause.)

Together, we will create millions of good American jobs -- also, so many energy jobs -- and really lead to unbelievable prosperity all throughout our country. And Rick Perry is going to have a lot to do with that.

I want to just thank everybody in this room. You're all very special people. In particular, I want to thank the miners. You know, my guys, they'll get enough thanks. These people haven't had enough thanks. They've had a hard time for a long time. (Applause.)

They're tough-looking guys, too. I'll tell you what -- not going to mess around with this group, right?

All right. Thank you, fellas. **I made my promise and I keep my promise.**

So I want to thank everybody in the room. God bless you,

and God bless America. Thank you very much. Thank you. (Applause.)

THE PRESIDENT: Come on, fellas. Basically, you know what this is? You know what it says, right? You're going back to work.

PARTICIPANT: Good. (Applause.)

THE PRESIDENT: You're going back to work. Ready?

PARTICIPANT: We're ready.

THE PRESIDENT: Okay. (Applause.)

(The Executive Order is signed.)

Come on. What about a miner? One of the miners -- who's the miner back there? Only a miner. (Laughter.)

Come on, fellas. You split it up. Cut it in -- (laughter) -- come on, where's Ryan? Where's Ryan? Okay, Rick, you'll split that up with Ryan.

I want to thank everybody very much. This is a great honor today. Very special, special people. And you're going to see a lot of progress.

And Shelley, thank you very much. You have been fantastic. Really fantastic. Appreciate it. Thank you. (Applause.)

END
2:26 P.M. EDT

Chapter 113

**REMARKS BY THE FIRST LADY MELANIA TRUMP
AT THE 2017 INTERNATIONAL WOMEN
OF COURAGE AWARDS CEREMONY**

WASHINGTON, DC

29 March 2017

Background:
First Lady Melania Trump and Under Secretary of State for Political Affairs Thomas A. Shannon presented the 2017 Secretary of State's International Women of Courage (IWOC) Award to a group of extraordinary women from around the world on March 29 at the State Department.

The Secretary of State's International Women of Courage Award annually recognizes women around the globe who have demonstrated exceptional courage and leadership in advocating for peace, justice, human rights, gender equality, and women's empowerment, often at great personal risk. Since the inception of this award in 2007, the State Department has honored over 100 women from more than 60 different countries.

The 2017 awardees are:

- Sharmin Akter, Activist Against Early/ Forced Marriage, Bangladesh
- Malebogo Molefhe, Human Rights Activist, Botswana
- Natalia Ponce de Leon, President, Natalia Ponce de Leon Foundation, Colombia
- Rebecca Kabugho, Political and Social Activist, Demo-

cratic Republic of Congo
•Jannat Al Ghezi, Deputy Director of The Organization of Women's Freedom in Iraq, Iraq
•Major Aichatou Ousmane Issaka, Deputy Director of Social Work at the Military Hospital of Niamey, Niger
•Veronica Simogun, Director and Founder, Family for Change Association, Papua New Guinea
•Cindy Arlette Contreras Bautista, Lawyer and Founder of Not One Woman Less, Peru
•Sandya Eknelygoda, Human Rights Activist, Sri Lanka
•Sister Carolin Tahhan Fachakh, Member, Daughters of Mary Help of Christians (F.M.A.), Syria
•Saadet Ozkan, Educator and Gender Activist, Turkey
•Nguyen Ngoc Nhu Quynh, Blogger and Environmental Activist, Vietnam
•Fadia Najib Thabet, Human Rights Activist, Yemen

THOMAS A SHANNON JR. (ACTING DEPUTY SECRETARY OF STATE): Good Morning. It's my great pleasure to welcome you to the State Department and the 2017 International Women of Courage Awards Ceremony.

Madam First Lady, Mrs Melania Trump, thank you so much for being with us today. We are deeply honored by your participation in this important celebration and grateful for your commitment and that of the President to the wellbeing and success of Women and girls across the globe.

Please join me again in welcoming The First Lady. [Applause]

I would also like to welcome the members of The Diplomatic Corps who are with us here today and, of course, the women joining us on this stage, The 2017 International Women of Courage.

Thank you very much. [Applause]

The Secretary of State's Award for International Women of Courage is part of our celebration of Women's History Month and International Women's Day.

The Secretary wanted to be here to present these awards himself; regrettably, he is on his way to Ankara and Brussels, but extends his heartfelt congratulation to these Honorees.

Since 2007, this award has honored women from around the world who have exhibited exceptional courage and leadership; who have drawn strength from adversity to help transform their societies.

These women have mobilized public sentiment and their governments to expose and address injustice, speak against corruption, prevent violent extremism and stand up for the rule of law and peace, often with little more than their voices and sheer determination.

We are honored to recognize this incredible group.

Shortly you will hear each woman's story. They are an inspiring reminder of how individuals can make a difference.

Taken together, they provide a powerful message of courage and leadership. As we celebrate the accomplishments of these women, we also provide them with a platform fro telling their stories.

After this celebration, they will participate in a State Department sponsored exchange program to engage with American audiences around our country, contributing to the tradition of people to people diplomacy.

The United States is proud to honor these leaders as part of our commitment to advance the status of women and girls around the world. I want to take a moment to thank my colleagues in the Secretary's Office of Global Women's Issues for the work they do to ensure that gender equality and women's empowerment are integrated into our foreign policy.

I also want to recognize the Bureau of Education and Cultural Affairs whose programs like the International Visitor's Leadership program on which these women are about to embark, are an important element of our Diplomacy. The work of our colleagues here at The State Department embodies a commitment that comes from the very top of our Administration.

As Secretary Tillerson has said, there is a study after study to confirm that when you empower women in these developing parts of the world, you change the future of the country, because you change the cycle within the families.

Women's Empowerment is not just a moral imperative; it is a strategic investment in our collective security.

In short, when women do better, countries do better. Women's security is a matter of international security. Without it, we all lose. President Trump and his administration are committed to expanding opportunities for women and girls domestically and across the globe.

On February 13 [2017], President Trump and Canadian Prime Minister Trudeau launched the United States of Canada Council for The Advancement of Women

Entrepreneurs and Business Leaders.

On February 28 [2017], President Trump signed two bills into law. First, The Inspiring the Next Space Pioneers and Innovators and Explorers Act; and second, The Promoting Women and Entrepreneurship Act. Both of which encourage women to pursue careers in engineering, science and mathematics, and to provide support for women's entrepreneurial programs through The National Science Foundation.

So, it gives me great pleasure to introduce someone who has played a central role in that effort.

As a philanthropist and humanitarian, The First Lady has been a driving force behind the Administration's efforts to promote the empowerment of women and child in our society.

Mrs Trump has been an Honorary Chairwoman for The Boys Club of New York for five consecutive years, and in 2005 was awarded the title of Goodwill Ambassador by the American Red Cross.

She helped launch – National Child Abuse Prevention Month in April 2008 and has been a champion for the American Heart Association.

Her deep concern for issues affection [sic.] women and children continue as she has focused as First Lady on the challenge of Cyber Bullying among our youth.

Ladies and gentlemen, please join me in welcoming The First Lady of the United States, Mrs Melanie Trump. [Applause.]

FIRST LADY MELANIA TRUMP: Thank you, thank you.
Ambassador Shannon, Dignitaries, esteemed guests, ladies
and gentlemen.

I am deeply humbled to be here today, to honor these
twelve remarkable and inspirational women who have
given so much for so many, regardless of the unimaginable
threat to their own personal **safety**.

Each one of these heroic women has an extraordinary
story of courage, which must inspire each of us to also
achieve more than we have are ever imagined possible.
Their lives remind us of the boundless capacity of the human **Spirit**, when guided by moral clarity and desire to do
good.

These honorees on the stage with me, have fought for
their rights and for the rights so [sic.] others. Each battled
forces such as government, the courts, gender bias, terrorism, war and corruption; and were willing, in each moment
to face harsh penalties, including imprisonment and death.

As they continue to persevere against unimaginable odds,
these women are extraordinary examples of reaching within to find the courage that lies inside us all to change the
world. While learning the stories of these twelve honorees,
I would like to ask each of us to take this moment and try
to image what it would be like to experience the trying ob-
stacles, domestic abuse, gender biased violence or government oppression that some of these women have faced.

Let us try to envision ourselves in their place, struggling
against gender bias and discriminatory laws which serve to
protect the predators of unthinkable crimes while punish-
ing their victims, should they even dare to speak out.

Ask yourself if you would have the fortitude of **Spirit**, the courage of your convictions, and the enormous inner strength required to stand up and fight against such overwhelming odds.

Amazingly, each of our honorees has courageously answered – YES to those questions.

For it is their strength and the strength of others like them, which will unite a global battle against inhumanity.

Together with the international community, the United States must send a clear message that we are watching.

It is therefore our duty to continue to shine the light on each miraculous victory achieved by women, all capable of trying, truly leading the change to fight for those that cannot fight for themselves.

Theirs are the stories of human greatness that will continue to inspire and therefore must be told far and wide. These honorees, who have fought on the front lines against injustice are true heroes. Their stores of individual bravery remind us that there in always hope whenever the human spirit is brought to bear in the service of others, and the healing and person empowerment are often born from such deeds.

I believe bravery is the ability to live one's life refusing to be discouraged and instead choosing a life of purpose. Only when we do this are we able to surpass what we previously believed to be possible.

Each of these twelve women represents a life of enormous courage, to save a child, to help a family, to make a neighborhood or school safe, or to boldly speak out against evil by refusing to back down no matter the personal cost.

To the young people here today, I ask you to allow the triumphs exemplified by these heroic women to inspire you in your own lives and to remind yourself that you, too are capable of greatness.

I urge you to not be afraid to fail. As failure will never have the power to define you as long as you learn from it, and realize that your first steps will always involve taking a leap of faith, but believing in yourself while choosing to replace fear with hope. Let these brave women service as daily inspiration, as it is now up to each of you to remain vigilant against injustice in all it's many forms.

As you go forward, remember, their journeys to push ahead and strive to bring about a better community. A better country and a better world in an ongoing fight for right over might. We must continue once again to shine the light on the horrendous atrocities taking place in neigborhoods around the corner and around the globe, where innocent families are crying out to live in safety.

We must continue to fight injustice in all it's forms, in whatever scale or shape it takes in our lives. Together, we must declare that the era of allowing the brutality against women and children is over; while affirming that the time for empowering women around the world is now.

For wherever women are diminished, the entire world is diminished with them.

However, wherever women are empowered; towns and villages schools and economies are empowered and together we are all made stronger with them. We must begin now to challenge old fears.

Fight long held injustices and stand up against evil and injustice wherever it may be. As leaders of our shared global community, we must continue to work towards gender empowerment and respect for people from all backgrounds and ethnicity, remembering always that we are all ultimately members of one race, the human race, each one of us is uniquely gifted.

We must continually affirm our American values as we join with the international community to make our world **safer** through acts of collaborative and individual bravery.

Thank you, honorees, for your courage; and thank you Ambassador Shannon, for your support.

God bless you and God bless this great nation.

Thank you. [Applause]

> *"These honorees on the stage with me,*
> *have fought for their rights*
> *and for the rights so [sic.] others.*
> *Each battled forces such as government,*
> *the courts, gender bias, terrorism,*
> *war and corruption;*
> *and were willing, in each moment to face*
> *harsh penalties, including imprisonment and*
> *death."*

Chapter 114

29 March 2017

11:32 A.M. EDT

THE PRESIDENT: Hello, everybody. Thank you for being here with us this morning. During my campaign, I promised to take action to keep drugs from pouring into our country.

And I want to just thank Secretary Kelly; he's done an amazing job.

Down 61 percent at the border right now in terms of people and the drugs that are being stopped. It will take longer, and there's great cooperation with Mexico and others. But we're doing a good job.

And we want to help those who have become so badly addicted. Drug abuse has become a crippling problem throughout the United States. **Drug overdoses are now the leading cause of accidental death in our country. And opioid overdose deaths have nearly quadrupled since 1999.** This is a total epidemic, and I think it's probably almost untalked about compared to the severity that we're witnessing.

Today, we're bringing together leaders from inside our government and outside of our government, and courageous people who have been affected -- and really affected -- by this terrible affliction. In a joint campaign, we want to battle drug addiction and combat opioid, and we have to do it -- a crisis.

We're fortunate to have Governor Chris Christie with us, a friend of mine -- a great friend of mine -- a very, very early endorser -- in fact, an immediate endorser -- once he got out of the race. (Laughter.)

He liked himself more than he liked me. (Laughter.)

But other than that --

GOVERNOR CHRISTIE: I still do, sir, but that's all right. (Laughter.)

THE PRESIDENT: Other than that, he's been great. And he's a very effective guy, I will tell you -- to have you working on this -- and a great moment, actually, if people remember, was you talking about your friend. That was probably your greatest moment during the campaign for President, and it showed how much you knew about this issue. So, thank you very much, Chris.

We'll work directly with representatives from state and local governments, law enforcement, medical professionals, and victims.

I especially want to thank Pam Garozzo -- where's Pam? Hi, Pam. How are you? -- for being here. Pam sadly lost her son, beautiful boy, to drug addiction. And, Pam, we mourn your terrible loss, and we honor your strength and the fact that you're here. And he will not have died in vain, okay? We'll make sure -- he will not have died in vain. So thank you, Pam. We appreciate it.

We're also thankful to welcome AJ Solomon and Vanessa Vitolo, both of whom have fought addiction and are now symbols of hope and recovery, right? Good job.

We must get our citizens to help, and we need help. Everybody has to help. And we will not have to go through what Pam has gone through and so many other families in this country have gone through. We want to help people like AJ and Vanessa, who struggled through the dark depths of addiction. Not easy. Not easy. And they found this bright promise of recovery.

We wish to also focus on prevention and law enforcement, which is why I've issued previous executive actions to strengthen law enforcement and dismantle criminal cartels. Drug cartels have spread their deadly industry across our nation, and the availability of cheap narcotics -- the cheap narcotics -- some of it comes in cheaper than candy -- has devastated our communities.

It's really one of the biggest problems our country has, and nobody really wants to talk about it.

Vice President Pence mentioned this coming into the room. He said, this is a problem like nobody understands. And I think they're going to start to understand it. And, more importantly, we have to solve the problem.

Our Attorney General, Jeff Sessions, is working very hard on this problem. It takes a lot of his time, because this causes so much of the problem that you have to solve -- that problem.

So solving the drug crisis will require cooperation across government and across society, including early intervention to keep America's youth off this destructive path.

We must work together, trust each other, and forge a true partnership based on the common ground of cherishing human life.

So this is a very, very important meeting, and maybe we'll go around the room and we'll just say hello to everybody so we all know who we are. And then the press will leave and we'll start talking.

General Sessions, we know who you are. Go ahead.

SECRETARY DeVOS: Betsey DeVos, Secretary of Education. Secretary Shulkin: David Shulkin, Secretary of the VA.

MS. GAROZZO: Pam Garozzo, parent of Carlos.

MR. SOLOMON: AJ Solomon. Thanks for introducing me, Mr. President.

MS. VITOLO: Vanessa. Thank you so much for having me.

SECRETARY KELLY: Secretary Kelly, Homeland Security.

DR. WRIGHT: Don Wright, Acting Assistant Secretary for Health.

MR. ROSENBERG: Chuck Rosenberg. I run the DEA.

MR. BAUM: Richard Baum, Acting Director of the Office of National Drug Control Policy.

MS. MADRAS: Bertha Madras, Harvard Medical School.

MS. BONDI: Pam Bondi, Attorney General of Florida.

MR. RIVERA: Mariano Rivera, founder of the Mariano Rivera Foundation.

THE PRESIDENT: Oh, they could use you now. (Laughter.)

You know, I think you'd make $100 million a year right. I tell you, I watched for many years Mariano. I'd sit with George, and George always felt good when Mariano was --

MR. RIVERA: That's right.

THE PRESIDENT: He threw the heaviest pitch any time. I don't know -- you made the ball like -- it weighed 30 pounds, right?

MR. RIVERA: Something like that.

THE PRESIDENT: How about the broken bats? (Laughter.) How many broken bats?

MR. RIVERA: Too many.

THE PRESIDENT: Those bats used to crack, right? Thank you. Great honor.

And, Jared, thank you, and Chris. Chris, why don't you say a few words?

GOVERNOR CHRISTIE: Mr. President, first, to the President and the Vice President, thank you so much for focusing on this issue. As you know, Mr. Vice President, as the gover-

nor of Indiana for four years, this issue causes enormous
pain and destruction to everyday families in every state
in this country. And that's why, Mr. President, I thought it
was so important to bring Pam and AJ and Vanessa here
today for you meet them and hear directly from them their
stories.

I'm just so honored that the President would ask me to
take on this task with the group that we put together. And
I'm thrilled to work with the Attorney General, as well, on
the issues of prevention and interdiction of drugs, so we
don't get people hooked in the first place.

But the most important thing to me is, I think the President
and I both agree that addiction is a disease, and it's a disease that can be treated, and that we need to make sure
we let people know -- the President talked about how folks
don't talk about it.

We talked about cancer, we talk about heart disease, we
talk about diabetes, and we're not afraid to talk about
it. But people are afraid and ashamed to talk about drug
addiction. And while they don't talk about it, we lose lives
-- lives of good people.

In the end, the President ended by saying -- talking about
life. And he and I are both pro-life. The difference with
the President and I is we're pro-life for the whole life, not
just for the nine months in the womb, but for the whole
life. Every life is an individual gift from God. And no
life is irredeemable, and people make mistakes -- we all
have. The people who mistakes of drug use -- and it is a
mistake -- we can't throw their life away.

The President and I believe that every life is an individual gift from God and is precious.

And I think that's why it was such an important issue to him in the campaign, and why I'm so honored to work with a President who understands the value of life and the value of second chances. And that's what this commission, I hope, is going to be about, to be able to give he and the Vice President the best suggestions we possible can about how to have a national fight against this epidemic.

Mr. President, thank you for your confidence in all of us, and thank you for your support.

[Photo: screengrab.]

THE PRESIDENT: Thank you very much. Maybe, Vanessa, you can tell a little bit of your story. We're so proud of you.

MS. VITOLO: Don't put me on the spot, but -- (laughter) -- so, first of all, I would like to take this opportunity to thank you so much to brining this whole platform to a national level. You are literally -- everyone at this table is saving lives. There are people dying every single day, and it's heartbreaking.

And, Governor Christie, I need you to know that I draw so much strength and courage from you, standing up for people that had nearly given up completely. That's extraordinary.

I come from a small town in South Jersey. My aunt is a teacher, and she taught me the importance of education. My uncle is a fire fighter. He taught me the importance of law and order. I went to a private high school. I was a cheerleader. I went to college, where I joined a sorority. After I left college, I had an injury and was prescribed pain killers, and so quickly it took off from there. I didn't know anything about heroin. I was never warned -- not that it's anybody else's fault; I take full responsibility.

THE PRESIDENT: So this all began very innocently with an injury.

MS. VITOLO: Absolutely, yes -- with a prescription of pain killers.

THE PRESIDENT: And what was it? What was the drug they gave?

MS. VITOLO: Percocet.

THE PRESIDENT: I see.

MS. VITOLO: And then from Percocet, it went to Oxy. And then from Oxy, it went to heroin, because it is definitely, like you said, more accessible and so much cheaper. Very quickly, I lost everything. I was homeless. I chose to be homeless. I was living on the streets of Atlantic City.

I was in and out of jail, and I was lucky enough to see some kind of light where I became a drug court participant -- a drug court system that we have in New Jersey, which saved my life. They sent me to a long-term treatment facility, Integrity House, in New Jersey, and they saved my life.

THE PRESIDENT: How hard was that, getting off this horrible stuff? How hard was it for you?

MS. VITOLO: Physically, it was so hard. And I felt that was the hardest part. But then, a couple of months later, comes the psychological aspect of it, and you still think that you need it, because you're still not as happy when you're happy, you're still not as sad. You have no feelings. It's like you're a shell. And it takes over your whole life -- to choose to be homeless instead of live with your parents; to choose not to speak to your family.

THE PRESIDENT: And what did your parents say during this whole process? Because I'm looking at you, you're like all-American -- perfect. You're a perfect person. And I'm saying it's hard to believe that you're living on the streets.

MS. VITOLO: Well, it was so hard for my family. My mom would drive the streets of Atlantic City begging people to find me. She couldn't find me. I was that lost in every aspect of the word. In jail -- like I said, I was sent to Integrity House, and they saved my life.

They gave me a second chance at life. And from there, I went to a halfway house, I got a job where I quickly moved up. I'm now a manager. Got my own apartment. I'm graduating drug court this year. And it's amazing the opportunities that have been given to me. I'm sitting across from you right now. (Laughter.)

Three years ago, I didn't have a place to live, and today I'm here to represent the light that can be born out of the defeat of this darkness.

There is hope, and there is a tomorrow, and there is a day after that. You just have to fight for it. And people have to know that there's people fighting for them too, because you give up. There comes a point where you feel as if you have nothing. You already ruined everything, so there's no point to get sober.

But I'm here to show you that there is hope. You can get better. There is a better way, and there is a better life.

And I wish I could tell you the heartbreak that I feel with the people that are overdosing every day and dying, and the families that have to go through that suffering -- because there is no need.

We can help somebody. We can change this. And that's the most amazing thing I've ever been a part of in my whole life.

And I would like to thank each and every one of you for giving me this opportunity. It means the world to me. It is my life. I used to think that being an addict was my downfall. But look at me, I'm here today; it's obviously made me a stronger and better person.

THE PRESIDENT: Incredible story. Thank you very much. (Applause.)

Amazing, amazing job. Thank you very much, Vanessa. And we'll talk to you in a little while.

The First 100 Days   **905**

AJ? And I know how successful your father is and what
a great man he is, so that also put pressure on you in a
different way, right?

MR. SOLOMON: Yeah, well, I didn't end up going into politics, so... (Laughter.)

THE PRESIDENT: Don't do it. (Laughter.)

MR. SOLOMON: So Vanessa really spelled it out. But I
grew up in a little town in South Jersey, called
Haddonfield. It's a picturesque town, really good
schools. My dad now is a Supreme Court justice in the
state of New Jersey. Thank you for the appointment, Governor. (Laughter.)

And my mom also serves in state government. And I grew
up, I was a good student. I was an athlete. And I found alcohol and other drugs, and I was probably well on my way
to having an issue, but then I found OxyContin.

My dad got in an accident, and I decided that it would
be a good idea to try it. And that's really where my story
started.

THE PRESIDENT: Immediately hooked? Because I hear so
much about OxyContin. Were you immediately hooked?

MR. SOLOMON: Yeah. When I did my first one, I remember doing it and thinking, this is how I want to live the rest
of my life. I was always searching for something outside of
myself that would make me feel better. People think the
drug is the problem, and to some extent its accessibility is.

But addiction is a disease that I always had, and just had to

be unlocked. And that's what I feel OxyContin did for me.
And when that happened -- you know, now I'm a brother and a son, and a business owner -- I own a treatment
center, which is awesome. And I love it. I'm so happy I
went that route instead of -- I was on track -- I was on the
Governor's advance team. Not that I didn't love it. (Laughter.)

But I really enjoy what I do helping other alcoholics and
addicts. Back then I was --

THE PRESIDENT: Do you have still an alcohol problem?

MR. SOLOMON: I don't drink. I don't do any drugs.

THE PRESIDENT: But that was -- you could see you were
going to have that problem. But you found this
OxyContin?

MR. SOLOMON: Yes. And I was a thief and a liar, and I
ended up homeless. Different story -- my parents did not
want me home. I was living out of my car, and then I ended up going to a long-term treatment center. And I accepted what I was, that I was an addict. And I would rather
have died than live with that. So I left. My plan was to kill
myself. I wasn't able to get home. So I surrendered.

And a lot of people don't believe this part of the story
-- and whatever someone's conception of God or a higher
power is --I got on my knees on a shuttle back to treatment; I hadn't used. And I said, God either please just let
me die -- because my plan was to shoot myself; I didn't
have a gun -- let me die, or just let me get this. And I
swear to you that that obsession that Vanessa talked about
to use was lifted that day. And my goal now in life is to

help another alcoholic and an addict.

And I think -- back then I would have rather died than had this disease. But now, a normal person can be miserable, and they can be angry and resentful, and that's just how they'll live their life. Me, if I get angry, resentful, if I'm miserable, I'll drink and then I'll do dope -- heroin. And then I will die. So I'm grateful.

THE PRESIDENT: But not -- not anymore, right?

MR. SOLOMON: I don't have -- I'm not allowed to be miserable. I have to be trying to get the most out of life. Normal people don't have that. They won't die if they don't do that. So I'm grateful that I am what I am. Yes, I guess that's it.

THE PRESIDENT: That's an amazing story. How did you get off it? How did you get -- did you go to a center or something? Or what happened?

MR. SOLOMON: I did. I went in the mountains in Arizona to this place, and I was only coming off of opiates. And they said -- it was this tall guy, I'll never forget -- his name was Bird -- he said, what are you coming off of?

I said, opiates. He said, you don't need detox. You'll feel like you're going to die, but you won't die. And they put me in the center, and I detoxed cold turkey. And --

THE PRESIDENT: And what was that like?

MR. SOLOMON: It's like 20 times worse than the flu, but the anxiety is the worst part, the suicidal ideations crawling out of your skin. I mean, if I had drugs in front of me, I would have done them.

THE PRESIDENT: So he was right?

MR. SOLOMON: Oh, yeah. Yeah, he was right.

THE PRESIDENT: But you got through it? How long did
that take?

MR. SOLOMON: Two weeks.

THE PRESIDENT: It was two weeks of -- they used to call it
cold turkey, right?

MR. SOLOMON: Cold turkey.

THE PRESIDENT: Do they still do that?

MR. SOLOMON: Yeah.

THE PRESIDENT: No way. So you went through two weeks
of that, and that was hell?

MR. SOLOMON: Yes.

THE PRESIDENT: But then you knew you were going to get
better?

MR. SOLOMON: No, then the mental obsession came,
and I wanted to use so badly, but I had accepted what I
was, and I knew I couldn't. So I wanted the obsession to
stop. I wanted my brain to stop yelling at me to pick up. I
didn't want to be that person anymore. So I figured I'd kill
myself, and it would stop. But my dad -- you talked about
how powerful he is, he somehow cancelled all my personal

credit cards. I still don't know how he did it. (Laughter.)

And I wasn't able to get on a plane to get home to get what I needed to end my life. And so I got on my knees and prayed, and that was really the beginning.

THE PRESIDENT: So he did you a great service when he did that?

MR. SOLOMON: He did.

THE PRESIDENT: Smart guy. You have done an amazing job. It's so great. Not easy. Not easy, right, AJ?

MR. SOLOMON: No, not easy.

THE PRESIDENT: But we're very proud of you. (Applause.)

Chris.

GOVERNOR CHRISTIE: Mr. President, Pam works in the New Jersey State Department of Education. And she's someone who came to the candlelight vigil that I held right before Christmas for addicts in New Jersey and their families. And Pam wants to tell you the story about her son, Carlos.

MS. GAROZZO: Yes. First of all, Mr. President, Mr. Vice President, Cabinet, and guests, this is an extreme honor. I am here unfortunately because my son is no longer here.

As Governor Christie said, I came to his candlelight vigil celebrating the fact -- with our Education Commissioner, who is my boss -- that my son was 10 months clean. He had been a year and a half clean before that, before he

had a relapse -- one of many, one of several. Just celebrating his life and celebrating the lives of everybody who are
in recovery.

And then later in December -- actually before that, I just
want to introduce you. This is my son, Carlos. He's wearing a suit because on December 3rd -- this is not his -- was
not his normal attire as a 23-year-old. On December 3rd,
he was here at my church with my husband, Mike, and me
-- Mike, who is seated behind me and to the left -- walking
me down the aisle on my wedding day, one of the happiest
days of my life. Carlos was healthy, happy, thriving, working, getting ready to go back to school, had a job, had a
steady girlfriend, had everything together -- 10 and a half
months clean.

So celebrating him at the candlelight vigil, previously having been at our wedding on December 3rd, and then three
weeks later, on December 23rd, two police detectives
show up at our door and tell me the news that no parent
ever wants to hear. And we just didn't understand. Because this is a disease, you don't understand the dynamics
of it. You can't -- you're not -- nothing prepares you for
this journey.

Unfortunately, my son OD'd after having been clean for 10
and a half months -- OD'd on a drug that was laced with
fentanyl. So he died pretty quickly.

THE PRESIDENT: Which is getting worse and worse I hear,
Jeff.

MS. GAROZZO: Yes.

THE PRESIDENT: Getting just out of control.

MS. GAROZZO: So Carlos started smoking marijuana when he was 15 and a half years old, and for him -- and he'd be the first to tell you this -- it's absolutely for him a gateway drug. It led to heroin, cocaine, crystal meth. At 18, when he was a senior in high school, with months to graduate, he had a crystal meth overdose. And by the time I got to the hospital -- because his friend drove him there; I didn't even know that he was doing this to this extent -- by the time I got to the hospital, the ER doctor came out and said, you need to call your family now; we don't think there's anything we can do for your son.

We managed to transfer him to another hospital. He got the care that he needed. He was in a coma for three days and suffered some minor memory loss from that.

And of course, at this time as an 18-year-old, said, oh, I'm never going to touch anything again, I'm going to stay clean. We had him in a program. But less than a couple months later, he's back on the streets not only taking drugs, but got caught smoking pot, ended up in jail. I had told him early on, I will put every penny, every dime I have into your recovery and getting you clean and helping you stay clean and supporting you 100 percent. But if you end up in trouble with the law, there is nothing I'm doing for you because you have to figure out the way out of that.

So he was in jail a couple of times. He actually went through cold turkey in jail getting clean. When he was clean for a period of almost a year and a half, during that time he was going back to school. He was at this point around 20 years old -- 20, 21 -- was working, volunteering at a recovery house, working with people trying to help them work through their program. He spoke regionally at a conference in West Virginia. They selected him because

he's a young kid, and they figured he would be a good
spokesperson, maybe be able to speak to people's hearts.

Sadly, as I said, he did pass. Nothing in parenting prepares
you to deal with the fact that Mike and I will outlive our
son; that his sisters, who he idolized and who were so
close to him, won't see him anymore; that there will be
empty seats at the Thanksgiving table; that Christmas presents -- we won't be able to give. I'll miss his laughter. I'll
miss his smile. I'll miss him, his hug. I'll miss his dry, witty
sense of humor.

When I asked him if he was walking down the aisle
for my wedding to Mike, he asked me, what does that
entail? Sure, I think I can do it. But what does that
mean? And I said -- I explained to him, and he said, oh, but
I'm pretty sure -- I've watched enough TV to know that I
have to take Mike on a fishing trip and see if he measures
up. (Laughter.)

He was constantly -- he's just that kind of guy. He was
just -- I had people coming up to us at the life celebration,
saying, your son is amazing. You don't know, your son
saved me. Your son was one of the people who came and
dragged me out of Philly, the tenement house that I was
living in, a flophouse, and took him in his place and gave
him money that he really didn't have, just to -- brought me
to meetings.

So this is why I'm here. I'm here because I'd like to see
nationally what's happening -- what Governor Christie has
managed to have happen in New Jersey, with, of course,
the help of the legislators there to make the programs for
recovery accessible and affordable to all. Because this is
-- I was fortunate to have a good insurance plan. But there

did come a point where Carlos needed to be in a program that wasn't entirely covered by insurance, and they wanted to exit him in four days.

Now, four days in a recovery program -- for those of you who have had no experience -- you guys know -- that's nothing. Carlos begged to stay in. So we scrambled, got the money, and were able to keep him in.

I'm here so that parents -- no parent should have to bury their child. No parent should have to wander -- as Vanessa said, I did the drives looking for Carlos all hours of the day and night. Nobody should have to go through this. This is entirely something that can be dealt with, and I appreciate what you are willing to do in shedding a light on this.

THE PRESIDENT: If Carlos stayed longer in the program, would he have been in better shape? Would it have possibly saved him? Or not really?

MS. GAROZZO: Well, I think so. He was in a couple of programs for a period of -- one program that was -- (Participant coughs.)

THE PRESIDENT: Do you want some water? Are you okay?

MS. GAROZZO: I'm good.

THE PRESIDENT: No, I'm just saying -- behind you. I thought she --

MS. GAROZZO: Oh, I'm sorry. (Laughter.)

He was in a program for 35 days. That was his most successful program. As AJ mentioned, Carlos had an underlying problem with self-esteem and feeling good about himself. He just never could quite get there -- even though he was an accomplished musician. He had a scholarship to a prestigious university. As a freshman going in, he was accepted into an engineering program that normally that didn't happen. He had a lot of gifts and talents, but he just never saw them. He was always looking for how can I escape. And like AJ, he also thought several times about suicide.

So I think it's treating the whole person. It's not just the disease of addiction, but it's what is causing you to go after the drugs, to seek it out, to stay with it. And once you're hooked, you're hooked. But how can you work within yourself, with help, to feel good about yourself, to feel that you're worthy. Everybody is loved. Everybody should feel loved. As Governor Christie said, every life is a precious life. And I believe, Governor, you also said that every life is worthy of being reclaimed. And unfortunately, Carlos couldn't entirely reclaim his life.

And behind everybody who is trying -- who's suffering with addiction or in recovery, there's parents and there's family just like me.

THE PRESIDENT: Thank you, Pam. Carlos sounds like he was a great guy, and I know how tough it is. So many people go through it, and we appreciate you being here.

MS. GAROZZO: Thank you, sir.

THE PRESIDENT: Jeff, do you have anything to say?

ATTORNEY GENERAL SESSIONS: Well, I just want to thank you for sharing your stories because that's what we're all here about, and we're seeing a surge in drug abuse and addiction.

The New England Journal of Medicine had -- I think our DEA commissioned it -- pointed out that with regard to heroin, we've got more availability, lower price, and much higher purity. That creates more addiction quicker, I think. And it's a very dangerous situation. You throw fentanyl into that too. And I do believe, Mr. President, we took -- when I became a United States attorney in '81, and the President and others led, the Education Department led -- and it took 20 years, but we reduced drug abuse in America, addiction and death dramatically.

It's begun now to start back up. And I think if we apply --

THE PRESIDENT: When did this start again? It's so bad. When did it start, would you say -- over the last how many years -- where it really took the big spike up?

ATTORNEY GENERAL SESSIONS: I think the fentanyl brought the -- if you noticed here -- Chuck, maybe -- the DEA Director Chuck Rosenberg --

THE PRESIDENT: You would know that. When do you think it really started spiking up, Chuck?

MR. ROSENBERG: Mr. President, there have been spikes in the past. We've seen spikes in '05, '06, and '07. I'd say in the last eight to ten years, though, the trajectory has been awful. And there's a number of pieces to it.

One is that we consume, as Americans, most of the world's supply of hydrocodone and oxycodone. And as these good folks have attested to, once you get hooked on that, heroin is cheaper and more plentiful. And folks just make that transition.

We have to change the culture. I think we can. One of the things we do at DEA -- and I'm extraordinarily proud of our men and women -- we do law enforcement really well. But ever since I was a brand, new federal prosecutor many, many years ago, I never thought we would enforce or prosecute our way out of this. That's part of it. It's a really important part of it.

But we've also at the DEA now turned to education, prevention. We talked about those things all the time. I want folks to know, if I may, sir, we do a national takeback program twice a year. The next one is on April 29th, and people can drop off at 5,000 sites around the country -- courtesy of DEA and our local partners -- anything in their medicine cabinet that they don't want. Last year, we took in 1.6 million pounds of stuff. It includes everything.

THE PRESIDENT: That's great.

MR. ROSENBERG: But we're going to do that relentlessly twice a year, encourage people to turn in these drugs, and try and break this cycle.

THE PRESIDENT: So it's been really -- it spiked over the last eight to ten years. Would that have anything to do with the weakening of the borders? Because a lot of it comes from the southern border.

MR. ROSENBERG: **A lot of it comes through Mexico**. A lot of it is in produced in Mexico. I should say this: We've worked closely with our Mexican counterparts. There are a lot of brave men and women down there trying to help us do what we do. Secretary Kelly knows that as well as anyone.

A lot of it also comes from Asia. I was recently in China; I met with our counterparts there. A lot of the synthetics, fentanyl and carfentanyl, which is even worse than fentanyl, is produced in China. Our Chinese counterparts have added some of those drugs to their banned list, precluding it from -- or hopefully precluding it from leaving China and coming to North America.

So there's a lot of work to be done. You got a lot of smart people around this table. But I can tell you from the perspective of the DEA, sir, law enforcement is crucial. Education and prevention and treatment is equally crucial.

THE PRESIDENT: Thank you very much, Chuck.

All right, thank you very much, folks.

Q   Will you talk about this on the road? Are you going to take this on the road, President Trump?

THE PRESIDENT: Yes, we will. It's a big issue -- very, very big issue. Thank you, thank you.

END
12:05 P.M. EDT

*"So Carlos started smoking
marijuana
when he was 15 and a half years old,
and for him
-- and he'd be the first to tell you
this
-- it's absolutely for him
a gateway drug.
It led to heroin, cocaine,
crystal meth."*

Ms Garozzo
Participant

Note: Further information

President's Commission:
Office Of National Drug Control Policy

On March 29, 2017, President Donald J. Trump signed an Executive Order establishing the President's Commission on Combating Drug Addiction and the Opioid Crisis. The Commission will be chaired by Governor Chris Christie and will study ways to combat and treat the scourge of drug abuse, addiction, and the opioid crisis, which was responsible for more than 50,000 deaths in 2015 and has caused families and communities across America to endure significant pain and suffering. The Commission will work closely with the White House Office of American Innovation led by Jared Kushner.

President Trump said, "I made a promise to the American people to take action to keep drugs from pouring into our country and to help those who have been so badly affected by them. Governor Christie will be instrumental in researching how best to combat this serious epidemic and how to treat those it has affected. He will work with people on both sides of the aisle to find the best ways for the Federal Government to treat and protect the American people from this serious problem. This is an epidemic that knows no boundaries and shows no mercy, and we will show great compassion and resolve as we work together on this important issue."

The Office of National Drug Control Policy (ONDCP) provides administrative and financial support for the Commission and its activities.

Source: The White House website

Chapter 115

REMARKS BY PRESIDENT TRUMP AT
WOMEN'S EMPOWERMENT PANEL
EAST ROOM

29 March 2017

3:50 P.M. EDT

THE PRESIDENT: Thank you very much. What an amazing audience this is. (Laughter.)

So many young faces that represent the future of leadership in our country. So true. Melania and I are deeply honored to join you. And, Melania, thank you for being here. (Applause.)

So as you know, Melania is a very highly accomplished woman and really an inspiration to so many. And she is doing some great job. In fact, I shouldn't say this, but her poll numbers went through the roof last week. (Laughter.)

What was that all about? Through the roof. (Applause.)

She has to give us the secret, Mike, right? (Laughter.)

Anyway, I appreciate it very much.

My Cabinet is full of really incredible women leaders. Administrator Linda McMahon, who has been a friend of mine for a long time -- (applause) -- long time. She's done an incredible job in business, by the way. Administrator Seema Verma, Secretary Betsy DeVos, and, of course, my good friend from South Carolina who is a very tough competitor, I want to tell you -- Nikki Haley, Ambassador. She is doing fantastically well. (Applause.)

And we're also joined, of course, by Florida Attorney General, highly respected, Pam Bondi. So I want to thank you, Pam. Thank you. (Applause.)

Elaine Chao, our Secretary of Transportation, who's a real expert. She was Secretary of Labor, but she said, I really wanted to be Secretary of Transportation. That's a real expertise, and she's doing incredibly. She would have been here, but she's celebrating the 50th anniversary of the Department of Transportation right now as we speak. And we're going to work on infrastructure and we're going to put up one of the big and great infrastructure bills of all time. (Applause.)

We're going to get our infrastructure fixed in our country, and we're going to rebuild our country, and that's what we need. Lots of jobs, also. (Applause.)

And I want to thank Ford -- you saw their big announcement yesterday. And so many others are announcing tremendous numbers of jobs. (Applause.)

They're not leaving our country anymore, folks. They're not leaving; they're staying and they're building right here. So we really have these incredibly strong and dedicated leaders, and they're with me and they're with us. And I'm very happy about it. And I want to thank you as being representative, very much, of our group. Thank you all very much. Thank you. (Applause.)

And I'm so proud that the White House and our administration is filled with so many women of such incredible talent. This week, as we conclude Women's History Month, we honor a great woman of American history. Since the very beginning, women have driven -- and I mean each generation of Americans -- toward a **more free** and **more prosperous** future.

Among these patriots are women like the legendary Abigail Adams ... Right? (Applause.)

Who, during the founding, urged her husband to remember the rights of women. She was very much a pioneer in that way.

We've been blessed with courageous heroes like Harriet Tubman, who escaped slavery --(applause) -- and went on to deliver hundreds of others to freedom, first on the Underground Railroad, and then as a spy for the Union Army. She was very, very courageous, believe me. (Applause.)

And we've had leaders like Susan B. Anthony -- have you heard of Susan B. Anthony? (Laughter.)

I'm shocked that you've heard of her -- who **dreamed** of a much more equal and fair future, an America where women themselves, as she said, "helped to make laws and elect the lawmakers." And that's what's happening more and more. Tough competition out there, I want to tell you.

From the untamed frontiers of the Western Plains to the skyscrapers of Manhattan, American women in every generation have shown extraordinary grit, courage, and devotion. Our present generation stands on the shoulders of these titans -- and that's what they were and are -- titans. Only by enlisting the full potential of women in our society will we be truly able to -- you have not heard this expression before -- **Make America Great Again**. (Laughter and applause.)

It's a good expression. (Applause.)

Thank you. Thank you, everybody. Thank you. It's been a lot of fun. (Laughter.)

And we didn't get that one from Madison Avenue, right? (Laughter.)

My administration will work every day to ensure that our economy is a place where women can work, succeed, and thrive like never before. That includes fighting to make sure that all mothers and all families have access to af-fordable childcare. (Applause.)

We want every **daughter in America** to grow up in a coun-try where she can believe in herself, believe in her future, and follow her heart and **realize her dreams**. (Applause.)

And **we want a country that celebrates family, that celebrates community,** and **that creates a safe and lov-ing home for every child** -- every child. That's what we want. (Applause.)

Earlier this year, I met with a remarkable group of lead-ers. They were women entrepreneurs from all across the country. They started their businesses from absolutely nothing, and today have grown them into successful enter-prises that employ hundreds -- and in certain cases, even thousands -- of people. Just think of what our country could achieve if we unleashed the power of women entrepreneurs nationwide. Think of that. (Applause.)

So, as a man, I stand before you as President. But if I weren't President, I wouldn't be happy to hear that statement. That would be a very scary statement to me because there's no way we can compete with you. (Laughter.)

So I would not be happy. (Applause.)

Just wouldn't be happy.

One of the business owners I met, Lisa Phillips, used to be homeless. She now is the owner of an event-planning company, and she trains homeless youth in Baltimore for good-paying jobs. Lisa had a message for all of us. As she put it, "This is a country of chances...if you're willing to work hard, you'll get the chance." And she means it, and she's become very successful. She's terrific.

Lisa is right -- but we have to fight to ensure that more people have the chance to succeed. To do that, **we must believe in each other**, and **we must dare to dream** of a better, brighter, and more prosperous future for all of our citizens. We have no choice. That's what we have to do.

And to be honest, whether you're a woman or whether you're a man, you have that same **dream**: You want to be able to **dream**. You just have a big advantage over us. (Laughter.)

You know why? Right there. (Applause.)

There's a lot of truth to that, Mike, right?

That's what I want for each and every one, and each and every one of our daughters and our granddaughters.

And I know, together, we will get there. I want every young person in the audience today, and watching from home -- and they're all over the place; those cameras are all over -- (laughter) -- to know that the future truly belongs to you.

We are Americans, and we will not stop until we have achieved our **dreams**.

I want to thank you very much for being here. It's my great honor, I will tell you, to be here.

In fact, Melania said, this is something I just have to be at. She feels so strongly about it. She feels so strongly about it. (Applause.)

So thank you, God bless you, and God bless America.

Thank you very much. Thank you. (Applause.)

END
4:00 P.M. EDT

Chapter 116

**REMARKS BY VICE PRESIDENT AND AMBASSADOR FRIEDMAN
AT A SWEARING-IN CEREMONY
THE INDIAN TREATY ROOM**

29 March 2017

5:23 P.M. EDT

THE VICE PRESIDENT: Good afternoon. On behalf of the President of the United States of America today it is my great privilege and honor to administer the oath of office to the 20th United States Ambassador Israel, David Friedman. (Applause.)

We're joined today by his beautiful family, beginning with his wife, Tammy; their five children. (Applause.)

And five of their beautiful and highly animated grandchildren. (Laughter.)

It is really an honor to have with us David's counterpart, as well, the Israeli ambassador to the United States, Ambassador Ron Dermer. Mr. Ambassador. (Applause.)

Thank you all for being here at this historic occasion. It's the greatest privilege of my life to serve as Vice President to President Donald Trump. (Applause.)

The President of the United States of America is a life-long friend of Israel and the Jewish people, and under his leadership, if the world knows nothing else, the world will know this: America stands with Israel. (Applause.)

One of the clearest signs of the President's commitment to
the State of Israel and to its people is in his choice of David
Friedman as America's Ambassador to Israel.

David, you literally were born for this job. It is because of
families like yours that the Jewish people are such a beautiful thread in the fabric of this nation.

Your father, Morris, was a rabbi in New York, and as the
Book of Proverbs teaches, he and your mother trained you
up in the way you should go.

And so you have. They raised you with the same faith as
your forefathers, and instilled in you a love for America and
for Israel from your very earliest days.

And that love has been evident throughout your life. In
over 35 years as a successful lawyer, you have always made
it a priority to support Israel's peace, security, and prosperity. And you've worked tirelessly to deepen the friendship
between our two nations.

Over the years, you have literally traveled to Israel more
75 times. You have been a leader in humanitarian phi-
lanthropy to help the people of Israel in their time of
need. You've always been quick to rise to Israel's defense
from those who would condemn her -- because in your
heart you know that those that hate Israel hate Israel not
for what she does wrong, but for what she does right.

David, your record of compassion and care for Israel and
her people is an inspiration to the President and an inspiration to us all. (Applause.)

President Trump has now called on you to represent our

nation as the ambassador to our most cherished ally. And this is a critical time for our two nations and our peoples. The challenges we face are many, but our resolve to overcome them has never been stronger.

Under President Trump's leadership, the United States will always be a faithful friend to the Jewish State of Israel. And David, the President and I both know that you will help us make the immutable bond between our people and the people of Israel even stronger still.

So, on behalf of President Trump, it's now my great privilege to administer to you the oath of office.

(The Oath is administered.) (Applause.)

AMBASSADOR FRIEDMAN: Thank you, Mr. Vice President, for your kind words and your extraordinary leadership. You have been a beacon of moral clarity in a world that increasingly needs such a beacon more and more. Thank you so much.

My thanks to President Trump for his courageous leadership, his friendship, and his guidance. I am humbled by the trust he has placed in me, and I will do everything that I can to justify his faith and confidence in my abilities.

I'm very proud to say that my nomination represents the first time in American history that the U.S. ambassador to Israel was nominated by the President as early as the first day of his presidency.

I was nominated on January 20th on Inauguration Day.

I'm equally proud to say that this is the first time in American history that the U.S. Ambassador to Israel was the first ambassador approved by the Senate and given the oath of office. Those facts speak volumes about how highly the Trump-Pence administration prioritizes our unbreakable bond with the State of Israel.

I've also been deeply inspired by the leadership of Secretary Tillerson, and I look forward to working with him to promote peace and stability within the Middle East.

A few days ago I left a legal practice that was a great source of professional pride and accomplishment.

My deepest gratitude to the partners of what was once called Kasowitz, Benson, Torres & Friedman. (Laughter.)

And especially to Marc Kasowitz for his deep friendship and understanding.

I have a few close friends who are here whose friendship I deeply value -- none more so than Eric Hirschman (ph), who has guided my transition from the private sector to public life. Thank you, Eric.

My children and most of my grandchildren are here. They are everything to me -- seeing the pride in their eyes inspires me to take on this new task with great energy and enthusiasm.

My wife and I have four parents. Our fathers are no longer of this world, and my mother is not well enough to travel. And so I welcome today Bunny Sand, my mother-in-law, as the representative of our beloved parents. And I know that her pride is felt by those who are no longer with us. (Applause.)

Finally, my undying love and devotion to my beautiful wife, Tammy. As I said at the confirmation hearing without her, none of this would have even been thinkable, let alone possible.

Thank you all very much. (Applause.)

END
5:32 P.M. EDT

Chapter 117

31 March 2017

Transcript:

My fellow Americans,
It's an exciting time for our country. Our new Administration has so much change underway – change that is going to strengthen our Union and improve so many people's lives.

In the next few days, the Senate will be taking a very important step – one that will **protect the rule of law** and **democratic way of life** that is absolutely a **birthright** of all Americans.

And it involves one of my most important actions as President. That was nominating Judge Neil Gorsuch to fill the seat of the late, great Justice Antonin Scalia.

Judge Gorsuch is incredibly qualified. He has a sterling record. He was confirmed unanimously to the Court of Appeals.

But Judge Gorsuch's nomination is about more than his incredible qualifications.

It's about preserving our Republic.

In their great wisdom, **the Founders placed legislative power in its own separate branch of government**.

Elected representatives from all across the country come together. They host hearings, they listen to the concerns of the people, and then, they try to write laws that address those concerns and make life better for all Americans.

It's a process that is meant to take time and energy to ensure that every new law will better serve our wonderful citizens. That's how our democratic process works.

The duty of judges, therefore, is not to re-write the laws – but to uphold the laws, and to apply the Constitution as written.

That is the solemn duty of every Justice on the Supreme Court – and this is what Judge Gorsuch will do.

In recent years, we've seen more and more judges make decisions not based on the Constitution or the rule of law, but based on their preferences, their personal views, or even their political opinions.

Each time a judge substitutes their own opinions for an unbiased reading of the law, they damage our democracy. They put their own will above the will of the people. And they undermine the legislative process that has always been the heartbeat of our democracy.

The Senate will soon have the chance **to help preserve our democratic institutions for our children** – by voting to confirm Judge Gorsuch to the Supreme Court.

Judge Gorsuch is going to serve our people by devoting

himself to our beloved Constitution. The Senate saw this first-hand in hours of Judge Gorsuch's impressive testimony. In every step of the process, what has been clear to all is that Judge Gorsuch is a man who respects the law. He **defends the Constitution**. And in doing so, he will **protect our freedoms**.

With Judge Gorsuch on the Supreme Court, **America will be a more free, fair, and just Nation for all of our citizens.**

Thank you, and God bless you.

Chapter 118

31 March 2017

12:09 P.M. EDT

THE PRESIDENT: We have some really good news today
that's really fantastic -- these numbers. Today I'm delighted to welcome the *National Association of Manufacturers*
to the White House. It's a great group of people. I know
many of them well.

And I want to thank your President and CEO, Jay Timmons,
for being here with us today. Great job.

MR. TIMMONS: Thank you.

THE PRESIDENT: Great job, Jay.

My administration is working every day **to make it easier
for manufacturers to build, hire, and grow in
America**. We're removing job-killing regulations and lifting
the burdens on American industry like I would say have
never been lifted before. We've done a lot of work over
the last 60, 70 days, and I think you're seeing some real
production.

I think we can say this, Mike -- like never before.

Earlier this week, I signed an executive order to end the

war on coal. We had coal miners up at the office. It was an amazing scene. You had very tough, very strong, very powerful men that were crying actually; and they were crying with happiness. And produce more American energy and more American jobs, which is how I got elected in the first place.

We've created the task force in every agency to eliminate wasteful regulations. And today at 3:30 p.m., with the Department of Commerce, Wilbur Ross, who will be up, and we're signing two very powerful executive orders. That will be something very important -- very, very special. And that will be with Commerce.

One of the reasons we're here today is to announce the extraordinary results of a new survey from the *National Association of Manufacturers*. Your survey shows that 93 percent of manufacturers now have a positive outlook on the future of their business in this country -- 93 [percent]. And it was just a few months ago, 56 [percent]. That's a slight difference. (Laughter.)

That's a slight difference. (Applause.)

That's a 20-year, record high -- highest it's been in 20 years, and it's going higher. Believe me, you could come back next month, Jay. (Laughter.)

I don't know how much higher it can go. And so I'm very proud of that, and we're all very proud of that. And the manufacturers are really starting to invest big money, and a lot of things are happening. **It's a new surge in optimism, which is sweeping all across our land.**

These survey results are a further vote of confidence in our plan to bring back jobs, lower taxes, and provide a level playing field for our workers. The manufacturing companies represent -- and represented here today -- are just an extraordinary group of people. They're leaders. They're brilliant in so many ways. The field has not been a level field. Jobs have been leaving our country, going to China and Mexico and lots of other places.

And you'll be seeing what's happening over the next few weeks. It should be very interesting for you to watch. As you know the President of China is coming to Florida. We're having a meeting -- big meeting -- at **Mar-a-Lago**. We call it the **Southern White House**, which it actually is. It was originally built as the **Southern White House**, a lot of people don't know. But it's sort of strange how it got there.

But it's going to be something I think very important, very special. I look very much forward to meeting him and the delegation, and we'll see what happens. But I am very, very proud of what you've been able to do in a short period of time -- just this little, short period of time, the optimism is so high. And I see the billions of dollars that are being invested by your people and your representatives in plant and equipment and jobs.

And I appreciate that, Jay, very much. Congratulations. You may want to say a few words.

MR. TIMMONS: Well, I do. And I want to re-emphasize for the media here that this quarterly survey of our 14,000 members has been going on for 20 years. And to the point you made, this was the **highest level of optimism that our manufacturers have expressed in 20 years**.

THE PRESIDENT: That's fantastic.

MR. TIMMONS: And the other statistic that I think you'll find interesting is the right-track/wrong-track question that our manufacturers answered. Just the month before Inauguration Day, the right-track number was only 26 percent. Today it is over 60 percent. So that's a huge growth, as well. And that's because of the focus on taxes, regulations, infrastructure investment. We appreciate your commitment to investment in job creation and manufacturing. And we're going to deliver.

THE PRESIDENT: Thank you very much, Jay. That's really nice.

MR. TIMMONS: Thank you.

THE PRESIDENT: Thank you very much. Patricia, would you like to say something? Pretty outstanding what you've done.

MS. MILLER: Thank you. I appreciate being here today. I own a plastics manufacturing company in the north-west suburbs of Chicago. We're a three-year entrepreneurial in growth phase with a 40-year legacy. It's great to be part of manufacturing in the U.S.

THE PRESIDENT: That's a really great job. You've done a great job. Really great.

Ed?

MR. PARADOWSKI: Good morning, Mr. President. I'm Ed Paradowski, President of Apache Stainless Equipment. We're in Beaver Dam, Wisconsin. We manufacture capital equipment out of stainless steel and other high alloys. We employ 175, and most of them are skilled trades people -- some of the best skilled trades people in the state of Wisconsin. We are a 100 percent S Corp, and we would love to have you out in Beaver Dam, Wisconsin.

THE PRESIDENT: Well, I love the state of Wisconsin.

MR. PARADOWSKI: As do I.

THE PRESIDENT: There was a little bit of an upset. I don't think -- (laughter) -- I don't think -- I thought we were going to do very well there. But people would -- they could consider that a slight upset, right? But we don't consider it that. Thank you. Very good.

Yes.

MR. STAUB: Mr. President, good to see you again. We enjoyed having you at our facility back in September. I'm Steve Staub with Staub Manufacturing Solutions in Dayton, Ohio.

THE PRESIDENT: I remember.

MR. STAUB: And hopefully you got a chance to see the "First Day" video that we did with the *National Association of Manufacturers.*

THE PRESIDENT: I did. Thank you. I did. Great job. And you've done a great job.

MR. STAUB: Thank you.

THE PRESIDENT: Yes.

MR. EDDY: Good morning, Mr. President. My name is Joe Eddy. I'm the President and CEO of a company in northern West Virginia called Eagle Manufacturing. We're 125 years old this year; a family-owned business.

We manufacture products out of steel and plastic. We make over a thousand industrial safety and hazardous materials handling products. And I bring from West Virginia a major thank you for the work you've done for coal.

THE PRESIDENT: Great state. Great people. Really. We really opened it up. Nobody thought it would happen that fast. They thought maybe at the end of the four-year term, maybe I'd sign it -- no. Nobody thought we were going to go that fast. And the people appreciate it.

Julie.

MS. COPELAND: Good morning, Mr. President. I am Julie Copeland. I am CEO and co-owner with my sister of Arbill, a Philadelphia-based company that protects people in the workplace. We partner with manufacturers to make sure that no one gets hurt. We have products and services and technologies. And it's a privilege to be here today. And we look forward to continuing --

THE PRESIDENT: Have you met these two guys? (Laughter.)

Thank you.

MR. WETHERINGTON: Thank you, Mr. President. Chuck Wetherington. I'm the President of BTE Technologies. We're based in Baltimore, Maryland and Denver, Colorado. We're a manufacturer of high-tech medical devices used in physical therapy and industrial rehab, and we also have a professional services business that focuses on workplace injury reduction. We are the safety corner here.

THE PRESIDENT: That's very good.

MR. WETHERINGTON: And we work with large employers around the United States and Canada doing that kind of work.

THE PRESIDENT: And you're starting to do really well.

MR. WETHERINGTONG: We are. Yes. Thank you.

THE PRESIDENT: That's good. You know our great Vice President.

MR. GREENBLATT: My name is Drew Greenblatt. I'm the owner of Marlin Steel. We're a steel factory, make wire baskets for the automotive industry and the pharmaceutical industry. We make everything in Baltimore City, Maryland. We import nothing. We use steel from Illinois, we use steel from Indiana. We're thrilled with the policies that you are pursuing. We feel great optimism, and we're thankful for those approaches you're taking. Obviously -- we're 45 miles from where you're sitting right now -- we'd love for you to come visit us.

THE PRESIDENT: Okay, good. Well, we're not finished yet, Drew. A lot of other things are happening, including -- you haven't seen this in 25 years. That's great.

MR. RIORDAN: Mr. President, good morning. My name is Tom Riordan. I'm the CEO of Neenah Enterprises. We're a casting and forging operation in Wisconsin

-- 145 years old. First products were plowshares back in
the Civil War. Today most of our product are related to
infrastructure in terms of street casting, sewer covers,
and so on. The other half of our business is really tied
to on/offload vehicles with folks like Caterpillar and John
Deere. We're very much dependent upon your policies
moving forward.

THE PRESIDENT: Good job.

MR. MAGYARI: Nice to meet you. My name is Doug
Magyari. I'm the CEO of IMMI, Inc. We're a Troy, Michigan
company, suburb of Detroit. And we're very much a lead-
ing-edge research and development company on advanced
technologies, and in particular, we've built the most advanced augmented reality and virtual reality glasses in the
world. And it's an extremely important technology that's
going to affect not only everybody at this table, but really
every facet of our lives. And there's military applications
and all sorts of medical applications, as well as entertainment.

And it's such an important technology that we've made
a commitment to manufacture it here in the United
States. And we really appreciate what you're doing to help
facilitate in making that happen.

THE PRESIDENT: We have a lot of plants going up now in
Michigan that were never going to be there if I -- if I didn't
win this election, those plants would never even think
about going back. They were gone. We're you thinking
about getting out?

MR. MAGYARI: I wouldn't abandon the United States
under any circumstances. But Michigan, we definitely have

had a rough go, and the things that **you're doing and a lot of initiatives are really bringing Michigan back.**

THE PRESIDENT: Big progress in Michigan.

MS. BUCHWALD-WRIGHT: Hello. It's nice to see you again. I'm Karen Buchwald-Wright. And I'm the President and CEO of a family business that manufactures natural gas compressors. We're from Mt. Vernon, Ohio. And gas compressors are used in both the oil and gas industry, so I'm especially thankful that you have gotten the Keystone --

THE PRESIDENT: Very busy.

MS. BUCHWALD-WRIGHT: Yes, we are going to be.

THE PRESIDENT: You have to be. Big difference. That industry has changed over the last couple of months -- actually, over the last couple of weeks, that industry has changed.

MS. BUCHWALD-WRIGHT: Yes. It's great.

THE PRESIDENT: A lot of jobs.

MR. BARR: Good morning, Mr. President. I'm Matt Barr with Carolina Color. We manufacture colors for the plastics industry. We're a family-owned business -- we also celebrated our 50th anniversary this year, 120 employees. We're in Delaware, Ohio, and we're headquartered in Salisbury, North Carolina.

THE PRESIDENT: Nice to have you.

MS. JOHNSON. Good morning, Mr. President. I'm Kellie

Johnson, President of ACE Clearwater Enterprises. It's a 16-year-old family business -- third generation. We're a supplier to the aerospace and power generation industries. We build products out of metal. If it flies or is launched, our parts are on it. We employ 200 of the best men and women in our industry. And on behalf of all of them, thank you for what you're doing.

And we would love to have you come and visit next time you're in southern California. In fact, I'll never forget my husband and I approaching you in the lobby of your golf course in Palos Verdes when the flag controversy was going on. And we respected your position and we are so proud that that flag is flying today. Thank you. It worked out well.

THE PRESIDENT: It worked out. That was a very good decision.

Thank you very much. Thank you, everybody. Thank you.

Q   Any comment on Michael Flynn, Mr. President?

Q   Are you looking forward to your visit with the Chinese President?

THE PRESIDENT: Yes, I am.

END
10:23 A.M. EDT

Chapter 119

**REMARKS BY PRESIDENT TRUMP ET AL. AT
SIGNING OF TRADE EXECUTIVE ORDERS
OVAL OFFICE**

31 March 2017

3:44 P.M. EDT

THE PRESIDENT: During the campaign, I traveled the nation and visited the cities and towns devastated by unfair trade policies, probably one of the major reasons I'm here today -- trade. Nobody has ever made bad trade deals like our country has made.

I saw the shuttered factories and spent time with the laid-off factory workers. I heard their stories, and I **promised action** and I **promised them a solution**. And all over America, you're already seeing solutions start to take place. Take a look at what's going on Michigan, with Ford and General Motors and Fiat-Chrysler, and so many more.

The jobs and wealth have been stripped from our country. Year after year, decade after decade, trade deficit upon trade deficit -- reaching more than $700 billion last year alone, and lots of jobs. Thousands of factories have been stolen from our country.

But these **voiceless Americans** now have a voice in the White House. Under my administration, the theft of **American Prosperity** will end. **We're going to defend our industry and create a level playing field for the American worker** -- finally.

Today, I am signing two executive orders that send this message loud and clear and that set the stage for **a great revival of American manufacturing**. And you saw that today; you saw what happened, you saw the kind of numbers we have. The survey actually showed 93 percent of manufacturers are now optimistic about the future -- a record high -- and that's up from about 56 percent just a couple of months ago. We're going to build on that tremendous momentum. We're bringing manufacturing and jobs back to our country.

First, I'm signing an executive order to ensure that we fully collect all duties imposed on foreign importers that cheat. They're cheaters. From now on, those who break the rules will face the consequences -- and they'll be very severe consequences.

Second, I am ordering the first-ever comprehensive review of America's trade deficits and all violations of trade rules that harm the United States and the workers of the United States, just as I **promised** during my campaign.

This review will be led by Secretary Wilbur Ross, who is joining us here today. Wilbur is an outstanding success story, an unbelievable businessman, a great but very, very fair negotiator, and on Wall Street he's simply known as Wilbur, and everybody knows him. And now we have him on our side. So I thank you, Wilbur. You're going to do a fantastic job.

We're going to investigate all trade abuses, and, based on those findings, we will take necessary and lawful action to end those many abuses.

I am not beholden to any political or financial interest. I

don't care. I'm here to do a job. I'm doing a job for
the American worker. I really don't care. I'm not thinking about my business or anybody's business. Wilbur
isn't. Peter isn't. None of the folks that we have up here
are. We're doing a job. It's an opportunity like nobody has
ever given. And we're here to do a great job for the American worker and for our companies where the American
workers are employed.

I work for the American people. Whether you're a Democrat, a Republican, or belong to no party at all, you are an
American and I'm here to represent you and your family. We're going to get this thing straightened out. We're
going to get these bad trade deals straightened out -- right,
Peter?

It's time.

You've been looking at it for years -- right, Wilbur? This
combination over here, it can't be beaten.

That's why I defied the special interests and followed
through on my pledge to withdraw immediately from the
Trans-Pacific Partnership. And that's why I am taking these
very historic steps today. **The wellbeing of America and
the American worker is my North Star**. And these two
orders will point out our nation, and point to everybody,
point to the world.

Next week, as you know, in Florida, the **Southern White
House**, we're having the President of China and a large
group from China as representatives. And we're going
to get down to some very serious business. So we look
forward to it. I've spoken to him numerous times on the
phone. We look very much forward to it. But it's been

very bad what's been happening to our country in terms of our companies and in terms of our jobs.

So we're going to start turning it around. We're going to turn it around fast; it's not going to take a long time. It's going to go fast.

So I just want to end by saying that we have a team that's second to none. And when everybody is assembled and fully in gear after these two orders, I think it's going to be something very special. I'd like to ask Wilbur to say a few words, and then, Peter, you could say a few words. And we're all set. Our Vice President -- I think I'm speaking for both, but I'm not 100 percent sure. I will tell you one thing -- he has one hell of a good marriage going. (Laughter.)

Come on, Wilbur.

SECRETARY ROSS: Thank you, Mr. President. If anyone had any doubt about the President's resolve to fix the trade problems, these two executive orders should end that speculation now and for all time. This marks the beginning of a totally new chapter in the American trade relationship with our partners overseas.

Thank you very much.

THE PRESIDENT: Thank you. Peter.

MR. NAVARRO: I remember well during the campaign, the day the President made the speech outside of Pittsburgh and laid down a set of **promises** to the American people on trade. And today, this is the beginning of the fulfill-ment of those **promises** in a grand way, with Wilbur Ross at the helm, and the President being the grand strategist of this. And we're going to get it done for the American people, workers, and domestic manufacturers.

Thank you.

THE PRESIDENT: Mr. Vice President.

THE VICE PRESIDENT: This is a great day for the American worker and a great day for the American economy.

Once again President Trump is **keeping his word.**

As we look for ways to expand exports from this country, imports to this country, this President is determined that we're going to have free trade, but it's going to be fair trade, and arms-length negotiations with nations, holding them accountable to the **promises** that they make.

And the review the President is initiating today and the work of members of this team on the President's behalf will ensure that we put **American First** when it comes to trade; we put **American jobs and American workers first.**

THE PRESIDENT: Thank you, Mike. Thank you, everybody. You're going to see some very, very strong results very, very quickly. Thank you very much. Thank you.

END
3:53 P.M. EDT

Chapter 120

01 April 2017

1:36 P.M. EDT

THE VICE PRESIDENT: Hello, Ohio!

AUDIENCE MEMBERS: Hello!

THE VICE PRESIDENT: It is great to be back. Last fall, thanks to all of you -- thanks to your hard work, your support, and your prayers -- Ohio voted to make Donald Trump the 45th President of the United States of America. (Applause.)

I spoke to the President this morning, and he asked me just simply to say thank you -- and to tell you, to **promise** you, we will never forget the support of the great people of the Buckeye State. (Applause.)

And let me say thank you to Senator Rob Portman for that kind introduction and for joining us today. The people of Ohio appreciate your principled leadership, and Karen and I truly cherish our friendship with you and Jane. Would you give Senator Rob Portman another vigorous round of applause for his great leadership? (Applause.)

Speaking of my wife, Karen, she's really sorry she couldn't be with us today. She already had dinner plans. (Laughter.)

All kidding aside, my wife of 31 years is an amazing woman.

This week alone, she traveled across the country to support military families and also went out and stood by children recovering from serious illness. I'm just so proud of her, and my wife and I are so grateful for your support and your prayers for our little family. Thank you all. (Applause.)

Let me also thank to my friend of so many years Congressman Pat Tiberi. He's a member of the ways and means committee. He is Chairman of the Health Sub-Committee. He's Chairman of the Joint Economic Committee. He's one of the most respected voices on tax reform in the United States Congress, Pat Tiberi, the hometown Congressman. Thank you so much, Pat. (Applause.)

And thank you to Mayor Brad McCloud for being here today and for your great leadership of this great community. It's a privilege to have all of you with us today, and the President and I are grateful for your support.

And finally, thank you to Gary James and the whole Dynalab team here for hosting us here today. Dynalab is a true American success story. Since 1981, you all have been doing here what our country does best -- **taking big ideas and bringing them to life** on the factory floor.

It's amazing to see what you've accomplished. Over 300 employees in a state-of-the-art facility, a great reputation -- congratulations to the whole Dynalab team. **You are American Dream**, and we congratulate you on your success. (Applause.)

Just so great to be with all the job creators that we met with for conversation earlier today, many of whom are still with us. People like the Flag Lady are here -- Mary Leavitt, from The Flag Lady Store; and Raine Neenan, from Tommy's Pizza.

I can personally testify that that is a great business. And all these great business leaders, thank you for coming out today and sharing your perspective on the challenges and opportunities we have to turn this economy loose.

So let me say from my heart, it is the greatest privilege of my life to be Vice President to President Donald Trump. (Applause.)

It's humbling for me to say it. The President of the United States is my friend. He loves his family. He loves this country with boundless energy, optimism, courage, and determination. And **President Trump has a three-part agenda. I hear about it every day: Jobs, Jobs, and Jobs!** And it's happening right here in Ohio already. (Applause.)

It's just amazing. The first two jobs reports under President Donald Trump are already out showing that nearly 500,000 jobs have been created this year -- including more than 135,000 new jobs in construction and manufacturing. (Applause.)

Thanks to our new President, it's been a great week for American jobs. On Monday, Ford Motor Company announced it would invest $1.2 billion right here in America to **protect** and create nearly 4,000 jobs. On Tuesday, the President signed a historic executive order to put America on the path to energy independence -- and give American job creators the kind of low-cost power that they need to grow. And yesterday, the President took decisive action to level the playing field on international trade. Under President Donald Trump, trade will mean jobs, but it's going to mean **American jobs and put American workers first**. (Applause.)

And American businesses are already getting the message. The President and I just yesterday were joined by the leadership of the *National Association of Manufacturers*, and they announced that manufacturing companies haven't been this optimistic in more 20 years. (Applause.)

Get this -- 93 percent of manufacturers are excited about what they have in store in President Trump's leadership. And so are the American people. People in this country haven't been this confident about our economy since the year 2000.

And they should be excited because President Trump knows what all of you know -- that **when manufacturing is strong, America is strong**. And he's fighting every day to bring American manufacturing back.

President Trump meant it when he said on Tuesday "we believe in those really magnificent words: **Made in the USA**." (Applause.)

Manufacturers are the engine of our economy, and thanks to President Trump, that engine is about to roar. It's not just this past week, but literally since day one, President Trump has been fighting to **get our economy moving again**. He's been signing bill after bill to roll back excessive regulations enacted in the closing days of the Obama administration.

He ordered every agency in Washington, D.C. to find two regulations to get rid of before issuing any new red tape on **American business and American job creators**. (Applause.)

And just last week, President Trump authorized the Keystone pipeline, creating tens of thousands of American jobs and strengthening America's energy future.

He's taken decisive action to **protect American jobs and American worke**rs, as well, by enforcing the laws of this country for the citizens of this country, and illegal immigration is already down by 60 percent since President Trump was elected. (Applause.)

And we're just getting started. Since the day the President was elected, he's worked tirelessly **to keep his promise** to repeal and replace Obamacare. (Applause.)

The President and I know what all of you know -- that every day Obamacare survives is another day that the American people struggle. We all know the truth about this failed law. Higher prices, lost plans, fewer choices -- Obamacare is a burden on the people of Ohio and it's a burden on Ohio's job creators.

That's why the President has worked so hard **to keep his promise** to the American people to repeal and replace Obamacare with something that actually works.

I've been incredibly inspired by the President's hands-on leadership on this issue. And the President and I are so grateful -- we're so grateful to Speaker Paul Ryan and all the House Republicans, like Congressman Pat Tiberi, who stood with us over the past month to begin the end of

Obamacare. Thank you, Congressman. (Applause.)

But as we saw about a week ago, Congress wasn't quite ready. With 100 percent of House Democrats -- every single one -- and a handful of Republicans, Congress basically said that they weren't ready yet to begin the end of Obamacare. It really is a shame. But as Congressman Tiberi just said to me a few minutes ago, it ain't over yet. (Applause.)

Obamacare is going to continue to explode, putting a great weight on millions of Americans. But the President and I have faith. We have faith that Congress is going to step and do the right thing. Even as we speak, I'm told the members of Congress are forging ahead -- working to craft legislation that will usher in the end of Obamacare. So be assured of this, folks here in the Buckeye State, when Congress finally decides to repeal and replace Obamacare, President Trump and I will be ready to work with them hand in glove. (Applause.)

You can take it to the bank: President Trump is never going to stop fighting **to keep the promises** he made to the American people -- and we will **Make America Great Again**. We will repeal and replace Obamacare and give the American people the world-class health-care they deserve. And once Obamacare is gone, we're going to cut taxes across the board for working families, small businesses, manufacturers, and family farms. (Applause.)

We're going to work with these great leaders in the Congress to pass the biggest tax cut since the days of Ronald Reagan. We'll make the tax code flatter and simpler and fairer for everybody.

There's an old joke about how the tax code is 10 times the size of the Bible, with none of the good news. (Laughter and applause.)

Well, here's some real good news -- President Trump's plan is going to put more money in your pocket and **Make American Business Competitive Again.**

We're going to cut the corporate tax rate in America, one of the highest in the world, so that companies in American jobs can invest and create opportunities for America's workers right here in Ohio. (Applause.)

And President Trump is going to keep slashing through the red tape that's strangling Ohio's small businesses and manufacturers. The truth is that bureaucrats in Washington, D.C. are too often standing in the way of job creators, making it harder for them to grow and thrive.

You know, complying with federal mandates actually costs businesses like this one here over $13,000 dollars a year for every single employee. All told, red tape from Washington, D.C. actually costs the economy over $2 trillion dollars a year. That's enough money to create more than 24 million new good-paying manufacturing jobs. But it's wasted on pushing papers and jumping through government hoops.

Folks, that's just not right, and that's why President Donald Trump is getting government out of the way. He's reining in unelected bureaucrats so they can no longer cripple Ohio's economy from the comfort of their taxpayer-funded metal desks in Washington, D.C., and we're going to keep that fight going. (Applause.)

And as President Trump announced just this week, a new era of American energy has begun -- the war on coal is over. (Applause.)

You know, it's really heartbreaking to think that nearly a quarter of Ohio's coal miners have lost their jobs in the past few years, and that nearly half the state's mines have shut down. Countless Ohio families have been forced to watch good-paying jobs disappear from their communities. But now they have hope.

From the first day of this administration, President Trump has been fighting for Ohio and fighting for American energy. The executive order President Trump signed on Tuesday will end Washington's assault on affordable energy and give hardworking Americans and manufacturers the relief they need.

And President Trump is going to put coal miners back to work. As he likes to say, we all like to say: President Trump digs coal. (Laughter.)

We're going to unlock our country's amazing national resources -- not just coal, but shale oil, natural gas, clean coal, you name it -- because lower energy costs mean more jobs, more growth, and more opportunity for American families and American businesses.

And folks, under President Donald Trump, we're also going to **rebuild America**. If you haven't noted it, the American people elected a builder to be President of the United States.

And with his **Hire American, Buy American strategy**, we're going to work with the Congress, and we're going to give

our nation the best roads, the best bridges, the best highways and airports that America has ever had. (Applause.)

Thanks to President Trump, **we're going to have jobs and
growth and prosperity like never before**. But **Making
America Great Again** isn't just about our economy. It also
means standing with those who are **protecting** our communities, our nation, and **protecting** our way of life.

I can tell you -- I'm with him every day -- President Trump
has no higher priority than the **safety and security** of the
American people. That's why the President every single
day is standing with the men and women in law enforcement here in Ohio and all across this country. (Applause.)

We've got a fair amount of men and women in uniform
who are with us today. Would you all mind getting on your
feet and showing these men and women in law enforcement just how much we appreciate the job they do protecting our families each and every day? (Applause.)

President Trump is strengthening our borders. **He's building a wall**, enforcing our laws, and as he said in his joint
address to Congress, we're taking measures to remove
all the "gang members, drug dealers, and criminals who
threaten our communities and prey on our citizens" off the
streets of Ohio and off the streets of America. (Applause.)

We're working with law enforcement every day -- Immigra-
tions and Customs Enforcement to accomplish that.

Beyond our borders, I have to tell you, I couldn't be more
grateful, couldn't be more proud, as the father of a United States Marine, that we now have a President who will
rebuild our military, restore the arsenal of democracy,

and give our Soldiers, Sailors, Airmen, Marines, and Coast Guard the resources and the training they need to accomplish their mission and come home safe. (Applause.)

And here in the homeland, in the wake of last November's terrorist-inspired attack on the grounds of Ohio State, I just want to assure all of you here in this community under President Donald Trump's leadership, America is standing strong and taking the fight to the terrorists on our terms, on their soil -- and ISIS is on the run. (Applause.)

And I'll make you a **promise**. President Donald Trump will not rest and will not relent until we hunt down and destroy ISIS at its source so it can no longer project violence around the world or inspire violence here at home. (Applause.)

So it's jobs. It's health care. It's energy, and it's the national security.

And this President is also keeping his **promise** to appoint a strict constructionist to the Supreme Court in the tradition of the late and great Justice Antonin Scalia. (Applause.)

By nominating Judge Neil Gorsuch, President Trump has kept his word to appoint to the Supreme Court a justice who will keep faith with our Constitution and uphold the God-given liberties enshrined there.

Next week the United States Senate will take his confirmation up. Let me just say emphatically, as America saw in those hearings just a little more than a week ago, Judge Neil Gorsuch is one of the most respected, qualified, and mainstream nominees to the Supreme Court in American history. (Applause.)

It's true.

But remarkably, yesterday your very own senator, Sherrod Brown, announced that he and the obstructionist Democrats in the Senate plan to filibuster Judge Gorsuch's nomination as an associate justice -- something that's never been successfully done in American history.

But let me say the President and I are confident, with the strong support of Senator Rob Portman, we know: For the sake of our Supreme Court, for the sake of our country, for the sake of our Constitution, we will overcome the obstructionists. And the United States Senate will confirm Judge Neil Gorsuch -- one way or the other. (Applause.)

My friends, the record is clear: President Donald Trump is **a man of his word**, and **he's a man of action**.

Before I wrap up, there's one other issue I'd like to address that I know also hits close to home here in Ohio, just as it did back in my home state of Indiana. I want you all to know, as America saw this week from the Cabinet Room in Washington, D.C., President Trump is working every day to end the opioid crisis that's ruining lives and tearing apart families and communities across Ohio and across America. Ohio knows all about the tragic consequences of this crisis. Over 2,500 Ohioans died from an opioid overdose in 2015, one of the hardest hit states in the nation. It grieves my heart to think of it. Tens of thousands more still suffer in the grip of addiction.

Let me say your own senator, Rob Portman, and Congressman Tiberi have been true leaders on this issue, and we're grateful for their leadership -- helping countless people through their work on Capitol Hill. And the President and I are grateful for their strong and compassionate leadership, as I know all of you are. (Applause.)

On Wednesday of this week in the Cabinet Room in the White House, President Trump and I met with a group of people who've seen opioid addiction up close and personal. We heard the inspiring stories of Vanessa and AJ, two young people who courageously overcame drug addiction, found hope and healing through counseling and medication to break the grip of addiction on their lives.

And tragically, we also heard from a mom, Pam Garozzo, who lost her son Carlos, the light of her life, a young man of incredible promise and creativity, to the scourge of drug addiction. President Trump told Pam -- with real emotion, he said, Pam, "your son will not have died in vain." And that very day, the President announced the creation of the President's Commission on Combating Drug Addiction and the Opioid Abuse.

Under President Trump's leadership, we're bringing together public servants, medical experts, community leaders. And we will find innovative solutions to stop the flow of drugs into our communities and help families who need it most.

As the President said in his joint address to the Congress, in his own words, we will "stop the drugs from pouring into our country and poisoning our youth, and we will expand treatment for those who have become so badly addicted." Those two **promises** will be kept by this President and this administration. (Applause.)

Under President Donald Trump's leadership, I just know our communities, our country are on the road to healing.

My friends, we've really come to **a pivotal moment in our nation's history**. I believe with all my heart in this moment, we need every **freedom-loving American** -- we need all of you -- to stand up and to speak out.

We need you to tell the world that you believe we can do better, that you know it; that **President Trump and his vision can renew and restore** this country and put us on a path to a brighter future.

For my part, I know we're going to get it done because I have faith. As your Ohio State motto says, "With God, all things are possible." (Applause.)

One of my favorite verses in the Old Book, comes out of the Book of Jeremiah. It's actually -- it was a gift from my wife the first year I was elected to Congress. It was the same year as your congressman, back in the year 2000. It hung over the mantle of our little home in Indiana when I served in Washington, D.C. It hung over the mantle in the Governor's Residence. And now these words hang over the mantle in the residence of the Vice President of the United States.

It simply says: "For I know the plans I have for you, plans to prosper you, and not to harm you, plans to give you a hope, and a future."

Those words a millennia ago have been words that Americans throughout our history have clung to, and I believe they're as true today as they were throughout our history.

In November, the people of Ohio voted to give America a President with the strength, the courage, and the **vision** to **Make America Safe Again**. You voted to give us a new leader who will **Make America Prosperous Again**.

And I believe with all my heart, that with your continued support, and with God's help, together we will **Make America Great Again**. (Applause.)

Thank you very much. Thank you for being here today. God bless you and God bless the United States of America. (Applause.)

END
2:00 P.M. EDT

Chapter 121

REMARKS BY PRESIDENT TRUMP AND PRESIDENT AL-SISI OF EGYPT BEFORE BILATERAL MEETING
OVAL OFFICE

03 April 2017

12:04 P.M. EDT

PRESIDENT TRUMP: It's great to be with the President of Egypt. And I will tell you, President Al-Sisi has been somebody that's been very close to me from the first time I met him. I met during the campaign, and at that point there were two of us, and we both met. And hopefully you like me a lot more. But it was very long. It was supposed to be just a quick brief meeting, and we were with each other for a long period of time. We agreed on so many things.

I just want to let everybody know, in case there was any doubt, that we are very much behind President Al-Sisi. He's done a fantastic job in a very difficult situation. We are very much behind Egypt and the people of Egypt.

And the United States has, believe me, backing, and we have strong backing. We are very much -- and as you and I will be soon talking -- we're building up our military to a level that will be the highest -- probably the highest that we've ever had -- plane orders, ship orders, aircraft carrier orders.

We are rejuvenating our military to the highest level I think in these times, probably more than ever before, or certain-

ly almost more than ever before. That's what we need.
And I just want to say to you, Mr. President, that you have
a great friend and ally in the United States and in me.

PRESIDENT AL-SISI: (As interpreted.) Your Excellency, allow
me to extend my thanks and appreciation for your kind
invitation for me to visit the United States. Actually, this
is MY FIRST STATE visit to the United States since my inauguration in office. AND, AS A MATTER OF FACT, THIS IS THE FIRST
VISIT IN EIGHT YEARS FROM AN EGYPTIAN PRESIDENT TO THE UNITED
STATES.

Your Excellency, since we met last September, I've had
a deep appreciation and admiration of your unique personality, especially as you are standing very strong in the
counter-terrorism field to counter this evil ideology that
is claiming innocent lives, that is bringing devastation to
communities and nations, and that is terrorizing innocent
people.

Your Excellency, very strongly and very openly, you will
find Egypt and myself always beside you in this, in bringing
about an effective strategy in the counter-terrorism.

The second point, Your Excellency, is that you'll find me
supporting you very strongly and very earnestly in finding
solution to the problem of the century. And I'm quite confident that you will be able to bring a solution to this issue.

PRESIDENT TRUMP: We will -- that I tell you. We will.

PRESIDENT AL-SISI: Yes. Thank you very much.

PRESIDENT TRUMP: We will do that together. We will fight
terrorism and other things, and we're going to be friends

for a long, long period of time. We have a great bond with
the people of Egypt, and I look forward to working with the
President. And we have some interesting conversations
going to start effective immediately, and then we're going
into the Cabinet Room and we're going to meet with your
representatives.

So again, thank you very much for coming. And I look forward to a very long and strong relationship.

END
12:09 P.M. EDT

[Photo: screengrab.]

Chapter 122

**REMARKS BY PRESIDENT TRUMP AND VICE PRESIDENT PENCE
AT CEO TOWN HALL ON UNLEASHING AMERICAN BUSINESS
SOUTH COURT AUDITORIUM**

04 April 2017

10:41 A.M. EDT

THE VICE PRESIDENT: It's a great privilege to be able to welcome you to the White House. Thank you so much. I want to thank everyone involved in the Partnership for New York City -- Michael Corbat, Stephen Schwarzman.

It's an honor to have the leaders that are gathered in the room here with us today. I know the President is on his way over, and it's my great privilege this morning to share a few thoughts, in the midst of this important conversation on the topics that you're covering before I introduce my friend and the 45th President of the United States.

But let me say first and foremost, though, the companies represented in the Partnership for New York City are all American success stories. You have our admiration. You have our appreciation. Your businesses account for more than 7 million jobs and you add over $1 trillion to our economy each and every year.

What's more important is the people behind the numbers, and the topics that you've covered today are all about creating more jobs and more opportunities for Americans who are anxious to climb the ladder of success in the or-ganizations that you represent and in companies all across this country.

So, first and foremost, on behalf of the President and the whole team that you've heard from this morning, and distinguished members of our Cabinet, thank you. Thank you for what you do. Thank you for your leadership.

I think as you will hear this morning in the dialogue that is about to commence THAT AMERICA HAS ELECTED A BUSINESSMAN AS PRESIDENT OF THE UNITED STATES, and he is committed to being the best friend business has ever had in the White House. (Applause.)

We've already seen the results. Since literally when the election was called at -- I think it was about 4 a.m. in the morning, wasn't it, **Ivanka**, that we were all together -- literally we've seen renewed energy and dynamism in the American economy.

The first two jobs reports, as I'm sure you are aware, thanks in no small part to the leadership represented in businesses here in the room today, the first two jobs report show that under President Trump, nearly 500,000 new jobs have been created in the first two months of this year.

Businesses and consumers haven't been this **optimistic** in decades. In fact, we just learned from the *National Association of Manufacturers* that in their historic quarterly report, **93 percent of manufacturers are optimistic about the future**. That represented almost a 40-point increase in optimism since the last report. (Applause.)

We think that is **evidence of a vote of confidence** in our new President and in **his vision** to get this economy moving **Again** by putting common-sense principles into practice. From the very outset of this administration, the President has been **energetically working to roll back excessive regulation and red tape.**

Leaders in Congress -- and I see Leader McCarthy, who is with us today -- have been producing under what's known as the **Congressional Review Act, legislation to roll back onerous regulations that emerged in the waning days of the Obama administration.** And in the coming days, President Trump will be signing even more bills into law, rolling back that avalanche of red tape.

The President has also taken decisive executive action on **expanding American energy** -- the Keystone Pipeline and the Dakota Pipeline.

We continue to work earnestly with Congress for a new future on healthcare reform. The President and I remain confident that working with the Congress we will repeal and replace Obamacare with healthcare reform that will work for the American people and work for the American economy.

And of course, in the offing before we reached the end of the year, the President is determined to roll his sleeves up, work with the Congress and pass the largest tax reform in a generation.

Business -- as I said in those numbers about optimism -- business has clearly gotten the message.

But today's conversation is all about learning from job creators represented in this room how we can continue to build on the momentum in this economy, particularly focusing on infrastructure, government modernization and workforce.

I can tell you that the subject that I came in at the end of and I know was much a topic today with **Ivanka** and with Wilbur, having to do with improving the quality of our workforce, expanding opportunities for what is known as **career and technical education** -- what we back in Indiana call **vocational education** -- is A REAL PASSION for our new President. And we look forward to partnering with you in ways that we can continue to encourage investment and create opportunities for expanded career and vocational education.

So today is all about really giving you an opportunity to share your thoughts. It's part of an ongoing conversation this administration has commenced since the very first day the President took office -- LISTENING to business leaders, LISTENING to everyday Americans about ways that we can bring about his agenda to **Make America Great Again** and to have our economy growing and expanding in a way that is consistent with the most powerful economy in the history of the world.

I think the President is in the side chamber, so let me say to all of you, the opportunity you have today is to hear from a man who I have a chance to sit with every day.

What you're going to see first-hand is what I see each and every day, and that is not only just **a businessman made President**, but you're going to see **a leader,** informed, focused, decisive, and absolutely committed to **Make America Great Again.**

It is my high honor and distinct privilege to introduce to all of you my friend, the 45th President of the United States of America, President Donald Trump. (Applause.)

[Photo: screengrab.]

THE PRESIDENT: Thank you, Mike. Good morning. Hello, **Ivanka**.

MR. CORDISH: I know you know a few of the people in this room.

[Photo: screengrab.]

THE PRESIDENT: I do. I do. **All the killers from New York** -- I'm looking at all those competitive -- those great, great talents, great builders.

MR. CORDISH: I have to give you a heads-up that **Ivanka** chaired one of the sessions before this -- tough act to follow.

THE PRESIDENT: Oh, she's tough. Very tough.

MR. CORDISH: Vice President Pence listed some of the amazing accomplishments that have taken place since your election and your 75 days in office.

The stock market has had almost unprecedented sustained growth, unprecedented confidence from our manufacturing sector and other business sectors, leading to massive private sector investment in job growth.

You have gotten rid of regulations that were unnecessary and were job-stifling. You have strengthened our borders and strengthened our military. You've nominated a great -- superb Supreme Court justice, amongst many other things. How does all that feel?

THE PRESIDENT: And we're getting unbelievable credit for what we've done, other than **the mainstream media, which just gives us no credit whatsoever**. But we are getting tremendous credit. And if you look at the real estate industry, the mining industry, the farming industry -- if you look at any of the major industries you see what's going.

In fact, even today I was very happy as I read this morning early that our trade deficit with others has gone down very considerably in the last short period of time. It's having a big impact.

And, as you know, I'm meeting with the President of China on Thursday and Friday in **Palm Beach, Florida**, and I think we're going to have a very interesting talk. We're having -- have a lot of respect for him. I've spoken to him numerous times. But we have to do better, because our deficit with China, as you know, $504 billion. That's a year. That's enough for a lifetime. Even Steve would say that. But **that's a year**.

So we're going to have a great meeting, I'm sure we're going to have a fantastic meeting. And we're going to talk about a lot of things, including, of course, North Korea, a problem. And that's really a humanity problem. So we're going to be talking about that also.

MR. CORDISH: You have made it a driving force in this administration to bring in the best minds we can from the private sector, to listen intently to them and to take decisive action. How important is that, and how important is it to reform government to bridge the gap between the private and public sectors?

THE PRESIDENT: Well, I did, I brought you, I brought Gary Cohn, I brought a lot of very great people -- my friend, Steve, is helping us out. We have a superstar committee of 22 people. And every time somebody calls me I say, Steve, put them on -- no, we want to keep it at this level. The heads of the biggest companies, they all want to be on our committee, right, Stephen? But Steve likes to keep it very small. But they will go off and they'll disappear and we'll put others on. But we've had some great meetings and we've all learned a lot.

One thing that did come up, and it came up yesterday, was Gary Cohn -- where's Gary? Is he here? Could you bring that chart, please? Do you mind? Let me see that chart. So this was just something -- this is sort of incredible. That's so beautiful. Yeah, no, you're not quite -- this is to build a highway in the United States -- now, this was just done yesterday. I saw it for the first time. I said, I'm speaking to some of my friends who are builders, really great builders, and they've gone through the process -- we've all gone through it in New York -- we call it the zoning process in New York.

But you start up here and this is anywhere from a 10 to 20-year process. You have -- is it 17 agencies. You have hundreds and hundreds of permits. Many of them are statutory, where you can't even apply for the second permit until six months go by. So this is to build a highway. This is a simple highway. And these are the agencies -- so it's 17 agencies. How many different steps is it?

[Photo: screengrab.]

Q: Sixteen different approvals.

THE PRESIDENT: Sixteen.

Q: Twenty-nine different statutes. Five different executive orders that all apply to this process. This is indicative, so this is not a specific project, but this is the type of process that a government -- this is a state government -- would have to go through to permit a highway federally. This is just federal, not state regulations.

THE PRESIDENT: **So it can take anywhere from 10** -- if you're really good, **10 years to 20 years**. And then they vote, and you lose. They don't want it. (Laughter.)

And it costs sometimes hundreds of millions of dollars just to go through the process.

Thank you very much. That was a great job you did. Be careful, don't fall. I don't want to have you fall. You'll be a big story in the paper if you go down. (Laughter.)

So I just saw that yesterday. Gary Cohn walked in and he showed it to me, and -- for no reason. I said, you have to do me a favor. But a lot of you, you're such pros, some of the best pros in the world sitting in this room, you under-stand it. It's a process.

Now, I've always liked it because it gave people that could go through that process an advantage, like Jerry, but it gave us an advantage if you could get through the pro-cess. But getting a building approved in New York is a hor-rible, horrible thing. And that's nothing compared to when you get into the highways and the dams -- they don't even talk about dams anymore. Hydropower is a great, great, form of power -- we don't even talk about it, because to get the environmental permits are virtually impossible. It's one of the best things you can do -- hydro. But we don't talk about it anymore.

So we've come to a halt. We have a tremendous person that we put in charge of EPA, Scott Pruitt, who is an environmental person. He wants clean air, he wants clean water, but he doesn't thing it takes you 26 years to get a permit to build a building and to have jobs, at which time those companies are usually gone, out of business, et cetera.

So we're really speeding up the process. **We're going to try and take that process from a minimum of 10 years down to one year.** I said can't we make it four months? Can't we do it in four months? And there is a certain logic to that, but we'll be satisfied with the year -- but it won't be any more than a year.

So we have to build roads. We have to build highways. We're talking about a very major infrastructure bill of a trillion dollars -- perhaps even more. And when we have to do -- our jobs -- I mean, if we say, we're giving to New York City hundreds of millions of dollars to build a road someplace, it doesn't help if they can't start because it's going to take seven and a half years to get the permits. Even to redo a road takes years to get the permits. You know, you have a road that's there and you want to redo it, and you have to get new permits for the kind of asphalt you're using, the kind of concrete you may want to use.

And if we're going to give all of this money -- you know, **there was very large infrastructure bill that was approved during the Obama administration -- a trillion dollars --** nobody ever saw anything being built. I mean, to this day,

     Chapter 122

I haven't heard of anything that's been built. They used most of that money -- it went, and they used it on social programs. And we want this to be on infrastructure.

I'm working with Steve Roth and with Richard LeFrak -- two friends of mine that are very good builders. They're great builders. And they know to get things done. They know how to cut red tape. We're going to give them the advantage of having what we have. I see Elaine is here, so important, who is doing an incredible job, by the way -- Secretary of Transportation. And Elaine will be working. But we're going to set up a committee headed by Steve and Richard, and we're going to cut a lot of red tape.

But we don't want to send a billion dollars to New York and find out, five years later, the money was never spent, because we're going to be very strong that it has to be spent on shovels, not on other programs. And in the last case, a lot of it was spent on other programs. But we're going to say, if you don't spend the money -- if you don't start -- if you have a job that you can't start within 90 days, we're not going to give you the money for it. Because it doesn't help -- doesn't help us. And we're going to be very strong on that. **They have to be able to start within 90 days.**

MR. CORDISH: Mr. President, we have some of the great business leaders in the country here. If okay with you, they have a few questions, if that's --

THE PRESIDENT: Sure.

MR. CORDISH: Great.

THE PRESIDENT: Hello, Jerry. (Laughter.)

MR. SPEYER: Hi, Mr. President. (Laughter.)

THE PRESIDENT: He didn't have to say his name. He was ready to say his name -- we know. Jerry Speyer, everybody.

MR. SPEYER: Mr. President, you're doing a great job, and we're all really grateful to you for the sacrifices you're making. Hope you heard that.

THE PRESIDENT: That sounds much better.

MR. SPEYER: I think from New York's point of view we send a lot of money into the economy. As a number of people have said, it's over a trillion dollars. We're worried we're going to have a problem with Congress.

THE PRESIDENT: With the deductions, right?

MR. SPEYER: Well, that, too. That, too. But we're worried about various programs that help the city. The city is doing fine right now -- even the Yankees are doing fine. But what we're really concerned about is the future. Do you have any advice for us?

THE PRESIDENT: Look, I love New York. And in some ways we're all lucky that I'm from New York, because New York has unique problems. So does Los Angeles, so does Chicago.

THERE ARE PLACES THAT HAVE UNIQUE PROBLEMS.

One of the problems that you have is debt and deductibility. That's a big one, because a lot of the states that don't have debt or have very little debt --like in the case of Mike Pence, where he did such a good job in Indiana, and it's a

AAA-rated bond, one of the strongest in the country, and deductibility is not that big of a deal because they don't have that much to deduct.

And over here, in New York, when you look at what's going on with us, we don't know in terms of the municipality and in terms of the state, we don't know if it can even make it if you don't have that. Are people going to buy? So it's a very big problem.

And the problem I have is that there are many places throughout the country that are in the exact opposite position. And they consider that a gift to the state and a gift to the people. And we know New York does things that a lot of people don't read about.

You look at what -- the money they contribute to our economy, to our country, and people don't know about that. They don't maybe want to know about that. So you do have -- I call it *a tale of two cities*. You have different interests.

But I am watching over everybody, Jerry. You're in good hands, okay? **You're in good hands, believe me**. You can tell the people of New York.

Even though I didn't win New York State. I should have won New York State, but I didn't. (Laughter and applause.)

MS. ENGELBERT: Mr. President, Cathy Engelbert with Deloitte. I want to return to a conversation we just had with **Ivanka**, Dina and Wilbur on jobs, the workforce of the future. And so as we think about that and we think about our skill-sets, **in New York City alone our high school -- public high school graduation rate is at 70 percent, but**

the readiness of our students for college and careers is only 37 -- it's assessed at 37 percent.

So as we look at the pace of change, we look at the digital transformation we all see in business and the marketplace, and we look at the skills that -- **this disconnect between what employers need and what our students coming into our workforces are prepared to deliver.** It would be great to get your thoughts on the priorities of the administration around education, around, again, what I like to call not the future of work but the work of the future. Because the future of work sounds a little ominous, but the work of the future actually sounds pretty visionary. So if you could give us those priorities --

THE PRESIDENT: Okay, so before you sit, so you're giving me numbers from New York. You're a proud New Yorker, but you're giving me numbers -- why is it doing so badly? Tell me. Why are the numbers so HORRIFIC in terms of education? And what happens when somebody goes through school and then they can't read after -- they graduate from high school and they can barely read. So what's the answer?

MS. ENGELBERT: Yes. So, first, I would say that as we look at New York, New York has made enormous progress in a decade. By the way, that 70 percent was 50 percent, so a 40 percent increase. So we're making enormous progress in making an impact on --

THE PRESIDENT: SEE HOW QUICKLY SHE'S CHANGING? See that? (Laughter.)

MS. ENGELBERT: Making enormous progress, but we're not done. We have a lot of work to do. And I think -- we

talked earlier about public/private partnerships, apprenticeship models, which -- **we have a beautiful apprenticeship model that works and brings them our next
generation of leaders**. So I do think there's a lot we can do
through re-looking at funding programs. We talked earlier about consolidating the many programs that are out
there. We're all trying to make our individual impact and
we can make a huge impact together.

THE PRESIDENT: Sure. I know you work very hard on it
and you have made progress. **Charter schools** are another
thing that people are talking about a lot, and some of the
charter schools in New York have been amazing. They've
done incredibly well. People can't get in. I mean, you
can't get in. I don't call it an experiment anymore, it's far
beyond an experiment.

If you look at so many elements of education, and it's so
sad to see what's coming -- what's happening in the country.

Even the numbers, as good -- you say we're doing better,
but the numbers in New York, the numbers in Chicago are
very rough. The numbers in Los Angeles, the cities, it's a
very rough situation.

Common Core -- I mean, we have to bring education more
local. We can't be managing education from Washington.

When I go out to Iowa, when I go out to the different
states and I talk, they want to run their school programs
locally, and they'll do a much better job than somebody --
and look, these are some very good people in Washington,
but you also have bureaucrats that make a lot of money
and don't really care that much about what they're doing

or about the community that they have never seen and they'll never meet, and they never will see.

And I like the fact of getting rid of -- Common Core to me is -- we have to end it. **We have to bring education local.** To me, I've always said it, I've been saying it during the campaign. And we're doing it. Betsy DeVos is -- she's doing a terrific job, highly respected, tremendous track record. But she's got one of the toughest jobs of any of our secretaries, to me. She's got one of the toughest jobs. There's some pretty tough jobs out there, but she's got one of the toughest jobs.

We're going to spend a lot of money and a lot of expertise. We're going to have great talent having to do with education, because there's nothing more important than education.

And we've got to get those numbers in New York better, and I think they will be better. And a lot of people -- a lot of the greatest people I know in New York, they're totally involved, including **Ivanka and Jared**, they're so much involved, and it's so important to them, the word "education."

And it's happening, and I see it happening in New York very much.

But it's happening elsewhere, too. I think we're going to have a great four years.

MR. CORDISH: Mr. President, I know you have --

THE PRESIDENT: Prior to running again.

MR. CORDISH: -- a pressing issue to deal with. Steve and Mike I think just wanted to thank you for attending today, and maybe make a final comment on behalf of --

MR. SCHWARZMAN: Well, thanks a lot for being here. And thanks for everybody for being here. It's been a really interesting day, and you've had everybody of importance at the event.

I think it's terrific in terms of the stuff you're trying to do to modernize the government, educate, and so forth. And I think we have to keep a focus on that, because the outside world doesn't always get the message that that's really what's going on -- because you're doing profound things, taking on enormous embedded issues.

And I think with the kind of effort that can be marshaled, you can do amazing things. And that's on behalf of Mike Corbat and myself who chaired the Partnership -- it's sort of trust, and gets rotated from person to person every two years.

I want to wish you really good luck with the Chinese. That's an important thing, as we all know. And I think there's a real opportunity to make progress with them. And you should have a good time in Florida. I hope the weather is good.

THE PRESIDENT: Yeah, the weather will be beautiful. Thank you, Steve.

I just want to finish by saying that we are absolutely destroying these horrible regulations that have been placed on your heads over not eight years, over the last 20 and 25 years. You have regulations that are horrendous. Dodd-

Frank is an example of what we're working on, and we're working on it right now. We're going to be coming out with some very strong -- far beyond recommendations -- we're going to be doing things that are going to be very good for the banking industry so that the banks can loan money to people that need it.

I speak to people all the time. They used to borrow money from banks to open up -- there's one in Nevada -- to open up a pizza shop here, three shops -- he had a bank, and he said, you know -- at that time he called me "Mr. Trump" because I hadn't won yet -- but he said, "Mr. Trump, I can't open up anything; I can't do anything. The banks don't even -- I had a bank for 20 years; now they don't even take my phone call. And I was always a very good customer. So I haven't been able to do what I do." They can't do it. I mean, the banks got so restricted.

And I've always said -- and some people get insulted -- but, you know, it's not necessarily the man that's making a lot of money that's running the bank.

You look at the folks from government that are running all over the banks, they're running the banks. And the people that are really the head people, they're petrified of the regulators. They're petrified. They can't move. The regulators are running the banks.

So we're going to do a very major haircut on Dodd-Frank. We want strong restrictions, we want strong regulation, but not regulation that makes it impossible for the banks to loan to people that are going to create jobs.

But we're doing -- that's just one example. We're doing so many cuts on regulations. And we have a book on regulations, and if you add them all up, **it goes up to the ceiling three times over**. It's just one after another after another. It's just like that chart. I thought that chart was so descriptive. And every industry is just like that chart, and that's to build a simple roadway or highway that's what you have to go through. And we're going to be able to get rid of 90, 95 percent of that and still have the same kind of protection.

And we want safety and we want environmental -- we want environmental protection. I've won awards on environmental protection. **I'm a big believer, believe it or not**. But we want that kind of protection. We want clean air and we want clean water, but we shouldn't have to get the approvals from 16 different agencies for almost the same thing.

So we have A COUNTRY WITH TREMENDOUS POTENTIAL. We have the greatest people on Earth, but we have to use that potential and we have to let those people do their thing.

And with that, I just want to thank you all. I think you're going to see a very much different environment than you've been used to over the last, again, 20, 25 years.

We're going to unleash the country. And I'm willing to take the heat, and that's okay. I've been taking the heat my whole life.

But in the end, I know it's the right thing to do.

And we're going to create a lot of jobs. **We have 100 million people,** if you look -- the real number is not 4.6 percent. They told me I had 4.6 percent last month, I'm doing great.

I said, yeah, but what about the 100 million people. A lot of those people came out and voted for me. **I call them the forgotten man, the forgotten woman**. But a lot of those people, a good percentage of them, would like to have jobs, and they don't.

One of the statistics that to me is just ridiculous -- so the 4.6 sounds good, but **when you look for a job, you can't find it and you give up** -- you are now considered statistically **employed**.

But I don't consider those people employed.

If you look at what's happened with Ford and with General Motors and with Fiat-Chrysler and so many other car companies, you see what they're doing back in Michigan and Ohio -- they were leaving. They were going to Mexico and many other places. They're now staying here.

Now, I did say -- Reed knows this very well, because you've seen me say it many times to the big auto companies at meetings -- it's okay, enjoy your new plant; please send me a picture, I'm sure it's going to be lovely. But when you make your car or when you make your air conditioner, and you think you're going to fire all of our workers and open up a new place in another country, and you're going to come through what will be **a very strong border,** which is already -- you see what's happened; 61 percent down now in terms of illegal people coming in.

Way, way down in terms of drugs pouring into our country and poisoning our youth. Way down. General Kelly has done a great job.

But when you think you're going to sell that car or that

air conditioner through our border, it's not going to happen. You're going to have a tax. And the tax may be 35
percent.

And you know what, every single major company that
I've had that conversation with has said, you know, we've
decided to stay in the United States. It's amazing. And you
would have thought they would have said this, frankly, for
years. But nobody has ever said it.

And we've lost close to 70,000 factories over a relatively
short period of time -- 70,000. You wouldn't believe it's
possible, Reed, to lose 70,000 factories -- 70,000. You
know, you look at a map of the United States -- how many
factories can you lose? **We lost almost 70,000 factories**.

And I will tell you, that's not happening, because now
they're staying here and they're all expanding here.

Ford announced last week a massive expansion of three of
its plants. That was not going to happen, believe me, if I
didn't win.

So, good luck, everybody. Enjoy yourselves. You're my
friends. You're amazing people. And we're going to put
you to work. Thank you. (Applause.)

END
11:12 A.M. EDT

Chapter 123

REMARKS BY PRESIDENT TRUMP AT 2017 NORTH AMERICA'S BUILDING TRADES UNIONS NATIONAL LEGISLATIVE CONFERENCE
WASHINGTON HILTON
WASHINGTON, D.C.

04 April 2017

12:25 P.M. EDT

THE PRESIDENT: I know these people well, you wouldn't believe it. **I know them too well**. (Applause.)

I know them too well. They cost me a lot of money. (Laughter.)

[Photo: screengrab.]

I spent a lot of money, but I love them, and they're great, and their people are fantastic. And nobody does it like you people, right? Nobody. We talked about that -- incredible. Incredible people.

So it's great to be back with **America's builders**. (Applause.)

So did you ever think you'd see a President who knows how much concrete and rebar you can lay down in a single day? Believe me, I know. I know. (Applause.)

We're a nation of builders, and it was about time we had a **builder in the White House**, right? (Applause.)

We have a builder.

I want to thank Sean McGarvey and the entire governing board of presidents for honoring me with this great invitation. And I love that it's in Washington, because I don't have to travel very far. Worked out pretty well, I have to tell you. Five minutes.

Sean took part in one of our very first meetings at the White House — he mentioned it -- and **I promise you that America's labor leaders will always find an open door with Donald Trump.**

Always. (Applause.)

Just look at the amazing talent assembled here. We have ironworkers, insulators -- (applause) -- never changes, does it, with the ironworkers? Let's hear it.

Laborers. (Applause.)

Painters. (Applause.)

Fitters. (Applause.)

Plumbers. (Applause.)

Operators -- they're operators, all right, I'll tell you
that. (Laughter.)

Electricians. (Applause.)

Not that good. Where's my Local 3? Where's Local
3? That wasn't that good, the electricians -- well, they
became so rich they don't have to -- (laughter) -- let's do
that again.

Electricians. (Applause.)

That's better.

Bricklayers. (Applause.)

Boilermakers. (Applause.)

Elevator constructors. (Applause.)

Good job. Sheet-metal workers. (Applause.)

Roofers. (Applause.)

Plasterers -- plaster, well, yeah, that's -- not using as much
plaster as we used to, fellas, right? No matter how you
cut it. Sorry about that. I'm not sure I can do much -- we
brought back the coalminers. I'm not so sure about the
plasterers. We'll do the best we can, okay? We're going to

do the best we can.

How about the cement masons. (Applause.)

And, of course, our wonderful Teamsters. (Applause.)

Oh, that wasn't very good, James.

But really, **you're the backbone of America**. With the
talent in this room, we could build any city at any time, and
we can build it better than anyone. (Applause.)

But we're going to do even better than that. Together, we
are going to **rebuild our nation**. (Applause.)

You're the keepers of the great trades and traditions that
built our country from the New York skyline to the
Golden Gate Bridge.

You represent the workers whose hands, skills, and **dreams**
will build the great landmarks of our future.

Every day, your members live out what I call the
American Creed. They're on the job before dawn and after
dusk, and they never quit until that job is done. You know
that. True. True. (Applause.)

We saw this grit on display when the construction trades
helped rebuild New York City after 9/11. (Applause.)

That was a terrible time -- we were all there -- that was a
terrible time in this country's history.

Worst attack in the history of our country. Worse than
Pearl Harbor. Pearl Harbor they were attacking mili-

tary. Here they were attacking civilians. Worst attack.

And I saw what happened. Within a very short period of time, we were back rebuilding, and rebuild you did. And I really congratulate -- that took a lot of courage and a lot of strength. Thank you. (Applause.)

The fact is you take pride in every part of your work -- every joist, bolt, and rivet. You're not only builders, but you're artisans, very talented people. A lot of people don't understand, you're very talented people -- enriching our cities and landscapes with works of great beauty. And just as you take pride in your work, our nation takes great, great pride in you, believe me. **And it's time that we give you the level playing field you deserve**. (Applause.)

Thank you. Thank you.

Washington and Wall Street have done very, very well for themselves.

Now it's your turn. And you're going to be also sharing the wealth. (Applause.)

And you know, for many years, we've been taken advantage of by other countries. All over the world they took advantage of us. We had leaders that didn't have a clue or worse. That's not going to happen anymore, folks. That's not going to happen anymore. And you see what's going on right now.

In fact, the trade deficit went way down -- just announced before I got on stage. And I will tell you, we're going to have a whole different set of values when it comes to representing our country. That I can tell you right now. (Ap-

plause.)

**This election was all about returning power to the peo-
ple**. I've spent my life working side-by-side with American
builders, and **now you have a builder as your
President**. (Applause.)

One of my first acts as President was to stop one of the
great sell-outs of the American worker -- I immediately
withdrew the United States from THE DISASTER -- this
would have been a disaster -- this would have been another NAFTA, which, by the way, is a disaster. I took you out of
the Trans-Pacific Partnership. (Applause.)

Thank you. That one wasn't even close. And you know it
and I know it, everybody knows it.

Next, I cleared the way for the construction of the Keystone XL and Dakota Access Pipelines. (Applause.)

And it's looking like that's going to have about 42,000 jobs
involved, those two jobs. That some number of great people. That's a big, big, beautiful -- lot of people. And Sean
actually, and a whole group joined me in the Oval Office
when we approved the Keystone permit.

And I joked that day -- I said, can you imagine the head of
this big Canadian company, in this case, they build pipelines -- and they failed. Didn't work.

They paid millions and millions and hundreds of millions of
dollars to consultants and lawyers, and they failed. And it
was over. And then one-day Trump wins, and a few days
later they get a knock on the door -- sir, the Keystone Pipeline was just approved.

The First 100 Days   993

Can you imagine? I want to see the expression on his face. And he's a nice guy. He actually -- they came to the office. (Applause.)

Because I did say you have to use American steel, you have to fabricate it here. Now, they had already bought 60-70 percent of it. So you can't be too wild, right?

But I was signing the order, and I said, where did they buy this steel? I didn't like the answer. I said, who fabricated the steel? I didn't like the answer. I said, from now on we're going to put a clause -- got to be **Made in America**. **We want American steel, Made in America**. (Applause.)

Right on the box. 100 percent, right? (Applause.)

And you'll be hearing more about this in the very near future. But as time goes by, let's say, **over the next seven and three-quarters years -- meaning eight years** … (Laughter.)

We believe in **two simple rules: Buy American, and Hire American**. That's what it's going to be. (Applause.)

And **that's not just a slogan, it's a promise**. Believe me, **that's a promise**. (Applause.)

The era of economic surrender has come to an end. It's come to an end. We have surrendered as a country to outside interests.

The era of economic victory for our country has just begun. You will see. No longer will we listen to those failed consultants who've made one wrong prediction after another -- delivering nothing but soaring trade deficits and a big, fat, shrinking workforce.

For decades now, we've watched as our factories have shuttered -- almost 70,000 factories -- our jobs have been stolen, and blue collar wages have declined. We've seen the economic pain inflicted on our fellow Americans in Pittsburgh and Detroit and Baltimore. We didn't just off-shore our jobs, we off-shored a big, big part of the **American Dream**.

We enriched foreign countries at the expense of our own country, the Great United States of America. But those days are over. (Applause.)

I'm not -- and I don't want to be -- the President of the World. I'm the President of the United States. And from now on, it's going to be **America First**. (Applause.)

We're going to **bring back our jobs** -- and, yes, we're going to **bring back the American Dream**. As I traveled the nation, I heard the pleas of the **forgotten men and women** of our country -- the people who work hard and play by the rules, but who don't have a voice. Together, we are their voice, and they will never, ever be forgotten **Again**. That I can tell you. (Applause.)

I don't know if you saw, but if you watch the Democrats now, the anger -- the anger and hatred, and they're trying to figure out where did all these people came that voted for Donald Trump?

Remember they said -- because the Electoral College is a very, very hard, they say, almost impossible for a Republican to win. The odds are stacked. And they would say

there's no way to 270 -- you need 270 -- there's no way to
270. I heard that so much for a year -- I kept saying, maybe
I shouldn't be running. You know, Sean, I said, maybe
I shouldn't run because there's no way. The people are
telling me -- the same people that say all of the bad stuff,
they're saying, there's no way to 270. But there was a way
to 306.

But wasn't that an exciting one? Places that nobody entered -- Donald Trump has won the state of
Michigan. They go, what?

Donald Trump has won the state of Wisconsin. They came
out of the blue, and we didn't even need them.

And we love those two states -- because we won the state
of Pennsylvania, and we won Ohio, and Iowa, and North
Carolina, and South Carolina, and Florida, and so many
others. We ran the coast. And if you don't run it, you
can't win. Huge disadvantage, Electoral College. It's very,
very tough. They say almost impossible for a Republican
to win. But I had the support of, I would say, I would say
almost everybody in this room.

We had tremendous -- we had tremendous support. Oh,
we did. We had tremendous support. (Applause.)

We had tremendous support. And I'll tell you, **we really
had the support of the workers**. We had tremendous support of the workers. But would you like to make a change,
folks? Would you like to make a change?

Because if anybody wants to make a change, you won't be
having so many jobs. That I can tell you. Your jobs will be
-- it will be a whole different story. Because in the last dec-

ade, **you lost over 750,000** -- think of this -- 750,000 construction jobs. Real wages in the construction sector have fallen more than 15 percent since the 1970s. We rank 39th in the world for construction permitting. And **approvals for infrastructure projects can take up to 10 years**.

Since taking office, I've signed one action after another to eliminate job-killing regulations that stand in the way. I had a chart -- is that chart around here someplace? Do you have that? I have to show this chart to you because it's amazing, actually.

[Photo: screengrab.]

This is -- if you want to build a highway in the United States, these are some of the permits that you need. It's a process that can take way over 10 years. And it just never happens. Then at the end of the period they vote against it. And we're getting rid of many of these regulations. (Applause.)

You have to go through 17 agencies, many permits in each agency.

In February alone, **we added almost 60,000 new construction jobs in the country**. I ordered expedited environmental reviews for infrastructure, environmental and energy projects all across the country. No longer will you have to wait year after year for approvals that never come.

I also took historic action to lift the restrictions on American energy production and to put our miners, who have been treated horribly, back to work. (Applause.)

They're great people.

Consumer confidence is at its highest level in more than a decade. You've seen all of the charts, all of the studies.

The *National Association of Manufacturers* just the other day reported the most optimism in the entire history of its survey -- which is a old survey -- 93 percent of manufacturers are optimistic about the future. It was almost 27 percent lower than that just a few months ago.

The *Home Builders Confidence Index* is at its highest level in 12 years.

And now in breaking news, it was just reported today, the monthly U.S. trade deficit declined by 10 percent -- for a reason. Not by accident, believe me. It was for a reason.

We're also **going to protect your jobs by protecting our borders**. My administration is -- just a matter of weeks, literally, a short period of time -- has brought record reductions to illegal immigration. Record reductions. (Applause.)

Down 61 percent since inauguration. General Kelly is

doing a fantastic job. And we'll crack down on visa abuses
that undermine the American worker. And we're doing
that right now. (Applause.)

These, and so many other great achievements, have defined our first 10 weeks in office. We've done so much for
the worker. Done so much for the military. We've done so
much for the police officers, our men in blue and women
in blue who are not treated fairly. We're fighting for workers of all backgrounds and from all walks of life.

But to achieve true progress, we must remember our
legacy. We're the nation that built the tallest skyscrapers
on what was once the Hudson River, and put neon lights of
Las Vegas in the middle of the desert. But if government
continues to punish America's builders, then we will not be
that nation any longer.

I'm calling on **all Americans** -- Democrat, Republican, independent -- **to come together** and take part in the great
rebuilding of our country. (Applause.)

That is why, in my address to Congress, I called on lawmakers to pass legislation that produces a $1-trillion invest-
ment in the infrastructure of our country. And we need it.
(Applause.)

With your help, we can **rebuild** our country's bridges,
airports, seaports, and water systems. We will streamline
the process to get approvals quickly, so that long-delayed
projects can finally move ahead. And with lower taxes on
America's middle class and businesses, we will see a new
surge of economic growth and development.

All of you have come to the nation's capital to call members of the House and Senate to action. You've also called your President to action. When you see them, you can tell Congress that America's building trades and its President are very much united. (Applause.)

Together, we are ready to break new ground. We will build in the **Spirit** of one of the great projects in our nation's history -- an enduring symbol of **American strength**.

The Empire State Building was forged in the Great Depression, and provided jobs for more than 3,000 workers. We've all seen the pictures -- rugged workers perched dozens and dozens of stories up in the air.

Workers like these moved almost 60,000 tons of steel, installed 200,000 cubic feet of stone, and laid 10 million bricks to build that American icon. And they did the job in a record time -- **13 months**. Hard to believe. Think of that -- the Empire State Building built in 13 months, during the Depression.

Nowadays, you couldn't even get a building permit or approval in that amount of time.

When the workers had secured the last piece of steel in that amazing and beautiful structure, they marked the moment -- as we still do today -- with what is called a "topping out" ceremony: 1.050 feet above the streets of New York City, **they hoisted a beautiful and great American flag**. (Applause.)

AUDIENCE MEMBER: The ironworkers!

THE PRESIDENT: They did a good job. They did a good -- those ironworkers, you better believe it.

It was an American flag that represented American projects -- the big, bold, and daring **dream** of one man, and then one city, and then finally, one people. **That banner marked our nation's proud climb to the top of the world**. Our people endured through the hardships of Depression and the battles of World War II, and they emerged from these trials stronger and more united than ever before.

Now, we must **Again** summon that same **national greatness** to meet the challenges of our time.

Only miles from the halls of Congress and the newsrooms of Washington, you will find once-thriving cities marred by empty lots and once-booming industrial towns that have become rusted and are in total disrepair.

Standing before me today, in this very hall, are the men and women who, if given the chance, can transform these communities. **You are** the citizens who can **rebuild** our cities, revive our industries, and **renew** our beloved country. **And I know you will stop at nothing to get the job done**. (Applause.)

For the rest of their lives, everyone who worked on the Empire State Building knew when they looked up at that great New York skyline that **they had lifted the Stars and Stripes atop the tallest flagpole on Earth**, and that somewhere high above the city streets, their place in history was carved into beams of steel.

In the future, when we become -- the trials -- and we are -- trials of our times -- we too will emerge stronger and more united than ever before. It's happening, you watch. When we rise above the cynics and critics who live only to defend the status quo, and to defend themselves from failure, then **we, too, will construct a lasting monument to national greatness.**

In this future, our nation's workers and craftsmen will look way out at the vast open landscape, and they will build new bridges and new schools and new landmarks, and **they will proudly raise up for all to see our bright and beautiful American flag.**

And when we see that flag, we will remember that we all **share one American home**, **one American heart**, and **one American destiny.**

May God bless our nation's builders. May God bless our nation's workers. And may God bless the United States of America. Thank you very much. Thank you. (Applause.)

END
12:54 P.M. EDT

Chapter 124

**REMARKS BY PRESIDENT TRUMP AND
HIS MAJESTY KING ABDULLAH II OF JORDAN
IN JOINT PRESS CONFERENCE
ROSE GARDEN**

05 April 2017

1:10 P.M. EDT

PRESIDENT TRUMP: Thank you very much. Your Majesty, thank you for being with us today. Very much appreciate it. This is our second meeting since my Inauguration, but our first at the White House. A very special place, I can tell you that. I've gotten to know it well. Long hours. Very special.

It's really an honor to welcome you here today. But before we begin, let me say a few words about recent events. Yesterday, a chemical attack -- a chemical attack that was so horrific, in Syria, against innocent people, including women, small children, and even beautiful little babies. Their deaths was an affront to humanity. These heinous actions by the Assad regime cannot be tolerate.

The United States stands with our allies across the globe to condemn this horrific attack and all other horrific attacks, for that matter.

Your Majesty, Jordanians are known for their legendary hospitality, and we will do our very best to be equally gracious hosts. They're also known, however -- I have to say this -- for their fighting ability. And **you are a great**

warrior, and we appreciate it. Thank you.

[Photo: screengrab.]

The historical ties and close friendship between our two countries dates back three-quarters of a century. In that time, the Middle East has faced many periods of crisis and unrest, perhaps never like it is today, however. Through them all, America has looked to Jordan as a valued partner, an advocate for the values of civilization, and a source of stability and hope.

I am deeply committed to preserving our strong relation-ship -- which I will -- and to strengthening America's long-standing support for Jordan. And you do have tremendous support within our country, I can tell you that.

As we know, the Middle East -- and the entire world -- is faced with one of its gravest threats in many, many years. Since the earliest days of the campaign against

ISIS, Jordan has been a staunch ally and partner, and we thank you for that. Jordanian service-members have made tremendous sacrifices in this battle against the enemies of civilization, and I want to thank all of them for their, really, just incredible courage. So many have been lost, and we pay homage. So many.

In King Abdullah, America is blessed with a thoughtful and determined partner. He is a man who has spent years commanding his country's special forces. He really knows what being a soldier is, that I can tell you.

And **he knows how to fight**. The King has been a leader in calling for a plan to defeat ISIS once and for all. And I'm with you on that. We're both leaders on that, believe me. That's what we speak about today, and that is what we are going to do. And it will be a shorter fight than a lot of people are thinking about, believe me. We've made tremendous strides as we discussed.

As you know, we had a very, very fine delegation come over from Egypt and also from Iraq, and they said more has been done in the last six weeks than has been done in years with the previous administration. And believe me, we're going to keep it that way.

We will destroy ISIS and we will protect civilization. We have no choice -- we will protect civilization.

King Abdullah and I also discussed measures to combat the evil ideology that inspires ISIS and plagues our planet.

In addition, we also acknowledge the vital role that Jordan has played in hosting refugees from the conflict in Syria. We have just announced that the United States will contribute additional funds to Jordan for humanitarian assistance.

This aid will help countries like Jordan host refugees until it is safe for them to return home.

The refugees want to return home. I know that from so many other instances. They want to return back to their home. And that's a goal of any responsible refugee policy.

Finally, we discussed to advance the cause of peace in the Middle East, including peace between the Israelis and Palestinians.

And I'm working very, very hard on trying to finally create peace between the Palestinians and Israel, and I think we'll be successful. I hope to be successful, I can tell you that.

The King has been a really tireless advocate for a solution, and he's going to help me with that and help me at the highest level. And we will be consulting with him closely in the days ahead.

King Abdullah, I want to take this opportunity to thank you for your partnership. Working together, the United States and Jordan can help bring peace and stability to the Middle East and, in fact, the entire world. And we will do that.

Thank you very, very much for being with us. (Applause.)

KING ABDULLAH: Thank you. Mr. President, thank you for such a kind and warm welcome to the White House. I fondly remember the meetings we've had many years ago and, more recently, several months ago. You've always been a generous host and have always looked after us. We

are very delighted with the way the discussions have gone
so far, and we're delighted to be here in such a wonderful
setting on such a beautiful day, which I think is a tremendous mark of how we are going to move into the future.

[Photo: screengrab.]

We've had a very good round of talks today, and I'm looking forward to continuing these discussions later on in our
meetings after the press conference.

What I do want to say is how much we deeply appreciate
the close relations we have with the United States, with
you, Mr. President, and with the American people.

This is a strategic partnership that we keep very close to
our hearts, and it is a partnership on so many levels that
we will continue, I think, with the frank discussions that
we had today to improve on as we face the challenges of
the future. And I am very delighted for your vision, your
holistic approach to all the challenges in our region, and to
the dedication of your team in being able to translate your

policies into action successfully, hopefully, as we move forward.

The challenges we face today are many and are not exclusive to my region, as I've just mentioned. They are global, and particularly the threats to global security. Terrorism has no borders, no nationality, no religion, and, therefore, joint action with a holistic approach, as I had just mentioned, Mr. President, is crucial. I am very delighted that you have the vision to be able to move in that direction, and I think that the world will be in a very good place as we move with all these challenges ahead.

No doubt, with all the challenges that we face in the world, the role of the U.S. is key to all the issues that we have around the world, but it's not just the fact that we should expect the United States to do all the heavy lifting.

The heavy lifting has to be done by all of us in the international community to support the United States in being able to translate that vision into the right direction.

So there's a lot of responsibility for all of us in the international community to support the President, the administration, and the American people to bring brighter days to all of us.

We are very encouraged with the President's determination to support Arab and Muslim states in their fight against terrorism.

But it is not only the fight of terrorism inside of our societies, but we, as Arab-Muslim states standing behind the international community in being able to defeat this international scourge.

In Syria, we need a political solution that ends the conflict in the country and preserve its unity and territorial integrity.

As the President mentioned, the issue we discussed was the Israeli-Palestinian conflict, which is essentially the core conflict in our region.

And the President's early engagement as beginning in bringing the Palestinians and Israelis together has been a very encouraging sign for all of us. And I think, sir, it was that initiative that allowed us at the Arab Summit last week to extend through the Arab Peace Initiative the message of peace to Israel, which we all hopefully will work together to make that come about.

All Arab countries -- we launched the *Arab Peace Initiative,* as I said, last week. It offers a historic reconciliation between Israel and the Palestinians, as well as all member states of the *Arab League*. It is the most comprehensive framework for lasting peace and it ensures statehood for the Palestinians, but also security, acceptance and normal ties for Israel with all Arab countries and hopefully all Islamic countries.

So we appreciate your commitment in all these issues where others have failed. You will find a strong ally in Jordan in supporting you in all your policies. And if I may just say, as you have, on Syria and the gas attack -- unfortunately, as you and I both agree, this is another testament to the failure of the international diplomacy to find the solutions to this crisis. But I believe under your leadership we will be able to unravel this very complicated situation.

This has been ongoing for seven years now, has descended

into proxy wars from different parties with dubious agendas. But at the end of the day, as you pointed out, Mr. President, it is the civilians -- women and children -- that are paying the heaviest price. This is happening on our watch, on our conscience, as well as the global community. And I know the passion and the emotion that the President has expressed and how this should not be tolerated whatsoever. And this threshold of inhumanity and savagery that are being crossed every day is something that I know the President will not allow to happen, wherever it may be. And I fully support and endorse the President in this issue.

So I want to thank you, sir, because you have the outlook of looking not just at the Syrian challenges but that of Iraq, Israel, Palestine, Libya, and everything that is in our region. So I think your message to all of us is a message of hope, and that's what I take away from this conference.

PRESIDENT TRUMP: Thank you very much.

KING ABDULLAH: And I thank you for all that you have done so far and all that you will do, sir. (Applause.)

PRESIDENT TRUMP: We'll take a few questions. Julie Pace.

Q   Thank you, sir. I have questions on Syria for both leaders. But if I could start with you, Mr. President. You've condemned the chemical attacks in Syria, but you also appeared in your statement yesterday to pin some of the blame on the Obama administration. You are the President now. Do you feel like you bear responsibility for responding to the chemical attack? And does the chemical attack cross a red line for you?

PRESIDENT TRUMP: Well, I think the Obama administration had a great opportunity to solve this crisis a long time ago when he said the red line in the sand.

And when he didn't cross that line after making the threat, I think that set us back a long ways, not only in Syria, but in many other parts of the world, because it was a blank threat.

I think it was something that was not one of our better days as a country.

So I do feel that, Julie. I feel it very strongly.

Q   So you feel like you now have the responsibility to respond to the chemical attack?

PRESIDENT TRUMP: I now have responsibility, and I will have that responsibility and carry it very proudly, I will tell you that. It is now my responsibility. It was a great opportunity missed.

As you know, I'll be meeting with the President of China very soon, **in Florida**, and that's another responsibility we have -- and that's called the country of North Korea. We have a big problem. We have somebody that is not doing the right thing.

And that's going to be my responsibility. But I'll tell you, that responsibility could have been made a lot easier if it was handled years ago.

Q   Before I move on to the King, could I just quickly ask you if the chemical attack crosses a red line for you?

PRESIDENT TRUMP: It crossed a lot of lines for me. When you kill innocent children, innocent babies -- babies, little babies -- with a chemical gas that is so lethal -- people were shocked to hear what gas it was -- that crosses many, many lines, beyond a red line. Many, many lines.

Thank you very much.

Q   And, Your Majesty, if I could ask about refugees. Your country has really borne the brunt of the refugee crisis in Syria. The President has signed travel bans that would block Syrians from coming to the U.S. If that goes into effect, what would the impact on your country and across the region be?

KING ABDULLAH: Well, I think as the President pointed out, most, if not all, Syrian refugees actually want to go back to Syria. And what we're working with the United States and the international community is to be able to stabilize the refugees in our country, give them the tools so that, as we're working with the solutions in Syria, we have the ability to be able to send them back as a positive influence into their economies.

And again, the President and the Europeans are being very forward-leaning in being able look after our host communi- ty -- tremendous burden on our country, but again, tre- mendous appreciation to the United States and the West- ern countries for being able to help us deliver that.

Q   Your Majesty, how does the outcome of the recent Arab Summit help the U.S. in its policy to advance Palestin- ian-Israeli negotiations?

KING ABDULLAH: Well, as I said, our peace initiative came

out with a resounding resolution to offer peace to the Israelis, to make them feel that they're accepted into the neighborhood, and to be able to support the President as he brings both parties together.

And again, I have to remind people that very early on there was an early engagement by the President and his team to the Israelis and the Palestinians to be able to see what he can do to bring them together. It is the core conflict for a lot of us in the region. The President knows this. He has his instincts in the right place. And working with his team, our job, as I said, is to do the heavy lifting. The Arabs are prepared to do whatever they can to bring Israelis and Palestinians together under the leadership of the President.

PRESIDENT TRUMP: Thank you. John Yang (ph).

Q   Thank you, Mr. President. I'd like to follow up on Julie's question and press you a little more on Syria. How will you distinguish your policy and your actions on Syria from the inaction that you criticized of the previous administration? You say it's now your responsibility. What should we see or what should we look for that will be different?

And, Your Majesty, I'd like to ask you, what gives you -- this is now your second meeting with the President -- what gives you the optimism that Mr. Trump will succeed in the Israeli-Palestinian conflict where so many others have failed before him to be a broker for peace?

PRESIDENT TRUMP: I like to think of myself as a **very flexible person**. I don't have to have one specific way, and if the world changes, I go the same way, I don't change.

Well, I do change and **I am flexible,** and I'm proud of

that **flexibility**. And I will tell you, that attack on children
yesterday had a big impact on me -- big impact. That was
a horrible, horrible thing. And I've been watching it and
seeing it, and it doesn't get any worse than that.

And I have that **flexibility**, and it's very, very possible --
and I will tell you, it's already happened that my attitude
toward Syria and Assad has changed very much.

And if you look back over the last few weeks, there were
other attacks using gas. You're now talking about a whole
different level.

And so, as you know, I would love to have never been in
the Middle East. I would love to have never seen that
whole big situation start. But once it started, we got out
the wrong way, and ISIS formed in the vacuum, and lots
of bad things happened. I will tell you, what happened
yesterday is unacceptable to me.

Q   Can I follow up, sir? Last year, you seemed to be reluc-
tant to get involved -- or to intervene in Syria directly. Is
that one thing that's changed after yesterday?

PRESIDENT TRUMP: Well, one of the things I think you've
noticed about me is, militarily, I don't like to say where
I'm going and what I doing. And I watched past administrations say, we will attack at such and such a day at such
and such an hour. And you, being a warrior -- you would
say, why are they saying that? And I'm sure you sat back in
Jordan, and you said, why are they saying that?

I watched Mosul, where the past administration was
saying, we will be attacking in four months. And I said,
why are they doing that? Then a month goes by, and they

say, we will be attacking in three months, and then two months, and then we will be attacking next week. And I'm saying, why are they doing that? And as you know, Mosul turned out to be a much harder fight than anyone thought, and a lot of people have been lost in that fight.

I'm not saying I'm doing anything one way or the other, but I'm certainly not going to be telling you, as much as I respect you, John. Thank you.

KING ABDULLAH: Sir, I think, on behalf of the President, what I saw was an early engagement by the President and his team, with all of us in the region, about the challenges between the Israelis and Palestinians. I had the honor of seeing the President and his team again in January where this was discussed. The President understands the nuances and the challenges. I think he has the courage and the dedication to be able to do this.

Like I said before, all of us have a responsibility to help the President push us over the finish line.

And so, his team had been in the region, they've been talking to all the partners, and it is our job to facilitate the atmospherics between Israelis and Palestinians to move together, and give the support to the President to be able to smooth the edges over between Israelis and Palestinians to achieve this. And the President understands that if we don't solve this problem, how are we going to win the global fight against terrorism, which is his number-one priority? So this is a core issue that he understands, and I think he has the commitment and he has my full support for this, as he does from many, many countries in our region.

PRESIDENT TRUMP: And I have to just say that the world is a mess. **I inherited a mess**. Whether it's the Middle East, whether it's North Korea, whether it's so many other things, whether it's in our country -- horrible trade deals -- **I inherited a mess**. We're going to fix it. We're going to fix it.

Okay.

Q   Thank you, Your Majesty. You touch upon the subject now, but if I ask you to look forward, how do you see the future of fighting terrorism post-Raqqa and Mosul, especially the role that Jordan will play in the eastern part of Iraq? And do you believe the real battle will start then?

And if I may, Mr. President, you know very well that the Iranian militias and Hezbollah has been propping the Syrian regime for a while -- over a few years now. Will you go after them? What message will you give them today? And will you work with the Russians to ground the Syrian air force and to establish safe zones? Thank you.

KING ABDULLAH: Well, the first part is that we are seeing, very recently, tremendous gains on the ground in Raqqa and Mosul.

Again, I think, as the President alluded to, it's very difficult to put time-lines on this issue because the battle space is always very fluid. But I think that the war is being won on the ground.

Having said that, terrorists are on the move. They'll be on the move inside of Iraq and inside of Syria, so that we have to make sure that we adapt our plans accordingly. And they move beyond borders, beyond our region and elsewhere. So as we and the administration have discussed, it's this holistic approach: How do we fight them wherev- er they are? And I think that is the understanding.

Terrorists have no respect for borders and religions and people. So it's the seriousness of how we do this holistic approach that I've mentioned several times. And what I am really delighted is that the understanding by the President and the administration in how to deal with this globally.

And I think you're seeing a move in the right direction be- cause the policy now is being charted out, and my discus- sions with the Defense Secretary and the Foreign Secretary allows us to be then able to decide how we adapt our- selves in the region to be able to come in line with interna- tional diplomacy.

PRESIDENT TRUMP: The Iran deal made by the previous administration is one of the worst deals I have ever wit- nessed -- and I've witnessed some beauties. It's one of the worst deals I've ever witnessed. It should never have been made. It was totally one-sided against the United States, and, frankly, against much of the Middle East.

I will do whatever I have to do. They have a deal. It was, some people say, not done properly even in the form of its finalization. There was no vote from Congress. There was no real ratification. But I will do what I have to do with respect to the Iran deal.

As far as ISIS is concerned, the United States will work with whoever it's appropriate to work with to totally eradi- cate ISIS and other terrorists. And, by the way, ISIS is one group, but others have formed.

Frankly, they're all over the place. We will do what we
have to do to eradicate terrorism.

Q   But, Sir, I'm talking about the Iranian militias in
Syria supporting the Syrian regime separate of the nuclear
deal. What message do you have for them today?

PRESIDENT TRUMP: You will see. They will have a message. You will see what the message will be. Okay? Thank
you.

Thank you all very much. Thank you. Thank you.

END
1:35 P.M. EDT

Chapter 125

**REMARKS BY PRESIDENT TRUMP TO THE PRESS
ABOARD AIR FORCE ONE
EN ROUTE WEST PALM BEACH, FLORIDA**

06 April 2017

2:08 P.M. EDT

Q (In progress.) -- the Chinese President?

THE PRESIDENT: North Korea and trade.

Q   And on North Korea, you had said in the -- inter-
view that you're willing to act alone if China doesn't step
up. What are you going to try to get from the Chinese?

THE PRESIDENT: Certainly, I would be. But I think China
will want to be stepping up.

Q   What do you want them to do specifically?

THE PRESIDENT: You're going to see. We'll be talking
about it.

Q   Have you told members of Congress --

THE PRESIDENT: The President just arrived. He just landed
in Palm Beach, so I just saw that.

Q   Mr. President, have you told members of Congress that
you're considering using military action in Syria?

THE PRESIDENT: I don't want to mention that, but the answer is no, I haven't.

Q   So what should we make now, going -- I think we're ending the 13th week or so -- how your staff is doing? Are you shaking things up and rebooting a little bit?

THE PRESIDENT: I've shaken them up, and I think we've had one of the most successful 13 weeks in the history of Presidents. If you look at all that we've done and all of the jobs we've created, if you look at the kind of cost-cutting we've been able to achieve with the military and at the same time ordering vast amounts of equipment -- saved hundreds of millions of dollars on airplanes, and really billions, because if you take that out over a period of years it's many billions of dollars -- I think we've had a tremendous success. And we've just begun. And we're going to have a very interesting couple of days.

Q   In terms of your staff, though, are you realigning your staff?

Q   Are you committed to doing something in Syria?

THE PRESIDENT: I don't want to say what I'm going to be doing with respect to Syria.

Q   What would you like the Chinese president to do regarding North Korea?

THE PRESIDENT: We have been treated unfairly and have made terrible deals -- trade deals with China for many, many years. So that's one of the things we're going to be talking about. The other thing, of course, is going to be North Korea, and somehow they will mix. They really do mix. So we're going to be talking about both trade, North Korea, and many other things.

Q   Will the use of nuclear option change how you consider which nominees to put before the Senate?

THE PRESIDENT: No, not at all. No. We have a great person right now in Judge Gorsuch, I mean a great person. And hopefully if there is a second one for me during my administration -- and there could be as many as four -- in fact, under a certain scenario there could even be more than that -- but no, I don't think the nuclear option has any impact on that at all.

Q   What do you think of Devin Nunes recusing himself this morning? Were you briefed on that? Was that a good decision?

THE PRESIDENT: He's a very good person. I just heard that he did. I think he's a very good person, he's a very honorable guy. And I think he did that maybe for his own reason. He's a high-quality person. And the gentleman replacing him, who I don't know, I hear is a very, very highly respected man, high-quality.

Q   For him sharing classified information? Did he share classified information?

THE PRESIDENT: With who? What?

Q   For the ethics investigation now undergoing for him sharing classified information. Do you think he's guilty of sharing classified information?

THE PRESIDENT: Nobody shared it with me, that I can tell

you --

Q   Mr. President --

THE PRESIDENT: -- because I haven't looked.

Q   Mr. President, two questions. Do you think Assad should leave power? And will you discuss the Syria --

THE PRESIDENT: What Assad did is terrible. I think what happened in Syria is one of the truly egregious crimes and it shouldn't have happened and it shouldn't be allowed to happen.

Q   Have you talked to Putin about this? Will you talk to the Russian president about what happened?

THE PRESIDENT: At some point, I may. I haven't, but at some point I may.

Q   Just to follow on that, though, do you think that Assad should leave power in Syria?

THE PRESIDENT: I think what happened in Syria is a disgrace to humanity. And he's there, and I guess he's running things, so something should happen.

Thanks, folks, I'll see you in a little while.

END
2:12 P.M. EDT

Chapter 126

06 April 2017

9:40 P.M. EDT

THE PRESIDENT: My fellow Americans: On Tuesday, Syrian dictator Bashar al-Assad launched a horrible chemical weapons attack on innocent civilians. Using a deadly nerve agent, Assad choked out the lives of helpless men, women, and children. It was a slow and brutal death for so many. Even beautiful babies were cruelly murdered in this very barbaric attack. No child of God should ever suffer such horror.

Tonight, I ordered a targeted military strike on the airfield in Syria from where the chemical attack was launched. It is in this vital national security interest of the United States to prevent and deter the spread and use of deadly chemical weapons. There can be no dispute that Syria used banned chemical weapons, violated its obligations under the Chemical Weapons Convention, and ignored the urging of the U.N. Security Council.

Years of previous attempts at changing Assad's behavior have all failed, and failed very dramatically. As a result, the refugee crisis continues to deepen and the region continues to destabilize, threatening the United States and its allies.

Tonight, I call on all civilized nations to join us in seeking to

end the slaughter and bloodshed in Syria, and also to end
terrorism of all kinds and all types.

We ask for God's wisdom as we face the challenge of our
very troubled world.

We pray for the lives of the wounded and for the souls
of those who have passed. And we hope that as long as
America stands for justice, then peace and harmony will, in
the end, prevail.

Goodnight. And God bless America and the entire
world. Thank you.

END
9:43 P.M. EDT

Chapter 127

07 April 2017

My Fellow Americans,
We're only 11 weeks in, but already my administration has achieved historic progress for the American people – in fact, 93% of our domestic manufacturers have expressed optimism in the future, a record.

The confidence we are seeing in our Nation is about **jobs and opportunity** – but it's also about **safety and security**.

Security begins at the border – as a candidate, **I pledged** to take swift and decisive action to **secure** the border, and that is exactly what I have done.

We inherited a full-fledged border crisis – it was a disaster. Yet, with quick and bold steps, we have so far exceeded even the most bullish predictions for the progress we could make in so short a period of time. Last month, we saw a 64% reduction in illegal immigration on our southern border.

At the same time, we are conducting enforcement actions across the country to remove dangerous criminal aliens from our society – and they'll be gone.

In just the last few days our Nation's ICE officers have arrested 153 criminal aliens in south Texas, 84 criminal aliens in the Pacific Northwest, and 31 criminal aliens in Long Island, New York – these arrests include aliens convicted of robbery, burglary, aggravated assault, sexual assault against a child, smuggling, drug dealing, and many more.

Much work needs to be done to reverse decades of harm caused by open border policies from Washington – but, with time, dedication, and effort, we will get the job done, and save countless lives in the process.

Providing **security** for the American People also means **restoring** America's standing in the world.

From the very start of my Presidency, I have worked to strengthen our alliances and improve our relationships all around the globe.

This week, I was honored to welcome the President of Egypt and the King of Jordan to the White House.

Now, I am hosting a summit with President Xi of China at the **Southern White House** to address the many critical issues affecting our two peoples.

In our dealings with other nations, our conversations have been candid, open, and grounded in mutual respect.

I have been clear about advocating for the national interests of the United States, something so important to me, and so important to our people – one of the reasons, certainly, that I got elected.

And I want to ensure that the decisions we make truly serve the **safety and security** of our citizens.

In matters both economic and military, we understand that a **strong America** is in the best interests of the world – that is why it is so important that as we strengthen international partnerships, we ensure these partnerships deliver real results for Americans and the American people.

Our decisions will be guided by our values and our goals – and we will reject the path of inflexible ideology that too often leads to unintended consequences.

A future of **peace, safety, and prosperity** – that is our guiding light, and always will be.

Together, we will bring about this future for the land we love, and for the people who call it home.

We love our country, and we love the American people.

Thank [you.]

Chapter 128

07 April 2017

11:22 A.M. EDT

PRESIDENT TRUMP: I just want to say that President Xi and all of his representatives have been really interesting to be with.

I think we have made tremendous progress in our relationship with China.

My representatives have been meeting one-on-one with their counterparts from China. And I think, truly, progress has been made. We'll be making a lot of additional progress.

The relationship developed by President Xi and myself I think is outstanding. We look forward to being together many times in the future. And I believe lots of very potentially bad problems will be going away.

So I just want to thank President Xi for being with us in the United States. It's a tremendous honor for me and all of my representatives to host the President and his representatives. And again, progress has been made.

Thank you very much. Thank you.

[President Xi's comments were not translated and presented on the White House website.]

PRESIDENT TRUMP: Well, I agree 100 percent, Mr.
President.

And thank you very much.

And again, a tremendous honor to have you in the United
States and in **Mar-A-Lago**. Thank you very much.

END
11:26 A.M. EDT

Chapter 129

10 April 2017

11:04 A.M. EDT

THE PRESIDENT: Thank you very much. Friends and distinguished guests, welcome to the White House. We are gathered here today for a truly momentous occasion in our democracy -- the swearing-in of a United States Supreme Court justice.

In particular, I'm greatly honored to welcome to these grounds every sitting justice of the United States Supreme Court. Welcome. (Applause.)

Thank you.

Mr. Chief Justice, and fellow justices, it's a privilege to have you here, to join in this historic moment on this very beautiful spring day in the Rose Garden. Spring is really the perfect backdrop for this joyful gathering of friends, because, together, we are in a process of reviewing and renewing, and also rebuilding, our country. A new optimism is sweeping across our land, and a new faith in America is filling our hearts and lifting our sights.

I'd also like to recognize Senator Cory Gardner, Mike Lee -- where's Mike? He's around here someplace -- thank you. And Mike Crapo. Good. Hi, Mike. Thank you very much, and for all your work. Thank you. (Applause.)

And although he could not be here today, I especially want to express our gratitude to Senator Mitch McConnell for all that he did to make this achievement possible. So, thank you, Mitch. (Applause.)

I'd also like to give my appreciation to Chairman Grassley for conducting such a fair and professional confirmation. Senator Grassley. Where is Senator Grassley? (Applause.)

Thank you. Thank you, Senator. Finally, a profound thank you to Louise Gorsuch, and to all of the Gorsuch family. Thank you. (Applause.)

And, Louise, I've heard it first-hand, I know what a total inspiration you are to your husband and to your entire family. So thank you very much. Fantastic. Thank you very much. (Applause.)

We are here to celebrate history -- the taking of the judicial oath by the newest member of the United States Supreme Court, Neil Gorsuch. Justice Gorsuch, I just want to congratulate you and your entire family. It's something so special. In fact, I've always heard that the most important thing that a President of the United States does is appoint people -- hopefully great people like this appointment -- to the United States Supreme Court. And I can say this is a great honor. (Applause.)

And **I got it done in the first 100 days** -- that's even nice. (Laughter.)

You think that's easy?

This ceremony has special meaning as Justice Gorsuch is filling the seat of one of the greatest Supreme Court judges in American history, and that's Antonin Scalia, who is a terrific -- was a terrific judge and a terrific person. Justice Scalia was a patriot who revered our Constitution. He was beloved by many, very many, who are here today, and he is deeply missed by all of us.

I want to at this time recognize his incredible wife, Maureen, who I got to know very well over the last short period of time. And, Maureen, please stand up. Thank you very much. (Applause.)

Thank you and your family. Thank you. Thank you, Maureen.

Americans are blessed to have in Neil Gorsuch a man who will, likewise, be a devoted servant of the law. Over the past two months, the American people have gotten to know, respect and truly admire our newest member of the United States Supreme Court. In Justice Gorsuch, they see a man of great and unquestioned integrity. They see a man of unmatched qualifications. And most of all, and most importantly, they see a man who is deeply faithful to the Constitution of the United States. He will decide cases based not on his personal preferences, but based on a fair and objective reading of the law.

Today, we have all three branches of government represented at this event. It is a very special thing -- and a very special happening. And it's worth taking just a minute to remember what it all means.

In our Founders' incredible wisdom, they gave each branch of government a different role in our Great Republic.

We have a Congress to write the laws on behalf of the people.

We have a President to enforce those laws and defend our nation.

And we have a Supreme Court to apply and interpret the law, in a fair and impartial manner, when disagreements arise.

The Founders separated power because they knew it was the best way to protect our citizens and keep our Constitution secure.

Justice Gorsuch, you are now entrusted with the sacred duty of defending our Constitution. Our country is counting on you to be wise, impartial and fair -- to serve under our laws, not over them, and to safegaurd the right of the people to govern their own affairs. I have no doubt you will rise to the occasion and that the decisions you will make will not only protect our Constitution today, but for many generations of Americans to come.

In just a moment, Justice Gorsuch will be sworn in by Justice Kennedy, a great man of outstanding accomplishment. Throughout his nearly 30 years on the Supreme Court, Justice Kennedy has been praised by all for his dedicated and dignified service.

We owe him an enormous debt of gratitude, and I am honored that he is with us today. (Applause.)

This is a very, very special moment, because many years ago a young Neil Gorsuch started his legal career as a law clerk to Justice Kennedy. You remember that, right? (Laughter.)

It is a fitting testament to Justice Kennedy's impact that, upon giving the oath to Justice Gorsuch, he will become the first ever Supreme Court justice to serve with one of his former law clerks. It's sort of a big deal, isn't it? (Applause.)

Sort of like that. That's sort of good. It has never happened before. That's pretty good.   Also shows you have a lot of respect for this man. Very good.

We're thrilled to share this historic moment with Justice Kennedy, with all of you here today, and with all Americans watching us at home.

Justice Gorsuch, I again congratulate you and your entire family, and I wish God's blessings on your amazing journey ahead. I have no doubt you will go down as one of the truly great justices in the history of the United States Supreme Court.

I now invite Justice Kennedy to say a few words. Thank you very much. (Applause.)

JUSTICE KENNEDY: Thank you, Mr. President. Mr. Chief Justice, Justice Gorsuch, and my fellow adherents to the idea and the reality of the rule of law: As many of you know, there are two oaths that a member of the federal judiciary must take. The first is the constitutional oath that so many of you are familiar with that applies to all three branches of the government. The second oath is one that applies just to federal judges.

Both of the oaths date from the founding of the Republic; the judicial oath dates from 1789. And both of these oaths remind us that we as a people are bound together, we as a people find our self-definition, our respect, our heritage, and our destiny in the Constitution.

And so, Justice Gorsuch, there is one oath remaining for you to take -- the judicial oath -- before you may receive and accept your commission from the President of the United States.

Are you ready, Justice Gorsuch, to take the oath?

(The Oath is administered.)

JUDGE GORSUCH: I see before me so many to whom I owe so much. I know I would not be here today without your friendship and support. Thank you all from the bottom of my heart.

I want to thank the President for nominating me and for the great confidence and trust he's reposed in me. I want to thank the Vice President for his constant encouragement and friendship throughout this process.

It's not possible to mention here everyone I should mention, but I'd be remiss if I didn't thank the President's counsel, Don McGahn, and Mark Paoletta, the Vice President's counsel, and every single person in the White House Counsel's Office for their tremendous and tireless support. I want thank Kelly Ayotte and my day-to-day team for their humor, for their sage advice, for their faith, as we spent months and so many miles trooping together through the

Senate complex. I want to thank every single person -- and
there are so many -- in the White House and the Department of Justice who worked through so many late nights
and long weeks on my behalf.

I want to thank, too, Senator McConnell and Senator
Grassley and their excellent teams for their support and
leadership. And I must thank my former law clerks and my
dear friends who gave so much of themselves so selflessly
through these last three months. You are dear to me. This
is truly your doing, and this is your day.

I wish I could mention each of you by name, but you know
who you are and you know your names are etched in my
heart forever.

This process has reminded me just how outrageously
blessed I am in my law clerks, and my family, and my
friends. And I hope that I may continue to rely on each of
you as I face this new challenge.

To my former colleagues and the wonderful staff of the
10th Circuit, I thank you for your faithful service and your
friendship over so many years.

To my new the very warm welcome. I look forward to
many happy years together.

And I cannot tell you how honored I am to have here today
my mentor, Justice Kennedy, administer the judicial oath,
a beautiful oath, as he did for me 11 years ago when I became a Circuit judge.

To the Scalia family, I won't ever forget that the seat I inherit today is that of a very, very great man.

To my wife, Louise, and my daughters, Emma and Bindi, thank you for your perseverance and your patience, your courage and your love. I simply could not have attempted this without you.

And to the American people, I am humbled by the trust placed in me today. I will never forget that to whom much is given, much will be expected.

And I promise you that I will do all my powers permit to be a faithful servant of the Constitution and laws of this great nation.

Thank you. (Applause.)

END
11:21 A.M. EDT

Chapter 130

**REMARKS BY PRESIDENT TRUMP IN STRATEGIC
AND POLICY CEO DISCUSSION
OLD STATE DEPARTMENT LIBRARY
EISENHOWER EXECUTIVE OFFICE BUILDING**

11 April 2017

10:55 A.M. EDT

THE PRESIDENT: Thank you all for being here. Very much appreciate it. I want to thank Steve Schwarzman for putting together this very incredible group of world-class business leaders. That's what you are. Also, joining us are Secretary Betsy DeVos, Secretary Wilbur Ross, Secretary Elaine Chao, EPA Administrator Scott Pruitt, and my budget director, Mick Mulvaney. That's an easy job. Where's Mick? (Laughter.)

Such an easy job. It's the easiest job of anybody in the government -- right, Mick?

At the top of **our agenda** is the **creation of great high-paying jobs for American workers.** And we've made a lot of process [sic.]. You see what's going on; you see the numbers. We've created over 600,000 jobs already in a very short period of time, and it's going to really start catching on now, because some of the things that we've done are big league and they are catching on.

Already, we've created more than almost 600,000 jobs. And yesterday, Toyota just announced that it will invest more than $1.3 billion -- it's probably going to be $1.9

billion -- into its Georgetown, Kentucky plant, an investment that would not have been made if we didn't win the election.

We have a lot of work to do. In the last two decades, our nation has lost a third of its manufacturing jobs, and our business tax is one of the highest in the world. It actually is, of developed countries, the single highest tax anywhere in the world.

For too long, we've punished production in America and rewarded companies for leaving our country. **And we're going to reverse that**. We would reward companies, give them incentives to leave. NAFTA is a disaster. It's been a disaster from the day it was devised. And we're going to have some very pleasant surprises for you on NAFTA, that I can tell you.

My administration has **already taken historic action to unleash job creation**. We've signed dozens of bills and executive actions to reduce federal overreach and expand domestic production.

On the environment, we're going to be very, very careful on the environment. It's very important to me and the administration. But we've allowed a lot of companies to go back to work. They were being restricted; their jobs were being restricted. We've unleashed a lot of companies, especially right now in the energy sector -- you see what's going on there. It was impossible for people to do what they had to do, and now they can do it. It's all done.

We're also working to modernize our economy and harness the full potential of women in the workforce, which is crucial to our economic success. **Economic confidence**

is sweeping the nation. You saw the new survey that
came out. It's at 93 -- which is the highest it's ever been
-- 93 percent of manufacturers are optimistic about the
future. It was a 27 percent increase over two months ago
when it was also high because of the administration, and
much higher than it's ever been -- 93 percent. Highest it's
ever been.

This is just the beginning. We're going to reduce taxes. We're going to eliminate wasteful regulations, which
we've already done -- probably 25 percent. You can take
a look at **Dodd-Frank**. For the bankers in the room, they'll
be very happy because **we're really doing a major stream-
lining and, perhaps, elimination, and replacing it** with
something else. But that will be the minimum. But we're
doing a major elimination of the horrendous Dodd-Frank
regulations, keeping some obviously, but getting rid of
many.

And **we're going to put many millions of people back to
work**.

The **banks will be able to lend Again**. So many people
come to see me, I see them all the time -- small businesses
-- they're unable to borrow from banks. They never had
a problem five, six, seven, ten years ago. They had great
bankers. They had great relationships. Now they can't
borrow. And we're going to let the banks loan them money, and they can build their businesses.

So with your help and insights, we will use the private
sector innovation to drive job creation and reform government. A lot of reform. We have a computer system in
this country that's 40 years old. So when you hear we're
hacked and we're this, that -- we're like easy targets. And

one of the things we're doing, in fact -- we're working with a very, very wonderful woman from IBM, and others -- and others, okay? (Laughter.)

Many others. It's like when I said to Lockheed, I like the F-35 fighter jet, but then I said, but I also like the Boeing F-18. Okay? (Laughter.)

So I love your computers, but we're also looking at others, all right?

But we are. We're going to have a massive program to modernize our equipment -- ideally get brand-new equip-ment. The cost of maintaining our computers is a number that is so high that it's not even a believable number. Now, I've heard anywhere -- is this possible? -- from $39 billion to $89 billion a year. Is that even possible? That's for keeping our computers updated and running. And I think we can buy a whole new system for less money than that, wouldn't you say? I mean, I hope so. We'll give you $10 billion right now -- modernize it. (Laughter.)

So I want to thank everybody for being here. I know most of you. You really are the top. And I want to thank my friend, Jack Welch, for being with us too. I've known Jack so long. We did deals together, right? Trump International -- a big success -- and the other one on Park Avenue.

We had great success together with your real estate group who are terrific people. Dale Fry and everybody -- right? Terrific. And John. So I just want to thank you. You've been a special guy for a long time.

And we'll get down to business. Maybe before the media leaves, we can go around the room, and we'll just introduce. We all know Steve, and I want to thank you, Steve, for putting the group together.

MR. SCHWARZMAN: Thank you.

THE PRESIDENT: Would you like to say something while all those cameras are running?

MR. SCHWARZMAN: I think we should say that we've had a really interesting day so far. What we did is we divided into five groups, meeting with each of the five Secretaries that the President mentioned. It's an open discussion. The Secretaries presented what they were trying to achieve, and we had several people from the forum meeting with them and making comments on what they were doing to hopefully make their jobs better.

We've been looking at trade, education and workforce development, energy and the environment, regulatory reform, and infrastructure.

All these things are really important, and we're focused. The people in the administration are also focused. And working together, hopefully we'll have a bunch of really good outcomes.

THE PRESIDENT: We will.

MR. LESSER: Rich Lesser, Boston Consulting Group.

MR. COSGROVE: Toby Cosgrove, Cleveland Clinic.

MS. ROMETTY: Ginni Rometty, IBM.

MS. BARRA: Mary Barra, General Motors.

MR. ATKINS: Paul Atkins, Patomak Global Partners.

MR. YERGIN: Dan Yergin, IHS Markit.

MR. PRUITT: Scott Pruitt, EPA Administrator.

MR. FINK: Larry Fink, BlackRock.

MR. WARSH: Kevin Warsh, Stanford University.

MR. WEINBERGER: Mark Weinberger, EY.

MR. MCNERNEY: Jim McNerney, Ex, Boeing.

MR. MCMILLION: Doug McMillon, Walmart.

MS. NOOYI: Indra Nooyi, PepsiCo.

MR. ROSE: Matt Rose, BNSF.

MR. HOWARD: Philip Howard, (inaudible).

MR. OGUNLESI: Bayo Ogunlesi, Global Infrastructure Partners.

THE PRESIDENT: Okay. Thank you very much. Thank you very much. Thank you.

END
11:02 A.M. EDT

Chapter 131

**JOINT PRESS CONFERENCE OF PRESIDENT TRUMP AND
NATO SECRETARY GENERAL STOLTENBERG
EAST ROOM**

12 April 2017

4:03 P.M. EDT

PRESIDENT TRUMP: Thank you. Secretary General
Stoltenberg, it's a pleasure to welcome you to the White
House -- especially at such an important moment in our
great Alliance.

I also want to acknowledge the great work being done
by our Secretary of State, Rex Tillerson, to strengthen the
NATO Alliance, as well as the Secretary's trip to Moscow to
promote the security interest of the United States and its
allies. He did a terrific job. Just watched parts of it -- an
absolutely terrific job.

Sixty-eight years ago this month, not far from where we
are gathered today, President Harry Truman spoke at the
signing of the North Atlantic Treaty. In the nearly seven
decades since Harry Truman spoke those words, the NATO
Alliance has been the bulwark of international peace and
security.

NATO allies defeated communism and liberated the captive
nations of the Cold War. They secured the longest period
of unbroken peace that Europe has ever known. This enduring partnership rooted out of so many different things,
but our common security is always number one, and our

common devotion to human dignity and freedom.

Since 1949, the NATO member states have more than doubled, increasing from 12 to 28. On Monday, I signed the protocol to approve the 29th -- the country of Montenegro. In the coming months and years, I'll work closely with all of our NATO allies to enhance this partnership and to adapt to the challenges of the future -- of which there will be many. This includes upgrading NATO to focus on today's most pressing security and all of its challenges, including migration and terrorism.

We must also work together to resolve the disaster currently taking place in Syria. We are grateful for the support of NATO members and partners in their condemnation of Assad's murderous attack, using the most horrible weapons. The vicious slaughter of innocent civilians with chemical weapons, including the barbaric killing of small and helpless children and babies, must be forcefully rejected by any nation that values human life. It is time to end this brutal civil war, defeat terrorists, and allow refugees to return home.

In facing our common challenges, we must also ensure that NATO members meet their financial obligations and pay what they owe. Many have not been doing that. The Secretary General and I agree that other member nations must satisfy their responsibility to contribute 2 percent of GDP to defense. If other countries make their fair share, instead of relying on the United States to make up the difference, we will all be much more secure and our partnership will be made that much stronger.

The Secretary General and I had a productive discussion about what more NATO can do in the fight against terrorism. I complained about that a long time ago and they made a change, and now they do fight terrorism. I said it was obsolete; it's no longer obsolete. It's my hope that NATO will take on an increased role in supporting our Iraqi partners in their battle against ISIS. I'm also sending General McMaster to Afghanistan to find out how we can make progress alongside our Afghan partners and NATO allies.

Every generation has strived to adapt the NATO Alliance to meet the challenges of their times -- and on my visit to Brussels this spring -- I look very much forward to -- we will work together to do the same. We must not be trapped by the tired thinking that so many have, but apply new solutions to face new circumstances. And that's all throughout the world. We're not here to stand on ceremony but to develop real strategies to achieve safety, security and peace. We're here to protect the freedom and prosperity of our citizens and to give them the future they so richly deserve.

Secretary General, I'm honored to have you here today, and to reaffirm our commitment to this Alliance and to the enduring values that we proudly -- and I mean, very proudly -- share. Thank you very much. Thank you for being here.

SECRETARY GENERAL STOLTENBERG: Thank you so much, sir, Mr. President.

We just had an excellent and very productive meeting, and it's really an honor to meet you for the first time here in the White House.

We agree that NATO is a bedrock of security, both for Europe and for the United States. Two world wars and a

Cold War have taught us all that peace in Europe is not only important for Europeans but is also important for the prosperity and the security of North America. So a strong NATO is good for Europe, but a strong NATO is also good for the United States.

And, therefore, I welcome the very strong commitment of the United States to the security of Europe. We see this commitment not only in words but also in deeds. Over the past months, thousands of U.S. troops have been deploying to Europe, a clear demonstration that America stands with allies to protect peace and defend our freedom. And yesterday, you announced the completion of the ratification of Montenegro's membership in NATO, another expression of your strong commitment to Europe and to the transatlantic bond. And we thank you for that.

In a more dangerous and more unpredictable world, it is important to have friends and allies. And in NATO, America has the best friends and the best allies in the world. Together, we represent half of the world's economic and military power. No other superpower has ever had such a strategic advantage. This makes the United States stronger and safer.

We saw that after the 9/11 attacks on the United States. That was the first time NATO invoked our Article 5, the collective defense clause. Allies sent AWACS surveillance planes to help patrol American skies, and we launched NATO's biggest military operation ever in Afghanistan. Hundreds of thousands of Europeans and Canadian soldiers have served shoulder-to-shoulder with American troops. More than a thousand have paid the ultimate price.

Earlier today, I laid a wreath at Arlington National Cemetery in tribute to the fallen. It was a deeply moving experience. We owe it to our servicemen and women to preserve the hard-earned gains we have made together in Afghanistan. We were reminded of their sacrifice just this week when a U.S. soldier was killed there fighting ISIL. Our mission in Afghanistan is a major contribution to the fight against international terrorism.

NATO plays a key role in many other ways also. All NATO allies are part of the global coalition to counter ISIL, and NATO provides support to the coalition with training for Iraqi forces in their fight against terrorists and more intelligence-sharing. And you are right, we have established a new division for intelligence, which enhances our ability to fight terrorism, and working together in the Alliance to fight terrorism in an even more effective way.

But we agreed today, you and I, that NATO can, and must, do more in the global fight against terrorism. In the fight against terrorism, training local forces is one of the best weapons we have. NATO has the experience, the expertise, and the staying power to make a real difference, and fighting terrorism will be an important topic when NATO leaders meet in Brussels in May.

The other major topic will be fair burden-sharing in our Alliance. And we had a total discussion on this issue today. And, Mr. President, I thank you for your attention to this issue. We are already seeing the effect of your strong focus on the importance of burden-sharing in the Alliance. We agree that allies need to redouble their efforts to meet the pledge we all made in 2014 to invest more in our Alliance.

It is about spending more on defense. It is about delivering the capabilities we need. And it is about contributing forces to NATO missions and operations. This means cash, capabilities, and contributions.

Fair burden-sharing has been my top priority since taking office. We have now turned a corner. In 2016, for the first time in many years, we saw an increase in defense spending across European allies and Canada -- a real increase of 3.8 percent or $10 billion more for our defense. We are now working to keep up the momentum, including by developing national plans outlining how to make good on what we agreed in 2014. We know that we all need to contribute our fair share because we need to keep our nations safe in a more dangerous world.

We discussed many different topics during our meeting today, including the horrendous use of chemical weapons in Syria. Any use of chemical weapons is unacceptable, cannot go unanswered, and those responsible must be held accountable.

So, Mr. President, thank you once again. I look forward to working with you to keeping the Alliance strong, and I look forward to welcoming you to Brussels in May when heads of state and government in the Alliance meet there to address the challenges and the need to continue to adapt the Alliance to a more challenging security environment, and to respond both to the need for fair burden-sharing, and stepping up our efforts to fight international terrorism. So thank you, once again.

THE PRESIDENT: Thank you very much. Great. Thank you. So we'll have a couple of questions.

Jeff Mason.

Q   Thank you. Thank you, Mr. President. I'd like to ask
you about two topics, if I may. First, has your view of
Vladimir Putin changed after what's happened in Syria? And what is the United States prepared to do if he
continues to support Assad?

And on a separate question, have you made a deal after
your chat last night with the President of China, about China helping to reign in North Korea? And is that one reason
you've decided not to label Beijing a currency manipulator?

THE PRESIDENT: Well, I'll be speaking to -- do you want to
go ahead. Go ahead.

Q   May I? For the Secretary General, do you believe NATO
should continue to bolster its presence along the Alliance's
eastern border? And do you have -- are you confident that
you have President Trump and the United States' support
for that? Thank you.

THE PRESIDENT: I'll be speaking with Rex Tillerson in a
little while -- he's calling in. I think he had a very successful meeting in Russia. We'll see. We'll see the end result,
which will be in a long period of time, perhaps. But the
end result is what's most important -- not just talk. And I
think that, based on everything I'm hearing, things went
pretty well, maybe better than anticipated.

It would be wonderful, as we were discussing just a little
while ago, if NATO and our country could get along with
Russia. Right now, we're not getting along with Russia at
all. We may be at an all-time low in terms of a relationship

with Russia. This has built for a long period of time. But we're going to see what happens. Putin is the leader of Russia. Russia is a strong country. We're a very, very strong country. We're going to see how that all works out. Last night, separately, I spoke with a man that I've gotten to know. I don't know Putin, but I do know this gentleman -- I've spent a lot of time with him over the last two days, and he is the President of China. You were there --most of you were there, and it was quite an interesting period of time.

President Xi wants to do the right thing. We had a very good bonding. I think we had a very good chemistry to-gether. I think he wants to help us with North Korea. We talked trade. We talked a lot of things. And I said, the way you're going to make a good trade deal is to help us with North Korea; otherwise we're just going to go it alone. That will be all right, too. But going it alone means going it with lots of other nations.

But I was very impressed with President Xi, and I think he means well and I think he wants to help. We'll see wheth-er or not he does.

Q   Do you feel like you have a deal with him? And if I could just --

THE PRESIDENT: Excuse me?

Q   Do you feel like you have a deal with him in terms of the currency manipulation designation? And have your views changed on Putin?

THE PRESIDENT: We're going to see, we're going to see about that. And I'll also see about Putin over a period of

time. It would be a fantastic thing if we got along with
Putin and if we got along with Russia. And that could happen, and it may not happen, it may be just the opposite.
I can only tell you what I would like to do. I would love to
be able to get along with everybody. Right now, the world
is a mess. But I think by the time we finish, I think it's going to be a lot better place to live. And I can tell you that,
speaking for myself, by the time I'm finished, it's going
to be a lot better place to live in -- because right now it's
nasty.

SECRETARY GENERAL STOLTENBERG: NATO is in the process of implementing the biggest reinforcement of our
collective defense since the end of the Cold War. And one
element of that is to increase our military presence in the
eastern part of the Alliance. And we are now deploying
four battle groups to the three Baltic countries and Poland,
and there have also been more U.S. forces in that part of
Europe.

And this is the first time in many, many years that we see
an increase in the military presence of the United States
in Europe. So we are increasing our presence, and we're
also increasing the readiness and the preparedness of our
forces so we can quickly reinforce if needed.

We consider the presence we will have when the four
battle groups are in place as sufficient given the current
security situation in Europe. But, of course, we will assess
the situation and follow the developments very closely.
The message from NATO is that what we do is proportionate; it is defensive. And we don't want a new Cold
War. We don't want a new arms race. And actually we
strongly believe that there is no contradiction between a
strong NATO, a credible deterrence on defense, and politi-

cal dialogue with Russia. Actually, we believe that a precondition for the political dialogue with Russia is that we are strong and that we are united. But based on that, we can talk to Russia because Russia is our neighbor, Russia is here to stay, so we have to find ways to manage our relationship with Russia.

And I am absolutely certain that the United States supports this approach -- partly because the United States is contributing with forces to our enhanced presence in the eastern part of the Alliance and also in the southeast of the Alliance in Romania, and the United States and the President has clearly expressed that they want dialogue with Russia, but based on unity and strength in the Alliance.

Then the next question is from Jon Sopel.

Q   Thank you very much. Secretary General, how long do you think it will take you to persuade the other European countries to burden-share? And what are you going to do to persuade them?

Mr. President, could I ask you --

PRESIDENT TRUMP: I like that question. (Laughter.)

Q   I'm here to help. (Laughter.)

And, Mr. President, do you think it's conceivable, what's your instinct -- was it possible that Syrian forces could have launched that attack in Idlib last week without the Russians knowing? And have you been disappointed, surprised by Vladimir Putin's reaction since then?

Thank you very much.

PRESIDENT TRUMP: I think it's certainly possible; I think it's probably unlikely. And I know they're doing investigations into that right now. I would like to think that they didn't know, but certainly they could have. They were there. So we'll find out. General Mattis is looking into it with the entire Pentagon group that does that kind of work.

So it was very disappointing to see. It's disappointing no matter who does it, but when you get into the gases -- especially that form -- it's vicious and violent. And everybody in this room saw it all too many times over the last three or four days -- young children dying, babies dying, fathers holding children in their arms that were dead. Dead children -- there can't be a worse sight, and it shouldn't be allowed. That's a butcher. That's a butcher.

So I felt we had to do something about it. I have absolutely no doubt we did the right thing, and it was very, very successfully done, as you well know. Thank you.

SECRETARY GENERAL STOLTENBERG: On defense spending and burden-sharing, that has been my top priority. I have raised it in all my meetings, in all capitals I visited, with Prime Ministers, Presidents, ministers of finance and, of course also defense and foreign ministers. And I expect, of course, all allies to make good on what they decided back in 2014.

And the very strong and clear message from President Trump has been very helpful. So now we see that things are starting to move in the right direction. For the first time after many, many years of decline in defense spending, we now see an increase in defense spending across Europe and Canada. So they have started to move in

the right direction -- 3.8 percent real increase in defense
spending across Europe and Canada is a significant step in
the right direction. It's not enough. We still have a long
way to go, but at least they have turned a corner -- the
European allies have turned a corner. Instead of reducing
defense spending, they have started to increase defense
spending.

Then I think it is important to remember that this something the Europeans do because they know that this is in
their own security interest. It is in their interest to invest
more in Europe defense because the world has become
more dangerous.

Many European allies, of course, reduced -- or all European
allies reduced defense spending after the end of the Cold
War because then tensions went down. But if you are de-
creasing defense spending when tensions are going down,
then you have to be able to increase the defense spending
when tensions are going up. And now they are going up.
So we have still a long way to go, but I'm encouraged by
the fact that we have started to move in the right direction. And last year there were five allies spending 2 percent. This year Romania has declared that they will reach
2 percent. Next year Latvia and Lithuania will also reach
2 percent, so we go from five to eight -- which is at least
going in the right direction. But still we have some work to
do.

PRESIDENT TRUMP: And I did ask about all the money that
hasn't been paid over the years, will that money be coming
back. We'll be talking about that, right? (Laughter.)

We want to talk about that, too.

Anita Kumar, where are you?

Hi. McClatchy.

Q   Mr. President, what's your reaction to the U.N. (inaudible) overall? Can you talk a little bit about your reaction to China -- we're you aware that was going to happen? Did President Xi talk to you about that? And how does that affect your relationship?

PRESIDENT TRUMP: We did talk last night. I think it's wonderful that they abstained. As you know very few people expected that. And, no, I was not surprised that China did abstain. Very, very few people thought that that was going to happen. So we're honored by the vote. That's the vote that should have taken place.

Q   Mr. Secretary General, you talked a little bit about Moscow, about Russia. How do you (inaudible) the impression in general? They've been interfering in recent democratic elections -- how do you counter Moscow's --

SECRETARY GENERAL STOLTENBERG: The most important thing is to have a strong Alliance, to stay united, and be firm and predictable in our approach to Russia. And that means that we have to invest in our collective defense. That's exactly what we are doing. Deploy more troops in the eastern part of the Alliance, increase the readiness of our forces, and increase defense spending. And I welcome the very strong message from President Trump on the importance of increased defense spending.

We have started to do this, so we are implementing the biggest reinforcement of our collective defense since the end of the Cold War, providing credible deterrence. But at the same time, we have to find ways to engage with Russia, to talk with Russia. Because Russia will not go away; Russia will be our biggest neighbor, and we have to find ways to live with them and to try to avoid a new Cold War, a new arms race.

And that's exactly why I am very much in favor of what we call the dual-track approach to Russia. And as a former Norwegian politician, I have the experience to work with the Russians, because Norway is bordering Russia. And Norway was able, even during the Cold War, to develop, I would call it, a pragmatic working relationship with Russia, cooperating with them on energy, on border issues, on environment, on fishery, and also in military affairs. And that was not despite our membership in NATO, but it was because of our membership in NATO. Because NATO provided the strength, the predictability, the platform for a small country to have a political dialogue with Russia.

So I strongly believe that the only way to deter Russia is to be strong. But the only way to avoid a new Cold War, avoid a new arms race and avoid increasing tensions is to continue to engage Russia is a political dialogue, and to make sure that what we do is defensive and proportionate in response to a more assertive Russia.

Q   Thank you. Mr. President, I'm from Norway. Russia is our neighboring country. What do you think Europe has to fear from Russia if this tension continues?

PRESIDENT TRUMP: Say it --

Q   What do you think that European countries have to fear from Russia if this tension continues?

PRESIDENT TRUMP: I cannot hear. I cannot understand --

SECRETARY GENERAL STOLTENBERG: She asked --

Q   I'll do it again. What do you think European countries have to fear from Russia if this tension continues to escalate?

And for you, Mr. Secretary General, the President has said the attack in Syria last week was warranted and was also an attack on U.S. allies. Do you think that this attack was warranted? And do you see NATO playing any supporting role in future actions in Syria?

PRESIDENT TRUMP: Well, I want to just start by saying hopefully they're going to have to fear nothing, ultimately. Right now there is a fear, and there are problems -- there are certainly problems. But ultimately, I hope that there won't be a fear and there won't be problems, and the world can get along. That would be the ideal situation. It's crazy what's going on -- whether it's the Middle East or you look at -- no matter where the -- Ukraine -- you look at -- whatever you look at, it's got problems, so many problems. And ultimately, I believe that we are going to get rid of most of those problems, and there won't be fear of anybody. That's the way it should be.

We have a very big problem in North Korea. And, as I said, I really think that China is going to try very hard, and has already started. A lot of the coal boats have already been turned back -- you saw that yesterday and today -- they've been turned back. The vast amount of coal that comes out of North Korea going to China, they've turned back the boats. That's a big step, and they have many other steps that I know about.

So we'll see what happens. It may be effective, it may not be effective. If it's not effective, we will be effective, I can promise you that. Thank you.

SECRETARY GENERAL STOLTENBERG: NATO has constantly condemned the use of chemical weapons in Syria. And the use of chemical weapons is horrendous and it's a clear violation of international law. And any use of chemical weapons is unacceptable and cannot go unanswered, so those responsible must be held accountable.

The strike against the airbase in Syria was a U.S. operation based on U.S. intelligence. But you have seen that within the Alliance, this has been something which has been met with a lot of understanding because NATO allies do not accept that chemical weapons are used. And therefore we also strongly support the efforts of the fact-finding com-mission to try to find out actually what happened and to make sure that we don't see any use of chemical weapons in the future.

PRESIDENT TRUMP: Thank you very much. Thank you.

END
4:34 P.M. EDT

Chapter 132

**REMARKS BY PRESIDENT TRUMP IN MEETING
WITH I-85 BRIDGE FIRST RESPONDERS
ROOSEVELT ROOM**

13 April 2017

2:26 P.M. EDT

THE PRESIDENT: Thank you, everybody. Sit down, please. Come on, get up here with me, everybody.

CHIEF BAKER: Sir, I bring you greetings on behalf of our honorable mayor, Mayor Kasim Reed. And our men and women of the Atlanta Fire Rescue Department would like to present you with a token of our appreciation.

THE PRESIDENT: That is beautiful. I think I should leave it right here, right? It fits so well. Thank you.

CHIEF BAKER: Thank you, sir.

THE PRESIDENT: Thank you very much. I didn't know I was going to get such a nice -- that is fantastic. Thank you, how are you?

CHIEF BAKER: I'm fine, sir.

THE PRESIDENT: We're going to go around and introduce ourselves, okay? We'll do this first. You know, these folks back here, they're very famous -- most of them -- it's called the media. (Laughter.)

They're very honorable people. But you are more honorable, I can tell you that.

CHIEF BAKER: Thank you, sir.

THE PRESIDENT: So I'm honored to be here with you today
and welcome you to the White House. The heroes who responded to the terrible bridge collapse on I-85 two weeks
ago in Atlanta. That was something. The whole world was
watching that one. Today we're joined by members of the
Georgia State Patrol, the Atlanta Fire Rescue Department,
and the Atlanta Police Department -- great people. On
that day, Georgia State police and Atlanta police took fast
action to get motorists away from danger. Then, our brave
fire-fighters battled 40-foot flames, which was incredible. What was the reason for those flames? It was something underneath that just was very combustible?

CHIEF BAKER: Yes, sir.

THE PRESIDENT: Yeah, those flames were amazing. They
pulled back, by battalion chiefs, and just minutes before
the bridge itself collapsed and everybody was safe. That
was an amazing thing, and everybody was watching. Your
skill and courage saved many lives and represented true
strength, and the true strength of America. Really great
job, fellas. I'm proud of you. Great job.

To the people of Georgia who were affected by the collapse, my administration stands with you. We've already
made a $10 million emergency relief fund available. And I
called your governor, who I know very well -- he's a terrific
guy -- and I approved it literally the day that it happened. I
had a feeling you'd need a little money -- (laughter) -- because I look like a big money deal, right, Elaine? But I

approved it immediately, and Elaine took care of it, and we gave fast action.

What happened in **Atlanta is a painful reminder of the critical importance of infrastructure**. We're going to be doing a lot with infrastructure. You'll be seeing that over the coming weeks -- a tremendous amount. I'm committed to funding a massive nationwide infrastructure program to rebuild, repair, and construct the roads and bridges of the future of this country. **This is necessary as a matter of both safety and economic growth, and it's necessary to improve our quality of life as Americans**.

We will also continue to seek proper funding for law enforcement and public safety in our country. On behalf of the entire nation, I salute you -- you're really amazing people -- and I honor your service. **I pledge** that you will have the support of our country -- the police, the fire-fighters, first responders -- you will always have the support of President Trump. I think you know that very well. And I thank you for the great job and the fast action. Really fantastic. A lot of bravery.

Maybe we could just go around and introduce yourselves. And, who knows, maybe you'll become a movie star after this. (Laughter.)

After all this, you'll become a movie star. If they like the way you look or sound, you'll become a star.

Go ahead.

CHIEF BAKER: Well, thank you again, sir. My name is Joel Baker, the Fire Chief of the City of Atlanta Fire Rescue Department.

THE PRESIDENT: And how tall are you, Joel?

CHIEF BAKER: I'm 6'6", sir.

THE PRESIDENT: That's all? I thought it was much more than that. I think you're taller than that. (Laughter.)

Okay, good. Thank you very much. I appreciate it.

Go ahead.

MR. BURKETT: I'm Trooper Thomas Burkett with the Georgia State Patrol.

MR. HEALD: And I'm Sergeant Ryan Heald from the Atlanta Police Department.

MR. MCLEMORE: I'm Battalion Chief James McLemore from the Atlanta Fire Rescue Department.

MR. GIUNTA: I'm Trooper John Giunta with the Georgia State Patrol.

MR. CAMPBELL: I'm Sergeant Anthony Campbell, Atlanta Fire Rescue Airport Division.

MR. BAKER: I'm senior police officer Michael Baker from the Atlanta Police Department.

SECRETARY CHAO: Elaine Chao, Secretary of Transportation.

MR. ADKINS: Captain Arthur Adkins, Atlanta Fire Rescue Department.

MR. TISDALE: I'm Trooper Harold Tisdale, Jr. with the Georgia State Patrol.

MR. MCKOY: Trooper First Class Kendell McKoy, Georgia State Patrol.

MR. BOSSERT: I'm Tom Bossert. I'm the President's Homeland Security Advisor.

MR. HATCHER: Battalion Chief Douglas Hatcher, Atlanta Fire Rescue Department.

MR. KUSRA: Sergeant First Class Thomas Kustra with Georgia State Patrol.

MR. BRYANT: Assistant Chief of Atlanta Police Department, Rodney Bryant.

THE PRESIDENT: Great, Rodney. Well, thank you very much. So who's the bravest person in this room? That's what I want to know. Raise your hands if you're the bravest person. Huh? Maybe it's -- (laughter) -- I thought so. I thought so.

SECRETARY CHAO: Do you want --

THE PRESIDENT: Go ahead.

MR. CRONIN: Sergeant First Class John Cronin, Georgia State Patrol.

MR. SEVERANCE: Officer Ryan Severance with the Atlanta Police Department.

THE PRESIDENT: Elaine, would you like to say something?

SECRETARY CHAO: Mr. President, beside you and around you are true heroes of our country. They demonstrate courage, steadfastness, commitment, and fealty to their oaths to serve our communities in need.

This fire was reported at 6:12 p.m., right in the middle of rush hour, on March 30th. By 6:20, this team was on site addressing the issues. Governor Nathan Deal also deserves some credit because he has, as a matter of policy, pre-positioned state troopers around I-85 to move any traffic incident right out of the way. So that helped a great deal. By 7:00, the bridge had collapsed. By 8:00, these brave men, leaders of their own communities, basically had the fire under control. The U.S. Department of Transportation was on site, and we worked hand-in-hand with these great heroes. And as you mentioned, $10 million from your administration went out within one hour of the governor making this request.

The good story following all of this is also that the repairs and recovery of this whole scene will occur very quickly. You will like them, because they will come in under budget and on time.

THE PRESIDENT: That's good. I love to hear the words "under budget" and "under schedule," right? (Laughter.)

We used to call it "ahead of schedule." Now we say "under schedule." But that will be great.

And I have to tell you, Governor Nathan Deal did call me immediately as this was happening, and he sort of said, could you be ready? Because we're going to need some emergency money fast. And we were ready and we got him the money immediately.

And again, we want to thank everybody in the room very much. And, Secretary, congratulations.

SECRETARY CHAO: Not at all. Again, I told them that you are really approachable and that you would enjoy meeting them so much. They were a little bit apprehensive about meeting you, so they're just so thrilled. And Chief Baker and also Chief Bryant, these are the two leaders here, and they both said what an honor it is to be at the White House, to be with you. And you have done the first responder community a tremendous honor by honoring them. And they want to make sure -- because they're saying that you are sending a message to all the first responders that you value them. So, Chief Bryant, why don't you say that to the President? (Laughter.)

CHIEF BRYANT: Yes, ma'am. I stand with her, Mr. President, that this is not only a great day for the city of Atlanta and Atlanta Fire Rescue Department, but it's a great day for all the public safety personnel throughout the country to include the department of fire, police, state patrols throughout the country, corrections department. But all the public safety really appreciate the opportunity that you're recognizing public safety members.

THE PRESIDENT: Well, Chief, I have great respect for the people that do what you do. It's amazing bravery. And the speed is incredible. So, again, I want to thank you. And I think what we'll do is, when we're finished here we'll talk, and then, unless you don't want to do this, but I know you do, we'll go right across the hall to the Oval Office and we'll have some pictures. Is that okay? The Oval Office. It is -- believe me, I've been in a lot of good offices. (Laughter.)

It is a special office, okay? So we'll go over there, we'll take some pictures, okay?

CHIEF BRYANT: Yes, sir.

THE PRESIDENT: Thank you all very much.

Q   (Inaudible) bomb in Afghanistan?

THE PRESIDENT: It was really another successful
job. We're very, very proud of our military. Just like we're
proud of the folks in this room, we're so proud of our military. And it was another successful event.

Q   Did you authorize this --

THE PRESIDENT: Everybody knows exactly what happened. And what I do is I authorize my military. We have
the greatest military in the world, and they've done their
job as usual. So we have given them total authorization,
and that's what they're doing. And, frankly, that's why
they've been so successful lately. If you look at what's
happened over the last eight weeks and compare that really to what's happened over the last eight years, you'll see
there's a tremendous difference -- tremendous difference.
So we have incredible leaders in the military, and we have
incredible military. And we are very proud of them. And
this was another very, very successful mission.

Thank you very much.

Q   Does this send a message to North Korea?

THE PRESIDENT: I don't know if this sends a message. It
doesn't make any difference if it does or not. North Korea
is a problem. The problem will be taken care of. I will say

this: I think China has really been working very hard. I have really gotten to like and respect, as you know, President Xi. He's a terrific person. We spent a lot of time together in **Florida.** And he's a very special man, so we'll see how it goes. I think he's going to try very hard.

Thank you.

END
2:37 P.M. EDT

Chapter 133

14 April 2017

Transcript:

My fellow Americans,
This is a season of great hope.

This week, Jewish families across our country, and around the world, celebrate Passover and retell the story of God's deliverance of the Jewish people.

The story of the Exodus is a story of freedom. It is the story of an incredible people who were liberated from oppression and raised up the face of humankind.

Down through the centuries, the Jewish People have lived through one persecution after another—and yet, they persevered and thrived and uplifted the world beyond measure. And now, the State of Israel stands as a monument to their faith and endurance.

Another day of faith and celebration is also upon us.

This Easter Sunday, Christians celebrate the resurrection of Christ and the promise of eternal salvation. It is a holy day of reverence and worship; it is a sacred time that fills the spirit of our Nation with the faith of our people.

America is a Nation of believers.

As families gather in houses of worship across the Nation, we are grateful for the tremendous blessings of this land, our home. We have a beautiful country, an abundant countryside, and an amazing people with a truly bright and wonderful future.

From the beginning, America has been a place that has cherished the freedom of worship. That is the promise the first settlers saw in our vast continent—and it is the promise that our bravest warriors have protected for all of our citizens in centuries since, a long time ago.

Sadly, many around the globe do not enjoy this freedom— and one of the gravest threats to religious freedom remains the threat of terror.

On Palm Sunday, as Christians around the world celebrate the beginning of Holy Week, ISIS murdered at least 45 people and injured over 100 others at two Christian churches in Egypt.

We condemn this barbaric attack. We mourn for those who lost loved ones. And we pray for the strength and wisdom to achieve a better tomorrow—one where good people of all faiths, Christians and Muslims and Jewish and Hindu, can follow their hearts and worship according to their conscience.

With God's grace, life always triumphs over death, freedom overcomes oppression, and faith extinguishes fear. This is the source of our hope—and our confidence in the future. I also want to give a special message to those struggling Americans who have felt for too long the bitter taste of hardship. I want you to know: this White House is fighting for you. We are fighting for every American who has been left behind. We are fighting for the right of all citizens to enjoy safety and peace—and to work and live with the dignity that all Children of God are entitled to know.

As long as we have faith in each other, and trust in God, we will succeed.

Thank you. Have a Happy Easter, and a Happy Passover.

God bless you. And God bless America.

Chapter 134

16 April 2017

THE VICE PRESIDENT: Marc, thank you for that kind introduction. Thank you for your leadership of the U.S. embassy as our charge d'affaires. Thank you for your long career in the Asian Pacific representing the United States of America in so many different capacities. I'm grateful for your service as I know is all of our administration. Thank you, Marc.

To Ambassador Ahn Ho-young, members of the American Chamber of Commerce in Korea, distinguished leaders of the American and South Korean business communities, honored guests, it is an honor to be here with you today for my first stop in the Asian Pacific as Vice President of the United States of America. It's here in South Korea that we came first. (Applause.)

And it's a special honor for me to have with us today a man who I've had the opportunity to spend time with, traveling around, going to the Demilitarized Zone, being briefed on the circumstances taking place across this region. To General Vince Brooks, the commander of the Combined Forces Command of U.S. Forces Korea, who proudly leads some 37,500 U.S. soldiers, sailors, airmen, Marines in close cooperation with more than 600,000 courageous South Korean forces, General, we are grateful for your leadership and even more grateful for those who serve under your command. (Applause.)

I bring greetings this morning from the 45th President of the United States of America, President Donald Trump. The President asked me to come here to South Korea as a sign of our commitment and his personal commitment to the United States' long-term alliance with this great country and to our not only strategic but economic partnership with South Korea.

The bonds of security and commerce between our nations stretch back for decades. More than 60 years ago, the United States helped establish the foundation for South Korea's security and economic strength through great sacrifice. And ever since the relationship between our two countries has grown for the benefit of both our nations and all who call them home.

Yesterday I had the privilege to meet with Acting President Hwang Kyo-ahn and leaders of the National Assembly here in South Korea. My message to them, to the people of South Korea, to the business enterprises in this country, and to all of you, on behalf of the President of the United States is simply this: We are with you 100 percent. (Applause.)

Don't doubt it for a second. Even in these challenging times we stand with you for a free and secure future. The alliance between South Korea and the United States is the linchpin of peace and security not only on the Korean Peninsula but indeed throughout the Asian Pacific. The United States' commitment to South Korea is ironclad and immutable. As I told acting President Hwang yesterday, our alliance will be stronger. Our nations will be safer, and the Asian Pacific will be more secure. And together we will address this nation's most dangerous and urgent threat to peace and security, the regime in North Korea, and we will address it together. (Applause.)

As examples we will continue to work closely with our military to deploy the THAAD missile defense system as a defensive measure, called for by the alliance for the alliance. We'll continue to evolve a comprehensive set of capabilities to ensure the security of South Korea.

And while all options are on the table, the United States will continue to marshal economic and diplomatic pressure from regional powers and the entire international community to demand that North Korea once and for all abandon its nuclear and ballistic missile programs, turn away from renewed hostility toward its neighbors, and end the repression of its own people. (Applause.)

As an example of that outreach, earlier this month President Trump met with President Xi of China at the Southern White House. The two leaders noted in their meeting, which was productive, the urgency of the threat posed by North Korea's weapons program. And both of them -- I'm pleased to say both of them -- reaffirmed both of our nations' commitment to a denuclearized Korean Peninsula.

Now, China has taken some initial steps to bring economic and diplomatic pressure on North Korea. And we welcome those steps. It's heartening to see China take these actions, and we're hopeful that they will do more in the days ahead.

While the United States is troubled by China's economic retaliation against businesses here in South Korea for taking appropriate steps to defend themselves, you may be assured we will continue to communicate to China that a better path for their country would be for them to join with us to address the circumstances in North Korea that make such defensive measures necessary.

Now while issues will remain, the President and I have great confidence that China will properly deal with North Korea. But as President Trump made it clear just a few days ago, if China is unable to deal with North Korea, the United States and our allies will.

Beyond the issues of security and stability, our alliance with South Korea is also grounded in the shared values of freedom, free markets, and a strong and vibrant economic partnership between our two nations and our people. The businesses represented here today -- American and Ko-rean -- have helped build a strong relationship between the United States and Korea. In fact, AMCHAM Korea has been here since the very beginning. Since your founding in 1953, you've brought together businesses large and small to invest in both of our economies. Today you boast roughly 700 members spanning dozens of industries, and you foster jobs and growth and prosperity on both sides of the Pacific.

And thank you. I want to thank all of you who came out here today and the businesses that I spent time with this morning over coffee for your insights -- American and Ko-rean companies, Ford, Boeing, Pfizer, Visa, and really all of you. You're pillars of our economy and pillars of a partner-ship between America and South Korea, and you have our thanks. (Applause.)

Each of these businesses creates jobs and drive innovation

in the United States and Korea. Each of you have done a tremendous work in strengthening the bond between our peoples over the last several decades. Today thanks in no smart to all of you, South Korea is, in fact, the United States' sixth largest trading partner. America's high quality products and services have made tremendous impact on South Korea's way of life. And South Korea's firms have made and continue to make significant contributions and investments in the American economy, as well.

Now last month marked the fifth anniversary of the implementation of the United States-Korea Free Trade Agreement. Since KORUS went into effect, our two-way trade in goods and services has grown by nearly $20 billion. The United States' goods and services exports have increased by more than 6 percent. Service exports alone have risen by nearly 30 percent to a record high of $21.6 billion. And today South Korea is one of the fastest growing sources of foreign direct investment in the United States of America with more than $40 billion and growing invested in the United States so far. And that's worth a round of applause. (Applause.)

But despite the strong economic ties between the United States and South Korea, we have to be honest about where our trade relationship is falling short. Most concerning is the fact that the United States' trade deficit with South Korea has more than doubled since KORUS came into effect. That's the hard truth of it.

And our businesses continue to face too many barriers to entry, which tilts the playing field against American workers and American growth. President Trump has made it clear that the United States will pursue and America First policy in trade and exchange. We'll pursue trade that is both free and fair, and that will be true in all of our trade relationships, including KORUS.

We're reviewing all of our trade agreements across the world to ensure that they benefit our economy as much as they benefit our trading partners. As members of the business community, President Trump and I value your continued input on the issues that you face. And we know that you can help us level that playing field between our two countries and move toward a system that will maximize jobs and growth and a brighter future for the people of the United States of America and the people of South Korea. And we will work with you toward that end as we reform KORUS in the days ahead. (Applause.)

The truth is a stronger American economy means a stronger economy for South Korea, and for all of our trading partners. And you'll be glad to know the United States will continue to be a driver of global growth. And under President Donald Trump, we'll drive that growth like never before. I promise you.

President Trump and our administration are working around the clock to pass an aggressive agenda to get the American economy moving again -- lower taxes, less regulation, better infrastructure, and a renewed focus on American energy. And tax reform will be one of our top priorities.

I don't have to tell you in this room how the American tax code tends to hamper the business community at home and abroad. The ability for American companies like those that are located here in South Korea to bring profits back to the United States of America is much in need of reform. Our corporate tax rate is actually one of the highest

in the developed world. It's more than 10 percent higher
than the tax rate here in South Korea.

Well, President Trump's tax plan will slash the corporate
rate, reform the tax code to make it simpler, flatter, and
fairer. Rest assured, our tax reform plan will make the
strongest economy in the world stronger still, and that will
benefit America and benefit all of America's trading partners.

The same is true of the President's actions to reduce the
regulatory burden in America. The President has already
ordered every agency in Washington, D.C. to find two regulations to get rid of before issuing any new ones. And
President Trump has already signed more than a dozen
bills turning back the last administration's mandates. And
we'll continue to work with Congress to slash through
mountains of red tape that are a barrier to economic
growth and jobs.

Make no mistake about it, under President Donald Trump,
over-regulations' days are over. And there's a new era of
jobs and growth and prosperity in the United States of
America.

Now, these are only a few of the policies that the
President and I could discuss today. There are many more
from healthcare to infrastructure. But I'm grateful to
have had the opportunity to meet with businesses -- great
American businesses included -- that are located here in
South Korea to reassure you that we're going to continue
to promote the policies in the United States of America
that will cause investment to occur and businesses to
thrive and jobs to be created.

Rest assured, President Trump's agenda will continue to renew America's reputation as the premier investment destination in the world, and as America grows, all of our partners will grow with us.

And our success will further strengthen the bond of commerce and the bond of friendship between the American people and the people of South Korea. Of that I'm very confident.

Today it's my privilege really to conclude by trip here to South Korea on behalf of President Donald Trump with a simple message to reaffirm the United States' enduring commitment to the security and prosperity of South Korea, and to assure the people of South Korea of our unbreakable bond.

We're bound together by our shared values. But also as I said yesterday following my meeting with acting President Hwang, we've also been bonded together by our shared sacrifice. A free and democratic South Korea was forged in the fires of sacrifice by soldiers from both of our lands. And my father was one of them. Sixty-five years ago Second Lieutenant Edward J. Pence, Jr., of the 45th Infantry Division of the United States Army, fought alongside brave South Korea forces to win the freedom of this land. It was my great privilege to stand with the General and look out over the landscape past the DMZ and see the very hills on which my father fought, Mount Baldy and Pork Chop Hill. For me, for my wife, for our two daughters, it was a deeply meaningful time.

My dad was able to come home to raise a family, but he had friends in uniform -- America and Korean -- who went home to eternity, and he carried the faces and the names of those heroes in his heart his whole life.

My dad any time -- and people would look at the medal
that he had earned over here and been awarded -- and an-
ytime anyone would refer to my dad as a hero, he'd shake
his head and say the heroes were the ones that didn't
come home. And he bore that burden his whole life. But I
can't help but feel that Dad looking down from Glory today
wouldn't be proud of their sacrifice and proud of his service in this great country. To see now more than six decades on the freedom that he fought and labored to win for
the people of South Korea continuing to thrive, continuing
to stand, continuing to prosper. Truly the friendship between our two nations -- our two free nations is as eternal
as the bonds between those who fought to win it.

As I said yesterday we have bled together. We have prospered together. And on that foundation, the people of
the United States of America and South Korea will face the
future together. With courage, determination and faith,
we go together. Katchi Kapshida.

Thank you very much and God bless you. (Applause.)

END

Chapter 135

**REMARKS BY THE VICE PRESIDENT AND MRS. PENCE
TO THE TROOPS, SEOUL, SOUTH KOREA
U.S. ARMY GARRISON YONGSAN
SEOUL, REPUBLIC OF KOREA**

16 April 2017

THE VICE PRESIDENT: Thank you so much, General
Brooks. It is an honor to be with you today on this Easter
Sunday, and let me invite a round of applause from all the
great soldiers and their families who are gathered here for
General Vincent Brooks, and the great leadership that he
provides here to United States Forces Korea. (Applause.)

General, we are proud -- grateful for your leadership.
To Chaplain Kim, to Chaplain Wasaki (ph), and to all of
those who made the service so special to us, my daughter
Audrey already told me that was one of the best sermons
she's heard in a year and a half. So what a special Easter
sermon. (Applause.)

And we are just honored to be with you all today and
looking forward just to some good food and to some good
fellowship. But it is a pleasure to be with you today. On
behalf of my wife, Karen, and our two daughters, happy
Easter in South Korea. It's a joy to be with you all. (Applause.)

I bring greetings this morning from your Commander-in-Chief, President Donald Trump. (Applause.)

I spoke to the President early today, and I spoke to him on

the way over. And he asked me to be here, and he told me in no uncertain terms to make sure that I told all of you we're proud of you, and we are grateful for your service to the United States of America on this frontier of freedom that is South Korea. (Applause.)

In fact, I can say with confidence that every American is PROUD of your service here, and the attention that this part of the world has gotten from people back home is probably no surprise to all of you who are gathered here today. This morning's provocation from the north is just the latest reminder of the risks each one of you face every day in the **defense of the freedom** of the people of South Korea and the **defense of America** in this part of the world. Your willingness to step forward, to serve, to stand firm without fear inspires our nation and inspires the world. And it's an honor for us to share this meal with you today. Thank you for your service. (Applause.)

And let me say, as the General mentioned, as proud parents of a United States Marine --

AUDIENCE MEMBER: Ooorahh! (Laughter.)

THE VICE PRESIDENT: It is the greatest privilege of my life to serve as Vice President to a President who cares so deeply about the men and women of our armed forces and their families.

Now days like today make me think of the separation that comes at special times of the year for those who serve. And so would all of you in uniform join me in giving a rousing round of applause to the family members who are here and the family members far away. We appreciate their service and their support as you serve our nation in uniform. (Applause.)

And let me **promise** those family members and all of you in uniform here today that under President Trump's leadership, we're going to rebuild our military. We're going to restore the **arsenal of democracy**. We're going to give our Soldiers, Sailors, Airmen, Marines, and Coast Guard the resources you need and deserve to accomplish the mission you are given and come home safe. That's a **promise** from your Commander-in-Chief. (Applause.)

This is a challenging time all over the world, but especially here in the Asia Pacific. The opportunity for me to be here today at such a time as this is a great privilege for me, but let me assure you under President Trump's leadership, our resolve has never been stronger. Our commitment to this historic alliance with the courageous people of South Korea has never been stronger. And with your help and with God's help, **freedom** will ever prevail on this peninsula. (Applause.)

But it is Easter Sunday, and as I look out at all these courageous Americans and courageous Koreans who are gathered here today, I'm deeply humbled. I truly am. We celebrate today what Karen and I and those of us gathered here recall as that Resurrection Sunday, and that worship service was so sublime.

But it puts me to mind of one of my favorite stories in the Old Book. It's the story of a moment where the Nazarene encountered a soldier. The soldier walked up to him and told him that he had someone ill in his home, and he asked if he might take action to be helpful. And as Jesus began to walk with him, he said, no, you don't need to come with me. He said, I'm a man under authority. He said, I tell one to do this and he does it. I tell another to do this and he does it. He said, you just say the word and that servant under my household will be healed.

The words that ever struck me from that story were there at that crossroads, the story recalls in a little town called Capernaum. It simply said that Jesus was amazed.

At no other point in any of the stories of his life do I hear that he was amazed, except when he was speaking to a soldier. Because he saw orientation to authority and he saw faith.

Let me say on this most holy of days, for those of us who claim Christ as Lord, we're amazed too. We're humbled. We look out today and we see courage writ large in the soldiers and the families who are gathered here. And I just want to assure you on behalf of the people all across the United States that in these troubled times, in this part of the world, your courage and your valor still amazes the American people.

So we just wanted to come and say thank you, say thank you for your service, and thank you, General, for your leadership and the leadership and service of all those represented here, carrying on a tradition and a commitment to freedom here on this peninsula that is now more than six decades in the running; and succeeding far beyond those who carved this free society in this ancient land could possibly have imagined, perhaps, is the American soldier shoulder-to-shoulder with the Korean people who fought for and won the freedom more than six decades ago.

And I stand before you today very moved on this Easter Sunday because one of those soldiers more than six days ago -- 60 years ago was my dad. As we landed today on the peninsula, I looked out at those rolling hills, and I thought about Second Lieutenant Edward J. Pence, who was with the 45th Infantry Division of the United States Army. Dad served here in combat. It was in this month -- this very week -- in 1953 that my dad was awarded a Bronze Star here in Korea for action in combat.

But like so many who have worn the uniform and come home, my dad didn't think the heroes were the ones that came home. Whenever he spoke of his time here in Korea, he spoke of the ones that didn't come home. He spoke of friends lost, sacrifices made. And so on this day I think of my dad, gone 29 years now, but still enshrined in the hearts of everyone in our family. And I think of what dad would be thinking about and I believe is thinking about as he looks down to see his third son return to that place that he left so many years ago, and to see that the sacrifices that were made here, and the commitment that endures here has resulted in a free and prosperous South Korea. And so it shall ever be.

So for the sake of all of you who wear the uniform today, for the sake of all who have gone before, thank you for your service and Happy Easter. (Applause.)

Now, the prayer-in-chief in our family is my wife, Karen. And she said that we could impose on her to maybe return thanks for this meal, and then we look forward to meeting as many of you as we have time to meet today. So, everyone, my wife, Karen Pence. (Applause.)

MRS. PENCE: If you would bow with me. Heavenly Father, we thank you for your son who died on the cross for each one of us in this room. We thank you for the privilege of being able to fellowship today together. Thank you for the sacrifices of the families here. And in this Month of the Military Child, thank you for the sacrifices that the children make as well.

And, Lord, we just thank you as well for the hands that prepared this wonderful meal. We pray that you would bless our conversation and that you would just pour out your blessings on these amazing people in this amazing country. In your son's name we pray, amen.

AUDIENCE MEMBERS: Amen.

THE VICE PRESIDENT: Thanks, everybody.

END

Chapter 136

**REMARKS TO THE TROOPS BY THE VICE PRESIDENT
WITH Q&A, DEMILITARIZED ZONE, SOUTH KOREA
FREEDOM HOUSE
DEMILITARIZED ZONE, REPUBLIC OF KOREA**

17 April 2017

THE VICE PRESIDENT: Thank you all for being here. It's my great honor to represent the President of the United States here in the Demilitarized Zone. And I'm very grateful for the leadership of General Brooks and General Lee and the ironclad and immutable alliance that is represented here by these two strong military leaders.

To stand here in this place to be able to (inaudible) of the commitment of the people of the United States to our long-term alliance for the people of South Korea is a great honor for me.

And I bring greetings to our soldiers here and to soldiers of South Korea from the President of the United States. We commend them for their vigilance here along this historic frontier of **freedom**, and we express the resolve of the people of the United States of America to stand together in the months and years ahead with the people of South Korea to both **preserve their freedom**, and ensure the objective of a denuclearized Korean Peninsula. It is an objective not just shared by the United States and the people of South Korea, but by our allies across the globe.

We are heartened by the support of allies across the Asia Pacific, including China, who will continue to advance this objective on the Korean Peninsula.

And I'm here to express the resolve of the people of the United States and the President of the United States to achieve that objective through peaceable means, through negotiations, but all options are on the table as we continue to stand shoulder-to-shoulder with the people of South Korea for the de-nuclearization of this peninsula and for the **long-term prosperity and freedom** of the people of South Korea.

Let me say it's also very humbling for me to be here because my father served here in Korea in the United States Army more than 64 years ago.

The General favored me this morning with a few reflections on my father's service here. And it seems altogether fitting that as Vice President I could be here to personally express the timeless bond between the people of South Korea and the people of the United States of America.

People across the world should know that the bonds between our people are not simply strategic and military and economic, but they are personal, and they span generations of Americans and South Koreans.

And on that foundation, **we will see freedom through**. We will see the interests of the **security and prosperity** of the people of South Korea. And in a word, we go together. Any questions?

Q   Mr. Vice President, question for you. You said that everything is still on the table. Does that include a potential U.S. pre-emptive strike?

And secondly on China, what concrete steps did China lay out to President Trump that led him to believe that China is working very hard to put pressure on North Korea?

THE VICE PRESIDENT: I think President Trump and President Xi had a very frank and productive discussion about a broad range of international issues, including the de-nuclearization of the Korean Peninsula. I know the President is hopeful that China will use its influence here on the Korean Peninsula with North Korea to achieve that objective.

And we are heartened by some initial steps that China has taken in this regard, but we look for them to do more. And our hope is that we'll be able -- working with China, working with our partners here in South Korea, working with Japan and other allies across the region -- to achieve this objective through peaceable means.

Q   And a pre-emptive strike would be on the table?

THE VICE PRESIDENT: As the President has made clear, we will never discuss military tactical decisions. But the President has made clear, our administration has made clear, we stand with the people of South Korea. And all options are on the table to achieve the objectives and ensure the security of the people of this country and the stability of this region.

Q   Mr. Vice President, do you have a message for the people on the other side of this line?

THE VICE PRESIDENT: I think the message of the people of the United States of America is that we seek peace, but **America has always sought peace through strength**. And my message here today standing with U.S. Forces Korea, standing with courageous soldiers from the Republic of Korea is a message of resolve.

The people of North Korea, the military of North Korea should not mistake the resolve of the United States of America to stand with our ally.

The alliance between South Korea and the United States is ironclad. We will fulfill that alliance for the sake of our people and the people of South Korea. And we will continue to stand strong to achieve our shared objective across this region and across the world of a denuclearized Korean Peninsula.

Q   Mr. Vice President, how is this a different policy that the Trump administration is pursuing compared to the Obama administration?

And why do you believe that you can trust China this time to follow through? Past administrations have sought help from China and they often haven't come through?

THE VICE PRESIDENT: I know President Trump is very hopeful that China will take actions necessary to bring about a change in policy in North Korea, an abandonment of its nuclear program and its ballistic missile program. We're hopeful that they'll use the extraordinary levers that they have and relationship they have with North Korea to achieve that objective.

But as the President has made very clear, either China will deal with this problem or the United States and our allies will.

Now with regard to a change, we have literally gone through decades -- it was more than some quarter century ago that we first learned of the presence of nuclear weapons on the Korean Peninsula in the possession of North Korea. There was an agreed framework. There was a period of strategic patience. But the era of strategic patience is over.

President Trump has made it clear that the patience of the United States and our allies in this region has run out, and we want to see change.

We want to see North Korea abandon its reckless path of the development of nuclear weapons. And also its continual use of and testing of ballistic missiles is unacceptable.

That clarity we hope will be received in North Korea, and that they will understand that the United States of America, the people of South Korea, our allies across the region are resolved to achieve our objectives through peaceable means or ultimately by whatever means are necessary to protect the interest, the security of the people of South Korea and to bring stability to the region.

END

Chapter 137

**REMARKS BY THE VICE PRESIDENT AND SOUTH KOREAN ACTING PRESIDENT HWANG AT A JOINT PRESS STATEMENT
THE PRIME MINISTER'S RESIDENCE
SEOUL, REPUBLIC OF KOREA**

17 April 2017

ACTING PRESIDENT HWANG: (As interpreted.) Good afternoon. First of all I would like to wholeheartedly welcome Vice President Pence on his first visit to Korea, and I would also like to extend my warmest welcome to his family and delegation.

Vice President Pence's late father was a Korean War veteran who had devoted himself to the defense of our freedom and democracy during the Korean War. And this morning, Vice President Pence visited the Demilitarized Zone to inspect our stalwart combined defense posture and reconfirm our strong will to deter North Korea. This symbolizes not only a special personal tie, but also the depth and sturdiness of our alliance that has lasted over 60 years.

In particular, at this time when the security situation on the Korean Peninsula is dire due to North Korea's nuclear and missile provocations, Vice President Pence's visit to Korea as his first destination in Asia since taking office shows the firm stance of the new U.S. administration on developing our alliance and responding to North Korea's nuclear and missile threats. As such, I believe Vice President Pence's visit is timely and meaningful.

Today, the Vice President and I shared the view that on the

basis of close cooperation and collaboration, the ROK-U.S. alliance has grown into an indispensable linchpin for peace and security on the Korean Peninsula and in Northeast Asia, as well as a successful strategic alliance that works together to resolve global challenges.

We have also reconfirmed our unwavering will to continue to make our alliance even stronger through further cooperation in the areas of security, economy and trade, and global issues.

Ten days ago on April 10th, I spoke with President Trump on the results of the U.S.-China summit and ways to work together going forward. Today with Vice President Pence we shared the understanding of the gravity and urgency of North Korea's nuclear and missile threat and agreed to double our efforts to change North Korea's strategic calculations by further tightening the global network of pressure on North Korea and thoroughly implementing sanctions under the unwavering principle of denying North Korea nuclear weapons.

Furthermore under the shared view that China's constructive efforts and role are critical, we applaud the results of the recent U.S.-China summit, and we will closely strengthen our cooperation with China. If North Korea commits another provocation, we will swiftly implement intensive punitive measures based on our cooperation with China.

At the same time in response to North Korea's continuously advancing nuclear and missile threat, we have agreed to continue to pursue various measures to strengthen our deterrence capabilities and combined defense posture to include extended deterrence. We have also agreed to further strengthen the readiness posture of the ROK-U.S.

alliance in response to North Korea's growing threat by ensuring the early deployment and operation of the USFK's THAAD system.

In this respect I appreciate the United States taking a clear position on various occasions, including at the U.S.-China summit with regard to China's unfair actions in connection with USFK's deployment of THAAD. We have agree to continue to work together so that such unfair actions may come to an end at an early date.

Furthermore, we fully shared the view that in responding to and resolving such critical issues the watertight collaboration between our two countries is of the utmost importance, and that all future policies and measures will be made under totally seamless cooperation and coordination.

Furthermore, as global partners we have also agreed to work together to resolve global issues.

It is truly meaningful that close cooperation and collaboration has continued to develop since the launch of the new U.S. administration. And I am confident that today's meeting with Vice President Pence will serve as yet another meaningful occasion for the further development of the ROK-U.S. alliance. Thank you.

THE VICE PRESIDENT: Good afternoon. Ahn-young Ha-shim-nika.

To Acting President Hwang Kyo-ahn, thank you for the kind words and the hospitality you have shown me and my family in welcoming us to the Republic of Korea, my very first stop in the Asia Pacific as Vice President of the United

States.

It's a great honor for me to be in South Korea today. And I bring greetings from the President of the United States, President Donald Trump, and on his behalf, I am here to express the unwavering support of the United States for our long-standing alliance with South Korea.

President Trump and I are grateful for your strong partnership with the United States. We commend you personally for your steady hand in this time of transition in South Korea. The President and our entire administration admire the South Korean people's commitment to the rule of law and the democratic process -- and we look forward to the upcoming election with great anticipation.

While change is coming on May 9th, the people of South Korea may be assured -- whatever change happens in your elections, the commitment of the United States to South Korea's safety and security will remain unchanged.

On behalf of the President of the United States, my message to the people of South Korea is this: We are with you 100 percent. Even in these troubled times, we stand with you for a free and secure future.

The United States of America stands shoulder-to-shoulder with the Republic of Korea, and the service and vigilance of some 37,500 U.S. soldiers, sailors, airmen, and Marines on this frontier of freedom stand as a testament to the enduring partnership between our people.

The alliance between South Korea and the United States is the linchpin of peace and security on the Korean Peninsula and indeed throughout the Asia Pacific.

The United States' commitment to South Korea is ironclad and immutable. And under President Trump's leadership, I know our alliance will even be stronger, our nations will be **safer**, and the Asia Pacific will be more secure.

Nowhere is that more evident than with our commitment to confront the region's most dangerous and urgent threat to peace and security -- the regime in North Korea.

Since 1992, the United States and our allies have stood together for a denuclearized Korean Peninsula. We hope to achieve this objective through peaceable means. But all options are on the table.

Just in the past two weeks, the world witnessed the strength and resolve of our new President in actions taken in Syria and Afghanistan. North Korea would do well not to test his resolve -- or the strength of the Armed Forces of the United States in this region.

We will continue to deploy the THAAD missile-defense system as a defensive measure -- called for by the alliance, and for the alliance. We will continue to evolve a comprehensive set of capabilities to ensure the security of South Korea. And as our Secretary of Defense made clear here in South Korea not long ago, we will defeat any attack, and we will meet any use of conventional or nuclear weapons with an overwhelming and effective response.

Strategic patience has been the approach of the last American administration and beyond. For more than two decades, the United States and our allies have worked to peacefully dismantle North Korea's nuclear program and alleviate the suffering of their people. But at every step of the way, North Korea answered our overtures with willful deception, broken promises, and nuclear and missile tests.

Over the past 18 months, North Korea has conducted two unlawful nuclear tests and an unprecedented number of ballistic missile tests, even conducting a failed missile launch as I traveled here for this visit.

The era of strategic patience is over.

Earlier this month, President Trump spoke with you, Acting President Hwang, to reaffirm the strength of our alliance. As I reassured you today, we will continue to closely consult with South Korea and your leadership as we make decisions moving forward.

We also call on other regional powers and the entire international community to join us to confront North Korea and demand that it abandon its nuclear and ballistic missile programs, to turn away from renewed hostility towards its neighbors, and to end the repression of its own people.

Earlier this month, President Trump met with Chinese President Xi at the Southern White House. The two leaders noted the urgency of the threat posed by North Korea's weapons programs and each of them reaffirmed their commitment to a denuclearized Korean Peninsula during that meeting on April 7th.

They also committed to fully implement U.N. Security Council resolutions, and to increase cooperation to convince North Korea to abandon its illicit weapons programs.

It is heartening to see China commit to these actions. But the United States is troubled by China's economic retaliation against South Korea for taking appropriate steps to defend itself. The better path would be for China to address the North Korean threat that is actually making such defensive measures necessary.

Now while issues like that remain, the President and I have great confidence that China will properly deal with North Korea, but as President Trump made clear just a few short days ago, if China is unable to deal with North Korea, the United States, and our allies, will.

So today it is my privilege, on behalf of President Trump, to reaffirm the United States' enduring commitment to the security and prosperity of South Korea and to assure the people of South Korea of our unbreakable bond. We are bound together by our shared values, but also by our shared sacrifice. A free and democratic South Korea was forged in the fires of sacrifice by soldiers from both our lands. And my father was one of them.

Sixty-five years ago, Second Lieutenant Edward J. Pence, of the 45th Infantry Division in the United States Army, fought alongside brave South Korean forces, to win the freedom of this land.

While he came home to raise a family, he had friends in uniform, from America and Korea, who went home to eternity. So, too, the friendship between our two free nations is eternal. We have bled together. We have prospered together. And on that foundation, the people of the United States of America and South Korea, will face the future together.

With courage, determination, and faith -- we go together --Katchi Kapshida.

So thank you, Mr. Acting President, for your hospitality. It
is a great, great honor to be with you today. (Applause.)

END

Chapter 138

Remarks by President Trump and First Lady Melania Trump at the 2017 White House Easter Egg Roll South Lawn

17 April 2017

10:27 A.M. EDT

[Photo: screengrab.]

THE PRESIDENT: What a great voice. Thank you very much. Great job. I want to thank everybody.

This is the 139th Easter Egg Roll. Think of it -- 139. It began [a] long time ago -- 1878.

And we will be **stronger and bigger and better** as a nation than ever before.

We're right on track.

You see what's happening, and we're right on track.

So thank you, everybody, for being here.

We're going to do cards for soldiers in a little bit, Melania and Barron and myself. We're going downstairs, we're going to sign some cards to our great troops -- they're cards for troops -- and we look forward to that.

And then we're going to come out and join you, and enjoy your company for a roll, a great Easter Egg Roll. And I don't know if we're going to be successful, but I know a lot of people down there are going to be successful. I've seen those kids, and they're highly, highly competitive. (Laughter.)

That I can tell you.

I just want to thank First Lady Melania Trump. She's really worked hard on this. (Applause.)

She has been working on this for a long time to make it perfect, and we wanted to keep it just right. So I want to just ask her to speak. But before she speaks, I want to congratulate her on this wonderful, wonderful day. We're going to have a lot of people -- a lot of people -- and they're going to have a great time.

So, Melania, thank you very much. And, Barron, thank you very much for being here. Thank you very much. (Applause.)

Honey -- First Lady, Melania Trump.

Thank you, everybody.

MRS. TRUMP: Thank you. Welcome to the White House.

This is the first time that my husband and I [are] hosting this wonderful tradition, and it's great that you are all with us today. I hope you have a great time, with many activities.

I want to thank [the] military band, all the staff and volunteers who worked tirelessly to ensure that you have [a] memorable experience.

I want to thank all the military with us today -- (applause) -- and all military in this great nation, and servicemen and servicewomen all around the world keeping us **safe**.

As we renew this tradition, thank you for joining us.

On behalf of the President and Barron, we wish you great fun and beautiful day is coming ahead of us.

And Happy Easter.

Thank you. God bless you. (Applause.)

THE PRESIDENT: Happy Easter. And have a great, great time. Have a great day. Thank you, folks. Thank you very much. I'm coming down. I'm going to be joining you. Thank you very much.

My whole family is here. Thank you.

END
10:31 A.M. EDT

Chapter 139

**REMARKS BY FIRST LADY MELANIA TRUMP AT THE 2017
WHITE HOUSE AT THE 2017 EASTER EGG ROLL,
STORY TIME
FLOTUS READS PARTY ANIMALS BY KATHIE LEE GIFFORD
SOUTH LAWN**

17 April 2017

[Photo: screengrab.]

THE FIRST LADY: So for those who do not know me, I am Melania Trump. And Nice to meet you all. I will have a special book for you. 'Party Animals', did you know about the book?

No?

So Kathie Lee Gifford wrote it a while back and I really like that book, because it shows that we are all different, but we are all the same. So here is the story...

[The First Lady read the story.] [Applause.]

I hope you enjoyed the book.

Wishing you a Happy Easter and be well.

Have a great time.

Thank you.

Chapter 140

**REMARKS BY THE VICE PRESIDENT AND JAPANESE
DEPUTY PRIME MINISTER ASO AT A PRESS CONFERENCE
THE PRIME MINISTER'S RESIDENCE
TOKYO, JAPAN**

18 April 2017

DEPUTY PRIME MINISTER ASO: (As interpreted.) I'm delighted to welcome to Vice President Pence to Japan in April when some cherry blossoms are still remaining. Perhaps it reminded you of the big celebration of the Cherry Blossom Festival, which was held in Washington last month. So I hope you can still have some good impression about the cherry blossom.

Vice President Pence in his governor days in the state of Indiana visited Japan many times over and attracted many Japanese businesses to Indiana. He had really always worked very hard to strength Japan-U.S. relationship. Very soon after my visit to the United States where I had a very useful meeting with our dear, long-standing friend of Japan in February, I am very proud to say today that the Japan-U.S. Economic Dialogue was kicked off, opening up a new page for our bilateral relations.

I feel very proud about it. Security and economy are two wheels supporting Japan-U.S. alliance for the stability of the Asian Pacific region, economic prosperity is indispensable. At the dialogue today, from the perspective of further deepening win-win economic relations between Japan and the United States, Vice President Pence and I were able to have a good discussion.

Going forward in the dialogue we concurred to discuss three pillars, namely common strategy on trade and investment rule and issues; cooperation in economic and structural policy area; sectoral cooperation. Those three pillars will be discussed.

As for the common strategy for trade and investment rules and issues, at the Japan-U.S. summit meeting held a while ago, two leaders confirmed that they are fully committed to strengthening economic relationship bilaterally, as well as in the region based on the free and fair trade rules.

And based on this common recognition, Japan and U.S. relationship will further be strengthened. And under our bilateral leadership we will build high-level trade and investment standards and spread that to the Asian Pacific region, that is free and fair trade rules.

To rectify unfair trading practices in the region, Japan and the United States agree to further our mutual cooperation. Being mindful of WTO's dispute settlement procedures, Japan will push for Japan-U.S. authorities to work ever more closely, including the minister of foreign affairs dispute settlement section, as well as general counsel office, which was newly formed within METI.

On the cooperation on economic and structural policy area, Japan and the U.S. will actively use three-pronged approach of fiscal monetary and structural policy agreed at G7. And we'll discuss the ways to lead a balanced and strong growth. Views will be exchanged on international economic and financial developments, and we'll work closely.

On sectoral cooperation, infrastructure such as high-speed

rail and energy various themes where Japan-U.S. could cooperate will be taken up. And Japan-U.S. economic relationship will be deepened, a multi-faceted front along with these three pillars, Japan-U.S. economic relations will leap forward significantly. And Japan and U.S. together will lead strongly economic growth of the Asian Pacific region, as well as the rest of the world.

Also Vice President Pence and I agreed to hold the second economic dialogue meeting by the end of this year at a mutually convenient time.

To further deepen Japan-U.S. win-win economic relations and to build a new history of our bilateral relations going forward, Vice President Pence and I will continue to have constructive dialogue. As far as looking at the Japan-U.S. relationship, we started with a friction, but for the very first time, no longer it's a friction. But it's based on the cooperation now. This is a very important juncture where we are opening a new page.

Thank you so much.

Vice President Pence, please.

VICE PRESIDENT PENCE: Konnichiwa and hello. To Deputy Prime Minister Aso, thank you. Thank you for your great hospitality and your friendship and the kindness that you've shown us in the effort that begins today.

I thank you for your tireless work to strengthen the bond between your nation and mine. It is an honor to be back in Japan. On my very first visit to the Asian Pacific as Vice President of the United States, I had to come to Japan.

I bring greetings from the President of the United States of America, President Donald Trump. And earlier today on the President's behalf, I had the honor to meet with Prime Minister Abe to reaffirm the abiding friendship and the enduring alliance between Japan and the United States.

The United States-Japan alliance is the cornerstone of peace, prosperity, and freedom in the Asia Pacific. And under President Trump, America is committed to strengthening our alliance and deepening our friendship for the benefit of our people and for the benefit of the world.

Already our bond is growing stronger. Prime Minister Abe was one of the very first world leaders who President Trump hosted at the White House. They continued their meeting at the **Southern White House**, and I can attest personally that they have forged a good, personal relationship which is already benefitting both of our nations.

Their relationship truly demonstrates the extraordinary respect that President Trump has for our critically important ally Japan. Today as we have for more than half a century, the United States and Japan stand united in defense of democracy and the rule of law, not only in this region, but all across the world.

Tomorrow I will speak from the deck of the USS Ronald Reagan at Yokosuka Naval Base, a tangible sign of our unity with Japan and the United States' unyielding commitment to peace and security in the Asia Pacific.

Under President Trump, the United States will continue to work with Japan and with all our allies in the region, including South Korea to confront the most ominous threat posing this region of the world, the regime in North

Korea. And let me be clear, our commitment is unwavering and our resolve could not be stronger.

As President Trump told Prime Minister Abe at the Southern White House so I say on his behalf today to all the people of Japan, in these challenging times, we are with you 100 percent.

In the face of provocations across the Sea of Japan, the people of this country should know that we stand with you in the defense of your security and prosperity now and always. Now the United States will continue to work with Japan, our allies across the region, and China to bring economic and diplomatic pressure to bear until North Korea abandons its nuclear and ballistic missile programs. But all options are on the table.

Nevertheless, President Trump and I have great confidence that together with Japan and our allies in the region, we will protect the peace and security of this part of the world and achieve our shared goal of a nuclear-free Korean Peninsula.

Now security is the foundation of our prosperity. But promoting prosperity is actually the main reason that I had the privilege of meeting today with your Deputy Prime Minister. At the direction of President Trump and Prime Minister Abe, today Deputy Prime Minister Aso and I have the great privilege to formally launch the U.S.-Japan Economic Dialogue.

This dialogue presents the United States and Japan with an opportunity to deepen our bilateral economic ties and to foster jobs, prosperity, and growth on both sides of the Atlantic [sic]. We're building on a strong foundation. But as the Prime Minister said, our economies have been intertwined for generations, and this is a new day and a new chapter in relations between the United States and Japan. Every day, though, our nations already exchange goods and services that improve people's lives and help businesses on both sides of the Pacific succeed. Japan is the United States' fourth largest goods trading partner and our fourth largest goods export market. And Japan is one of America's leading investors. Japanese foreign direct investment in the United States now totals more than $400 billion, the second-most of any nation.

I saw that first-hand back in my old job when I was governor of Indiana, how trade and investment between our countries can be beneficial to us all. In 2013 and again in 2015, I led a group of Indiana businesses and community leaders here to Japan to foster closer economic ties, create jobs, and spur opportunity and growth.

Today the U.S.-Japan Economic Dialogue seeks the very same objectives for both of our countries in full. It signifies President Trump's commitment to strengthening our economic relationship with Japan using a bilateral approach.

Today's meeting with Deputy Prime Minister Aso was an opportunity for us to broadly discuss how we view the dialogue structure and goals. The Prime Minister and I agreed that the dialogue will focus on three key policy pillars, as he just discussed.

The first is a "common strategy on trade and investment rules and issues." Under President Trump's leadership, the United States seeks stronger and more balanced bilateral trade relationships with every country, including Japan. Our goal is simple: We seek trade that is free and we seek trade that is fair.

This requires breaking down barriers, leveling the playing field so that American companies and exporters can enjoy high levels of market access.

The second pillar involves economic and structural policies with a specific focus on fiscal and monetary issues. President Trump believes that both the United States and Japan can enact pro-growth and fiscally sustainable monetary and budgetary policies, a key to both of our long-term economic success.

The final pillar is what we call sectoral cooperation. The President and I are confident that we can find new ways to expand our economic ties with Japan in different sectors and different industries. American and Japanese business-es have much to offer each other. By working together, we can ensure that our two nations' economic leadership grows even stronger in the years ahead to the benefit of all of our people.

This is an important day for the partnership between the United States and Japan, and I'm deeply humbled to be a part of it. The U.S.-Japan Economic Dialogue will provide us with a new forum to address the economic issues that are crucial to our long-term success.

The relevant U.S. agencies -- the Department of Com-merce, the Department of Treasury, and the U.S. Trade Representative's Office will lead discussions for each of these three pillars, focusing on concrete economic results in the near term and reporting back to my office.

The Deputy Prime Minister and I look forward to receiving

input on the progress and accomplishment from these agencies over the coming months, and we have agreed to meet again by the end of the year to discuss the progress in each area.

President Trump and I are confident that working with Prime Minister Abe and Deputy Prime Minister Aso, we will open a new chapter of opportunity and agreement for both our people.

The President is working tirelessly to create forward momentum to deepen our bilateral economic partnership with Japan. And today's announcement is a reflection of that. President Trump and I are grateful that Prime Minister Abe and Deputy Prime Minister Aso share our goal of a mutually beneficial economic relationship, and we look forward to working with them through the U.S.-Japan Economic Dialogue to achieve our vision of an equal partnership that creates jobs and prosperity and growth in the United States and in Japan on an equal basis.

We have before us a historic opportunity, and today I say with confidence based on our first discussions we will seize this opportunity. We will take this moment to strengthen the ties of commerce and friendship that exist between our people. And I believe we will usher in a new era of prosperity for ourselves and for future generations.

There is a closeness between our people that is best described with a Japanese word, and it does not have a corollary in the English language. But I learned it a while ago. As governor of Indiana, I had the opportunity to understand and appreciate the more than 250 Japanese companies that had decided to make Indiana home. The word is kizuna, and it is a reflection of a close relationship -- a relationship of understanding and of mutual respect. And I can't help but feel today that we're renewing that relationship on that foundation as we initiate this important U.S.-Japan Economic Dialogue.

So thank you again, Mr. Deputy Prime Minister, for hosting me here today. I look forward to this work with great anticipation.

Q   (As interpreted.) I have both questions to Mr. Aso and Vice President Pence. Trump administration declared they would withdraw from TPP. And within Japan great attention is drawn to what is going to be the U.S. trade policy going forward. Mr. Lighthizer, USTR nominee, said that in the agricultural area trading and negotiation Japan will be the first to target. So what will be the trade negotiation going forward between Japan and U.S.? What is the outlook? Are you looking for concluding Japan-U.S. FTA in the end?

DEPUTY PRIME MINISTER ASO: Thank you, now can I answer your question first?

Well, at the Economic Dialogue this time as the common strategy on trade and investment rules and issues, free and fair rule-based trade and investment is an indispensable value and action principle for realizing the growth and prosperity not only for Japan and the United States but for the rest of the global economy, as well.

And on this course, once again Vice President Pence and I were able to confirm this. And based on that, having a good understanding about the situations underway in the Asian Pacific, it's important that Japan-U.S. should lead the rule-making process in the region. I think it's very important, and we've been discussing that concretely -- not only to strengthen trade and investment flow bilaterally, but also Japan-U.S. can play pivotal role in spreading high-level, fair rules over Asia and the Pacific region.

We like to strengthen economic aspect of Japan-U.S. alliance, and we've been discussing that.

And looking at the Japan-U.S. economic relationship, it used to be described as being an economic fiction. We started with the word fiction. And fiction used to be the symbol of our bilateral relationship, but no longer. We are now in the era of cooperation between our two countries. It's not a matter of which sides say what to the other side. From the big picture and strategic point of view, we would like to seek the best shape and forum of bilateral framework and define its significance and have a good constructive discussion. And I think we were able to mark a first step toward that.

Thank you.

VICE PRESIDENT PENCE: Well, thank you for your comments, Mr. Deputy Prime Minister.

And in response to the question let me say with great respect to those who worked on the Trans-Pacific Partnership in the past, the TPP is a thing of the past for the United States of America. The Trump administration has made a decision and taken steps to formally withdraw from the Trans-Pacific Partnership, and that will be our policy going forward.

But today I think gives evidence to the fact that the United States of America is determined to reach out to our partners here in the Asian Pacific and around the world to at least begin to explore the possibility of expanded economic opportunities, including trade, on a bilateral basis.

President Trump truly does believe that it's in the interests of the United States of America to negotiate trade agreements on a bilateral basis. That creates a framework within which countries can better assess whether the deal itself is -- what we call a **win-win** arrangement.

But today I think what the Deputy Prime Minister has said so eloquently is that today we're beginning a process of an economic dialogue, the end of which may result in bilateral trade negotiations in the future.

But we're beginning that conversation today, beginning to identify areas that we can enhance and strengthen the economic interaction between our two nations. And at some point in the future, there may be a decision made between our nations to take what we have learned in this dialogue and commence formal negotiations for a free-trade agreement.

But I'll leave that to the future, but tell you that these discussions are very much a reflection of the President's view that negotiating at arms' length on a bilateral basis with nations is the best path forward for the United States, the best path forward for the nations with whom we enter into such agreements, and I think in the days ahead you'll continue to see the United States work on a bilateral basis with countries around the world to expand jobs and opportunity for our people and the prosperity of the world at large.

Q   Thank you very much. Vice President Pence, you've

said that the United States will increase diplomatic and economic pressure on North Korea. Today we heard Prime Minister Abe say that while he agrees with that, and we shouldn't have dialogue for dialogues sake, Japan also places paramount importance on the need to seek a diplomatic effort to achieve a peaceful resolution to the crisis. My question is: What exactly must North Korea do? What are the conditions for beginning that dialogue? And what form should that dialogue take?

And for Deputy Prime Minister Aso, President Trump during his campaign often called on Japan to share more of the burden for common defense and pay more for U.S. security presence here in Japan. What specifically is Japan prepared to do to respond to President Trump's call?

(Speaks Japanese.)

VICE PRESIDENT PENCE: Thank you, Josh. De-nuclearization of the Korean Peninsula has been the long-standing policy of the United States of America, of South Korea, of Japan, of China, and it's been the long-standing policy of nations across the world.

For more than a generation, we've seen the very failure of dialogue writ large. First we remember the agreed framework of the 1990s, then we remember the six-party talks. And with good-faith efforts by nations around the world again and again, North Korea met those efforts and resolution with broken promises and more provocations. That's why we've said the era of strategic patience is over.

And President Trump has made it very clear: The policy of the United States of America will be to reach out to our allies in the region here in Japan where I just had a productive conversation with Prime Minister Abe on this topic. Yesterday, in South Korea, where I met with officials in the National Assembly and acting President Hwang.

President Trump recently met with President Xi, and the President of China reaffirmed China's commitment to a nuclear-free Korean Peninsula. It is our belief that by bringing together the family of nations with diplomatic and economic pressure, we have a chance -- we have a chance -- to achieve our objective of a nuclear-free Korean Peninsula.

Now all options are on the table, and there they will remain. But President Trump and I and our administration believes the most productive pathway forward is dialogue among the family of nations that can isolate and pressure North Korea into abandoning permanently and dismantling its nuclear weapons program and its ballistic missile program.

As Prime Minister Abe said today in our brief conversation, dialogue for the sake of dialogue is valueless. It is necessary for us to exercise pressure, and the United States of America believes the time has come for the international community to use both diplomatic and economic pressure to bring North Korea to a place that it has avoided successfully now for more than a generation. And we will not rest and we will not relent until we achieve the objective of a denuclearized Korean Peninsula.

DEPUTY PRIME MINISTER ASO: Washington Post, my English hearing is still good enough. But if I may say in Japanese.

(As interpreted.) Well, economic dialogue, TPP -- whether the TPP can be made as a foundation for a dialogue going forward, is that what you said?

Sorry. Then my English hearing is absolutely
wrong. Would you mind repeating the question again?

Q   Minister Aso, President Trump during his campaign
often called on Japan to share more of the burden for common defense and pay more money for U.S. security presence here in Japan. What is Japan willing to do to respond
to President Trump's calls for a better deal for the United
States in the U.S.-Japan security relationship?

DEPUTY PRIME MINISTER ASO: I think I got a picture. Response in Japanese is okay, right?

(As interpreted.) Now, responding to your question, let's
look at Japanese defense. Just the other day -- Mr. James
Mattis, Defense Secretary, came to Japan, at which occasion I had an opportunity to talk with him.

At least look at Okinawa's host nation's support -- host nation's support came up as a topic. And he said that Japan
is behaving like a textbook case -- 75 percent is paid to the
Okinawa host nation; ROK -- 40 percent; 30 percent Germany; and 20 percent Italy. That is a burden share. And I
think whole picture was understood by General Mattis.

And also just lately when the Abe Cabinet was formed,
look at the defense expenditure -- how it is being allocat-
ed. The navy is the crucial area where more budget allocation has been done, followed by air and the land. And I
think this is the most appropriate allocation of the defense
budget.

So at least -- ever since inclusive by General Mattis and

other military personnel of the United States with regard
to the Japanese defense or discontent, at least no message has been given to us from the United States as far
as I know. So we will continue to make mutual effort and
try to share the information as much as possible going
forward, and particularly look at the East China Sea and
Korean Peninsula and Sea of Japan. Certain fictions might
arise. So information exchange is particularly important
-- intelligence sharing and the information sharing has to
continue in appropriate manner most of all because of the
situation we are in.

END

Chapter 141

**REMARKS BY PRESIDENT TRUMP ON BUY AMERICAN,
HIRE AMERICAN EXECUTIVE ORDER
SNAP-ON TOOLS
KENOSHA, WISCONSIN**

18 April 2017

2:21 P.M. CDT

[Photo: screengrab.]

THE PRESIDENT: Thank you very much. (Applause.)

These are great, great people and these are real workers. I love the workers. We're doing a good job for the
workers. And I'm thrilled to be back in Wisconsin. The
optimism in this room is the same incredible **Spirit** that is
sweeping across our country -- and even **greater** than that
great day in November when I won the state of
Wisconsin and when we won the presidency. That was a

great day. (Applause.)

That was a great day. And thank you, Wisconsin.

[Photo: screengrab.]

No administration has accomplished more in the **first 90 days** -- that includes on military, on the border, on trade, on regulation, on law enforcement -- we love our law enforcement -- and on government reform.

Today, we're building on that **optimism**, and I'm proud to announce that we're about to take bold, new steps to follow through on **my pledge** to **Buy American and Hire American**. (Applause.)

I can't think of a better place to make this announcement than right here at *Snap-On* -- I just took a tour of the company -- good place, by the way; it's doing well, too -- standing among the workers who make the tools that will **rebuild** our nation. Your craftsmanship is incredible.

It's a pleasure to be see my good friend, Governor Scott Walker. He has been such a big help. He has been so incredible. (Applause.)

Stand up, Scott. Governor Walker. As well as Senator Ron Johnson. We worked hard together. Thank you, Ron. (Applause.)

And although he could not be here today, my thanks go to Speaker Ryan, who's represented this city for nearly two decades in Congress. And you know where he is? He's with NATO -- so he has a good excuse. And I said, Ron, make sure these countries start paying their bills a little bit more. They're way, way behind, Ron. We have to -- or I'm going to talk to you about that, Ron.

But Paul, you're over with NATO -- get them to pay their bills. And, Ron, you have to work on that, too. And, Scott, you're right here in Wisconsin -- you don't have to bother. We'll keep you right here. (Laughter.)

For a little while at least.

Also with us is a famous local resident, the pride of Kenosha -- Reince Priebus, my Chief of Staff. Where is Reince? (Applause.)

Where is he? What a good man. There he is. In fact, we flew over his house on the way up and he got all excited, he was taking pictures of it. (Laughter.)

Reince went to high school right here, just about a mile away, where he took his wife Sally to the prom. And that was a match made in heaven. Very nice.

I also want to thank Treasury Secretary Steven Mnuchin for being with us today. Secretary Mnuchin is working to put together a tax reform plan to make our industry more **competitive** and also to provide a level playing field for our workers. We don't have a level playing field, believe me. You're going to have one very soon. And our tax reform and tax plan is coming along very well. It's going to be out very soon. We're working on healthcare and we're going to get that done, too.

Our Education Secretary, Betsy DeVos, is also here. Where is Betsy? She's around here someplace. Stand up. Thank you, Betsy. (Applause.)

Secretary DeVos is working to ensure that our workers are trained for the skilled technical jobs that will, in the future, power our country.

I'm excited to be joined today by students from Gateway Technical College -- (applause) -- and remember the College President, Bryan Albrecht. Thank you. (Applause.)

Great job. Thank you very much. Thank you. Thank you, Bryan. Your partnership with *Snap-On* is a great example of why vocational education is the way of the future.

When I was growing up in Queens, we had vocational schools that were great. We don't have schools like that so much anymore, but we're bringing them back -- vocational schools. These are very talented people that love that type of work, and it's great work. It really is great work. So vocational schools are going to be a big factor in the Trump administration.

Together, we're going to do everything in our power to make sure that more products are stamped with those wonderful words: **"Made in the USA."** (Applause.)

In the old days, we used to use it. We don't use it so much anymore. We're going to start using it **Again -- Made in the USA**.

For too long, we've watched as our factories have been closed and our jobs have been sent to other faraway lands. We've lost 70,000 factories since China joined the World Trade Organization. And you've seen that and you've heard about it -- 70,000. The World Trade Organization -- another one of our disasters. But this election, the American people voted to end the theft of **American Prosperity**. They voted to bring back their jobs -- and to bring back their **dreams** into **our country**.

That's why I'm here today. In just a few moments, I will be signing a **Buy American** and **Hire American** executive order. You haven't heard about that in a long time in this country. With this action, we are sending a powerful signal to the world: We're going to **defend** our workers, **protect** our jobs, and finally put **America First**. (Applause.)

I see all the "**Make America Great Again**" hats, so it's a good crowd. Those are good hats.

Through the years, *Snap-On* tools have been at the center of our industrial life. Your tools have fixed the cars our families depend on. They've sailed with the fleets that patrol the oceans. They've fixed the planes that cross our skies. And *Snap-On* tools have reached the heights of space, used by astronauts in orbit to carry out their very, very important work. And I don't know if you noticed, recently I signed a very big order: We're going to spend again on the NASA space program, and that's something we need, and **we also need it psychologically**. (Applause.) But it's going to be very exciting.

For decades, this company has served the needs of American workers. It's time we had a federal government that does the same. The "**Buy and Hire American**" order I'm about to sign will help **protect** workers and students like those of you in the audience today. This historic action declares that the policy of our government is to aggressively promote and use **American-made goods** and to ensure that **American labor is hired** to do the job. It's **America First,** you better believe it. (Applause.)

It's time. It's time, right? It's time.

First, we will fully monitor, uphold and enforce our **Buy American laws** -- which we haven't done. **Buy American laws** require that when the federal government buys, builds or funds a project, domestic goods and products should be used. But over the years, these **Buy American** standards have been gutted by excessive waivers and reckless exemptions. The result has been countless jobs and countless contracts that have been lost to cheap, subsidized, and low-quality foreign goods.

With this order, I am directing every single agency in our government to strictly uphold our **Buy American laws**, to minimize the use of waivers, and to maximize **Made in America** content in all federal projects. (Applause.)

It's time. And for the first time ever, we are going to crack down on foreign bidders that used dumped steel and other subsidized goods to take contracts from workers like you. They take them away, and they've been doing it for a long time. Not going to happy anymore. (Applause.)

We are finally standing up for our workers and for our companies. In short, this order declares that **American**

projects should be **made with American goods**. No longer are we going to allow foreign countries to cheat our producers and our workers out of federal contracts. Everyone in my administration will be expected to enforce every last **Buy American provision** on behalf of the American worker, and we are going to investigate every single trade deal that undermines these provisions.

Secondly, we are going to enforce the **Hire American** rules that are designed to **protect** jobs and wages of workers in the United States. We believe jobs must be offered to **American workers First**. Does that make sense? (Applause.)

Right now, widespread abuse in our immigration system is allowing American workers of all backgrounds to be **replaced** by workers brought in from other countries to fill the same job for sometimes less pay. This will stop. American workers have long called for reforms to end these visa abuses. And today, their calls are being answered for the first time. That includes taking the first steps to set in motion a long-overdue reform of H1B visas.

Right now, H1B visas are awarded in a totally random lottery -- and that's wrong. Instead, they should be given to the most-skilled and highest-paid applicants, and they should never, ever be used to **replace Americans**. No one can compete with American workers when they're given a fair and level playing field, which has not happened for decades.

We're using every tool at our disposal to **restore the American Dream**. In fact, when it comes to wasteful, destructive, job-killing regulations, we are going to use a tool you all know very well -- it's called the sledgehammer. (Laugh-

ter.)

It's what we're going to use. We're also going to stand up
for our dairy farmers in Wisconsin -- (applause) -- and I've
been reading about it, and I've been talking about it for
a long time -- and that demands, really, immediately fair
trade with all of our trading partners, and that includes
Canada. (Applause.)

Because in Canada, some very unfair things have happened to our dairy farmers and others, and we're going to
strategy working on that with Ron and with Scott and with
Paul, with all of your representatives. What's happened to
you is very, very unfair. It's another typical one-sided deal
against the United States. And it's not going to be happening for long.

So, Scott, you and Ron and myself and Paul and everybody
else, we're going to get together and we're going to call
Canada, and we're going to say, "What happened?" And
they might give us an answer, but **we're going to get the
solution**, not just the answer, okay? Because **we know
what the solution is**, all right? (Applause.)

And if you guys can't do it, we'll bring maybe Reince. Reince, you ready, Reince? We better bring Reince back. No,
we'll get that done. We're going to work on that very
hard. We're going to work on it immediately; in fact, starting today. It's a terrible thing that happened to the farmers of Wisconsin.

The fact is, NAFTA has been a disaster for the United States
-- a complete and total disaster. And we're going to do
some things, and we have all sorts of rules and regulations
that are horrendous. Like we want to start to negotiate

with Mexico immediately, and we have these provisions
where you have to wait long periods of time, you have to
notify Congress, and after you notify Congress, you have
to get certified, and then you can't speak to them for 100
days. The whole thing is ridiculous.

NAFTA has been very, very bad for our country. It's been
very, very bad for our companies and for our workers, and
we're going to make some very big changes or we are going to get rid of NAFTA for once and for all. Cannot continue like this, believe me. (Applause.)

Big things will be happening on trade with other countries
over the coming months, and I mean very big. We're also
working with Congress on tax reform and simplification,
and we're on time if we get that healthcare approval. So
press every one of your congressmen, press everybody,
because we want to get that approval. And it just makes
the tax reform easier and it makes it better. **But it's going
to make it steeper, it's going to be bigger, and that's what
we want to do**.

So we're in very good shape on tax reform. We have the
concept of the plan. We're going to be announcing it
very soon. But healthcare -- we have to get the healthcare taken care of. And as soon as healthcare takes care
of -- we are going to march very quickly. You're going
to watch -- we're going to surprise you. Right, Steve
Mnuchin? Right? Secretary of Treasury. (Applause.)

I see Sean. Stand up, Sean. Stand up.

I had no idea -- I was told a year ago -- he's been so great
to me -- I was told a year ago he's like a world champion
climber; climbs the trees. And after that I look -- every

time I look at him, I look at him now differently. I'm very impressed with that, Sean. And he's also very good on television and very helpful. Thank you. Thank you, man. Thank you.

We'll be making big investments in **rebuilding** our military and **repairing** our badly depleted infrastructure. And that will happen soon also -- infrastructure. **Big infrastructure bill**, probably use it with something else that's a little bit harder to get approved in order to get that approved. But infrastructure is coming, and it's coming fast.

New ships, bridges, tunnels and airplanes will be construct-ed with **American hands, American steel**, and, yes, **American tools**. (Applause.)

As we work to **restore** the **American Dream at home**, we're also **working to restore America's standing abroad**. That means strengthening our partnerships and ensuring that our friends and allies pay their fair share, and that very much includes, as I've already said in my little statement to Paul, it also includes the NATO companies and countries. They are really sort of letting us down in that one respect, and **we don't want people taking advantage of the United States**. And that's not going to happen for very much longer. I'm going over there very soon and we're going to have it, and everybody is going to be pay-ing. And we're going to be a much happier country, we're going to be a much happier world.

No matter the circumstances, everyone will know we act from this core conviction that **America's strength** must be unmatched and **its first priority unquestioned -- the safety and security of our citizens**. This is the surest path to a more peaceful and prosperous world for us all.

Together, we can build a better future in the **Spirit** of this company's earliest days. Great company, great history. I recently learned that decades ago, in the 1920s, when your salesman entered a dusty repair shop, or stained, a nice, beautiful stained garage floor -- which I've seen many of -- they would find a spot to lay out a beautiful green felt mat. The people of the company know what that means. And on that green felt mat, he would carefully place a gleaming set of new *Snap-On* tools.

The founders of this company wanted their customers to know that the tools of the mechanic were just as important as the tools of the doctor, the dentist, the politician, or the business leader, and that his craft was a noble, noble craft, as noble as any. This is a wonderful story about your company and its Wisconsin heritage. And Wisconsin has a truly great heritage, and it's led by incredible people.

But it's also a story that tells us a lot about the **American Spirit**. In America, we honor work. We honor grit. We honor craftsmanship. We honor the men and women who turn **dreams** into reality with their own two hands. In America, we honor all of you.

We are a NATION OF BUILDERS. We are the country that dug out the Panama Canal, that put a man on the face of the moon, and that linked our cities with majestic railroads and curving highways. We are the country that is always on the cusp of the next invention. But we can only get there **with all of you**. We can only **restore this nation** we love so much by working and building with all of you.

We can only get there together. We are the one people sharing one **destiny,** saluting one great, beautiful American flag. I'm thrilled to be here today to celebrate **our**

great American heritage and to proudly embrace our great American future.

I want to thank the people of Wisconsin for doing so much for me. That's why I came back here -- not just for the company, frankly, for the people of Wisconsin. You have been so incredible to me and my administration, and **we will never, ever let you down.**

God bless you. God bless the American worker. God bless the **American Dream**.

And God bless the United States of America.

Thank you all very much.

Tremendous honor. Thank you. (Applause.)

END
2:42 P.M. CDT

Chapter 142

19 April 2017

THE VICE PRESIDENT: Well, good afternoon. Konnichiwa.
(Laughter.)

To Chris LaFleur, thank you for that gracious introduction
and for your great leadership; to Ambassador Sasae; to the
chargé d'affaires, Hyland; to our state minister, Sonuora
(ph); the members of the American Chamber of Commerce
in Japan; members of the Keidanren; representatives of
the Mount Fuji Dialogue, distinguished business leaders;
and my friend the Secretary of Commerce for the United
States of America, Wilbur Ross, who is with us today. (Applause.)

It is great to be back in Japan. This isn't my first time
here. As Governor of the state of Indiana, it was my great
privilege to come to Japan, which is a great partner with
the people of that heartland state, on two difference occasions. But it is my first trip to the Asian Pacific, so I had
to some to Japan as Vice President of the United States of
America. (Applause.)

I bring greetings from the President of the United States,
President Donald Trump.

Yesterday, under the President's behalf, I had the honor

to meet with Prime Minister Abe to reaffirm the abiding friendship and the enduring alliance between Japan and the United States.

The United States-Japan alliance is the cornerstone of peace, prosperity, and freedom in the Asia Pacific. And under President Donald Trump, America is firmly committed to strengthening our alliance and defending the prosperity and security that we have built together between our nations.

As President Trump told Prime Minister Abe, so I say on his behalf today to all of the business leaders that are gathered here, to all of the people of Japan: We are with you 100 percent. (Applause.)

Know that we stand with you, now and always, and together, we will address the challenges that we face in these uncertain times; and most especially, we will address the region's most dangerous and urgent threat to peace and security -- the regime in North Korea.

Now rest assured, under President Trump, the United States is unwavering in its commitment to defend Japan. Earlier today I had a great privilege to speak on the deck of USS Ronald Reagan at Yokosuka Naval Base. Her steel deck I said there signifies the ironclad alliance between the United States and Japan. And it is a testament to our commitment to our shared security. (Applause.)

Today, over 50,000 U.S. service-members and a further 50,000 civilians and family members are stationed here in Japan. And the United States will continue to deploy our most advanced military assets in the region. And with regard to this challenge, let me be clear: While all options are on the table, the United States will continue to work directly with Japan, our allies across the region, and China to bring economic and diplomatic pressure to bear on the regime in North Korea until they once and for all abandon their nuclear and ballistic missile programs. (Applause.)

The President and I have great confidence, that together with Japan, and our allies in the region, we will protect the peace and security of this region, and achieve our shared goal of a nuclear-free Korean Peninsula.

Security, of course, is the foundation of our prosperity, and prosperity is what I came to talk about with all of you today.

Under President Donald Trump, the United States is deeply committed to strengthening our economic ties with Japan. For more than 70 years, our nations have been partners in commerce, bringing our peoples together and generating growth and prosperity for generations to the benefit of both our nations.

Today, the United States' partnership with Japan is one of our most vibrant and one of our most cherished. And the American Chamber of Commerce Japan has played a pivotal role in that relationship for decades.

Since 1948, you've brought together hundreds of businesses, on both sides of the Pacific, to develop commerce between our nations and to invest in our shared future.

And the same goes to all the businesses represented here today. I just had the opportunity to meet with a number of great American and Japanese business executives -- companies like Aflac, IBM, Toyota, General Motors. All of you

are pillars of our shared prosperity. And join me in a round
of applause for these great business leaders who have
joined us here today. We are truly honored by your presence. (Applause.)

Your businesses create jobs and drive innovation in the
United States and in Japan. And thanks in no small part to
your hard work, the economic partnership between the
United States and Japan will continue to grow and flour-
ish. Of that I'm confident.

Our two nations have powered the global economy for
decades, and today, we account for nearly a third of the
world's gross domestic product. And the trade between us
is an important factor to our success.

In 2016, Japan was the United States' fourth-largest goods
exports market. From aircraft to medical devices, machinery to pharmaceuticals, the United States has sent more
than $63 billion worth of goods to Japan last year alone.
When you add in services, our annual exports are closing in on $110 billion, supporting more than 600,000
good-paying American jobs.

Our countries have also invested historic sums in each
other's economies. America is a top foreign direct investor
in Japan, with over $108 billion invested.

And the benefits flow both ways. Today, Japanese-owned
businesses employ 839,000 American workers, and Japanese foreign direct investment in the United States topped
a stunning $411 billion -- the second most of any nation in
the world. And America is grateful. (Applause.)

I know from first-hand experience how important Japan

is to the American economy. And some of these business
leaders I actually met in my old job. As governor of the
state of Indiana, in 2013 and 2015, I led a group of business and community leaders here to Japan. I'll always be
incredibly appreciative of the more than $1.8 billion in
planned investments and the nearly 7,000 jobs in the state
of Indiana that have been created by Japanese-owned
firms during my time in office.

I must tell you that I saw first-hand in the state of Indiana
more than 250 Japanese companies that came not just
to do business, but to help build communities. And the
relationship that I saw develop in communities large and
small across my heartland state could only be described
with that Japanese word kizuna. It's a bond. It's a bond of
friendship, of shared heritage and shared values.

And now, as Vice President, I'm grateful to all the Japanese
businesses that are investing all over the United States at
this very moment. I believe the best is yet to come.

Ever since President Donald Trump's election, Japanese
businesses have dramatically increased their commitment
to the American economy, and we're grateful. Last December, for instance, SoftBank announced a $50 billion invest-
ment in the United States, creating 50,000 new American
jobs.

And in January, Toyota unveiled a $10 billion investment
in America, and just last week dedicated more than $1.3
billion to a plant in the state of Kentucky.

These are only a couple of examples of many more that
I could name at the podium today. The truth is, though,
is that our economic partnership with Japan could still be

even stronger, and that's why President Trump is taking critical steps to strengthen our bond in the years ahead.

President Trump has made it clear that our administration will strengthen our international trade relationships using a bilateral approach, and yesterday, at the President's direction, I met with Japanese Deputy Prime Minister Aso to kick off the U.S.-Japan Economic Dialogue. And we've gone straight to work. (Applause.)

This dialogue presents the United States and Japan with the opportunity to deepen our bilateral economic ties, and to foster jobs, prosperity, and growth on both sides of the Pacific.

In yesterday's meeting with the Deputy Prime Minister, we broadly discussed how we view the dialogues structure and goals. That dialogue we decided will focus on three key policy pillars in the months ahead.

The first is to seek a common strategy on trade and investment rules and issues.

Under President Trump's leadership, the United States seeks a stronger and more balanced bilateral trade relationship with Japan. Our goal is simple: We seek trade that is both free and fair and benefits both our nations equally.

This requires breaking down barriers and leveling the playing field so that American companies and exporters enjoy high levels of market access.

The second pillar involves economic and structural policies, with a specific focus on fiscal and monetary issues.

The President believes that both the United States and Japan can enact pro-growth and fiscally sustainable monetary and budgetary policies, which are both key to our long-term economic success.

And the final pillar is what we call sectoral cooperation. The President and I are confident that we can find new ways to expand our economic ties with Japan in different sectors and industries. In fact, as we discussed earlier today with business leaders, one of the areas we agreed upon is to examine ways that we can promote and advance women empowerment in business in the United States and in Japan. (Applause.)

American and Japanese businesses have much to offer each other, and by working together, the President and I believe that we can ensure that our two nations' economic leadership grows even stronger in the years ahead to the benefit of the entire world.

President Trump and I are grateful that Prime Minister Abe and Deputy Prime Minister Aso share our goal of a mutually beneficial economic relationship.

And as members of the business community, all of you will play an integral role in helping us identify where and how we can make the most impact in the days ahead.

President Trump and I value your continued input on the issues that you face, and we know that you can help us move toward a system that maximizes jobs, growth, and a brighter future for Japan and the United States of America.

The truth is simply that a stronger American economy means a stronger economy for Japan and for all our trading partners. The United States and Japan are drivers of global growth, and under President Donald Trump, I can **promise** you, the United States will drive growth like never before. (Applause.)

President Trump and our entire administration are working around the clock to pass an agenda of lower taxes, less regulation, better infrastructure, and a **renewed** focus on American energy. I'm sure you'll be glad to know that tax reform is one of our top priorities. I don't have to tell you how complicated the American tax code is and how much harm it does to business investment in our country -- at home and, frankly, abroad.

Our corporate tax rate sadly is one of the highest in the developed world -- it's more than 10 percent higher than the tax rate here in Japan. President Trump's tax plan is to slash the corporate rate and reform the tax code and make it simpler, flatter, and fairer.

Rest assured, our tax reform plan will make the strongest economy in the world stronger still. And it will benefit every business represented here today. (Applause.)

The same is true of the President's energetic actions from the outset of our administration to reduce the regulatory burden in America. The President already ordered every agency in Washington, D.C. to find two regulations to get rid of before issuing any new red tape on the American economy and the American people.

The President has also signed more than a dozen bills turning back the last administration's excessive regulatory mandates, and we're going to continue to work with Con-gress to slash through the red tape.

Make no mistake about it: Under President Donald Trump,
the era of over-regulation in the American economy is
over, and a NEW ERA of jobs and growth has begun. (Applause.)

Now, these are just a few of the President's policies that I
could discuss today. I appreciate the feedback I received
from so many of you at our earlier conversation about
what our administration can continue to do to create an
environment on both sides of the Pacific where we can
grow and thrive.

Rest assured, President Trump's agenda in America will
renew our country's reputation as the premier investment
destination in the world, which will benefit both of our
countries and all the enterprises gathered here.

And our success will further strengthen our bond with the
businesses and the people of Japan. Of that I'm certain.
The truth is that both our nations seek the same thing.
We want good-paying jobs for our people. We want more
investment and higher growth. We want innovation and
high-tech companies. And we want our people to be
more prosperous tomorrow than they are today. These
are shared goals, and they're shared values. And I can tell
you that under President Trump's leadership, and working
closely with Prime Minister Abe, they're the shared ex-
pectations of both of our peoples. We're looking forward
to working with all of you and with the leadership here in
Japan to achieve that aim.

This is a historic time in the relationship between our nations. For more than 70 years, the United States and Japan
have built on a foundation of freedom and friendship, and
together we've become the pillars that support opportuni-

ty and prosperity around the world.

Today, I say with confidence: With your continued help, through an enduring alliance and economic partnership, and under President Donald Trump, our nations will reach new heights, for the benefit of all of our people, and for the benefit of the world.

Thank you so much for having me here today and thank you for the **opportunities** that the enterprises here represent in America and in Japan. And God bless you all. (Applause.)

(The Mount Fuji Dialogue Award is presented.)

END

Chapter 143

**REMARKS BY THE VICE PRESIDENT ABOARD
USS RONALD REAGAN
YOKOSUKA NAVAL BASE
YOKOSUKA CITY, JAPAN**

19 April 2017

THE VICE PRESIDENT: Lieutenant General Martinez, Major General Chiarotti, Vice Admiral Aucoin, Vice Admiral Doman, Rear Admiral Williams, Rear Admiral Carter, Rear Admiral Inoue, Rear Admiral Shimo, Captain Donnelly, Chargé Hyland, Ambassador Sasae, Director-General Mori, members of United States Forces of Japan, the Japan Self-Defense Forces, it is my high honor and distinct privilege to join you here today on America's flagship -- the USS Ronald Reagan -- where every day, all of you prove it can be done. (Applause.)

You all look sharp out there, but at ease. It's so good to be with you today.

I bring greetings from the President of the United States of America, your Commander-in-Chief, President Donald Trump. (Delayed applause and cheering.)

I spoke to the President this morning, just before I boarded the ship. He said to tell you that he's proud of you. And he said to me, "I wish I could be where you are." And I know he meant it, from the bottom of his heart.

The President sent me here today to thank you -- to thank you for your service -- all of you, American and Japanese, who have stood up, who've stepped forward to protect our countries, our values, and **our very way of life**.

You are the sons and daughters of **freedom**, willing to defend it with your life -- so that your families, your fellow countrymen, and future generations may continue to call themselves free. Give yourselves a round of applause. All of America is proud of you. (Applause.)

The Good Book tells us, "if you owe debts pay debts, if honor, then honor, if respect, then respect." I stand before you today, on behalf of your Commander-in-Chief, to pay a debt of gratitude to each of you and to express the well-deserved respect of the President of the United States and the American people for all of you who wear the uniform of this country.

Our prayers for you, for your families, your safety rise every day into the heart of heaven. In a word, you are the best of us -- heroes all. And you are here, the Americans among you so far away from home, because the United States of America and Japan are bound by history, a time-honored treaty, and the abiding oath of friendship.

The United States-Japan alliance is the cornerstone of peace, prosperity, and freedom in the Asia Pacific. And let me be clear: Under President Donald Trump, the United States stands unwavering in our alliance and unyielding in our resolve to defend all that we have built together over these generations. (Applause.)

Our bond with Japan is strong and growing stronger by the day. In February, only weeks after he took his oath of office, President Trump welcomed Prime Minister Abe to the White House, where they reaffirmed in their words "their strong determination to further strengthen the U.S.-Japan alliance."

You here, on the deck of this great ship, are the physical manifestation of that alliance, and I have to tell you it is deeply inspiring to stand before you today, and see what I see gathered here on this deck. Every American would be inspired and proud if they had this view, and I know I am. (Applause.)

As the President and the Prime Minister made clear, the United States will strengthen its presence in the Asia Pacific, Japan will assume a larger role and responsibility in our alliance in the years ahead, and both of our nations will continue to expand our cooperation for our common defense.

[Photo: screengrab.]

Under President Trump, the United States' commitment to Article 5 of our Security Treaty is unwavering. And our treaty covers all of the territories administered by Japan, including the Senkaku Islands.

It's fitting that today I deliver this message aboard this great ship, a majestic ship, the USS Ronald Reagan, here at Yokosuka Naval Base. Her steel deck literally signifies the ironclad alliance our country enjoys with Japan and our enduring commitment to the Asia Pacific. (Applause.)

And we are standing on a ship named after my second favorite President. Our 40th President, Ronald Reagan, was a great President who powerfully reminded us that peace only comes through strength. You are that strength.

Today, over 50,000 U.S. troops and a further 50,000 civilians and family members are stationed here in Japan. And the United States will continue to deploy more of our most advanced military assets to the region in the years ahead.

Beyond this noble ship and the carrier strike group that it leads, by the year 2020, this ocean will boast 60 percent of our Navy's fleet. And the skies above already have F-35 Joint Strike Fighters flying for freedom. (Applause.)

And you can rest assured, the full range of the United States military capability is dedicated to the protection of Japan. Japan, you are our friend -- you are our ally -- and on that foundation, we will face the future together.

Under President Donald Trump, the United States once again will stand with our allies and stand up to our enemies. (Applause.)

And I can assure you President Trump will unfailingly support the brave men and women in uniform who defend our freedom every single day.

We're the proud parents of a United States Marine, stationed as we speak at a naval air station in the South of the United States. And I have to tell you, as the parent of someone in the service, it is the greatest privilege of my life to serve as Vice President to a President who is so dedicated to the men and women of our armed forces, their families, and our veterans.

I can tell you from my heart: President Donald Trump will be the best friend America's Armed Forces will ever have. (Applause.)

The President and I will honor your commitment and secure America's safety through historic investments in our national defense.

Just as President Ronald Reagan **restored** the armed forces in his day, so too President Donald Trump will make the strongest fighting force in the world even stronger still.

Just look at what President Trump has already accomplished. In his **first 100 days**, President Trump has taken decisive action to end the era of budget cuts for America's military. (Applause.)

President Trump has submitted a budget which will **rebuild** our military and restore the arsenal of democracy with the largest increase in defense spending since the days the namesake of this ship sat in the Oval Office. (Applause.)

And in just the past two weeks, the world witnessed the strength and resolve of our new President in the decisive action that he took in Syria and Afghanistan.

The enemies of our freedom and this alliance would do well not to test the resolve of this President -- or the capabilities of the Armed Forces of the United States of America and our allies. (Loud applause and whistling.)

Make no mistake: Under President Donald Trump, the United States will be strong -- stronger than ever before. For as history attests, when America is strong, the world is safe. (Applause.)

A strong America -- militarily, economically, and diplomatically -- is vitally important to this region and all who call it home. It was through the bravery of our service-members and the **Spirit** of our people, that America established the foundation of peace and freedom that endures in the Asia Pacific to this very day.

And under President Trump, the United States will continue to defend prosperity and ensure security on these seas, and between our lands.

Today, as in ages past, American leadership lights the way. The United States stands with all our allies and our partners in the region to keep the peace, enrich our people, and advance the common good.

Together, we will defend the rules-based order upon which the region's progress, past and future, depends. We will protect the freedom of navigation and overflight and other lawful uses of the sea, in the South China Sea and elsewhere, and we will ensure the unimpeded flow of lawful commerce on the Seven Seas. (Applause.)

And we will uphold international rules and norms, promote peaceful diplomatic dialogue to address issues of regional and international concern, and we will defend human rights -- because the dignity and worth of every person is an eternal value of the United States of America.

Under President Trump, the United States will faithfully defend all that we hold dear -- for we know that if we falter, the light of truth and freedom in the world could swiftly be extinguished.

We gather here today, on this deck, and in this place, as storm clouds gather on the horizon. On Monday, I traveled to the front-lines of freedom, where the vibrancy of a free South Korea meets directly the repression of North Korea. At the Demilitarization Zone, I met with the brave men and women who watch over that land, day and night. They know what you who stand in the gap in this region already know -- North Korea is the most dangerous and urgent threat to the peace and security of the Asia Pacific.

[Photo: screengrab.]

For more than a generation, North Korea's leaders have sought to develop nuclear weapons and the ballistic missiles on which to deliver them. They have impoverished their people and embittered the region in their pursuit of this dangerous goal. For more than two decades, from the

Agreed Framework of 1994, the Six-Party Talks from year 2003 to '09, to the strategic patience of the recent past, the United States and our allies have worked to tirelessly to peacefully dismantle North Korea's nuclear program and alleviate the suffering of its people.

But at every step of the way, North Korea answered our overtures with willful deception, with broken promises, and nuclear and missile tests -- including a failed missile test they attempted just this past Sunday.

As President Trump has made clear to the world, the era of strategic patience is over. (Applause.)

At the President's direction, the policy of the United States will be to continue to work diligently with Japan, our allies across the region, China, and the wider world to bring economic and diplomatic pressure to bear on the regime in North Korea, and we will do so until they abandon their nuclear and ballistic missile programs.

But as all of you know, readiness is the key. And you, the instruments of American policy, should know -- all options are on the table. History will attest, the soldier "does not bear the sword in vain."

And those who would challenge our resolve or our readiness should know: We will defeat any attack and meet any use of conventional or nuclear weapons with an overwhelming and effective American response. (Loud applause and cheering.)

The United States of America will always seek peace, but under President Trump, the shield stands guard and the sword stands ready.

Rest assured, under President Trump's leadership, the United States will continue to **protect** our people and our allies and to strengthen the bonds between us -- today, tomorrow, and every day that follows.

As I look out across this deck, I see men and women -- American and Japanese -- who have answered the call to duty. And you have my deepest respect. In these challenging times, **it is you** -- through your voluntary service and your sacrifice -- **who guard the flame of freedom, undimmed and undiminished, to give to generations to come**.

The President and I have absolute faith that you will accomplish this mission and freedom will prevail because you follow in the footsteps also of those who defended freedom in the Asia Pacific in the past. I stand before you deeply humbled to be among so many in uniform because my own life's journey did not take me into the uniform of the United States. But it took my father.

Sixty-five years ago, a young Edward J. Pence left his home, in Illinois, put on the uniform and crossed this vast Pacific on which you serve. Like so many of his countrymen, that second lieutenant in the 45th Infantry Division of the United States Army landed on the shores of South Korea, in the midst of a battle for freedom, a rifle in hand, resolved to defend that freedom with his life.

Just two days ago, I stood at the Demilitarized Zone, and looked out across the landscape -- the very landscape where my father had fought, in the Battle for Old Baldy and the battle on Pork Chop Hill. It was a deeply emotional experience for me. There, alongside his brothers-in-arms, American and Korean, my dad had helped seize the

high ground, repulsing more than 20 enemy counter-at-
tacks. And they seized the high ground of freedom, which
prevails in South Korea to this day. (Applause.)

Sixty-four years ago last week, my dad was -- had a medal
pinned on his chest for his valor on the field of battle. But
like most of our nation's heroes, my dad never talked much
about his time in combat. I believe that he carried in his
heart something that you understand in ways that I perhaps never will.

My dad never thought of himself as a hero. He often
would say that the heroes were the ones that didn't get to
come home. He lost friends -- young shining faces filled
with promise -- who gave the last full measure of devotion
for your sake, and for mine to defend our freedom and to
plant freedom in that ancient land. And they succeeded.

So now it's our turn in this generation. And more to the
point, it's your turn. Today, we best honor the sacrifices
of those who have gone before by defending the freedom
they fought and bled and died to secure.

And on behalf of your Commander-in-Chief, this we know
you will do.

As President Ronald Reagan said in his time, "we must
realize that no arsenal, or no weapon in the arsenals of
the world, is so formidable as the will and moral courage
of free men and women. It is a weapon our adversaries in
today's world do not have." (Applause.)

For generations, the United States has stood guard over
the Asia Pacific, protecting freedom through our strength
of will and strength of arms.

With our friends and with our allies, with Japan and so many others, we have ushered in an era of unprecedented peace and prosperity on these seas and between our lands.

Our choice today is the same as in ages past: **Security through strength**, or an uncertain future of weakness and faltering will. Let me assure you, under President Donald Trump, the United States has again chosen the way of strength. (Applause.)

Under President Trump, the United States has chosen **prosperity and security** and an unwavering commitment to the Asia Pacific.

And in the name of the generations that came before, together with our allies, with confidence in all of you, and in the Commander-in-Chief who leads you, I know we will together go forth to meet the **glorious future that awaits**, a future of freedom for ourselves and our posterity.

Thank you. Godspeed on the USS Reagan's imminent deployment. God bless you. God bless Japan. And God bless the United States of America. (Applause.)

END

Chapter 144

**REMARKS BY PRESIDENT TRUMP AT SIGNING OF S. 544,
THE VETERANS CHOICE PROGRAM EXTENSION
AND IMPROVEMENT ACT
ROOSEVELT ROOM**

19 April 2017

11:32 A.M. EDT

THE PRESIDENT: Good morning. We're honored to join and be joined today by some absolutely tremendous people and great veterans. Thanks, as well -- and I have to thank them dearly -- but as well to Representative Phil Roe. Where is he? What a job you've done. And all the members of Congress who worked on the bill that we're about to sign. Such an important bill.

I especially want to thank Senator John McCain and Senator Johnny Isakson. They have been incredible in working with us. Let me also welcome my good friend, Florida Governor Rick Scott, a Navy veteran who's here with us to represent more than a million veterans from the state of Florida. We're also joined by the leaders of a number of veterans groups. I want to thank all of them for being here and all of the tremendous and important work that they do. We would not be here if it weren't for them, I can tell you that.

Finally, I want to thank our Secretary of the VA, David Shulkin, who, by the way, was approved with a vote of 100 to nothing. That's shocking, right? (Laughter.)

One hundred to nothing, really. Now, you wouldn't be getting 100 to nothing. (Laughter.)

We met earlier today in the Oval Office, and Secretary Shulkin updated me on the massive and chronic challenge he inherited at the VA, but also the great progress that he is making. He's got a group of people that are phenomenal at the VA. It's one of my most important things. I've been telling all of our friends at speeches and rallies for two years about the VA, how we're going to turn it around. And we're doing that.

And, actually, next week, on Thursday at 2 o'clock, we're going to have a news conference with David and some others to tell you about all of the tremendous things that are happening at the VA and what we've done in terms of progress and achievement.

The veterans have poured out their sweat and blood and tears for this country for so long, and it's time that they're recognized, and it's time that we now take care of them, and take care of them properly.

That's why I'm pleased today to sign into law the Veterans Choice Program Improvement Act. So this is called the Choice Program Improvement Act. It speaks for itself. This bill will extend and improve the Veterans Choice Program so that more veterans can see the doctor of their choice -- you got it? The doctor of their choice -- and don't have to wait and travel long distances for VA care. Some people have to travel five hours, eight hours, and they'll have to do it on a weekly basis, and even worse than that. It's not going to happen anymore.

This new law is a good start, but there is still much work

to do. We will fight each and every day to deliver the long-awaited reforms our veterans deserve, and to protect those who have so courageously protected each and every one of us.

So we've made a lot of strides for the veterans. These are, like, the most incredible people we have in our country as far as I'm concerned, and they have not been taken care of properly.

I want to thank David. You've done an incredible job. And you're going to see some of that on Thursday. So thank you all very much. And we're going to sign this. And I think I'm going to have to give this pen -- the way I look at it, we should probably give it to Phil. What do you think?

PARTICIPANT: I agree.

THE PRESIDENT: Does everybody agree? I think Phil is --

REPRESENTATIVE ROE: I'll agree with that. (Laughter.)

THE PRESIDENT: Phil agrees. But congratulations, every-body. Really fantastic. Thank you very much.

(Bill is signed.) (Applause.)

Phil, maybe you could say a few words, if you'd like.

REPRESENTATIVE ROE: Well, Mr. President, thank you very much. And this was a very, very important bill to get started with so we can get Choice 2.0 to get to the place exactly where the President said he wanted to be. And it's a privilege to work with all of these great people up here to help make the VA better.

I've spent the last week on the break going to Los Angeles and Phoenix to get a first-hand view of what's going on. And what we want to do is put the veteran in charge of these choices, not the bureaucracy. And I think Dr. Shulkin is just the person to see that happen. Mr. President, thank you so much.

THE PRESIDENT: Thank you very much. It's fantastic. And David? Where's David?

DR. SHULKIN: Yeah, I'm right behind you, Mr. President.

THE PRESIDENT: Go ahead. I won't look back. You just talk. (Laughter.)

DR. SHULKIN: Well, first of all, I want to thank everybody here as well, and thank Congress for seeing this done, and Mr. President to be signing this.

This is a good day for veterans. This is a great day to celebrate not only what veterans have contributed to the country, but how we're making things better for them. And by working together, we're going to continue this progress. I think, as the President said, we're actually going to do this a week from Thursday, Mr. President --

THE PRESIDENT: Right.

DR. SHULKIN: -- and talk about the tremendous accomplishments, but most importantly, about the great things that are to come to fulfill the President's commitments that he made to veterans. And so thank you all for being here today.

THE PRESIDENT: Thank you. Great job. So again, next

week, on Thursday, at 2 o'clock -- it may change a little bit, but about that time we're going to have a conference to talk about the progress and the achievement.

I'd like to ask Rick Scott, the governor of Florida -- he's done a fantastic job as governor, by the way, and really understands his subject, and really understands a lot of subjects. Rick, do you want to say a few words?

GOVERNOR SCOTT: Sure. Well, I was really proud. My father was in the 82nd Airborne, he did all the combat jumps, and I grew up listening to all his stories about the war. I had the opportunity to serve in the Navy. Unfortunately, in 2014, I had to sue the VA because we had -- our state healthcare agency couldn't go inspect their hospitals when we heard all the stories about deaths, delays, and poor conditions.

And so Mr. President and I want to thank Congress for doing this to create certainty of care while we figure out how to fix the VA system. And David, I want to thank you for what you're doing. You've got actually the right background to do this. I know President Trump has been focused on our veterans and our military before he was President, and I know he's going to continue to do a great job. We have 1.5 million veterans. I want them all to move to Florida. (Laughter.)

But thank you for doing this, Mr. President.

THE PRESIDENT: Thank you very much.

Most importantly, thank you, thank all of the great veterans. Would you like to say something to all of these people out there? You'll become a movie star tomorrow. (Laugh-

ter.)

PARTICIPANT: Well, our nation will be judged by how it treats its veterans, and I'm sure our country will allow generations -- right now, they're children, but they're going to be our future servicemen. And so we have to treat veterans well. It's about national security, it's about patriotism, and this is a great step forward to doing it.

THE PRESIDENT: Thank you very much. Nobody can say it better than that, so we're going to end. But I want to just thank you all.

Thank you for being here. Thank you. (Applause.)

END
11:40 A.M. EDT

Chapter 145

**REMARKS BY PRESIDENT TRUMP WELCOMING
THE SUPER BOWL LI CHAMPIONS,
NEW ENGLAND PATRIOTS
SOUTH LAWN**

19 April 2017

2:08 P.M. EDT

THE PRESIDENT: Thank you very much. Thank you very much. What a great day it is to be with all of our friends at the White House.

We celebrate the Super Bowl New England Patriots, world champions, Super Bowl champions -- champions, period -- and their historic win. (Applause.)

And they are champions.

Before we get started, I want to acknowledge some special guests. We're proud to be joined by seven wounded warriors who have bravely served and sacrificed for our nation.

Specialist Cameron Greenstreet. (Applause.)

Staff Sergeant Frederick Manning. (Applause.)

Specialist James Matthews. (Applause.)

Sergeant Christopher McGinnis. (Applause.)

Specialist Stephanie Morris. (Applause.)

Sergeant Major James Watson. (Applause.)

Staff Sergeant Sheldon Warner. (Applause.)

Special people. And America is very blessed to have you with us. Thank you.

The New England Patriots are big supporters of our military and America's veterans. Joe Cardona -- where's Joe? Where is Joe? There he is, in his beautiful navy -- (applause) --thank you, Joe.

Serves in the Navy Reserves and is a graduate of the Naval Academy. Coach Belichick is the son of a Navy veteran. And Bob -- that's Bob Kraft -- he's becoming a pretty famous guy for winning, I'll tell you that. Between him and Belichick, wow. You do so much to support our military. Bob has been my friend for a long time, and he wants to support our military.

So what a group of champions, all of them. And, Bob, I want to commend you for building such an extraordinary organization. Five Super Bowl victories since 2002 -- really unbelievable. And I'll say this right now: George Steinbrenner, as you know, was a very good friend of mine. And George was a great champ too, but there was a little more turmoil, right? A little more turmoil in his victories. And that's okay. He was another great one.

Since Bob bought the Patriots in 1994, they've won more division titles, conference championships and Super Bowl wins than any other team. No team has been this good for this long. (Applause.)

He's built a culture dedicated to winning. And he started it with his coach -- and I want to tell you, that is some special man -- it's called the Patriot Way. And that really starts with Coach Belichick.

And I want to thank all of you for being with us. The Patriots are an incredible organization, and this Super Bowl victory was a complete team effort. That's the beauty of what they do -- they win as a team. (Applause.)

With your backs against the wall, and the pundits -- good old pundits. Boy, they're wrong a lot, aren't they -- (laughter) -- saying you couldn't do it, the game was over, you pulled off the greatest Super Bowl comeback of all time, one of the greatest comebacks of all time -- but the greatest Super Bowl comeback of all time. And that was just special. I think I looked at odds and they gave you less than one half of 1 percent of winning the game.

And then the coach said, let's go for three. He's losing by so much, he said, let's go for three. And I say, what is he doing? That was a great decision, Coach. (Laughter.)

I tell him that all the time.

The fourth down conversion by Danny Amendola -- where's Danny? Where's Danny? (Applause.)

Way to go, Danny. The big sack by Trey Flowers. Big sack. Where's Trey? Come on, put your hand up, Trey. See, he's shy, a little bit. (Applause.)

You weren't shy when you hit that guy, were you? You weren't shy about -- he didn't mind hitting. Thank you, Trey. Great job. The incredible catch by Julian Edelman. (Applause.)

What a catch. We all said, no, that ball was dropped. Isn't that good? You know, in the old days, they might have said that was dropped. Those replays are good. You're starting to like the replay, right? (Laughter.)

Great going, Julian.

I think of guys like Marcus Cannon and the offensive line. Marcus? (Applause.)

That's some line. Or Matt Slater, who was awarded the 2017 Bart Starr Award for the character and leadership he has shown both on and off the field. Malcolm Mitchell -- (applause) -- it's true. (Applause.)

Malcolm Mitchell, who, as a rookie, handled the pressure of the Super Bowl like an absolute true veteran. Way to go, Malcolm. (Applause.)

Good job.

Or Nate Ebner, who played on our Olympic rugby team last summer. Pretty good athlete, right? And in Brazil -- he was in Brazil playing and doing really well, and is an All-Pro special team guy and player. So, Nate, congratulations. Where's Nate? (Applause.)

Which is the tougher sport, Nate, football or rugby?

MR. EBNER: I don't know. (Laughter.)

THE PRESIDENT: I had a feeling you might say that. But everyone played a role, and everybody played as champions. It was the first overtime game in Super Bowl history, and it ended with a legendary victory for this proud franchise and for these absolutely terrific players and coaches. You had the best record in football with 14 wins and only two losses. And that doesn't happen by accident. It takes hard work, dedication, and a commitment by every member of the team to work together in pursuit of the ultimate goal, a goal that very few people achieve. And you've achieved it five times, many of you, and our coach and our owner have achieved it five times. Great, great talents, great, great people.

Whether you're trying to win a Super Bowl or rebuild our country, as Coach Belichick would say, there are no days off. And just a quick story about the coach. So I had won the primaries, and I'm now in this rather heated election that a few of you have read about.

And he wrote me this beautiful letter after the primaries. "Congratulations," he said all sorts of things that were really good. I mean, it was really a beautiful letter. And it was very close to going before the election. And I called up, and I said, Coach, do you mind if I read the letter tonight to a stadium full of people in a very, very big and important state?

And he said, "You know what? I'd rather not have you do that. Could you send it back to me? I'm going to give you another one." I said, no that's okay. "Nope, I want to give you another one." Now, immediately to me, that means he's going to tone it down because what he said was so nice. And you know what he did? He toned it way up. It was much better. It was much better. He made that the greatest letter, and I did very well in that state. Thank you, Coach. That was very good.

But, you know, he's just a very special guy. And he's

tough. Is he tough, fellas, or a nice guy? Huh? A little tough, right? He's tough, he's smart, and he's got a great heart.

So the Patriot coaches and these great players have delivered iconic American sports moments that will last forever. We're going to watch that game over and over and over. That game will last forever. Five Super Bowl wins in the era of free agency, which is really, really tough. What an achievement.

So again, congratulations to Super Bowl Champion New England Patriots. And with that, I'd like to ask a very special and talented man, and a great friend of mine for a long time, Bob Kraft, to say a few words. Thank you all very much. (Applause.)

MR. KRAFT: Thank you, Mr. President. It's a true honor to be here for the fifth time celebrating a world championship. And every time that we have the privilege of coming here to the White House, I think about the long odds that were faced by our country's forefathers who fought for our freedom and independence.

Overcoming long odds through hard work, perseverance, and, most importantly, mental toughness is the foundation of everything that is great about this country. I am proud that the first time we came here as a team after winning a championship as 14-point underdogs but infinitely more important was it was the season of 9/11, 2001, at a time in which our nation showed its mental toughness to rally together and to rebound from an unthinkable tragedy.

This year's championship was achieved after falling behind by 25 points -- a deficit so great that in the 97-year history

of the NFL -- over 20,000 games -- that deficit had only
been overcome seven times. In that same year, a very
good friend of mine for over 25 years, a man who is mentally tough and hard-working as anybody I know, launched
a campaign for the presidency against 16 career politicians,
facing odds almost as long as we faced in the fourth quarter. He persevered to become the 45th President of the
United States. (Applause.)

It's a distinct honor for us to celebrate what was unequivocally our sweetest championship with a very good friend
and somebody whose mental toughness and strength I
greatly admire. And I would like to call upon our coach to
say a few words. But before, we'd like to jointly present --
(The President is presented with a jersey.) (Applause.)

A Super Bowl LI Championship jersey. (Applause.)

MR. BELICHICK: Thank you. On behalf of the team, the
organization, I just want to thank the President and his
great staff for wonderful day, a wonderful opportunity
here. We've had the great privilege to be here several
times, but this one -- the way we were treated and the
opportunities to be in the Oval Office, to meet with the
President, to see the inside of the White House has just
been fabulous.

So along with the parade, the ring ceremony -- as a team,
the opportunity and the privilege of coming to the White
House is just one of the great things about winning the
Super Bowl. And so we're very privileged to be here, and
we thank the President and his great staff for the hospitality that they have shown us.

Also, our great Patriot fans here and throughout Patriot

Nation, thank you for coming out today. (Applause.)

As Mr. Kraft said, this is really a special team. These guys
work incredibly hard all year. They put all the work in
in advance when we didn't have anything to show for
it. And then as the year went on -- you know, a total of 17
victories. They were all tough. These guys are mentally
tough. They're physically tough. They love to compete
and they knew how to compete under pressure, and that's
probably when we played our best football as we saw in
overtime in the Super Bowl.

So I'm incredibly proud and honored to coach this group
with our coaching staff. Our coaching staff did a tremendous job this year. I'm so appreciative of them. And then
this day really is -- you know, it's a great day for us, it's a
thrill to be here, and we appreciate your support, and we
appreciate, again, the great treatment that we received
from the President and his staff. Thank you very much.

And we have one other presentation to make. Super Bowl
LI helmet. (Applause.)

THE PRESIDENT: Thank you, everybody. Thank you very
much. (Applause.)

END
2:27 P.M. EDT

Chapter 146

**REMARKS BY THE VICE PRESIDENT AND
INDONESIAN PRESIDENT WIDODO TO THE PRESS
MERDEKA PALACE
JAKARTA, INDONESIA**

20 April 2017

PRESIDENT WIDODO: (As translated.) It is an honor for Indonesia to welcome the visit of the Vice President of the United States, His Excellency Michael Richard Pence.

This is my first meeting with the new administration of the United States. However, I have communicated with President Trump since January. And receiving the courtesy call of Vice President Pence, we discussed a number of bilateral and international issues.

The first is the commitment of the United States to enhance its strategic partnership with Indonesia. We'll focus on the issues of cooperation and investment. And next month, there will be a team that will discuss the arrangement of trade and investment bilateral between the countries based on the principles of **win-win** solution.

Second, as the largest Muslim population country in the world, as well as the third largest democracy in the world, Indonesia also agree to strengthen cooperation on peace. That is what I can convey to you all in this auspicious occasion. And I also send my best regards to President Trump through Vice President Pence. That is all from me. Thank you very much.

VICE PRESIDENT PENCE: Good morning. Thank you, President Widodo, for hosting me here today. Thank you for your warm hospitality to my family, and the extraordinarily colorful welcome that we received from all the children as we approached this morning will be a memory for a lifetime.

It is my great privilege to be here in Indonesia. My very first visit to Indonesia to represent the President of the United States of America, Donald Trump. And I bring his greetings to you and his appreciation for your kindness and outreach since his election in November.

I know I'm the first member of President Trump's administration to visit Southeast Asia, and the President sent me here -- sent me here as a sign of the high value the United States places on our strategic partnership with Indonesia.

As the second and third largest democracies in the world, our two countries share many common values -- including freedom, the rule of law, human rights, and religious diversity.

The United States is proud to partner with Indonesia to promote and protect these values, the birthright of all people.

And as President Widodo and I discussed under President Donald Trump, the United States and Indonesia are going to work even more closely together for the mutual benefit of our nations, our people, and for the benefit of Southeast Asia, as a whole.

Economically, President Trump and I seek to expand the United States' commercial relationship with

Indonesia. And the President and I spoke about that very openly today, and we look forward to those discussions continuing.

American companies have been doing business in Indonesia for years, and American products and services have contributed greatly to Indonesia's economic development. But we believe that we still have room for significant progress.

Under President Trump's leadership, the United States seeks trade relationships that are both free and fair, that spur job creation, and economic growth for both parties.

As you, President Widodo, have said so often, we're looking for a **win-win** relationship, and we're confident that we can find it on an increasing basis.

We believe we must level the playing field, break down barriers to ensure that American exporters can fully participate in the Indonesia market, the same freedom that Indonesia exporters have had in many sectors in the United States for many years.

Mr. President, President Trump and I look forward to working with you to make progress for this objective and are grateful for your openness to our teams beginning those conversations in the coming weeks.

The United States is also proud to be one of Indonesia's oldest and most engaged defense partners. And under President Trump we are firmly committed to continuing to collaborate on the security of both of our peoples. A stronger defense partnership will serve us well as we confront the various security threats and challenges that we now face. And of course, one of the greatest threats we face is the rise and spread of terrorism.

Sadly, Indonesia is no stranger to this evil, nor is the United States of America, as the President and I discussed. The world watched with heartbreak in January of last year when ISIS-linked terrorists struck in central Jakarta in a barbaric suicide bombing. Our hearts broke for your people. This vile attack claimed the lives of five innocents, injured more than two dozen others. What I can assure you and the people of Indonesia is that you had the condolences and the prayers of the American people as you confronted this tragedy.

We too know the terrible cost of terrorism, and the United States stands with you to condemn it and to confront it.

We will also continue to work with Indonesia to defend the rules-based system that is the foundation for Southeast Asia's peace and prosperity. The United States will uphold the fundamental freedoms of navigation and overflight in the South China Sea and throughout the Asia Pacific; will ensure the unimpeded flow of lawful commerce; and promote peaceful diplomatic dialogue to address issues of regional and global concern.

Finally, with President Trump's leadership, the United States intends to deepen our cultural ties with the nation and the good people of Indonesia. Later today I'm greatly humbled to have the privilege to visit Indonesia's national mosque, where I'll have the opportunity to speak with leaders of many faiths.

And, Mr. President, I'm very much looking forward to that visit and that honor.

As the largest majority Muslim country, Indonesia's tradition of moderate Islam, frankly, is an inspiration to the
world. And we commend you and your people.

In your nation, as in mine, religion unifies -- it doesn't
divide. It gives us hope for a brighter future, and we are all
grateful for the great inspiration that Indonesia provides
for the world.

Rest assured, under President Trump, the United States
welcomes all who share our values and strive for that
brighter future. Today on President Trump's behalf, I have
the privilege of reaffirming the United States' strategic
partnership with Indonesia and declaring our commitment
to strengthen our bonds of friendship, commerce, and
security.

Today I say with confidence through our continued partnership, the United States and Indonesia will continue to
maintain a peaceful, stable, and a prosperous Southeast
Asia for the benefit of both of our nations and for the benefit of the world.

So on behalf of President Trump, let me say again,
President Widodo, thank you. Thank you for your leadership. Thank you for your hospitality. And thank you for
the opportunity to build on a foundation of friendship and
partnership between our two nations.

END

Chapter 147

REMARKS BY THE VICE PRESIDENT AT ASEAN
ASEAN SECRETARIAT
JAKARTA, INDONESIA

20 April 2017

THE VICE PRESIDENT: Good afternoon. This is my first visit to the Asia Pacific as Vice President of the United States, and I bring greetings from the President of the United States, President Donald Trump.

And it is such an honor to be here today at ASEAN, the Association of Southeast Asian Nations.

Since 1967, ASEAN has fostered friendship and economic integration between its members. It's helped forge regional cooperation to tackle common challenges. It's promoted prosperity and security -- not just for ASEAN and its members, but for the Asia Pacific as a whole.

I want to thank the chargé d'affaires, Jane Bocklage, for that kind introduction. Thank you for faithfully representing the United States of America to ASEAN. The President and I are grateful for your work.

I also want to thank Secretary General Minh and Chairwoman Buensuceso and the ASEAN permanent members who are here with me today.

I was grateful to have the opportunity to meet with each of you today and appreciate our discussion about our shared values and shared opportunities.

Today on President Trump's behalf, I'd like to congratulate
ASEAN on its 50th anniversary. This year also marks the
40th anniversary of the United States' diplomatic relationship with ASEAN. Our relationship without a doubt
has benefitted both ASEAN and America -- diplomatically,
economically, and from the standpoint of national security.

The relationship between the United States and ASEAN is a
strategic partnership. And under President Trump's leadership, the United States is already taking steps to strengthen
our partnership with ASEAN and deepen our friendship.

I spoke to President Trump this morning, and he gave me
the great privilege to inform the Secretary General and the
permanent members of ASEAN that the President of the
United States will attend the U.S.-ASEAN Summit, the East
Asia Summit, and the APEC Leaders Meeting in Vietnam
and the Philippines this November. (Applause.)

The President asked me to deliver this message directly to
the leadership here at ASEAN and to express how enthusiastic he is to join the U.S.-ASEAN Summit during the golden
anniversary year of this organization.

It is a testament to the value that President Trump places
on the U.S.-ASEAN strategic partnership and the Asia Pacific as a whole. And it's a sign, I hope, to all of our firm and
unwavering commitment to build on the strong foundation
that we already share.

By strengthening our economic ties, the United States
and ASEAN member nations can foster jobs, prosperity,
and growth in new and unprecedented ways. American
exports to ASEAN member nations already support more
than 550,000 jobs in the United States, and almost 42,000

U.S. companies export more than $100 billion in goods and services to ASEAN nations every year. At the same time, the United States imports a significant amount from ASEAN member nations, as well. But amazingly, U.S. companies invest more in ASEAN and its members than any other part of Asia, nearly $274 billion, which is an investment -- which is more, in fact, than our investment in China, India, and Japan combined.

Now to protect that prosperity and to ensure our continued growth, the United States will redouble our cooperation with ASEAN on issues of regional security. The menace and the reality of global terrorism threatens all our nations. And under President Trump, we will continue to support increasing information sharing and security efforts to protect our people and our way of life across this region and across the wider world.

We'll continue to work closely with ASEAN to promote peace and stability in the South China Sea by upholding a rules-based order, ensuring the lawful and unimpeded flow of commerce, and encouraging the peaceful and diplomatic resolution of disputes.

For 40 years, the United States has worked side by side with ASEAN to foster peace and prosperity on these seas and between our lands; and President Trump and I are confident that through our continued partnership, which even now, today, is growing stronger, together we will build on our firm foundation to reach even greater heights in the next 50 years of this great organization.

So I want to say thank you. Thank you to the permanent members, thank you to the Secretary General for the warm hospitality today. President Trump and I look forward to

reaffirming our commitment to each of you in the days
ahead, and I know he looks forward to seeing you all at the
summits this November.

Thank you very much for giving me the opportunity to
make this announcement. It is an honor to be with you
all. (Applause.)

END

Chapter 148

**REMARKS BY PRESIDENT TRUMP AT
SIGNING OF THE
MEMORANDUM REGARDING THE
INVESTIGATION PURSUANT TO
SECTION 232(B) OF THE TRADE EXPANSION ACT
OVAL OFFICE**

20 April 2017

12:13 P.M. EDT

THE PRESIDENT: Thank you very much. We appreciate everybody for being here. It's a historic day for American steel and, most importantly, for American steelworkers. Thanks, especially, to Secretary Wilbur Ross for helping to lead this critical effort. We've been working on it since I came to office, and long before I came to office.

We're going to fight for American workers and American-made steel. And that's beginning immediately.

For decades, America has lost our jobs and our factories to unfair foreign trade. And one steel mill after another has been shut down, abandoned, and closed, and we're going to reverse that.

Other countries have made a living taking advantage of the United States in so many ways, as you know, and I've been talking about that for a long time.

As I traveled the country, I saw the shuttered factories, of the shuttered **dreams**, and **I pledged** that I would take action. And I think it's probably one of the primary reasons I'm sitting here today as President.

And since the day I entered office, I have followed through on that **pledge**, big league, beginning with our withdrawal from the Trans-Pacific Partnership, which would have been a catastrophe for our businesses and for our workers. I'm very proud of that withdrawal.

Some people say, oh, gee, I wish you didn't do that, but the smart people say, thank you, thank you, thank you. That would have been another NAFTA disaster. And NAFTA, believe me, was a disaster and continues to be a disaster for our country.

On Tuesday, I signed an order to enforce the **Buy American laws and stop foreign countries from stealing contracts from American companies** and, essentially, from American workers.

Today, I'm directing the Department of Commerce to immediately prioritize the investigation that began yesterday and really long before that -- because Wilbur and I have been working on this for a long time -- into foreign steel arriving into our markets, and to submit a report on the effects of these foreign steel products on the national security of the United States. It's not just the pricing, it's not just employment, it also has to do with the national security of our country, which people never talk about. I talked about it.

Maintaining the production of American steel is extremely important to our national security and our defense industrial base. **Steel is critical to both our economy and our military**. This is not an area where we can afford to be-

come dependent on foreign countries. We have a product
where we actually need foreign countries to be nice to us
in order to fight for our people.

And that's not going to happen any longer, believe me --
especially as it comes to steel.

This investigation will look at how steel imports are impact-
ing the United States national security, taking into account
foreign practices such as steel dumping. Dumping is a tremendous problem in this country. They're dumping vast
amounts of steel in our country, and they're really hurting
not only our country, but our companies. Their targeting
of American industry and other foreign strategies designed
to undermine American industry as a whole.

Based on the findings of this report, Secretary Wilbur Ross
will make formal recommendations to the White House
in a very, very, near future. He'll be back very soon with
those recommendations that we will implement.

From now on, we're going to stand up for American jobs,
workers, their security, and for American steel companies
and companies generally. Today's action is the next vital
step toward making America strong and prosperous once
again.

And I want to just add -- I wasn't going to do this -- but
I was in Wisconsin the other day, and I want to end and
add by saying that Canada, what they've done to our dairy
farm workers is a disgrace. It's a disgrace. I spent time
with some of the farmers in Wisconsin, and, as you know,
rules, regulations, different things have changed. And our
farmers in Wisconsin and New York State are being put
out of business, our dairy farmers. And that also includes

what's happening along our northern border states with Canada, having to do with lumber and timber.

The fact is, NAFTA -- whether it's Mexico or Canada -- is a disaster for our country. It's a disaster. It's a trading disaster. And we'll be reporting back sometime over the next two weeks as to NAFTA and what we're going to do about it. But what happened to our dairy farmers in Wisconsin and New York State -- we're not going to let it happen. We can't let Canada or anybody else take advantage and do what they did to our workers and to our farmers. And again, I want to also just mention, included in there is lumber, timber, and energy. So we're going to have to get to the negotiating table with Canada very, very quickly. Again, just to tell you, this is another NAFTA disaster, and we're not going to let it continue onward.

I think what I'd like to do is ask a few of the people if they'd like to -- these are some of the great steel companies of our country. Now, some of those companies were much bigger years ago. U.S. Steel would be an example, and others would be examples. But they were much -- these were the greatest companies in the world years ago.

And today, they've been hurt but they'll be **Great Again**.

And they'll be great, I think, very soon. We're going to impose very, very strict regulations on unfair competition from the outside world.

Perhaps I could ask the head of United States Steel to say a few words.

MR. LONGHI: An honor, Mr. President, Mr. Secretary. I think the signing of this executive order clearly demonstrates your understanding of the fundamental importance that our industry has, not just to the national economy, but to our national defense.

THE PRESIDENT: Thank you very much. Anybody like to say something on behalf of your company or your workers?

PARTICIPANT: I would just like to thank you, Mr. President and Secretary Ross, for this action to protect not only our industries, our employees, but, frankly, our country. So thank you for this bold move.

THE PRESIDENT: Thank you very much.

MR. GERARD: Mr. President, on behalf of the workers in the industry -- President of the Steelworkers Union -- I have worked a long time with Wilbur, and we've been fighting this unfair trade for more than 30 years. Hopefully, this executive order will give us the tools we need to grow our companies back and put people back to work. And I have lots of faith that Secretary Wilbur Ross will help make that happen.

THE PRESIDENT: I have to say, the unions have been working with us very closely, and they've been great. So I appreciate that. Thank you very much.

So we're going to sign, and this is a very important signing. And we'll be back over a period of the next 30 to 50 days, I would say, and maybe sooner than that. But statutorily, we probably want to take a very good, strong, hard study.

And we're going to do something really great for our industry, but in this particular case, for the steel industry. I look forward to it too.

(The President signs the Executive Order.)

So should I give this pen to labor or to steel? (Laughter.)

And I'm going to look at it, and they're going to be a partnership. So how about we give it to the union for a change? Should we do that? Come on. You treat us fairly, that's all. Okay, you treat us fairly.

Q   Mr. President, how will this affect your dealing with China on North Korea? Are you concerned that this will affect that at all?

THE PRESIDENT: This has nothing to do with China. This has to do with worldwide, what's happening. The dumping problem is a worldwide problem.

Thank you, everybody. (Applause.)

END
12:22 P.M. EDT

Chapter 149

**REMARKS BY PRESIDENT TRUMP AND
PRIME MINISTER GENTILONI OF ITALY
IN JOINT PRESS CONFERENCE
EAST ROOM**

20 April 2017

3:56 P.M. EDT

PRESIDENT TRUMP: Prime Minister Gentiloni, welcome. Great honor. Thank you.

It's wonderful to have you in our wonderful People's House, known as the White House. And so many great Italian friends are with us today.

And we renew, always, the deep ties of history and friendship that link together the American and the Italian peoples. That history traces its roots to the timeless contributions of Italy to civilization and human progress -- so true -- stretching all the way back to Ancient Rome.

Through the ages, your country has been a beacon of artistic and scientific achievement -- and that continues today -- from Venice to Florence, from Verdi to Pavarotti, a friend of mine. Great friend of mine.

These bonds of history and culture have only grown stronger as our two nations have become close partners, dear friends, and very vital allies.

Mr. Prime Minister, I'm thrilled that you are here today to

discuss how we can make this great relationship even more productive in the years to come.

On the economy, Italy is one of America's largest trading partners. A lot of people don't know that. We both seek a trading relationship that is balanced, reciprocal -- I love the word "reciprocal," because we don't have too many recip-rocal trading partnerships, I will tell you that, but we will very soon -- and fair, benefitting both of our countries.

And we can work together to achieve that outcome, and that will happen.

Italy is also a key partner in the fight against terrorism.

Italy is now the second-largest contributor of troops to the conflicts in Iraq and Afghanistan. I would also like to thank you, Prime Minister, for your leadership on seeking stabi-lization in Libya, and for your crucial efforts to deny ISIS a foothold in the Mediterranean. You fought hard.

We're grateful for your role in the anti-ISIS campaign. All nations must condemn this barbaric enemy and support the effort to achieve its total and complete destruction.

Also, as you know, Mr. Prime Minister, we have more than 30,000 American service-members, families, and person-nel who are stationed across your country. As we reaffirm our support for historic institutions, we must also reaffirm the requirement that everyone must pay their full and fair share for the cost of defense.

Together, we can address many pressing challenges, includ-ing two that greatly affect both of our countries, those of large-scale migration and international smuggling. Maintaining strong borders is a vital component of any security policy, and a responsible approach to refugees is one that seeks the eventual return of refugees to their home countries so that they can help to rebuild their own nations.

Finally, I want to say how much I look forward to visiting Sicily for the G7, as we seek to foster cooperation not only on matters of security, but also science, commerce, health, and technology. Our two countries have shared interests and shared values, and we can each make great contributions to the other.

Mr. Prime Minister, I again want to thank you for being with us and being our true friend. Italy is a spectacular place; I know it well. I love the people of Italy. We have 18 million Italians living in the United States, people originally from Italy. And it's a great honor to have many of them as my friends. Thank you for being here.

PRIME MINISTER GENTILONI: Thank you for hosting us here. It's an honor to be here at the White House today. And I'll now switch to Italian.

(As interpreted.) We had a very fruitful meeting which reflects an ancient friendship, as the President reminded us with his words.

This friendship is also a sign of the 18 million Italian Americans who have such an important role in our country -- in this country. And this friendship is witnessed also by the fact that Italy is the second choice of American students to study abroad, and we're very proud of this.

And this confirms the importance that the United States gives to the cultural dimension of our country, as the

President, himself, just said.

This friendship is based on a common commitment against terrorism. This commitment is a commitment in which we are both very active -- our country is very active in Iraq and in Afghanistan, and I think that the stabilization work will be decisive, the civilization work of Iraq, after the military defeat that we expect for Daesh.

We know that this action against terrorism must take place within our individual countries. In Europe, with the social and cultural commitment against radicalization, by cooperating with Islamic communities, Italy contributes to peace and to stability in the Mediterranean.

In Syria, where I believe the U.S. choice to react to the use of chemical weapons by Bashar al-Assad, and where a negotiated solution is more necessary than ever.

 In Libya -- and we discussed this in our meeting -- where we need to work against the division of the country in order to stabilize it.

This is a very decisive task if we want to manage the migratory flows without giving up on our values and our humanitarian principles. And we need to contrast the horrible traffic of people and clandestine refugees.

Italy is convinced of its strategic commitment in favor of the transatlantic relationship. We have also spoken about common commitments in NATO and the goals that were identified in 2014, and the commitments on military expenses and the contribution that each country must make towards collective security. We are proud of our contribution.

And finally, Italy is a country of dialogue. We are proud because we succeeded in keeping open the doors in difficult
crises. Dialogue can be useful even vis-à-vis Russia, without obviously giving up our unity and our principles, and
without giving up our strength and our values.

I also told President Trump that we have confidence --
even though this is a difficult moment, and we all know it's
difficult right now -- we have confidence in the future of
the European Union and certainly in the importance of the
relationship between the U.S. and Italy.

These are the two pillars that the transatlantic relationship
is based on and a great part of peace and freedom in the
world. We are going through a difficult time, but I have
confidence that the European Union will continue to be a
positive response to this.

And, finally, we are expecting and I look forward to the
President's visit to the summit in Taormina, and I trust that
this will be the opportunity to show him the unity of our
leaders and of the principal free economies of the planet. Because right now, we really do need this unity. Once
again, thank you, Mr. President.

PRESIDENT TRUMP: Thank you very much. Thank
you. Appreciate it.

I'll take a few questions. John Roberts of Fox, please.

Q   Mr. President, thanks so much. I hope you'll forgive
me for asking you a three-part question -- it's been a
while. In just the last few minutes -- I believe it was while
you were meeting with the Prime Minister -- there was a
shooting in downtown Paris.

PRESIDENT TRUMP: I see that.

Q   It's being described as a potential terrorist attack. I wonder if you have something on that.

And further to that, to the big trouble spots that you're dealing with right now, North Korea and Iran.

Do you believe that the leader of North Korea, Kim Jong-un, is mentally unstable?

Is that one of the reasons why you're so concerned about these latest developments?

Is he a man who can be reasoned with?

And on Iran, do you have reason to suspect that they are cheating on the JCPOA?

And to Mr. Prime Minister, you talked just a moment ago about your commitment to NATO. President Trump would like to see all NATO members contribute 2 percent of their GDP to NATO.

Your contribution is slightly less than 1 percent. Will you commit to committing 2 percent of your GDP to the Alliance going forward? Thank you.

PRESIDENT TRUMP: Well, first of all, I love the question you asked the Prime Minister. I look forward to his answer -- (laughter) -- because I'm going to be asking him that same question very soon.

Well, first of all, our condolences from our country to the people of France. Again, it's happening, it seems. I just saw it as I was walking in, so that's a terrible thing and it's a very, very terrible thing that's going on in the world today. But it looks like another terrorist attack. And what can you say -- it just never ends.

We have to be strong and we have to be vigilant. And I've been saying it for a long time.

As far as North Korea is concerned, we are in very good shape. We're building our military rapidly. A lot of things have happened over the last short period of time.

I've been here for approximately **91 days**; we're doing a lot of work. We're in very good position. We're going to see what happens.

I can't ask your -- answer your question on stability. I hope the answer is a positive one, not a negative one. But hopefully that will be something that gets taken care of.

I have great respect for the President of China.

As you know, we had a great summit in Florida, and Palm Beach, and got to know each other and I think like each other. I can say from my standpoint I liked him very much. I respect him very much. And I think he's working very hard.

I can say that all of the pundits out there are saying they never have seen China work like they're working right now.

Many coal ships have sent back. Many other things have happened. Some very unusual moves have been made over the last two or three hours. And I really have confidence that the President will try very hard. We don't know

whether or not they're able to do that, but I have absolute
confidence that he will be trying very, very hard.

And one of the reasons that we're talking about trade
deals and we're talking about all of the different things --
but we're slowing up a little bit. I actually told him, I said,
you'll make a much better deal on trade if you get rid of
this menace or do something about the menace of North
Korea. Because that's what it is, it's a menace right now.

So we'll see what happens. As far as Iran is concerned, I
think they are doing a tremendous disservice to an agreement that was signed. It was a terrible agreement. It
shouldn't have been signed. It shouldn't have been negotiated the way it was negotiated. I'm all for agreements, but
that was a bad one, as bad as I've ever seen negotiated.

They are not living up to the spirit of the agreement, I can
tell you that. And we're analyzing it very, very carefully
and we'll have something to say about it in the not-too-
distant future. But Iran has not lived up to the spirit of the
agreement. And they have to do that. They have to do
that. So we will see what happens. Thank you very much,
John.

PRIME MINISTER GENTILONI: Thank you, Mr.
President. (As interpreted.) First of all, allow me to
join President Trump's words for what happened in Paris. These words of condolences and closeness to the
French people. And this is a very delicate period for them,
just three days before the election.

As far as the question is concerned, the commitment has
been made. It was made during a NATO summit. And we
are used to respecting our commitments. We know that

this will be a gradual process; it has already begun. And we know that Italy has certain limitations when it comes to its budget, but despite these limitations our commitment for common defense is very clear.

And, as I said earlier, I'm very proud not only of the progress made in our financial commitment, but also proud of the contribution that we give to the security of the Alliance in so many areas of the world. We talked about Iraq and Afghanistan, but we could also talk about the Baltic Sea or the Balkans. And in all of these areas, you will see the presence of Italian forces within the Alliance, and we are proud of that.

Q   Sky Italia. (As interpreted.) First, for you, President [sic] Gentiloni, I wanted to ask you -- we saw from this new administration a new type of policy on the international scene, very different from what we had in the past. And one of the last important operations which was carried out by President Trump was in Syria with a bombing following the use of chemical weapons by the Assad regime. I wanted to ask you, does Italy think or conceive a possibility to take action in -- more action in Syria? (In progress.)

(In English.) -- since my colleague from Fox News did, so I'm going to take as well the possibility to ask you two questions.

First of all, about European Union. You have said in the past that Brexit was a great thing, and that you think that other country will follow.

So you know that Italy is an important player and supporter of European integration. Do you believe that actually a strong Europe is important for the United States, also looking forward at a French election?

And on the second question, is that you said that you're looking forward to come to Italy for the G7, and I wanted to know if you're also looking forward, if it's going to be possible, to meet Pope Francis during your Italian trip. Thank you.

PRIME MINISTER GENTILONI: (As interpreted.) Syria: We immediately assessed the operation that was ordered by President Trump and decided that this was a motivated response to the use of chemical weapons. We added that it's up to everyone to consider negotiation as the road through which we hopefully can put an end to this infinite dramatic war and come to peace.

Italy is not directly involved in the operations and military operations in Syria other than marginal aspects, but it's not our plan to change this attitude.

PRESIDENT TRUMP: Yes, a strong Europe is very, very important to me as President of the United States. And it's also, in my opinion, in my very strong opinion, important for the United States. We want to see it. We will help it be strong, and it's very much to everybody's advantage.

And I look very much forward to meeting the Pope.

Fabian of The Hill. Fabian. Yes.

Q   Thank you, Mr. President. Some people on Capitol Hill believe you can get one of two things next week: a vote on healthcare or a vote on a government funding bill.

So my question is, which one is more important to you

have: a vote on healthcare or a vote on a bill to keep the government open?

And, Mr. Prime Minister, I want to get your thoughts on a referendum in Turkey that occurred last week. You spoke about democratic values in the European continent, so are you concerned with the result of the Turkish referendum?

Is that something that you discussed with President Trump?

PRESIDENT TRUMP: Okay, I want to get both. Are you shocked to hear that?

And we're doing very well on healthcare. We'll see what happens. But this is a great bill. There's a great plan. And this will be great healthcare. It's evolving. You know, there was never a give-up.

The press sort of reported there was like a give-up. There's no give-up. We started. Remember, it took Obamacare 17 months. I've really been negotiating this for two months, maybe even less than that, because we had a 30-day period where we did lots of other things the first 30 days.

But this has really been two months. And this is a continuation. And the plan gets better and better and better. And it's gotten really, really good. And a lot of people are liking it a lot. We have a good chance of getting it soon. I'd like to say next week, but it will be -- I believe we will get it. And whether it's next week or shortly thereafter. As far as keeping the government open, I think we want to keep the government open. Don't you agree? So, yeah, I think we'll get both. Thank you.

PRIME MINISTER GENTILONI: (As interpreted.) The Turkish referendum is a fact that we must take note of, leaving aside any debates that can take place about how the vote took place. But I believe the European leadership have taken note of the vote.

The consequences will depend a great deal on how the Turkish government and President Erdogan, especially, will take into account almost half of the population's expression of a different opinion.

Will there be an inclusive approach, or will there be a confrontation in this part of Turkey?

This will be very important for us and the European Union.

The other thing that's going to be very important is the respect of the certain fundamental principles.

We are members of the Atlantic alliance -- Italy and Turkey -- and Italy contributes to Turkey's defense with its own military assets. We believe that, among our countries, there should be a cooperation, and hopefully -- and we trust -- that this cooperation will have, among its consequences, the solution of the case concerning the journalist who's been detained over the last few days in Turkey.

Q   (As interpreted.) President Gentiloni, you have focused a lot on the leadership -- Italian leadership and American leadership -- in order to stabilize Libya.

What do you expect exactly from Washington?

And especially, I am asking you, what is necessary in this process, in this relationship of cooperation with Russia?

(In English.) President Trump, do you see a role for your administration in helping stabilizing Libya?

And do you agree that stabilizing Libya means combating terrorism and ISIS?

PRESIDENT GENTILONI: (As interpreted.) America has played a very key role -- first of all, to prevent the consolidation of an important basis for terrorism while Daesh was undergoing defeat in Iraq and Syria. There were operations that were sustained by the U.S. against Daesh in the city of Sirte which were successful. Now the commitment must be political. And, therefore, in the cooperation of U.S. and Italy and other key partners in the region, the goal is to broaden the basis -- the consensus for the Tripoli government, which is recognized by the international community, but which must be able to count on a broader consensus.

I believe that one clear goal should be this: We need the region, and we need countries like Egypt and Tunisia that are close to Libya. We need a stable and unified Libya. A divided country and in conflict would make stability worse. The U.S. role in this is very critical.

PRESIDENT TRUMP: I do not see a role in Libya. I think the United States has right now enough roles.

We're in a role everywhere. So I do not see that.

I do see a role in getting rid of ISIS. We're being very effective in that regard. We are doing a job, with respect to ISIS, that has not been done anywhere near the numbers that we're producing right now.

It's a very effective force we have. We have no choice. It's
a horrible thing to say, but we have no choice. And we are
effectively ridding the world of ISIS.

I see that as a primary role, and that's what we're going to
do, whether it's in Iraq or in Libya or anywhere else.

And that role will come to an end at a certain point, and
we'll be able to go back home and **rebuild** our country,
which is what I want to do.

Thank you all very much. I appreciate it. Thank you.

END
4:21 P.M. EDT

Chapter 150

21 April 2017

Transcript:

My Fellow Americans,
A **new optimism** is sweeping our country as we return power from Washington and **give it back to the American People**, where it belongs.

For too long, **American workers were forgotten by their government** – and I mean totally forgotten. Their interests were pushed aside for global projects, and their wealth was taken from their communities and shipped across the world, all across the seas.

My Administration has offered a new vision. The well-being of the American citizen and worker will be placed second to none – and boy do I mean second to none.

Since Day One, I have been fighting for the hard-working people of this country – and **this week we took historic action to continue delivering on that promise**.

We did so in one of the many proud industrial towns of our nation – Kenosha, Wisconsin – with the men and women of *Snap-On*, who make American tools for workers around the world. They were there, and they loved what they heard, and they loved what they saw.

In Wisconsin, I signed an Executive Order to **Buy American and Hire American**.

I took historic action to ensure that Federal Projects are made with **American Goods** – and **to keep American workers** and companies from being cheated out of contracts by countries that break the rules and break every regulation in the book to take advantage of the United States. That's not going to happen anymore.

I also took action to reform our immigration system so that it **puts the needs of American workers first** – the duty of government is to represent the citizens of the United States, and that is what we will do.

Whether it's removing job-killing regulations, protecting our borders, or unleashing American energy, **we are keeping our promises** and delivering for the American Worker.

During my visit, I talked about how America is a nation that honors work. **We honor grit.** We honor craftsmanship. We honor the skilled tradespeople who turn rock and steel and iron and cement into works of art and grace and beauty. There's tremendous talent there, believe me.

The wrench and ratchet are not only tools, but instruments that help build cities out of deserts and send ships across oceans. And the tools of craftsmen and the masons are just as important as the tools of the doctor and the dentist or the CEO, or even the tools of politicians, believe it or not – and their work is every bit as noble. They take pride in their jobs, and we take pride in them.

No longer will the concerns of these hard-working Americans go unanswered.

By making government answer to our citizens, we are
removing the limits on our future and setting free the
dreams of our people.

As long as we do this, **optimism will continue to
soar.** Hope will continue to spring. And this country we
love will grow stronger and stronger day by day.

Thank you, God Bless you, and God Bless America.

Chapter 151

21 April 2017

2:55 P.M. EDT

THE PRESIDENT: Thank you very much, Steve. Great honor, I must say. It's a great pleasure to be at the United States Treasury Department and to meet so many dedicated public servants.

I went through that beautiful hallway where those incredible paintings of past secretaries, and it was really very interesting. I want to read every one, I want to learn about every one of them, but we have one that I hope will go down as one of the greats.

I think Hamilton is tough to beat, but maybe you can do that too. We'll take it, right? But thank you very much.

The Treasury Department is the guardian of America's wealth and a worldwide symbol of American prestige.

This department was first led by the same gentleman, Alexander Hamilton, a man who understood that the **government must protect** the jobs of its citizens and the wealth of our nation.

Secretary Mnuchin, who I've known for so long, and he's

so good and so smart and so financially adept, is working
very hard every day to do just that -- to **protect** the working citizen of America, and **to safeguard** our finances from
anyone, anybody, any nation who would try to take advantage of the United States.

His vast experience and financial talent are now being put
into service on behalf of the American people. And you'll
see what I mean very soon.

We have taken unprecedented action to bring back our
jobs and return power to our citizens. It's been taken
away. We've lifted one terrible regulation after another
at a record clip, from the energy sector to the auto sector. And we have many more to go, and that's going to be
happening over the next, I would say, four to five weeks.

And we've begun a historic effort to protect our manufacturing and our manufacturing businesses, companies and
our workers from unfair foreign trade.

Protecting our Treasury also means getting other countries
to finally pay their fair share for the cost of defense, and
many other global projects that for too long have fallen under our guidance and, unfortunately, fallen under the United States taxpayer expense. And we're going to end that;
we're going to end it quickly. We want fairness. We don't
want to take advantage of anyone. We want fairness.

We're now in the process of **rebuilding** America, and
there's a **new optimism** sweeping across our country like
people have not seen in many, many decades. We're here
today to continue this great economic revival. **I will be
signing three presidential directives to further protect our
workers and our taxpayers.**

The first executive action instructs Secretary Mnuchin to begin the process of tax simplification. Such a big thing. People can't do their returns. They have no idea what they're doing. They're too complicated.

This regulatory reduction is the first step toward a tax reform that reduces rates, provides relief to our middle class, and lowers our business tax, which is one of the highest in the world and has stopped us from so much wealth and productivity.

Secretary Mnuchin is a leader in our effort to **Make America Competitive Again**. We're going to **Make It Great Again**, we're going to **Make It Strong Again**, we're going to **Make It Safe Again**, and we're going to **Make It Competitive Again**.

I'm also issuing two directives that instruct Secretary Mnuchin to review the damaging Dodd-Frank regulations that failed to hold Wall Street firms accountable. I mean, they've done really, in many cases, the opposite of what they were supposed to. These regulations enshrine "too big to fail" and encourage risky behavior.

We're taking steps to make our economy more fair and **prosperous** for all. As part of our broader financial strategy, we're working to open up lending to small businesses and entrepreneurs, including our incredible women entrepreneurs who are doing better and better and better. We want opportunity for everyone and in every single part of our country.

Secretary Mnuchin and my entire administration are working around the clock **to help struggling Americans achieve their financial dreams**, earn a great pay-check, have a job that they love going to every single day, and have real confidence in the future.

Together, **we will restore prosperity to this nation**, a nation that we so dearly love, and to bring people -- who call this home -- into a great, great way of living and **a great way of life**. They're going to be thrilled. We're going to be thrilled.

And you're going to be seeing some very, very major changes. You've already seen them. I don't know if anybody has looked recently, but if you looked at optimism indexes that are just coming out, manufacturing in particular, where it's up to the highest point it's ever been -- 93 percent -- it was a 27 percent increase over the past, over the last one.

So I just want to thank everybody for being here. This is such a privilege for me to sign. **This is really the beginning of a whole new way of life that this country hasn't seen in really many, many years.**

I want to thank you, and I want to God bless America. Thank you. Thank you, everybody.

So this is identifying and reducing tax regulatory burdens. That covers a lot of territory, believe me.

(The President signs the Executive Order.)

This is the subject of Financial Stability, the Oversight Council. Very important.

(The President signs the Executive Order.)

This is Orderly Liquidation Authority. It doesn't sound like much, but it is.

That's a **biggie**. It doesn't sound good, but it is.

(The President signs the Executive Order.)

And we'll be having a big announcement on Wednesday having to do with tax reform.

The process has begun long ago, but it really formally begins on Wednesday. So go to it.

Thank you very much, everybody. Thank you.

END
3:03 P.M. EDT

Chapter 152

**REMARKS BY THE VICE PRESIDENT AND
AUSTRALIAN PRIME MINISTER TURNBULL
AT A PRESS CONFERENCE
KIRRIBILLI HOUSE
SYDNEY, AUSTRALIA**

22 April 2017

PRIME MINISTER TURNBULL: Well, Vice President, it has been a great honor to welcome you to Australia. **This is the earliest visit to Australia of any Vice President in a new administration.** And your commitment to our alliance, your commitment to the region, the commitment of the Trump administration to the security and the stability, the maintenance of the rule of law in our region, in the Indo-Pacific is one that we welcome.

We are delighted that you're here.

And it's been great, too, we discussed earlier for Lucy and I to welcome you and Karen and your daughters with our family -- or many of them, two out of our three grandchildren. And as we observed earlier, your Karen was showing great ability in nursing Baby Alice. So that all augurs well.

So we've had a very productive discussion this morning. We have the strongest and the closest ties between our two nations at every level. And the Vice President's visit is an opportunity for both our nations emphatically to reaffirm those ties and our deep commitment to the alliance.

The alliance is as important today as it was more than

60 years ago, indeed, as it has been for the 99 years that
-- since Australian and American troops went into battle
together. It will be 100 years from the *Battle of Hamel* in
2018.

And through all of that time, the people of the United
States understand that they have no stronger, no more
committed, no more loyal partner, ally than Australia -- in
every major conflict for 99 years, we have stood side-by-
side in **freedom's cause**.

And this year is also the 75th anniversary of the Battle of
the *Coral Sea*, when American and Australian naval forces
turned back the Japanese invaders, and then went on to
turn them back again and again and keep Australia and our
region free.

We have stood side-by-side in **freedom's cause** through all
those years, and today the brave men and women -- the
Australian Defense Forces -- and their American allies and
our partners are fighting together with the common goal
of utterly destroying ISIS in the field in the Middle East.

That is our commitment.

In that theater of war and around the world, we are in
absolute lock-step, totally united with a common purpose,
and a resolute intent to destroy the threat of terrorism,
and to destroy it in the field, and to combat it around the
world -- whether at home or abroad. Our freedom depends on it. And we're committed to it.

And again, today, as 99 years ago, as 75 years ago, in all of
those conflicts, we have stood side-by-side because we are
united by values, a commitment to freedom, democracy,

and the rule of law. Our two great nations -- we share so much. But above all, we share -- and, Mr. Vice President, you know you come here on the eve of *ANZAC Day* where we honor the sacrifice of thousands of Australians -- over 100,000 Australians who've paid the supreme sacrifice to keep us free, and they have done that again and again, side-by-side in *mateship* -- an Australian term, but well understood across the Pacific, in *mateship* -- a hundred years of *mateship* side-by-side with our American allies.

Mr. Vice President, we also stand with you and with President Trump in condemning the behavior, the criminal, abhorrent use of chemical weapons in Syria by President Assad's regime. We welcomed and endorsed and supported the quick and calibrated and proportionate response of the United States in answer to that shocking crime.

And here in our region, we have spent a lot of time this morning talking about the threat from North Korea. This reckless and dangerous regime puts the peace, the stability, the prosperity of our region at risk. And we endorse and, indeed, have echoed and made directly the calls to China to step up, to take responsibility.

Because China has a leverage, an ability to influence North Korea that far exceeds any others -- with their economy, the North Korean economy is entirely dependent on China.

So as I've said earlier this week, the eyes of the world are on Beijing, and we seek leadership from China to join the leadership shown by the United States and Japan and Australia and other nations around the world committed to peace; call on China to make that stronger commitment to ensure that North Korea stops this reckless and dangerous conduct.

We are very, very heartened by your visit, Mr. Vice President. The United States' commitment to our region has underpinned the prosperity of the last 40 years. We would not have seen the extraordinary lifting out of poverty of billions of people in our region had it not been for the peace and the stability, the *Pax Americana*, if you like, that has been delivered by that continuing American commitment.

And your presence so early in the administration, and of the Secretary of State, and of the Defense Secretary, and as you've confirmed on your visit, the commitment of President Trump to attend the *East Asia Summit*, all of this sends a strong commitment, a strong message that the United States is committed to our region, committed to the peace and stability upon which so much depends in every nation.

We've also discussed matters economic. The United States is by some considerable margin Australia's largest source of foreign investment. And the United States is also the leading destination for Australian foreign investment.

In 2015, Australian investment in the United States was worth $594 billion, representing almost double what it was in 2005; while the United States' investment in Australia has almost tripled since then and now represents about $860 billion.

We have a very successful free trade agreement. Bilateral trade has grown from $41 billion to $70 billion since the Australia-United States Free Trade Agreement entered into force in that year, 2005. And the U.S. is Australia's second-largest trading partner.

We'll continue this close cooperation on trade and investment.

And we had a very good discussion, too, about [the] President Trump's commitment to reduce company tax and tax generally in the United States. We too recognize that reducing business taxes is vital to deliver stronger economic growth.

Businesses that can retain more of their profits for investment will grow. They'll hire more employees. Investment, employment are driven by lower business taxes. And we applaud the commitment of President Trump to that, and we're grateful for your update on those plans.

We will continue to work more closely together in every field. The relationship is a very deep -- it's a very intimate one. It is carried by millions of Australians and Americans over a century and more. **We have a shared destiny**. We always have. We grow closer together, built on those ties, defense, common strategic goals, shared values, stronger economic relationship, and above all, those connections of family that extend across the Pacific. It's a close relationship. **It's a family relationship**. And our family gathering this morning underpin the nature of this very deep friendship, Mr. Vice President.

So I thank you very much for visiting Australia. We've had a very good meeting with the foreign minister this morning, following on her meetings with you in Washington. And you'll meet more of our ministers today, including the deputy prime minister and the trade minister. We have a very deep commitment to growing and strengthening this relationship so important to our region, so important to our world, so important for the security and the prosperity, the opportunity of both our peoples. Welcome, Mr. Vice President.

THE VICE PRESIDENT: Prime Minister Turnbull, thank you so much for those gracious words, for the hospitality you have shown me and my family upon our arrival in Australia today. The warm welcome that you and the Australian people have given us is something that we will cherish for the rest of our lives.

I am honored to be in Australia today to offer greetings from the President of the United States, President Donald Trump. And as I spoke to the President this morning, Mr. Prime Minister, he wanted me to offer his best wishes to you and his congratulations for your strong leadership of the Commonwealth.

Mr. Prime Minister, with the strong encouragement of your administration, only two days ago, as you mentioned, it was my privilege to announce that President Trump will attend the *APEC Leaders Summit*, the *East Asia Summit*, and the *U.S.-ASEAN Summit* in Vietnam and the Philippines this November.

I trust that my visit here today -- on my very first trip to the Asia Pacific as Vice President of the United States -- and the President's plans to travel to this region this fall, are a strong sign of our enduring commitment to the historic alliance between the people of the United States of America and the people of Australia. As I told Prime Minister Turnbull today, Australia is, and always will be, one of America's closest allies and truest friends.

We are partners in security, we are partners in prosperity, and together we are bound by our historic alliance. And under President Trump, I can assure you, that the United States is committed to strengthening our bond for the benefit of our people, and for the benefit of our world.

The relationship between our nations stretches back for generations, as the Prime Minister just said. From the *Coral Sea* to *Kandahar,* our friendship has been forged in the fires of sacrifice.

Very humbling for me to say that only three days from now, on April 25th, Australia will commemorate *ANZAC Day*, to honor those brave Australians and New Zealanders who gave their lives in defense of freedom, often-times shoulder-to-shoulder with Americans.

The sons and daughters of both our lands have fought together in every major conflict for the past 100 years.

From World Wars One and Two, to Korea, to Vietnam, and most recently, in the conflicts in Iraq and Afghanistan, our grandparents, our parents, and now our children have served together and sacrificed together, and have defended our freedom and all that we hold dear. That represents the foundation of an unshakeable bond between America and Australia.

Even now our citizens serve together, in Afghanistan and in the fight against ISIS. And around the world, we are deepening our defense collaboration, and as Prime Minister Turnbull and I discussed today, we will continue to deepen our defense and security collaboration in the days ahead. The historic United States-Australia alliance is more vital than ever to regional security and prosperity.

In recent years, we have dramatically stepped up our intelligence sharing, increased our emphasis on shared cyber capabilities, and we have conducted and will continue to conduct joint military exercises to ensure our readiness, including the Talisman Saber later this year.

As the Prime Minister and I discussed, together, our nations will continue to uphold a rules-based system that is the foundation of peace and prosperity in the Asia Pacific. In the *South China Sea* and throughout the region, we will defend the fundamental freedoms of navigation and overflight, and ensure the unimpeded flow of lawful commerce, and promote peaceful diplomatic dialogue to address issues of regional and global concern.

And as the Prime Minister and I just reaffirmed, under President Trump's leadership, and yours, the United States and Australia will continue to stand firm and stand strong to confront the most urgent and dangerous threat to peace and security in the Asia Pacific, the regime in North Korea.

While all options are on the table, let me assure you, the United States will continue to work closely with Australia, our other allies in the region, and with China to bring economic and diplomatic pressure to bear on the regime in Pyongyang until they abandon their nuclear and ballistic missile programs.

Mr. Prime Minister, know that President Trump and I are truly grateful -- truly grateful -- to you for calling on China even this week to play an even more active and constructive role in addressing the North Korean threat.

The President and I have in his words great confidence that China will properly deal with North Korea. And I know you share that hope. But as President Trump made clear just a few days ago, if China is unable to deal with North Korea, the United States, and our allies, will.

The United States and Australia face this threat, and every other, together -- because we know that our security is the foundation of our prosperity. And today, Prime Minister Turnbull and I discussed ways for us to promote renewed prosperity for our people.

We are already building on a sturdy foundation. The *U.S.-Australia Free Trade Agreement* is a case study in success. And while we can still make additional progress, it's a model for what a mutually beneficial trade agreement can be.

Today, the United States is far and away Australia's largest economic partner -- not just in the region, but all across the world. Our economic relationship is worth a stunning $1.5 trillion, and our two-way investment has grown by 50 percent in just the last three years alone.

And we still have room to grow. Today, the Prime Minister and I discussed the need to break down barriers and encourage the kind of policies that will encourage even more trade and investment, more innovation and more opportunities for both our peoples.

We're confident that, working together, we'll build on our strong foundation in a way that will be beneficial to the people of America and the people of Australia.

Beyond our commercial partnership, the President and I are confident that this historic alliance between the United States and Australia will grow even stronger in the years ahead. Nowhere is our enduring commitment to each other and to our shared future more evident than in the topic that the Prime Minister just addressed so eloquently and so passionately -- the global fight against terror.

The people of the United States will never forget that Australia invoked our *ANZUS Security Treaty* for the first and only time following the September 11th terrorist attacks, which claimed the lives of nearly 3,000 innocent people, including 11 Australians. The support that Australia showed America in our darkest hour will never be forgotten.

Australia, like the United States, has not been spared. The four-lone wolf terror attacks over the past 31 months were all inspired by this global cancer. The people of Australia can rest assured: Under President Trump's leadership and under your capable leadership in Australia, we will not rest, we will not relent until, together, we drive this evil from the face of the Earth.

As I close, let me simply say it's an honor to be here on behalf of President Donald Trump to say simply from our hearts that the historic alliance between the United States and Australia is inviolate. It's immutable. And it's a beacon that shines throughout the Asia Pacific and inspires the wider world.

Our shared history, our shared values bind us together, and as we look toward what lies ahead, it's always heartening to stand beside a friend, and I do so today.

Prime Minister Turnbull, know that under President Donald Trump, the historic alliance between the United States and Australia will grow stronger, our people will grow closer, enhancing our security and our prosperity for generations to come.

And so we go forward with **faith** -- with **faith** in our historic alliance, faith in our shared values, and faith that the best days for America and for Australia are yet to come.

Thank you, Mr. Prime Minister. It's an honor to be with you.

PRIME MINISTER TURNBULL: Thank you, Mr. Vice President, for those eloquent words -- heartfelt, passionate, committed. Thank you so much.

Now, we have some questions.

Q   [...] Very well said, Mr. Prime Minister. This question is actually for both of you, if I may, does Australia have an increased role to play in helping moderate the North Korea threat? If so, what is that role?

And could it, indeed, be a military one down the track?

PRIME MINISTER TURNBULL: Well, thank you. We work very closely with our ally -- our ally and our friends in the region. The global community is committed to the end of this reckless and dangerous conduct, and the challenge now is obviously for China because they have, as I've said, and this is not a political point, this is a statement of fact, **China has the greatest leverage over North Korea**. There is no question about that.

So I've made this point to Chinese leaders over a long period of time, in fact, before I was Prime Minister. It is self-evident that China has the opportunity and we say the responsibility to bring pressure to bear on North Korea to stop this reckless and dangerous trajectory upon which they are embarked.

Now we will work closely with the United States as we always do. At this stage, the support that we are providing at the level of diplomacy and public diplomacy -- both public and private diplomacy is of critical importance. And we share the -- we are quietly confident I would say that China will step up to this challenge and responsibility.

Vice President.

VICE PRESIDENT PENCE: For more than a generation there has been a consensus in the world community for a nuclear-free Korean Peninsula. In the 1990s, it was a subject of negotiations and an agreed framework was arrived at. *Six-Party Talks* would follow sometime later. The last administration embraced a policy of strategic patience. All along the way the regime in North Korea answered the entreaties of the world community with broken promises and with continued pursuit -- headlong pursuit of their nuclear and ballistic missile ambitions.

And as President Trump has made clear, and I've made clear as I've traveled on this behalf throughout the region, the era of strategic patience is over. Under the President's leadership and working closely with our allies, with Prime Minister Turnbull, in my meetings with Prime Minister Abe, and with acting President Hwang in South Korea, and others, the United States is determined to bring economic and diplomatic pressure to bear working with all of our allies -- and China -- to ensure that we achieve a nuclear-free Korean Peninsula.

Now all options are on the table, and the United States is

prepared to do what's necessary in conjunction with our allies to see to the security of this region and of our own people. But we are hopeful -- in fact, in President Trump's words, we have great confidence that China, with the encouragement of the United States, of our allies, and we're grateful to say with the strong encouragement of the leadership here in Australia, that China will take advantage of the unique position and relationship that it has with North Korea to bring an end to their nuclear program and to their ballistic missile programs. We call on them to do that.

The President observed recently that China in a very real sense is the economic lifeline for North Korea. They've already taken steps, which we greatly welcome -- intervening in coal shipments and intervening in commercial travel. But we believe China can do more, and on behalf of the President, I'm just very grateful that even this week, Australia has taken steps to engage with China directly and encourage them to take even more steps to bring that economic and diplomatic pressure to bear.

But make no mistake about it, the United States of America is committed to seeing this way forward and achieve what's eluded the world community for a generation. And that is to achieve the de-nuclearization of the Korean Peninsula. [...]

Q   Thank you. Prime Minister, I wanted to ask you about trade, and if there are specific steps the U.S. has asked you to take, or that you will be taking to improve bilateral trade after President Trump pulled out of TPP.

I'm also wondering what you see is the best way to improve regional trade after the collapse of that agreement. And then, Mr. Vice President, I just wanted to follow on

North Korea but ask specifically about some recent statements from the administration earlier this week there was some **controversy regarding the timing of the armada** that President Trump said that he'd send to the region. **It's led to mockery** in North Korean and Chinese press and criticism from a South Korean presidential candidate who said that it potentially undermined your administration's credibility. Is the lack of rhetorical clarity making your job with allies and partners like China harder?

And to that point, can I ask you explain the President's recent statement that China is just now taking "some unusual moves" towards North Korea?

PRIME MINISTER TURNBULL: Well, thank you. And in terms of trade, we have obviously continuing discussions. But at this stage, the *Australia-U.S. Free Trade Agreement* is working very, very well.

In terms of trade generally, Australia has been a great beneficiary of free trade and open markets. Just let that helicopter pass.

We've been a great beneficiary of free trade and open markets. We strongly supported the TPP as being in our national interest. President Trump has discontinued America's engagement in it. That is his right. Absolutely each nation must -- look, each nation is committed to protecting its economic interests, first and foremost. That's the duty each leader has to their own people.

So the United States government must make its own judgments on that. We look forward to more trade. **President Trump is an international businessman. So he's not -- he can hardly be described as somebody who is unused to**

the benefits of international trade and international commerce. He understands it very well.

But he obviously will decide, as the Vice President and I were discussing today, he will decide how agreements, new trade deals, whether and to what extent they work in America's interest. That is the sovereign right, and, in fact, the solemn obligation of every nation and every leader.

But at this stage, in terms of the bilateral relationship, it is proceeding very, very well. It's proceeding apace, actually. And the economic engagement and the prosperity that flows from that has been demonstrated over the years since it came into force in 2005.

THE VICE PRESIDENT: First on trade, with great respect to the Prime Minister's view and Australia's view of TPP, the President has made it clear and America has taken steps -- the Trans-Pacific Partnership is a thing of the past for the United States.

As we **move forward with the President's philosophy of an America First foreign policy and trade policy**, we'll continue to pursue opportunities for expanded commerce, but do so on bilateral basis.

I trust that my travels throughout the Asia Pacific this week give evidence of the fact that this administration is committed to building both our security and economic relationships with countries all across this region.

We do believe that the bilateral agreement, trade agreement between the United States and Australia is a win-win for our countries. It is -- as I said earlier, we think it's a model agreement for how to encourage investment and encourage trade between nations.

I think in the days ahead we initiated an economic dialogue that I and the deputy prime minister of Japan will be
heading up to begin to explore the possibility of expanded
economic relations with Japan. We had discussions about
our free trade agreement while I was in South Korea. But I
think you'll continue to see President Trump engaging with
nations across this region, but again on a bilateral basis.

With regard to the *USS Carl Vinson* and the carrier group,
our expectation is that they will be in the *Sea of Japan*,
in position in a matter of days -- before the end of this
month. That decision was set into motion some time
ago. And the one thing that nations -- most especially the
regime in North Korea -- should make no mistake about is
that the United States has the resources, the personnel,
and the presence in this region of the world to see to our
interests, and to see to the security of our... those interests
and our allies.

I think what the President was referring to with regard to
China is encouraging news. In **his summit at the Southern
White House** with President Xi, President Trump engaged
President Xi in a candid and respectful discussion about
China's engagement with North Korea. And now the steps
we're seeing China take, in many ways **unprecedented
steps**, bringing economic pressure to bear on North Korea
are very welcome.

We do believe China can do more. And as I mentioned,
we're very grateful for the clear message that Prime Minister Turnbull's government and Australia are sending to
the Chinese to do just that. But this is a time when I think
you'll continue to see the United States and our allies in

the region work together to encourage China to take those steps necessary to bring about a peaceable solution to achieve a nuclear-free Korean Peninsula.

Q   Thank you. My question -- the refugee deal last year. Mr. Vice President, in February, President Trump said of the refugees deal, "I will study this dumb deal" -- seemingly contradicting assurances given to Mr. Turnbull. In recent weeks we've seen officials (inaudible) can we infer that President Trump has given final approval to that deal proceeding?

And if so, how many refugees will be resettled in the United States?

THE VICE PRESIDENT: Let me make it clear the United States intends to honor the agreement, subject to the results of the vetting processes that now apply to all refugees considered for admission to the United States of America. President Trump has made it clear that we'll honor the agreement. It doesn't mean we admire the agreement.

Frankly, looking back on the last administration, the President has never been shy about expressing frustration with other international agreements, most notably the so-called *Nuclear Agreement* with Iran. But rest assured, as I confirmed today with the Prime Minister, the United States of America will honor the agreement.

And actually we've initiated the process of fulfilling that agreement, subject to the results of the vetting processes that now apply to all refugees in the United States.

PRIME MINISTER TURNBULL: Thank you. And, Mr. Vice President, as I said to the President, we thank you for honoring the commitment made by the President's predecessor. The commitment to honoring that deal is -- that agreement is very important, and it's one that speaks whatever the reservations of the President are -- and we know what they are about the deal -- nonetheless, it speaks volumes for the commitment, the integrity of President Trump and your administration, sir, to honor that commitment as you have committed to and, indeed, as you are doing. So we thank you for that commitment. That's -- it's a very important commitment, and we thank you for restating that today.

VICE PRESIDENT PENCE: I would just add, if I may, Mr. Prime Minister, that as this topic came up early in the administration, Prime Minister Turnbull made a case for the agreement with the President, and the decision to go forward I think can rightly be seen as a reflection of the enormous importance of the historic alliance between the United States and Australia.

And whatever reservations the President may have about the details of agreements reached by the prior administration, we'll honor this agreement out of respect for that enormous and important alliance.

PRIME MINISTER TURNBULL: Thank you, sir.

Q   Mr. Vice President, the administration is ramping up pressure on North Korea at the same time you seem to have ruled out talks. I'm wondering what you think the endgame is here. What makes you believe that the regime will give up the weapons systems and weapons that it has to ensure its -- are perhaps guarantee of its own survival?

And for the Prime Minister, did you get any clarity on the

U.S. position with regards to the *South China Sea*?

Do you think that there is a need for more freedom of navigation operations in the region?

Would you consider more joint operations in the region? Thank you.

VICE PRESIDENT PENCE: This is just a very serious time. And the President sent me to this region to engage with our allies to reaffirm the alliances that we enjoy, but also to make it very, very clear that the era of strategic partnership -- strategic patience is over; that the United States of America is determined to work with our allies and especially with China to achieve the objective of a nuclear-free Korean Peninsula.

We believe that that can occur peaceably, largely owing to the new engagement of China. In this regard, I think the world is seeing President Trump's leadership in high relief. He is in a very real sense -- like the Prime Minister of Australia -- **he is a bottom-line person** that likes to get to the point.

And in his meeting with President Xi, they had a very candid conversation about a broad range of issues. But on the issue of North Korea, the President made it very clear to President Xi that we were looking to China to step up and use that unique relationship that it has with North Korea to achieve an end to the nuclear ambitions and the ballistic missile ambitions of that regime.

And as I said, we're encouraged by the steps that China has taken thus far. That being said, we also wanted to make it clear that all options are on the table, and that the United

States is prepared to work with our allies to ensure the security of our allies in the region, and ensure the security of the people of the United States of America.

Nuclear weapons in the hands of the regime in Pyongyang with a ballistic missile program and with the **potential for intercontinental ballistic missiles represents a threat to the stability and security of this region, and potentially a threat to the continental United States**. And continuing on the path the world has been on with North Korea over the last 25 years is just unacceptable.

But again, we continue to be hopeful and continue to have great confidence that we can finally after a generation achieve a peaceable solution.

And I want to reiterate again the gratitude of the United States of America for the strong support that our ally here in Australia has provided to this effort; **even this week**, meeting with high-ranking officials from China urging them to do more to bring economic and diplomatic pressure to bear on China is welcome. We truly believe that as our allies in the region and China bring that pressure to bear that there is a chance that we can achieve a historic objective of a nuclear-free Korean Peninsula by peaceable means.

PRIME MINISTER TURNBULL: Thank you, Mr. Vice President. And as we've described, we share that commitment.

And we are absolutely united in our determination to achieve a nuclear-free Korean Peninsula. That has been the goal, as the Vice President described, of the global community for many years. The time has come now to realize it.

You asked about the *South China Sea*, and I just repeat what we have said consistently for many years and that is this, that **Australia has no territorial claims** in the *South China Sea*. We are committed to freedom of navigation and freedom of overflight. Any territorial dispute should be resolved peacefully and in accordance with international law. And we call on all parties to refrain from actions that would exacerbate tensions. And in particular, we call on all parties to refrain from militarizing any features in the *South China Sea*, any disputed features in particular in the *South China Sea*.

The critical thing to understand in our region, as we said at the outset -- both the Vice President and I observed -- is the prosperity of everybody in this region, in every nation has been underpinned by decades of peace and stability, supported by the strong commitment of the United States to this region.

The maintenance of peace and stability in this region has had as its sheet anchor the strong commitment of the United States. And that is why we so welcome the commitment of President Trump's new administration shown by the visit here today and through the region over the last week of the Vice President.

This is **a historic visit**, and it underlines the importance of the **American commitment to our region -- the sheet anchor, the foundation, the bedrock of the peace and the stability upon which the security and the prosperity of billions depend.**

Thank you all very much, indeed.
END

Chapter 153

22 April 2017

THE VICE PRESIDENT: Well, g'day. Minister Steven Ciobo, thank you for that kind introduction and those eloquent words about the relationship between the United States and Australia. And I want thank you for tireless work strengthening the economic partnership between your nation and mine. And it's an honor for you to be joining us here today.

To all of our honored guests, to our host, Deputy Prime Minister Barnaby Joyce, who I'll be meeting with momentarily, to Minister Arthur Sinodinos, Ambassador Joe Hockey, our Chargé d'Affaires, Jim Carouso, Consul General Valerie Fowler, to Maureen Dougherty, and members of the American Chamber of Commerce for Australia hosting us today, distinguished leaders of the business community, honored guests, it is my great honor to be here today in Australia on behalf of the President of the United States of America -- on my first visit to the Asia Pacific as Vice President I had to come to our ally and friend Australia. (Applause.)

And I bring greetings from the 45th President of the United States, President Donald Trump, to all of you who are gathered here today, and especially to the business leaders who are gathered here and have been a part of such a dynamic economic relationship between the United States and Australia.

The President sent me here as the first member of his administration to visit Australia, and I am tremendously grateful for the opportunity to be with all of you.

Earlier today, on President Trump's behalf, I had the great privilege of meeting with your Prime Minister, Malcolm Turnbull. I reaffirmed to him what I would reaffirm to all of you today and to the people of Australia who may be looking on: Australia is, and always will be, one of America's closest allies and truest friends. We are partners in security. We are partners in prosperity, and together we are bound by our historic alliance.

And under President Trump, the United States is dedicated to strengthening our bond, strengthening our ties for the benefit of our people of both of our nations and people all over the world. (Applause.)

The relationship between our nations stretches back literally generations. From the *Coral Sea* to *Kandahar*, our friendship has been forged ultimately in the fires of sacrifice.

Only three days from now, it's humbling for me to say that I stand here on the eve of when Australia will commemorate that extraordinary moment every year, *ANZAC Day*, to honor those brave Australian and New Zealand veterans who gave their lives in the defense of freedom, often alongside Americans. We call a similar commemoration *Memorial Day in America*, and it's humbling for me to stand before you today just a few short days before this annual commemoration of those who gave the last full measure of devotion.

The sons and daughters of both our lands have fought shoulder-to-shoulder in every conflict for the past 100 years. From World Wars One and Two, to Korea, to Vietnam, and most recently, in the conflicts in Iraq and Afghanistan -- it's remarkable to consider it -- our grandparents, our parents, and now our children are serving together.

They have sacrificed together to defend the freedom that we all hold dear. And we honor them this day and every day.

Even now our citizens serve together in Afghanistan and in the fight against ISIS. And around the world, we are deepening our defense collaboration, and we will continue to do so to ensure the safety and security of our people.

The historic United States-Australia alliance is more vital than ever to regional security and prosperity. In recent years, we have dramatically stepped up our collaboration and cooperation between the United States and Australia -- intelligence sharing, increasing our emphasis on cyber capabilities, and we've conducted and will continue to conduct joint military exercises to ensure readiness, including the Talisman Saber, which will take place later this year. Together, our nations will continue to uphold a rules-based system as the foundation of peace and prosperity in the Asia Pacific.

In the *South China Sea* and throughout the region, we will defend the fundamental freedoms of navigation and overflight, and the United States of America with Australia will ensure the unimpeded flow of lawful commerce, and promote a peaceful dialogue to address every issue that arises of regional and global concern. (Applause.)

Under President Trump's leadership, the United States and Australia will continue to stand firm and to stand strong, as well, to confront the most urgent and dangerous threat to peace and security in the Asia Pacific, the regime in North Korea.

While all options are on the table, the United States will continue to work closely with our allies, including Australia and other allies across the region, and with China to bring economic and diplomatic pressure to bear on the regime in Pyongyang until they finally and permanently abandon their nuclear and ballistic missile programs.

President Trump and I are truly grateful -- truly grateful to Prime Minister Turnbull and all the people of Australia -- for calling on China to play a more constructive role in addressing the North Korean threat.

The President and I have great confidence that China will properly deal with Korea. But as President Trump made clear just a few days ago, if China is unable to deal with North Korea, the United States, and our allies, will.

The United States and Australia face this threat, and every other one, together -- because we know that our security is the foundation of our prosperity. And strengthening our prosperity is what I came to this forum mostly to talk about today, so let me begin by simply saying thank you. All the businesses represented in this room are why the United States and Australia are such close economic partners.

Just look at the *American Chamber of Commerce in Australia*. Since 1961, *AMCHAM* has brought together American and Australian businesses to foster investment and opportunity on both sides of the Pacific, and your 600 corporate members are a testament to our collective success. On behalf of President Trump, let me just say thank you for your tireless work to draw the United States and Australia closer together.

And thank you to all the businesses that are represented here today -- ConocoPhillips, Microsoft, GE, and really, all of you in this room -- you're titans of industry and you're pillars of the U.S.-Australia economic partnership.

You create jobs in both of our countries. You drive innovation. You open up opportunity. And you've helped build a strong and durable bond between the United States and Australia.

In fact, thanks in no small part to you, the United States is far and away Australia's largest economic partner -- not just in this region, but across the wider world.

All told, our economic partnership is worth a staggering $1.5 trillion - and investment has grown by 50 percent in the last three years alone.

Countless American companies export tens of billions of dollars' worth of goods and services to Australia every year -- machines, appliances, automobiles, parts, electrical machinery, textiles, apparel, you name it.

Today, more than a quarter of a million American jobs depend on exports to Australia. The American people are grateful.

American companies also are investing in Australia like never before. More than 1,000 U.S. businesses large and small, have operations here today. My own brother who works with Cummins engine company spent five memorable years with his family here in Sydney as he worked in their Australia operation.

To name just another one of these companies, Chevron's gas facilities are now the largest single foreign investment ever in the history of Australia. And U.S. investment here has contributed greatly to Australia's huge commodity exports to Asia.

And the investments flow both ways. Today, the United States is Australia's leading destination for investment, and we're grateful. Australian companies have invested just under $45 billion in America, where they employ over 95,000 Americans in good-paying jobs.

I know the benefits of Australian investment first-hand. In my home state of Indiana, IFM Investors, who are represented here today, invested more than $5 billion in the Indiana toll road. The bottom line is that our economies are inextricably intertwined in a **win-win** relationship that's creating jobs and opportunity for both our nations.

From energy to agriculture, advanced manufacturing to aerospace, our economic partnership is vital to the American people and vital to the people of Australia.

And today, under President Trump, I'm very pleased to **pledge** that the United States will continue to work together with Australia to forge even greater opportunity and prosperity for both our nations and our people.

President Trump is committed to fostering free and fair bilateral trade relationships with Australia and throughout the Asia Pacific.

The good news is that the U.S.-Australia Free Trade Agreement is already working. In fact, the United States believes our agreement with Australia is a case study in success -- and while we can always make additional progress, and the Prime Minister and I talked about identifying areas that we might lower barriers to trade and investment, we consider the U.S.-Australia trade agreement to be model for a mutually beneficial trade agreement and a model for the world. Ever since it came into force in 2005, bilateral trade and investment between our nations has soared. Minister Ciobo, know that your contribution to our trade relationship is deeply appreciated.

But we think we can still do better. This morning, Prime Minister Turnbull and I discussed the need to take those additional steps that I mentioned to break down barriers to foster even more investment and exchange between our nations.

It is just the beginning of a conversation that will continue. But President Trump and I look forward to continuing our dialogue with Australia's leaders in the months and years ahead to the benefit of all of our people.

And we hope that all of you in this room will join that conversation. We had a good one earlier today with some of the business leaders who gathered for our listening session. As members of the business community, you can help us identify the barriers that we need to break down and areas that we can improve to make more economic progress possible.

President Trump and I value your continued input on the issues that you face, and we know the job creators in this room can help us move toward a system that maximizes jobs and growth, and a brighter future here in Australia and in the United States.

The truth is that a stronger American economy also means a stronger economy for all of our trading partners, including Australia.

And let me **promise you**, under President Trump's leadership, the United States is going to drive growth like never before.

President Trump has already taken decisive action to get our **American economy moving Again**. Our administration is working around the clock to pass an agenda of lower taxes, less regulation, better infrastructure, and a **renewed focus on American energy**.

I'm sure you'll be glad to know that American businesses represented here today and businesses that are investing in our country -- that tax reform is one of our very top priorities, including a reform of corporate taxes. I don't have to tell you how the American tax code harms our business community, at home and abroad.

Our corporate tax rate today is one of the highest in the developed world -- and it's 5 percent higher than the tax rate here in Australia. President Trump's tax plan would slash the corporate rate and reform the tax code to make it simpler, flatter, and fairer.

Rest assured, our tax reform will make the strongest economy in the world stronger still, and it will benefit the

American people, American workers, and it will benefit the economy of Australia.

And the same is true of President Trump's decisive action on regulation. He's already announced that our various agencies have to find two regulations to get rid of before they create any one new piece of red tape on the American people.

The President has already signed dozens bills turning back the last administration's burdensome mandates, and he'll continue to work with Congress to slash through red tape so jobs and opportunities can flow in the United States.

Make no mistake: Under President Donald Trump, the era of over-taxation and over-regulation is over, and **a new era of jobs and growth and prosperity has just begun**.

Now these are a couple of the policies that the President is advancing, and I could keep on going. But I'll go easy on you. I just appreciate the feedback I received from so many of you earlier today in our roundtable about what our administration can continue to do to foster jobs and investment and growth.

And rest assured, **President Trump's agenda will renew America's reputation** as the premier investment destination in the world. And as America's economy grows, all of our trading partners and Australia's economy will benefit as a result.

And we're confident that working together with you and with Australia's leaders, we're going to build on a strong foundation. And we're going to reach even new heights in our partnership, in our relationship, strategically, and economically.

And the President and I are also confident that the historic alliance between the United States and Australia will grow even stronger in the years ahead. Nowhere is our enduring commitment to each other and to our shared future more evident than in our shared struggle against global terrorism.

The people of the United States will never forget that Australia invoked our *ANZUS Security Treaty* for the first and only time following the attack on our nation on September the 11th, an attack which claimed the lives of nearly 3,000 innocent people, including 11 Australians. The support that Australia showed in our darkest hour will never be forgotten by the American people.

Australia, like the United States, has not been spared in this regard. The four-lone wolf terror attacks over the past 31 months were all inspired by this global cancer.

And as the Prime Minister and I discussed today, the people of Australia can rest assured: Under your leadership here in this nation and under President Trump's leadership, we will not rest, we will not relent until, together, we drive the evil of global terrorism from the face of this Earth. (Applause.)

As I close, let me simply say that the historic alliance between Australia and the United States is a beacon that shines not only throughout the Asia Pacific, but across the wider world. Our shared history and our shared values bind us together. And as we look toward what lies ahead, we do so with confidence as we stand here today with a true friend and a true friendship between the United

States and Australia.

And I am confident that in the days ahead, I have faith that our relationship will only grow stronger, our historic alliance will benefit the people of our country and yours. And the best days for America and Australia are yet to come.

Thank you. God bless you all. God bless Australia. And God bless the United States of America. (Applause.)

END

Chapter 154

24 April 2017

VICE PRESIDENT PENCE: How about a big round of applause for Admiral Harry Harris, everybody? This is a great, great leader. (Applause.)

Admiral, thank you for that kind introduction. Thank you for your resolute leadership of the U.S. Pacific Command at this pivotal time in the life of our nation.

I'm very humbled to be with all of you. Thank you so much for the warm welcome. And most especially, I bring greetings on behalf of your Commander-in-Chief, President Donald Trump. (Applause.)

The President -- we're on our way back to Washington, D.C. We'll be back to work at the White House tomorrow morning, but the President wanted me to come by today just to tell you how grateful we all are for your service.

And as he said to me, just tell them I'm proud of them. And I **promise** all of you, the American people are **proud** of every man and woman in this room.

Give yourselves another round of applause. Thank you for serving your country. (Applause.)

I just had a chance to visit with a family member of mine,

Master Sergeant Jimmy Leseune (ph), who is Air Force.

AUDIENCE MEMBERS: Ooorah!

THE VICE PRESIDENT: He and his family are here in Hawaii, and he's been in the service I think upwards to 18 years. And as the Admiral said, I'm not a soldier.

My life didn't take me into the uniform that every one of you have put on voluntarily, but I am the son of a soldier, a combat veteran who served in the Korean War.

And I'm the proud father of a United States Marine. And so I stand before you today deeply humbled -- deeply humbled because I really speak on behalf of the hundreds of millions of Americans, who each and every day benefit by the services and the sacrifices that you and your families make on our behalf.

And I just really came by to say thanks. Thank you for stepping forward to serve your country; and also to assure you that in these days that lie ahead, in these uncertain times, people who serve here at U.S. Pacific Command will know that in your Commander-in-Chief, you have a President who is going to fight to **rebuild our military, restore the arsenal of democracy**. And we're going to give our Soldiers, Sailors, Airmen, Marines, and Coast Guard the resources you need to accomplish your mission for the American people. We're going to do it. (Applause.)

Even this week, my fellow Americans, I can tell you I'm headed back to Capitol Hill. There's a spending bill that's being considered as we speak. The President is working even in what remains of this budget year to begin to supplement our military spending.

The President truly believes that the time has come for us to **rebuild this military**. And the budget that the President submitted you may be glad to know had the largest single-year increase in military spending since the days of the Reagan administration. (Applause.)

It is the greatest privilege of my life to serve as Vice President to a President who cares so deeply about the men and women of our armed forces, their families, and our veterans.

And I know in my heart President Donald Trump is going to be the best friend the American Armed Forces have ever had in the White House.

With that said, let me close by simply thanking you. Thanking you from the bottom of my heart for being willing to step forward and volunteer to wear the uniform of the United States of America.

It's not lost on any American that the way that you arrive in those uniforms which you're wearing from all the different branches of the service are because you stepped forward.

I was speaking to one young airman a little bit ago, and she told me that she just felt early on the calling to serve. And I thanked her for answering that call.

And each one of you have responded to the call of your country. And I just want you to know that it is going to be to your eternal credit that here in this time in the life of our nation, you stepped forward and you said yes to America.

So I'm here basically to do two things:

To assure you of our thanks, the admiration and gratitude of your Commander-in-Chief, and the gratitude of the American people for the service that you render here in this place.

But also I'm here to assure you of their prayers.

The American people are grateful every day for those who serve around the globe -- whether it be the U.S. Pacific Command or in far-flung places in the world, often-times separated for months at a time from your families, I want you to know that as you go, you go with our gratitude. And you go with our prayers.

Each one of you carries with you the **strength of this nation** and the **pride of this nation**.

And on behalf of your President and on behalf of the American people, I say from my heart, God bless you.

Thank you for your service and God bless America. (Applause.)

END

Chapter 155

**Remarks by President Trump in Video Call
with NASA Astronauts Aboard
the International Space Station
Via Videoconference
Oval Office**

24 April 2017

10:00 A.M. EDT

NASA: White House, this is Mission Control,
Houston. Please call Station for a voice check.

THE PRESIDENT: Do you hear me?

[Photo: screengrab.]

CMDR. WHITSON: Yes, sir. We have you loud and clear.

THE PRESIDENT: Well, that's what we like -- great American equipment that works. And this isn't easy. (Laughter.)

I want to say it's very exciting to be here today -- very, very exciting -- and to speak to you live with three brave American astronauts. These are our finest.

These are great, great Americans, great people. Two join us from orbit aboard the International Space Station: Commander Peggy Whitson and Colonel Jack Fischer. And Peggy Whitson has been setting records, and we're going to talk about that very soon.

I'm here in the Oval Office, **along with my daughter Ivanka** and astronaut Kate Rubins, who recently returned from space and from the Space Station.

[Photo: screengrab.]

Together, we are being joined by students all across America, thousands and thousands of students who are learning -- they're learning about space, learning about a lot of other things -- and they're watching this conversation from the classroom. And, all over, we have astronauts and we have everybody, who are flying right now, 17,000 miles per hour. That's about as fast as I've ever heard. I wouldn't want to be flying 17,000 miles an hour. But that's what you do.

Peggy, Jack, and Kate, I know that America's students are thrilled to hear from you. But first, I want to say that this is a very special day in the glorious history of American space-flight. Today, Commander Whitson, you have broken the record for the most total time spent in space by an American astronaut -- 534 days and counting. That's an incredible record to break.

And on behalf of our nation and, frankly, on behalf of the world, I'd like to congratulate you. That is really something. And I'd like to know, how does it feel to have broken such a big and important record?

CMDR. WHITSON: Well, it's actually a huge honor to break a record like this, but it's an honor for me basically to be representing all the folks at NASA who make this space-flight possible and who make me setting this record feasible. And so it's a very exciting time to be at NASA. We are all very much looking forward, as directed by your new NASA bill -- we're excited about the missions to Mars in the 2030s. And so we actually, physically, have hardware on the ground that's being built for the SLS rocket that's going to take us there. And, of course, the hardware being built now is going to be for the test flights that will eventually get us there.

But it's a very exciting time, and I'm so proud of the team.

THE PRESIDENT: Great. And what are we learning from having you spending your time up there? I know so much research is done; I'm getting a glimpse of some of it right here in the Oval Office. What are we learning by being in space?

CMDR. WHITSON: Well, I think probably the International
Space Station is providing a key bridge from us living on
Earth to going somewhere into deep space. So on those
Mars missions, we need to better understand how micro-
gravity is really affecting our body, and we need to understand it in great detail. So, many of the studies are looking
at the human body. We're also looking at things that
involve operations of a space vehicles on these long-dura-
tion missions and the technological advancements that will
be required.

For instance, on a multi-year Mars mission, we're going to
need to be able to close the life support system, and that
means we, right now, for instance, are taking solar power
that we collect, and using it to break apart water into oxygen and hydrogen. The oxygen, we breathe, of course. We
use the hydrogen, combine it back with the CO_2 that we
take out of the air, and make more water. But water is
such a precious resource up here that we also are cleaning
up our urine and making it drinkable. And it's really not as
bad as it sounds.

THE PRESIDENT: Well, that's good. I'm glad to hear
that. (Laughter.)

Better you than me. I will say, Colonel Fischer, you just
arrived, and how was your trip? Complicated? Easy? How
did it go?

COL. FISCHER: Oh, sir, it was awesome. It made even my
beloved F-22 feel a little bit underpowered. I launched in a
Russian vehicle with my Russian friend, Fyodor
Yurchikhin, from Kazakhstan. Got the immediate perspective change as we got to orbit, and I saw that frail, thin
blue line of life around the Earth. Six hours later, we're

docked at the station.

The next day, I install an experiment in the Japanese module that's going to be looking at new drugs and how we can make those drugs for muscular dystrophy, Alzheimer's, multi-drug-resistant bacteria -- all sorts of things.

A couple hours later, I watched our crew-mate, Thomas Pesquet, a Frenchman, drive a Canadian robotic arm to capture a spaceship from Virginia, carrying 3.5 tons of cargo and science that's going to keep us busy for the next few months, and dock that to the station.

Sir, it's amazing. Oh, and then, you know, now I'm talking to the President of the United States while hanging from a wall. It's amazing. The International Space Station is, by far, the best example of international cooperation and what we can do when we work together in the history of humanity. And I am so proud to be a part of it. And it's just cool. (Laughter.)

Like, yesterday, I had -- well, there you go -- there's our resident space ninja doing the gravity demonstration. And yesterday morning, I had my coffee in floaty ball form, and, sir, it was delicious. So, it's awesome.

THE PRESIDENT: Tell me, Mars -- what do you see a timing for actually sending humans to Mars? Is there a schedule? And when would you see that happening?

CMDR. WHITSON: Well, I think as your bill directed, it will be approximately in the 2030s. As I mentioned, we actually are building hardware to test the new heavy launch vehicle, and this vehicle will take us further than we've ever been away from this planet.

Unfortunately, space-flight takes a lot of time and money, so getting there will require some international cooperation to get it to be a planet-wide approach in order to make it successful, just because it is a very expensive endeavor. But it so worthwhile doing.

THE PRESIDENT: Well, we want to try and do it during my first term or, at worst, during my second term. So we'll have to speed that up a little bit, okay?

CMDR. WHITSON: (Laughter.)

We'll do our best.

THE PRESIDENT: Oh, you will. And I have great respect for you folks. It's amazing what you do. And I just want to introduce another great one. Kate Rubins is with us today, and she has been so impressive with research and so many other things having to do with NASA. And, Kate, I understand you're the first person to sequence DNA in space. Can you tell us about that?

DR. RUBINS: Yeah. So that was actually just this last summer, and it's a real example of what we can do with technology and innovation. We've got a sequencer down to the size of your cellphone, and we were actually able to fly that on-board the space station and sequence DNA. It's not just the technology demonstration, but we can actually use that to do things like detect microbes on the space station, look at astronaut health. We can easily use that in Earth-based settings, too, to look for disease outbreaks and to do rural healthcare as well.

THE PRESIDENT: That's fantastic. That is really great. I saw some of the work, and it's incredible. You know, I've been dealing with politicians so much, I'm so much more impressed with these people. You have no idea.

Now, speaking of another impressive person -- **Ivanka,** you've been very much interested in this program. Tell us something about it.

MS. TRUMP: Hi, Dr. Whitson. First of all, congratulations on your incredible milestone today. You may know that my father recently signed the *Inspire Women Act* to encourage female participation in STEM fields across all aerospace areas, and really with a focus on NASA. So encouraging women and girls to pursue STEM careers is a major priority for this administration.

And today we are sitting with an amazing example of that -- Dr. Rubins, and you, Dr. Whitson. So I would love to hear from you, what was the impetus for you to get involved in the sciences?

DR. RUBINS: Yeah, so when I around fifteen, I actually went to a conference, and that was very inspiring for me. It was sort of the beginning of recombinant DNA and understanding biology. And so just that exposure to scientists and the kinds of things that you can do with science and technology innovation.

MS. TRUMP: Amazing. Dr. Whitson?

CMDR. WHITSON: For me, it was actually the Apollo program was my inspiration, and that was when it became a dream to become an astronaut. But I don't really think it became a goal until I graduated from high school, when the first female astronauts were selected.

And seeing those role models, and with the encouragement of my parents and various mentors in college and
graduate school, and when I started working at Rice,
that's what made it possible, I think, to become an astronaut. And it took me a lot longer to become an astronaut
than I ever really wanted it to take, but I do think I'm better
at my job because of the journey.

MS. TRUMP: You're an incredible inspiration to us all. So I
would also like to ask you one more question. I'm incredibly curious, as I'm sure all the students across the country
are, to know what a day in the life in space is like. Could
you share what a typical day looks like, what the challenges are, just any special moments?

CMDR. WHITSON: Well, a typical day, we wake up and look
at the messages from the ground, because we have a huge
ground team that's working overnight to prepare changes
or the details of the tests that we're going to be perform-
ing over the course of the day. So first thing I do is check
out that, see what's changed.

But on any given day, it can be so dramatically different. On one day, we might be focusing on science. On
another day, we might be repairing the carbon dioxide
removal system. On another day, soon Jack and I are going
to do a space-walk. We talked about, last Saturday, we did
robotics operations. I love the diversity of the different
activities that we do. Plus, you know, we have over 200
investigations ongoing on-board the space station, and I
just think that's a phenomenal part of the day.

Of course, there's also just the living and, on-board the
space station, it's such a unique and novel environment. Nothing that we're used to on the ground. And it's

so special to just be in zero gravity. So Jack is the new guy here, and I think he can probably give you a better perspective on what that's like.

COL. FISCHER: Well, you know, everything here -- my dad always said that if you love what you do, you never work a day in your life. And we work really hard up here, but it's not really work, it's just fun. It's like playing fort almost, only you're changing the world while you do it.

And then on the off time, the other morning I was working out, and on our machine that we work out on, right below it is the Cupola window. And so when you're on the device where you do crunches, every time you come up, you see out the window. And it's awesome because you kind of go, crunch, "Oh, my gosh, that's beautiful! I got to do that again." Crunch, "Oh my gosh, that's beautiful." It's awesome. Everything we do here is fun, and it feels so great to know that we're making a difference on the ground and for the future of humanity as well. So it's an incredible, incredible job.

THE PRESIDENT: You're making a great difference, I have to say. And this is a very exciting time for our country, and you see what's happening with our country in terms of jobs, in terms of business, and there's such excitement and such enthusiasm.

Many American entrepreneurs are racing into space. I have many friends that are so excited about space. They want to get involved in space from the standpoint of entrepreneurship and business.

Tell us about the opportunities that could exist for the next generation of scientists and engineers. Is that something

that you think a student -- because you have so many
students, hundreds of thousands watching -- is that something that you think that students should be focusing, or
should they be thinking about other subjects?

What do you think are the opportunities for young students wanting to be involved in space?

COL. FISCHER: Sir, absolutely. I think that this is probably the most exciting in space exploration, certainly in my
lifetime. We are about to just have an explosion of activi-
ty. There is so much involvement on the space station with
commercial industries and commercial partners. We have
an entire program to manage the science. NASA has done
a wonderful job of seeding a new industry with the Commercial Crew Program and the Commercial Cargo Program
so that we can build the infrastructure we need for the
future exploration.

One thing I love about American entrepreneurs is, once
you get them going, you better stand out of their way
because they're going to start chucking. And we're about
to that point. NASA is taking on that expensive, hard,
complex task of going further and deeper into space with
the wonderful new rocket, Space Launch System and
Orion. And then, as soon as we break open that door, this
incredible infrastructure that we've been building is going
to be right there to pick up the baton and continue into the
stars.

I would say to all the students that are watching, the time
to get excited is now. If you aren't studying science and
math, you might want to think about that because our future in the stars starts now, and you can be a part of that if,
like Dr. Whitson, you can find that passion and work really

hard. And we're going to find a permanent foothold in the stars for humanity if you do that.

THE PRESIDENT: Well, thank you. So well said. And I have to say, there's tremendous military application in space. **We're rebuilding our military** like never before. We're ordering equipment, and we're going to have the strongest military that we've ever had, the strongest military that the world has ever seen, and there's been no time where we need it more. And I'm sure that every student watching wants to know, what is next for Americans in space.

I'm very proud that I just signed a bill committing NASA to the aim of sending America astronauts to Mars. So we'll do that. I think we'll do it a lot sooner than we're even thinking. So which one of you is ready to go to Mars?

Are you ready? And I think you're ready. I know you're ready, right? We just discussed that. She'd like to go to Mars very quickly. Who's ready to go to Mars up there?

CMDR. WHITSON: We are absolutely ready to go to Mars. It's going to be a fantastic journey getting there, and very exciting times, and all of us would be happy to go.

But I want all the young people out there to recognize that the real steps are going to be taken in a few years.

And so by studying math, science, engineering, any kind of technology, you're going to have a part in that, and that will be very exciting.

THE PRESIDENT: I just want to thank you very much. And, Dr. Whitson, I just -- congratulations. Amazing. What an amazing thing that you've done. Everybody here -- I know you're family -- but everybody here is incredibly proud of the record you just broke.

I hope that every young American watching today finds, in your example, a reason to love space and think about space because many great things are going to come out, tremendous discoveries in medicine and so many other fields.

So thank you very much. I want to say God bless you, God bless America. We are very, very proud of you, and very proud of your bravery. Thank you very much.

END
10:19 A.M. ED

Chapter 156

**REMARKS BY PRESIDENT TRUMP AT
A WORKING LUNCH WITH
U.N. SECURITY COUNCIL AMBASSADORS
STATE DINING ROOM**

24 April 2017

11:50 A.M. EDT

THE PRESIDENT: This is a very, very important and powerful group of people, and it's really wonderful to have you with us. And I have to say, welcome to the White House. It's a privilege to have all of the ambassadors and their spouses. You know, they were going to leave out the spouses, and I said, you must bring your spouses. (Laughter.)

You know, I heard there were a lot of very angry spouses – (laughter) -- and this is their first time to the White House. So it's a great honor to those of you that brought your wife or spouse.

As you know, the United States holds the presidency of the Security Council this month, and I'm glad that we are continuing the tradition of hosting the Council's ambassadors in our nation's capital. It's our great honor, believe me.

I want to thank Ambassador Nikki Haley for her outstanding leadership, and for acting as my personal envoy on the Security Council. She's doing a good job. Now, does everybody like Nikki? Because if you don't -- (laughter) -- otherwise, she can easily be replaced. (Laughter.)

No, we won't do that, **I promise**. We won't do that. She's
doing a fantastic job. And everyone, I see -- even as we
took pictures before -- the friendship that you've developed, all of you together. That's really a fantastic thing.
The mission of the United Nations and the U.N. Security
Council is to maintain international peace and security. These are important aims and shared interests. But
as we look around the world, it's clear that there is much
work for you to achieve. You're going to be very busy people, I suspect, over these coming months and years.

Our nation faces serious and growing threats, and many of
them stem from problems that have been unaddressed for
far too long. In fact, the United Nations doesn't like taking on certain problems. But I have a feeling that people
in this room -- and I know for a fact that Nikki feels very,
very strongly about taking on problems that really people
steered away from.

I encourage the Security Council to come together and
take action to counter all of these many threats. On Syria,
the Council failed again this month to respond to Syria's
use of chemical weapons. A great disappointment; I was
very disappointed by that.

The status quo in North Korea is also unacceptable, and
the Council must be prepared to impose additional and
stronger sanctions on North Korean nuclear and ballistic missile programs. This is a real threat to the world,
whether we want to talk about it or not. North Korea is
a big world problem, and it's a problem we have to finally solve. People have put blindfolds on for decades, and
now it's time to solve the problem. For the United Nations
to play an effective role in solving these and other security challenges, big reforms will be required. In addition,

we must also take a close look at the U.N. budget. Costs have been -- absolutely gone out of control. But I will say this: If we do a great job, I care much less about the budget, because you're talking about peanuts compared to the important work you're doing. You really are. You're talking about the most important things ever. And I must say, I'm a budget person. You see the way I'm talking about NATO, the same thing, but if you do a great job at the United Nations, I feel much differently about it because we're talking pennies compared to the kind of lives and money that you'll be saving. The United States, just one of 193 countries in the U.N., pays for 22 percent of the budget and almost 30 percent of the United Nations peacekeeping, which is unfair. We need the member states to come together to eliminate inefficiency and bloat, and to ensure that no one nation shoulders a disproportionate share of the burden militarily or financially. This is only fair to our taxpayers.

I look forward to a productive discussion about our shared role in keeping the peace, advancing reforms, and getting everyone to do their fair share.

I also want to say to you that I have long felt the United Nations is an under-performer but has tremendous potential. There are those people that think it's an under-performer and will never perform. I think -- and I think especially I'm so happy with the job that Nikki is doing and our representatives -- but Nikki and the group -- and I see the relationship that she has already developed.

I think that the United Nations has tremendous potential -- tremendous potential -- far greater than what I would say any other candidate in the last 30 years would have even thought to say. I don't think it's lived up -- I know it hasn't

lived up to the potential. I mean, I see a day when there's
a conflict where the United Nations, you get together,
and you solve the conflict. You just don't see the United
Nations, like, solving conflicts. I think that's going to start
happening now. I can see it. And the United Nations will
get together and solve conflicts. It won't be two countries;
it will be the United Nations mediating or arbitrating with
those countries. So I see fantastic potential and fantastic
things ahead for the United Nations. And I have to say, it's
a tremendous honor to know you and to meet you. And
Nikki has given me a little briefing on each and every one
of you, and I must tell you -- I will tell you, you know, I'm
a very blunt person, if she didn't like I would tell you right
now -- (laughter) -- but she gets along with everybody and
respects everybody in this room.

I'll end by saying that -- unless you would rather not do it
-- so we have an office in the White House, you may have
heard of it, called the Oval Office. So what we'll do is we'll
go down as a group and we'll take some pictures in the
Oval Office. I know you've never seen it. Nobody seems
to get to see the Oval Office very much, but we're going
to show you the Oval Office. So we'll go down, take some
pictures of the Oval Office, and we'll have a good luncheon, and we'll talk about the United Nations and we'll talk
about peace.

Thank you all very much for being here. It's a great honor,
and I'm glad you brought your spouses. Thank you. (Applause.)

END
11:56 A.M. EDT

Chapter 157

**REMARKS BY PRESIDENT TRUMP AT
UNITED STATES HOLOCAUST MEMORIAL MUSEUM
NATIONAL DAYS OF REMEMBRANCE
UNITED STATES CAPITOL
WASHINGTON, D.C.**

25 April 2017

11:30 A.M. EDT

THE PRESIDENT: Thank you very much. Thank
you. Friends, members of Congress, ambassadors, veterans, and, most especially, to the survivors here with us
today, it's an honor to join you on this very, very solemn
occasion. I am deeply moved to stand before those who
survived history's darkest hour. Your cherished presence
transforms this place into a sacred gathering.

Thank you, Tom Bernstein, Alan Holt, Sara Bloomfield, and
everyone at the Holocaust Memorial Council and Museum
for your vital work and tireless contributions.

We are privileged to be joined by Israel's Ambassador to
the United States, friend of mine -- he's done a great job
and said some wonderful words -- Ron Dermer. The State
of Israel is an eternal monument to the undying strength
of the Jewish people. The fervent dream that burned in
the hearts of the oppressed is now filled with the breath of
life, and the Star of David waves atop a great nation arisen
from the desert.

To those in the audience who have served America in

uniform, our country eternally thanks you. We are proud
and grateful to be joined today by veterans of the Second
World War who liberated survivors from the camps. Your
sacrifice helped save freedom for the world -- for the entire world. (Applause.)

Sadly, this year marks the first Day of Remembrance since
the passing of **Elie Wiesel,** a great person, a great man. His
absence leaves an empty space in our hearts, but his spirit
fills this room. It is the kind of gentle spirit of an angel
who lived through hell, and whose courage still lights the
path from darkness. Though Elie's story is well known by
so many people, it's always worth repeating. He suffered
the unthinkable horrors of the Holocaust. His mother and
sister perished in Auschwitz. He watched his father slowly
dying before his own young eyes in Buchenwald. He lived
through an endless nightmare of murder and death, and
he inscribed on our collective conscience the duty we have
to remember that long, dark night so as never to again
repeat it.

The survivors in this hall, through their testimony, fulfill
the righteous duty to never forget, and engrave into the
world's memory the Nazi genocide of the Jewish people. You witnessed evil, and what you saw is beyond
description, beyond any description. Many of you lost
your entire family, everything and everyone you loved,
gone. You saw mothers and children led to mass slaughter. You saw the starvation and the torture. You saw the
organized attempt at the extermination of an entire people
-- and great people, I must add. You survived the ghet-
tos, the concentration camps and the death camps. And
you persevered to tell your stories. You tell of these living
nightmares because, despite your great pain, you believe
in Elie's famous plea, that "For the dead and the living, we

must bear witness."

That is why we are here today -- to remember and to bear witness. To make sure that humanity never, ever forgets.

The Nazis massacred 6 million Jews. Two out of every three Jews in Europe were murdered in the genocide. Millions more innocent people were imprisoned and executed by the Nazis without mercy, without even a sign of mercy.

Yet, even today, there are those who want to forget the past. Worse still, there are even those filled with such hate, total hate, that they want to erase the Holocaust from history. Those who deny the Holocaust are an accomplice to this horrible evil. And we'll never be silent -- we just won't -- we will never, ever be silent in the face of evil again. (Applause.)

Denying the Holocaust is only one of many forms of dangerous anti-Semitism that continues all around the world. We've seen anti-Semitism on university campuses, in the public square, and in threats against Jewish citizens. Even worse, it's been on display in the most sinister manner when terrorists attack Jewish communities, or when aggressors threaten Israel with total and complete destruction.

This is my pledge to you: We will confront anti-Semitism (Applause.)

We will stamp out prejudice. We will condemn hatred. We will bear witness. And we will act. As President of the United States, I will always stand with the Jewish people -- and I will always stand with our great friend and partner, the State of Israel.

So today, we remember the 6 million Jewish men, women and children whose lives and dreams were stolen from this Earth.

We remember the millions of other innocent victims the Nazis so brutally targeted and so brutally killed. We remember the survivors who bore more than we can imagine. We remember the hatred and evil that sought to extinguish human life, dignity, and freedom.

But we also remember the light that shone through the darkness. We remember sisters and brothers who gave everything to those they loved -- survivors like **Steven Springfield**, who, in the long death march, carried his brother on his back. As he said, "I just couldn't give in." We remember the brave souls who banded together to save the lives of their neighbors -- even at the risk of their own life. And we remember those first hopeful moments of liberation, when at long last the American soldiers arrived in camps and cities throughout occupied Europe, waving the same beautiful flags before us today, speaking those three glorious words: "You are free."

It is this love of freedom, this embrace of human dignity, this call to courage in the face of evil that the survivors here today have helped to write onto our hearts. The Jewish people have endured oppression, persecution, and those who have sought and planned their destruction. Yet, through the suffering, they have persevered. They have thrived. And they have enlightened the world. We stand in awe of the unbreakable spirit of the Jewish people.

I want to close with a story enshrined in the Museum that captures the moment of liberation in the final days of the war.

It is the story of **Gerda Klein**, a young Jewish woman from Poland. Some of you know her. Gerda's family was murdered by the Nazis. She spent three years imprisoned in labor camps, and the last four months of the war on a terrible death march. She assumed it was over. At the end, on the eve of her 21st birthday, her hair had lost all of its color, and she weighed a mere 68 pounds. Yet she had the will to live another day. It was tough.

Gerda later recalled the moment she realized that her long-awaited deliverance had arrived. She saw a car coming towards her. Many cars had driven up before, but this one was different. On its hood, in place of that wretched swastika, was a bright, beautiful, gleaming white star. Two American soldiers got out. One walked up to her. The first thing Gerda said was what she had been trained to say: "We are Jewish, you know." "We are Jewish." And then he said, "So am I." It was a beautiful moment after so much darkness, after so much evil.

As Gerda took this solider to see the other prisoners, the American did something she had long forgotten to even expect -- he opened the door for her. In Gerda's words, "that was the moment of restoration of humanity, of humanness, of dignity, and of freedom."

But the story does not end there. Because, as some of you know, that young American soldier who liberated her and who showed her such decency would soon become her husband. A year later, they were married. In her words, "He opened not only the door for me, but the door to my life and to my future."

Gerda has since spent her life telling the world of what she witnessed. She, like those survivors who are among us today, has dedicated her life to shining a light of hope through the dark of night.

Your courage strengthens us. Your voices inspire us. And your stories remind us that we must never, ever shrink away from telling the truth about evil in our time. Evil is always seeking to wage war against the innocent and to destroy all that is good and beautiful about our common humanity. But evil can only thrive in darkness. And what you have brought us today is so much more powerful than evil. You have brought us hope -- hope that love will conquer hatred, that right will defeat wrong, and that peace will rise from the ashes of war.

Each survivor here today is a beacon of light, and it only takes one light to illuminate even the darkest space. Just like it takes only one truth to crush a thousand lies and one hero to change the course of history. We know that in the end, good will triumph over evil, and that as long as we refuse to close our eyes or to silence our voices, we know that justice will ultimately prevail.

So today we mourn. We remember. We pray. And we pledge: Never again.

Thank you. God bless you, and God bless America. Thank you very much. Thank you. (Applause.)

END
11:45 A.M. EDT

Chapter 158

**REMARKS BY PRESIDENT TRUMP IN
FARMERS ROUNDTABLE AND EXECUTIVE ORDER
SIGNING PROMOTING
AGRICULTURE AND RURAL PROSPERITY IN AMERICA
ROOSEVELT ROOM**

25 April 2017

3:14 P.M. EDT

THE PRESIDENT: Busy day. They had a very busy day -- had a good day. We're doing well, very well. Things are turning around. I know they're turning around for you folks, so I just want to welcome you very much to the White House -- special place -- America's farmers and ranchers.

I especially want to congratulate Secretary -- now I can say, Secretary Sonny Perdue, who was just sworn in as the Secretary of Agriculture -- (applause) -- sworn in by Justice Thomas. And it was a beautiful ceremony, and we're going to celebrate a little bit later, and that's great. We're very happy. And you had a good vote too.

SECRETARY PERDUE: Yes, sir.

THE PRESIDENT: You didn't have one of those 51-49 votes. (Laughter.)

He had a very big vote, so thank Justice Thomas too -- great man, great person. We appreciate it.

America's noble farming tradition stretches back to its earliest days. **Farmers led the way across the Great Plains**, and put down roots from coast to coast. Today, America's farmers feed not only our nation, but millions of people around the world, and we're going to open that up much more for you folks because, as you know, it's not totally open, to put it mildly. We learned that yesterday, frankly, with Canada, where the dairy farmers up in Wisconsin, Upstate New York, different places -- a lot of border states in particular -- are not able to sell their dairy products into Canada. And this has been going on for a while, and we're not going to put up with it.

And separately, we put a very big tax -- we will be putting a very big tariff on lumber -- timber -- coming into this country. People don't realize Canada has been very rough on the United States. Everyone thinks of Canada as being wonderful, and so do I. I love Canada. But they've out-smarted our politicians for many years, and you people understand that. **So we did institute a very big tariff; we announced it yesterday**. And we're going to take care of our dairy farmers in Wisconsin, and Upstate New York, and lots of other places. So I think you people all probably agree with that, right? Would you agree with that? You better believe it.

Our **farmers deserve a government that serves their in-terest and empowers them** to do the hard work that they love to do so much. And that's what today's executive order is all about. With this order, I'm directing Secretary Perdue to work with other members of my Cabinet to identify and eliminate unnecessary regulations that hurt our nation's farmers and rural communities.

Now, Sonny, I've already signed a lot of regulations and ter-minations that really help the farmer a lot. You know what

I'm talking about. But we have some left, and you'll identify them. But we've really gotten rid of some of the biggest ones. And that was a big help, right? I mean, they won't tell you about it, but they're big numbers, and it's going to mean a lot to the farmers.

This order also establishes the *Inter-agency Task Force on Agriculture and Rural Prosperity*, to be led by Secretary Perdue. I just want to tell you that it's an honor to be with you because, among many other things, with this order, we continue a very relentless effort to make life better for hard-working Americans, and that includes the farmers and all of the people gathered around this table, including our ranchers, our rural community folks. We're having a very, very big impact. It's already started. Sonny is going to now identify additional areas where we can get rid of unnecessary regulations, and you people are going to be so **prosperous**, and you're going to **hire** so many more people than currently work for you, and that's going to make me very happy, okay?

So I want to thank you very much. So do we have the executive order, please?

So this is **promoting agriculture and rural prosperity in America**. And, now, there's a lot of words I won't bother reading everything. But **agriculture and rural prosperity in America, that's what we want**. And we don't want to be taken advantage of by other countries -- and that's stopping, and that's stopping fast. Okay, thank you.

(The President signs the Executive Order.)

Well, perhaps I should give this pen to Sonny Perdue. What do you think? (Laughter and applause.)

Thank you very much, everybody.

Q   Mr. President, do you fear a trade war with Canada, sir?

THE PRESIDENT: No, not at all.

Q   Why not?

THE PRESIDENT: They have a tremendous surplus with the United States. Whenever they have a surplus, I have no fear. By the way, virtually every country has a surplus with the United States. We have massive trade deficits. So when we're the country with the deficits, we have no fear.

Q   Will you sign a CR if it doesn't include funding for the wall?

THE PRESIDENT: Say it?

Q   Will you sign a CR to continue funding the government if it doesn't include --

THE PRESIDENT: The **wall is going to get built**, by the way. Just in case anybody has any question: The **wall is going to get built**, and the wall is going to stop drugs, and it's going to stop a lot of people from coming in that shouldn't be here, and it's going to have a huge effect on human trafficking, which is a tremendous problem in this world -- a problem that nobody talks about -- but it's a problem that's probably worse than any time in the history of this world. Human trafficking, what's going on.

The **wall is going to get built**, and we're setting record numbers in terms of stopping people from coming in, and stopping drugs from coming in. You see the numbers down 73, 74 percent. I will say, Secretary Kelly -- formerly General Kelly -- is doing an incredible job. And I was just with him a little while ago, and **he said we definitely, desperately need the wall. And we're going to have the wall built**. I mean, I don't know why people are talking. I watch these shows, and the pundits in the morning -- they don't know what they're talking about. **The wall gets built -- 100 percent**. Thank you very much.

Q   When will the wall get built?

THE PRESIDENT: Soon. We're already preparing. We're doing plans. We're doing specifications. We're doing a lot of work on the wall, and the wall gets built. **The wall is very, very important**.

Q   In your first term?

THE PRESIDENT: Well, it's certainly going to -- yeah, yeah, sure.

Q   In your first term?

THE PRESIDENT: We have plenty of time -- got a lot of time.

Thank you.

END
3:21 P.M. EDT

CHAPTER 159

**PRESS BRIEFING BY SECRETARY OF INTERIOR RYAN ZINKE ON THE EXECUTIVE ORDER TO
REVIEW THE DESIGNATIONS UNDER THE ANTIQUITIES ACT
JAMES S. BRADY PRESS BRIEFING ROOM**

April 25, 2017

5:11 P.M. EDT

MS. WALTERS: Hello, everyone. As you guys knows, we're going to go through an EO for tomorrow. The speaker this evening is Secretary Zinke. This is embargoed until 9:00 p.m. It is on the record, so everything discussed here will be on the record. The embargo is until 9:00 p.m. tonight.

Again, this falls underneath Kelly's issue area, so if you have any additional follow-up questions, please reach out to Kelly Love. For those of you on the phone, there will be a handout during this session, so if you would like the handout please email Kelly as well, and we will get it to you.

With that, I'll turn it over.

SECRETARY ZINKE: So I'll read this and then I'll answer some questions. Tomorrow, the President will come to the Department of Interior, to my office, and sign the executive order to review the Antiquities Act. The executive order will direct me, as the Secretary, to review prior monument designations and to suggest legislative changes or modifications to the monuments. The monument designation period stretches from 1 January 1996 under which the act — and it has to include acts and monuments that are 100,000 acres or more — so the beginning date is January 1st, 1996, and the other condition is they have to be a total of 100,000 acres or more. That should include about 24 to 40 monuments. That gives you kind of a thumbnail.

The executive order directs the Interior to provide an interim report to the President within 45 days of the day of the order and a final report to the President within 120 days of that order.

For the record, in the last 20 years, in particular, that would cover about, oh, tens of millions of acres to include marine area sanctuaries. Some of these areas were put off limits for traditional uses, like farming, ranching, timber harvest, mining, oil and gas exploration, fishing, and motorized recreation.

The designations on kind of the bookends are the Grand Staircase-Escalante National Monument of 1996. And that was the first BLM land designation, all the way to really the Bears Ears National Monument in 2016, which has been in the news a lot. So those are the kind of two bookends. Again, it's monuments that are 100,000 acres or larger, so it hits the big ones.

The President's — the authority on such matters is singular, so you know. There's no requirement for public input before the designation of a monument and there's no NEPA requirement. Normally, when you do a land use project, we normally NEPA. The Antiquities Act is the exception. Again, we don't have to go through legislative process; the President determines it, and it does not have to go through NEPA.

In this case, the administration, as you all know, has heard from members of Congress and states and, in some cases, the designation of the monuments may have resulted in loss of jobs, reduced wages and reduced public access. And in the case of sign public land use, we feel that the public, the people that the monuments affect, should be considered. And that's why the President is asking for a review of the monuments designated in the last 20 years to see what changes, if any, improvements can be made, and give states and local communities a meaningful voice in the process.

And I can tell you, from a kid who grew up in Montana, or grew up in the West, where much-needed monuments have taken place, I think today's executive order and review of the Antiquities Act over the past two decades is long overdue.

And the policy is consistent with the President's promise to give Americans a voice and make sure their voices are heard. Like many of the actions he's taken since assuming the role of the President, the office, this is yet another example the President is doing exactly what he was saying in his campaign promises, and he's delivering.

The President believes, like I do, that many of the neighbors in the Western states of the federal government can be a good neighbor. We can protect areas of cultural and economic importance, and they can use the federal lands for economic development when appropriate, just as Teddy Roosevelt envisioned it. I am a lifetime supporter and admirer of Teddy Roosevelt's policies, and the President is the same.

The Antiquities Act of 1906 — and that was under President Roosevelt — it did give the President the authority to declare historic monuments, landmarks, prehistoric structures, and other objects of historic and scientific interest on federal lands. Also in the Antiquities Act, authors specified the scope of the authority to "designate the smallest area compatible with proper care and management of the objects to be protected." That's verbiage from the act itself.

So with the average size of the monument's designations over the past years has increased. I think that should be worthy of notice. Since the 1990s, when the act was first used, the average size of the national monuments came from 422 acres to, today, in the millions of acres.

So here's what the executive order does in summary. It restores the trust between local communities in Washington that the local communities and states will have a voice — those states that are affected, and local communities. The executive order puts America and the Department of Interior back on track to manage our federal lands in accordance with traditional multiple use, as laid out by Pinchot and the President, and directs the Department of Interior to make recommendations to the President on whether a monument should be rescinded, resized, modified in order to better manage our federal lands. And this executive order gives rural communities across America, again, a voice, as his campaign promised and is delivering that.

Here's what the executive order does not do. The executive order does not strip any monument of a designation. The executive order does not loosen any environmental or conservation regulation on any land or marine areas. It is a review of the last 20 years, and the review has time-lines in which I am obligated to uphold.

So I have with me my advisor, Downey Magallanes, with me. Downey is there, and she'll help me answer questions if I cannot field them. So, questions? Sir.

Q   Does this executive order presuppose that the President has the authority to unilaterally withdraw weigh-ins or revoke a national monument designation? Or is that one of the issues that —

SECRETARY ZINKE: No. As I said in my hearing, it's undisputed the President has the authority to modify a monument. It's pretty premature to suggest we do the review in which I'm going to review and recommend to the President whether to rescind a monument completely or modify it. It is untested, as you know, whether the President can do that, but at this point, I haven't gone through the list — and I'm sure someone is going to ask me how I'm going to go through and review, so I'll be glad to answer that.

Yes, sir.

Q   Thank you very much. First, just to clarify, it was extended to 21 years just to include Grand Staircase in this review? And secondly, do you believe, at the end of this review process, you'll recommend changes to the Antiquities Act?

SECRETARY ZINKE: The bookends really are from the Grand Staircase to Bear's Ears, so that's the period of time, roughly — about 20 years.

Q   So it's included on purpose?

SECRETARY ZINKE: Well, it went back 20 years. So I'm not going to predispose what the outcome is going to be. How

I'm going to proceed is this — is I'm going to talk to congressional delegations and review the list. I'm going to talk to governors. I'm going to talk to the stakeholders involved and formulate recommendations that are appropriate.

Up front, I'm a Teddy Roosevelt guy. And so I think, when the Antiquities Act came out, I think we should all recognize that, by and large, the Antiquities Act and the monuments that we have protected have done a great service to the public and are some of our most treasured lands in this country. So this is an enormous responsibility I have to make recommendations that are appropriate, that follow the law. But no one loves our public lands more than I. You could love them as much, but you can't love them more than I do. And that's one of the reasons why I love my job.

Q   During your confirmation hearing, you told Maria Cantwell, I am absolutely against the transfer and sale of public lands, it can't be more clear. Do you still believe that? And I have a follow-up.

SECRETARY ZINKE: Absolutely, unequivocally, I stand by — matter of fact, with a recreational guide this morning, I made the same statement again, is that I am opposed to transfer or sale of public land.

What I am strongly supportive of is managing our land. And there's no doubt if you — especially out West. You look at the catastrophic forest fires, our wildlife corridors, our water management — that we can do a lot better as a government of managing our land. And, to a degree, we've drifted too far away from multiple use into single use.

Q   Do you worry, though, that this will lead to the transfer of land?

SECRETARY ZINKE: No. I've heard that argument; I think that argument is false.

Q   It just won't happen?

SECRETARY ZINKE: And remember, the monuments before this happened were public land. And when they designate a monument, what it does is it restricts it and sometimes it restricts it from traditional uses like grazing. Public access, in some cases, can be restricted because gates go up.

So I think you have to proceed carefully on it. But multiple use on much of our land was designed under Pinchot to use for the public good for all of us, and not necessarily single use. And that's where we are.

Q   You said in your last response that in general you feel like in most of these cases the designations have provided some kind of public service and they've done a good job. Can you talk about the flip side of that coin — cases where you feel like maybe they actually haven't? And then just one clarification — does this apply to monuments that were designated earlier than 1996 but then modified after 1996? Apparently there are a number that fall into that category.

SECRETARY ZINKE: On your second point, if the modification was significant, we'll look at that. My understanding is there's about 30 or so monuments that fall into the category of 100,000 acres or larger and the modification was significant. But by and large, it's the bookends we talked about.

I think the concern that I have and the President has that when you designate a monument, the local community that's affected should have a voice. And he said that in the campaign, he said that American citizens should have a voice. The little community, the loggers, the fishermen, those areas that are affected should have a say and a voice.

And so, again, this executive order doesn't predispose any action other than having the Secretary that he chose — me —review them. And I'm going to review it in a transparent matter to make sure, A, we have a voice, the process is transparent. And at the end of it, we're going to follow the law as Teddy Roosevelt laid out.

Q   Just want to get back to concern swirling around the EO. What's your response to people who believe that the review is setting the stage for an assault on public lands for the purposes of oil and gas development?

SECRETARY ZINKE: I've heard that many times about — and I think it's the modern media that we live in today. We're so polarized as a country, and action is perceived as doing something that's not — and this, the executive order is carefully crafted to review. It doesn't predispose an outcome.

Again, the President — I was honored to be chosen and confirmed as his Secretary of Interior. I've laid out my beliefs, as well as the President shares, about public land. But again, the core of this is to make sure the public has a voice. That's who I work for. That's who the President works for, is the people. And that's — love to get the people a voice on that. But I think it's a false narrative that we're going to predispose any particular action until the review.

Q   Are you anticipating any legal challenges from environmental groups? And what are you doing to prepare for
some pretty staunch opposition from some of these groups
opposed to the President's —

SECRETARY ZINKE: It's interesting, in the first days of my
office, I think I got sued six times before lunch. So prudent
public policy should be the right policy, and I'm not in fear
of getting sued. I get sued all the time. I don't think law-
suits should shape public policy. I think our public policy
should do what's right. The courts are free to challenge,
and we live in a great country that people are free to challenge. I'm not going to make my judgments on the basis of
getting sued or not sued doing the right thing.

Q   Mr. Secretary, you referred to lost jobs. Could you
provide a concrete example, going back to 1996, of where
there's community that — in terms of net job loss, it exceeded the gains from being designated a national monument? And in terms of your recommendations, obviously,
you and White House officials have indicated that it might
include legislative recommendations. To what extent do
you think Congress is the one that should redraw the lines
based on community input, as opposed to, say, the White
House and the Interior Department redrawing any lines for
these monuments?

SECRETARY ZINKE: Great question. Jobs, that's part of the
study we're going to look at. Because you have, on the
side — some jobs would probably be created by recreation
opportunities. So in the parks, we had 330 million visitors
last year. Some of our parks alone are at record capacity. And so I was this morning in our parks, and I think our

economic driver is at $34.9 billion a year. And if you look at the recreation industry, it's quite a bit more than that.

So there's jobs across — we'll look at what sectors were affected, plus or minus, and that will be part of the recommendation. I can't give you any numbers until we look at it, but jobs — I recognize on both sides.

Secondly, I'm sorry, your second point was?

Q   My second question is, to what extent should it be Congress that actually redraws the lines for any of these monuments, or to what extent do you think that the White House and the Interior Department can unilaterally redraw them?

SECRETARY ZINKE: From an Antiquities Act point — this is — the President has singular authority. But I think the philosophy on public lands should be what's inscribed in the Roosevelt Arch, Yellowstone Park — it's for the benefit and enjoyment of the people. That's what's ascribed in stone at the Yellowstone Arch. And oddly enough, in one of the pillars, it says "Enacted by Congress."

So I think it's appropriate, the three branches of government — at least the Congress and the President — should work together. Certainly in Utah, you have a congressional delegation — this is the two we've talked about in Utah. I think that the delegation that represents the people should be coordinated with, the governor should be coordinated — and the principals on the ground on both sides, their voice needs to be heard.

Q   Yes, thank you. Is it your opinion that (inaudible) will be used in the Antiquities Act?

SECRETARY ZINKE: Well, certainly, that's a concern. If
you're out in Utah, the Utah legislature — on a state side,
they're vehemently opposed to it. Those out in the West
would probably say it's abused. My position is I'm going
into it and evaluating on a legal basis, and making sure
people have a say. But I'm not going in with a political
judgment either way. I just want to make a firm judgment
based on the facts on the ground and giving people a
voice.

Certainly the governor is going to have an influence. Jobs
are going to have an influence. The congressional folks are
going to have an influence on it. But given my personality,
I'm going to be transparent about it.

And, sir, I'm going to give you the last question.

Q   Thank you. So you said there's going to be a 45-day
interim review. We've seen the President sign other executive orders where he just asks for a final review. Is there a
particular reason why there's a shorter window for that —

SECRETARY ZINKE: The 45-day review is pretty much cen-
tered on Bears Ears, because that's the most current one.
My obligation is to wrap up at least my recommendation
in 120 days. The recommendation I could save for further
review.

So that's part of it, is I have some latitude as the Secretary
to look at whether I have the facts on the ground. Again, a
lot of it's going to be driven on talking to elected officials,
local governments, the stakeholders, and making a reason-
able decision so we, the people, have a voice.

And I think it's appropriate to — a couple mentions whether the President — this President has some plan to sell or transfer public lands — no. This executive order simply, I think, initiates a review, which is appropriate. When an administration comes in — a new administration, that was one of his campaign promises. He's delivering on a promise. He selected me to review it. I may be the most popular individual in the world, or I may be the most unpopular position in the world, but it's a job that — I can't be more thrilled being the Secretary of Interior. I mean, to be the steward of a fifth of our country and the majesty — it's an enormous responsibility, but also it's a gift. So I'm going to use that authority I think to the benefit of us all.

So thank you, everybody.

Q   Just to clear up, do you expect to have a decision on Bears Ears in 45 days?

SECRETARY ZINKE: I expect to have a recommendation.

Q   A recommendation on Bears Ears in 45 days.

SECRETARY ZINKE: I do.

Q   And are you planning on going in that amount of time?

SECRETARY ZINKE: I am going to be out there. There's no doubt I'm going out there. And I would have been sooner, but we had the first Cabinet meeting. I was delayed in the hearings. So no doubt that my travel schedule is going to be busier than it already is.

Q   Mr. Secretary, just on (inaudible) — can you just say anything about your philosophy about that upcoming executive order, which we also expect this year

MS. WALTERS: We'll be able to comment on that on Thursday. We're going to put together a background briefing. Thank you.

SECRETARY ZINKE: Keep the faith. It's all good.

Q   Thank you, Mr. Secretary.

Q   Thank you.

END
5:34 P.M. EDT

Continuation

26 April 2017

11:34 A.M. EDT

[SECRETARY ZINKE: ...]

[THE VICE PRESIDENT: ...]

THE PRESIDENT: Thank you, Mike. He's been a great Vice President, a great help. And everybody loves Mike Pence. I just want to thank you for your service. Been incredible. (Applause.)

It's a real pleasure to be at the Department of Interior, where you help preserve the splendor and the beauty of America's natural resources. And I can tell you the group that's in here right now, they really do the job. Right, Lisa? They're doing a good job. We're going to take care of Alaska, too. Don't worry about it. (Laughter.)

And they protect the ability of the people to access and utilize the land which truly belongs to them and belongs to all of us.

Secretary Ryan Zinke is doing an incredible job -- and he never overlooks the details. He's a detail person. Soon after he was confirmed, we had a snowstorm, big one, and

he was out there on the steps of the Lincoln
Memorial shoveling the snow all by himself. And he's a
strong guy. He did a good job. (Laughter.)

He did a very, very good job. But we're proud of him.
In the **first 100 days**, we have **taken historic action to
eliminate wasteful regulation**s. They're being eliminated
like nobody has ever seen before. There has never been
anything like it. Sometimes I look at some of the things I'm
signing I say maybe people won't like it, but I'm doing the
right thing. And no regular politician is going do it. (Laughter.)

I don't know if you folks would do -- I will tell you literally
some politicians have said, you're doing the right thing. I
don't know if I would have had the courage to do some of
these things. But we're doing them because it's the right
thing to do. And it's for the good of the nation.

We're **returning power back to the people**. We've eliminated job-destroying regulations on farmers, ranchers, and
coal miners, on auto-workers, and so many other American
workers and businesses.

Today, I am signing a new executive order to end another
egregious abuse of federal power, and to give that power
back to the states and to the people, where it belongs.

The **previous administration used a 100-year-old law
known as the Antiquities Act to unilaterally put millions
of acres of land and water under strict federal control --**
have you heard about that? -- eliminating the ability of the
people who actually live in those states to decide how best
to use that land.

Today, we are putting the states back in charge. It's a big thing.

I am pleased to be joined by so many members of Congress and governors who have been waiting for this moment, including Governor Herbert of Utah.

Thank you, thank you, Governor. Governor LePage of Maine, who, by the way, has lost a lot of weight. (Laughter.)

I knew him when he was heavy, and now I know him when he's thin, and I like him both ways, okay? (Laughter.)

Done a great job. Governor Calvo of Guam. Thank you. Governor Torres from the Northern Mariana Islands. Thank you, thank you, Governor.

I also want to recognize Senator Orrin Hatch, who -- believe me, he's tough. He would call me and call me and say, you got to do this. Is that right, Orrin?

SENATOR HATCH: That's right.

THE PRESIDENT: You didn't stop. He doesn't give up. And he's shocked that I'm doing it, but I'm doing it because it's the right thing to do. But I really have to point you out, you didn't stop.

And, Mike, the same thing. So many people feel -- Mike Lee -- so many people feel so strongly about this, and so I appreciate your support and your prodding, and your never-ending prodding, I should say, because we're now getting something done that many people thought would never ever get done, and I'm very proud to be doing it in honor of you guys, okay? Thank you. (Applause.)

Altogether, the previous administration bypassed the states to place over 265 million acres -- that's a lot of land, million acres.

Think of it -- 265 million acres of land and water under federal control through the abuse of the monuments designation. That's larger than the entire state of Texas.

In December of last year alone, **the federal government asserted this power over 1.35 million acres of land in Utah, known as Bears Ears** -- I've heard a lot about Bears Ears, and I hear it's beautiful -- over the profound objections of the citizens of Utah.

The ***Antiquities Act*** does not give the federal government unlimited power to lock up millions of acres of land and water, and it's time we ended this abusive practice.

I've spoken with many state and local leaders -- a number of them here today -- who care very much about preserving our land, and who are gravely concerned about this massive federal land grab. And it's gotten worse and worse and worse, and now we're going to free it up, which is what should have happened in the first place. This should never have happened.

That's why today I am signing this order and directing Secretary Zinke to end these abuses and return control to the people -- the people of Utah, the people of all of the states, the people of the United States.
Every day, we are going to continue pushing ahead with our reform agenda to put the American people back in charge of their government and their lives.

And again, I want to congratulate the Secretary. I want to congratulate Orrin and Mike and all of the people that worked so hard on bringing it to this point. And tremendously positive things are going to happen on that incredible land, the likes of which there is nothing more beautiful anywhere in the world. But now tremendously positive things will happen.

So I want to thank you. I want to thank everybody for being here. God bless you all and God bless America.

Thank you. Thank you very much. So I'll sign.

(The Executive Order is signed.) (Applause.)

Q   Are you surprised about this 9th Circuit ruling?

THE PRESIDENT: I'm never surprised by the 9th Circuit. (Laughter.)

As I said, we'll see them in the Supreme Court. (Laughter and applause.)

END
11:42 A.M. EDT

[Note: As President Trump made reference to the previous administrations use of the **Antiquities Act**, to add context the following information is provided.

On 28 December 2016, President Obama made a Presidential Proclamation:

ESTABLISHMENT OF THE BEARS EARS NATIONAL MONUMENT
ESTABLISHMENT OF
THE BEARS EARS NATIONAL MONUMENT

~

BY THE PRESIDENT OF THE UNITED STATES OF AMERICA

A PROCLAMATION

Rising from the center of the south-eastern Utah landscape and visible from every direction are twin buttes so distinctive that in each of the native languages of the region their name is the same: Hoon'Naqvut, Shash Jáa, Kwiyagatu Nukavachi, Ansh An Lashokdiwe, or "Bears Ears." For hundreds of generations, native peoples lived in the surrounding deep sandstone canyons, desert mesas, and meadow mountaintops, which constitute one of the densest and most significant cultural landscapes in the United States. Abundant rock art, ancient cliff dwellings, ceremonial sites, and countless other artifacts provide an extraordinary archaeological and cultural record that is important to us all, but most notably the land is profoundly sacred to many Native American tribes, including the Ute Mountain Ute Tribe, Navajo Nation, Ute Indian Tribe of the Uintah Ouray, Hopi Nation, and Zuni Tribe.

The area's human history is as vibrant and diverse as the ruggedly beautiful landscape. From the earliest occupation, native peoples left traces of their presence. Clovis people hunted among the cliffs and canyons of Cedar Mesa as early as 13,000 years ago, leaving behind tools and projectile points in places like the Lime Ridge Clovis Site, one of the oldest known archaeological sites in Utah. Archaeologists believe that these early people hunted mammoths, ground sloths, and other now-extinct megafauna, a narrative echoed by native creation stories. Hunters and gatherers continued to live in this region in the Archaic Period, with sites dating as far back as 8,500 years ago.

Ancestral Puebloans followed, beginning to occupy the area at least 2,500 years ago, leaving behind items from their daily life such as baskets, pottery, and weapons. These early farmers of Basketmaker II, and III and builders of Pueblo I, II and III left their marks on the land. The remains of single family dwellings, granaries, kivas, towers, and large villages and roads linking them together reveal a complex cultural history. "Moki steps," hand and toe holds carved into steep canyon walls by the Ancestral Puebloans, illustrate the early people's ingenuity and perseverance and are still used today to access dwellings along cliff walls. Other, distinct cultures have thrived here as well -- the Fremont People, Numic- and Athabaskan-speaking hunter-gatherers, and Utes and Navajos. Resources such as the Doll House Ruin in Dark Canyon Wilderness Area and the Moon House Ruin on Cedar Mesa allow visitors to marvel at artistry and architecture that have withstood thousands of seasons in this harsh climate.

The landscape is a milieu of the accessible and observable together with the inaccessible and hidden. The area's petroglyphs and pictographs capture the imagination with images dating back at least 5,000 years and spanning a range of styles and traditions. From life-size ghostlike figures that defy categorization, to the more literal depictions of bighorn sheep, birds, and lizards, these drawings enable us to feel the humanity of these ancient artists. The Indian Creek area contains spectacular rock art, including hundreds of petroglyphs at Newspaper Rock. Visitors to Bears Ears can also discover more recent rock art left by the Ute, Navajo, and Paiute peoples. It is also the less visible sites, however -- those that supported the food gathering, subsistence and ceremony of daily life -- that tell the story of the people who lived here. Historic remnants of Native American sheep-herding and farming are scattered throughout the area, and pottery and Navajo hogans record the lifeways of native peoples in the 19th and 20th centuries.

For thousands of years, humans have occupied and stewarded this land. With respect to most of these people, their contribution to the historical record is unknown, but some have played a more public role. Famed Navajo headman K'aayélii was born around 1800 near the twin Bears Ears buttes. His band used the area's remote canyons to elude capture by the U.S. Army and avoid the fate that befell many other Navajo bands: surrender, the Long Walk, and forced relocation to Bosque Redondo. Another renowned 19th century Navajo leader, "Hastiin Ch'ihaajin" Manuelito, was also born near the Bears Ears.

The area's cultural importance to Native American tribes continues to this day. As they have for generations, these tribes and their members come here for ceremonies and to visit sacred sites. Throughout the region, many landscape features, such as Comb Ridge, the San Juan River, and Cedar Mesa, are closely tied to native stories of creation, danger, protection, and healing. The towering spires in the Valley of the Gods are sacred to the Navajo, representing ancient Navajo warriors frozen in stone. Traditions of hunting, fishing, gathering, and wood cutting are still practiced by tribal members, as is collection of medicinal and ceremonial plants, edible herbs, and materials for crafting items like baskets and footwear. The traditional ecological knowledge amassed by the Native Americans whose ancestors inhabited this region, passed down from generation to generation, offers critical insight into the historic and scientific significance of the area. Such knowledge is, itself, a resource to be protected and used in understanding and managing this landscape sustainably for generations to come.

Euro-Americans first explored the Bears Ears area during the 18th century, and Mormon settlers followed in the late 19th century. The San Juan Mission expedition traversed this rugged country in 1880 on their journey to establish a new settlement in what is now Bluff, Utah. To ease the passage of wagons over the slick rock slopes and through the canyonlands, the settlers smoothed sections of the rock surface and constructed dugways and other features still visible along their route, known as the Hole-in-the-Rock Trail. Cabins, corrals, trails, and carved inscriptions in the rock reveal the lives of ranchers, prospectors, and early archaeologists. Cattle rustlers and other outlaws created a convoluted trail network known as the Outlaw Trail, said to be used by Butch Cassidy and the Sundance Kid. These outlaws took advantage of the area's network of canyons, including the aptly-named Hideout Canyon, to avoid detection.

The area's stunning geology, from sharp pinnacles to broad mesas, labyrinthine canyons to solitary hoodoos, and verdant hanging gardens to bare stone arches and natural bridges, provides vital insights to geologists. In the east, the Abajo Mountains tower, reaching elevations of more than 11,000 feet. A long geologic history is documented in the colorful rock layers visible in the area's canyons.

For long periods over 300 million years ago, these lands were inundated by tropical seas and hosted thriving coral reefs. These seas infused the area's black rock shale with salts as they receded. Later, the lands were bucked upwards multiple times by the Monument Upwarp, and near-volcanoes punched up through the rock, leaving their marks on the landscape without reaching the surface. In the sandstone of Cedar Mesa, fossil evidence has revealed large, mammal-like reptiles that burrowed into the sand to survive the blistering heat of the end of the Permian Period, when the region was dominated by a seaside desert. Later, in the Late Triassic Period more than 200 million years ago, seasonal monsoons flooded an ancient river system that fed a vast desert here.

The paleontological resources in the Bears Ears area are among the richest and most significant in the United States, and protection of this area will provide important opportunities for further archaeological and paleontological study. Many sites, such as Arch Canyon, are teeming with fossils, and research conducted in the Bears Ears area is revealing new insights into the transition of vertebrate life from reptiles to mammals and from sea to land. Numerous ray-finned fish fossils from the Permian Period have been discovered, along with other late Paleozoic Era fossils, including giant amphibians, synapsid reptiles, and important plant fossils. Fossilized traces of marine and aquatic creatures such as clams, crayfish, fish, and aquatic reptiles have been found in Indian Creek's Chinle Formation, dating to the Triassic Period, and phytosaur and dinosaur fossils from the same period have been found along Comb Ridge. Paleontologists have identified new species of plant-eating crocodile-like reptiles and mass graves of lumbering sauropods, along with metoposarus, crocodiles, and other dinosaur fossils. Fossilized trackways of early tetrapods can be seen in the Valley of the Gods and in Indian Creek, where paleontologists have also discovered exceptional examples of fossilized ferns, horsetails, and cycads. The Chinle Formation and the Wingate, Kayenta, and Navajo Formations above it provide one of the best continuous rock records of the Triassic-Jurassic transition in the world, crucial to understanding how dinosaurs dominated terrestrial ecosystems and how our mammalian ancestors evolved. In Pleistocene Epoch sediments, scientists have found traces of mammoths, short-faced bears, ground sloths, primates, and camels.

From earth to sky, the region is unsurpassed in wonders.

The star-filled nights and natural quiet of the Bears Ears area transport visitors to an earlier eon. Against an absolutely black night sky, our galaxy and others more distant leap into view. As one of the most intact and least roaded areas in the contiguous United States, Bears Ears has that rare and arresting quality of deafening silence.

Communities have depended on the resources of the region for hundreds of generations. Understanding the important role of the green highlands in providing habitat for subsistence plants and animals, as well as capturing and filtering water from passing storms, the Navajo refer to such places as "Nahodishgish," or places to be left alone. Local communities seeking to protect the mountains for their watershed values have long recognized the importance of the Bears Ears' headwaters. Wildfires, both natural and human-set, have shaped and maintained forests and grasslands of this area for millennia. Ranchers have relied on the forests and grasslands of the region for ages, and hunters come from across the globe for a chance at a bull elk or other big game. Today, ecological restoration through the careful use of wildfire and management of grazing and timber is working to restore and maintain the health of these vital watersheds and grasslands.

The diversity of the soils and micro-environments in the Bears Ears area provide habitat for a wide variety of vegetation. The highest elevations, in the Elk Ridge area of the Manti-La Sal National Forest, contain pockets of ancient Engelmann spruce, ponderosa pine, aspen, and subalpine fir. Mesa tops include pinyon-juniper woodlands along with big sagebrush, low sage, blackbrush, rabbitbrush, bitterbrush, four-wing saltbush, shadscale, winterfat, Utah serviceberry, western chokecherry, hackberry, barberry, cliff rose, and greasewood. Canyons contain diverse vegetation ranging from yucca and cacti such as prickly pear, claret cup, and Whipple's fishhook to mountain mahogany, ponderosa pine, alder, sagebrush, birch, dogwood, and Gambel's oak, along with occasional stands of aspen. Grasses and herbaceous species such as bluegrass, bluestem, giant ryegrass, ricegrass, needle and thread, yarrow, common mallow, balsamroot, low larkspur, horsetail, and peppergrass also grow here, as well as pinnate spring parsley, Navajo penstemon, Canyonlands lomatium, and the Abajo daisy.

Tucked into winding canyons are vibrant riparian communities characterized by Fremont cottonwood, western sandbar willow, yellow willow, and box elder. Numerous seeps provide year-round water and support delicate hanging gardens, moisture-loving plants, and relict species such as Douglas fir. A few populations of the rare Kachina daisy, endemic to the Colorado Plateau, hide in shaded seeps and alcoves of the area's canyons. A genetically distinct population of Kachina daisy was also found on Elk Ridge. The alcove columbine and cave primrose, also regionally endemic, grow in seeps and hanging gardens in the Bears Ears landscape. Wildflowers such as beardtongue, evening primrose, aster, Indian paintbrush, yellow and purple beeflower, straight bladderpod, Durango tumble mustard, scarlet gilia, globe mallow, sand verbena, sego lily, cliffrose, sacred datura, monkey flower, sunflower, prince's plume, hedgehog cactus, and columbine, bring bursts of color to the landscape.

The diverse vegetation and topography of the Bears Ears area, in turn, support a variety of wildlife species. Mule deer and elk range on the mesas and near canyon heads, which provide crucial habitat for both species. The Cedar Mesa landscape is home to bighorn sheep which were once abundant but still live in Indian Creek, and in the canyons north of the San Juan River. Small mammals such as desert cottontail, black-tailed jackrabbit, prairie dog, Botta's pocket gopher, white-tailed antelope squirrel, Colorado chipmunk, canyon mouse, deer mouse, pinyon mouse, and desert woodrat, as well as Utah's only population of Abert's tassel-eared squirrels, find shelter and sustenance in the landscape's canyons and uplands. Rare shrews, including a variant of Merriam's shrew and the dwarf shrew can be found in this area.

Carnivores, including badger, coyote, striped skunk, ringtail, gray fox, bobcat, and the occasional mountain lion, all hunt here, while porcupines use their sharp quills and climbing abilities to escape these predators. Oral histories from the Ute describe the historic presence of bison, antelope, and abundant bighorn sheep, which are also depicted in ancient rock art. Black bear pass through the area but are rarely seen, though they are common in the oral histories and legends of this region, including those of the Navajo.

Consistent sources of water in a dry landscape draw diverse wildlife species to the area's riparian habitats, including an array of amphibian species such as tiger salamander, red-spotted toad, Woodhouse's toad, canyon tree frog, Great Basin spadefoot, and northern leopard frog. Even the most sharp-eyed visitors probably will not catch a glimpse of the secretive Utah night lizard. Other reptiles in the area include the sagebrush lizard, eastern fence lizard, tree lizard, side-blotched lizard, plateau striped whiptail, western rattlesnake, night snake, striped whipsnake, and gopher snake.

Raptors such as the golden eagle, peregrine falcon, bald eagle, northern harrier, northern goshawk, red-tailed hawk, ferruginous hawk, American kestrel, flammulated owl, and great horned owl hunt their prey on the mesa tops with deadly speed and accuracy. The largest contiguous critical habitat for the threatened Mexican spotted owl is on the Manti-La Sal National Forest. Other bird species found in the area include Merriam's turkey, Williamson's sapsucker, common nighthawk, white-throated swift, ash-throated flycatcher, violet-green swallow, cliff swallow, mourning dove, pinyon jay, sagebrush sparrow, canyon towhee, rock wren, sage thrasher, and the endangered south-western willow flycatcher.

As the skies darken in the evenings, visitors may catch a glimpse of some the area's at least 15 species of bats, including the big free-tailed bat, pallid bat, Townsend's big-eared bat, spotted bat, and silver-haired bat. Tinajas, rock depressions filled with rainwater, provide habitat for many specialized aquatic species, including pothole beetles and freshwater shrimp. Eucosma navajoensis, an endemic moth that has only been described near Valley of the Gods, is unique to this area.

Protection of the Bears Ears area will preserve its cultural, prehistoric, and historic legacy and maintain its diverse array of natural and scientific resources, ensuring that the prehistoric, historic, and scientific values of this area remain for the benefit of all Americans. **The Bears Ears area has been proposed for protection by members of Congress, Secretaries of the Interior, State and tribal leaders, and local conservationists for at least 80 years.** The area contains numerous objects of historic and of scientific interest, and it provides world class outdoor recreation opportunities, including rock climbing, hunting, hiking, backpacking, canyoneering, whitewater rafting, mountain biking, and horseback riding. Because visitors travel from near and far, these lands support a growing travel and tourism sector that is a source of economic opportunity for the region.

WHEREAS, **section 320301 of title 54, United States Code (known as the "Antiquities Act")**, authorizes the President, in his discretion, to declare by public proclamation historic landmarks, historic and prehistoric structures, and other objects of historic or scientific interest that are situated upon the lands owned or controlled by the Federal Government to be national monuments, and to reserve as a part thereof parcels of land, the limits of which shall be confined to the smallest area compatible with the proper care and management of the objects to be protected; WHEREAS, it is in the public interest to preserve the objects of scientific and historic interest on the Bears Ears lands;

NOW, THEREFORE, I, BARACK OBAMA, President of the United States of America, by the authority vested in me by section 320301 of title 54, United States Code, hereby proclaim the objects identified above that are situated upon lands and interests in lands owned or controlled by the Federal Government to be the **Bears Ears National Monument** (monument) and, for the purpose of protecting those objects, reserve as part thereof all lands and interests in lands owned or controlled by the Federal Government within the boundaries described on the accompanying map, which is attached to and forms a part of this proclamation. These reserved Federal lands and interests in lands encompass approximately 1.35 million acres. The boundaries described on the accompanying map are confined to the smallest area compatible with the proper care and management of the objects to be protected.

All Federal lands and interests in lands within the boundaries of the monument are hereby appropriated and withdrawn from all forms of entry, location, selection, sale, or other disposition under the public land laws or laws applicable to the U.S. Forest Service, from location, entry, and patent under the mining laws, and from disposition under all laws relating to mineral and geothermal leasing, other than by exchange that furthers the protective purposes of the monument.

The establishment of the monument is subject to valid existing rights, including valid existing water rights. If the Federal Government acquires ownership or control of any lands or interests in lands that it did not previously own or control within the boundaries described on the accompanying map, such lands and interests in lands shall be reserved as a part of the monument, and objects identified above that are situated upon those lands and interests in lands shall be part of the monument, upon acquisition of ownership or control by the Federal Government.

The Secretary of Agriculture and the Secretary of the Interior (Secretaries) shall manage the monument through the U.S. Forest Service (USFS) and the Bureau of Land Management (BLM), pursuant to their respective applicable legal authorities, to implement the purposes of this proclamation. The USFS shall manage that portion of the monument within the boundaries of the National Forest System (NFS), and the BLM shall manage the remainder of the monument. The lands administered by the USFS shall be managed as part of the Manti-La Sal National Forest. The lands administered by the BLM shall be managed as a unit of the National Landscape Conservation System, pursuant to applicable legal authorities.

For purposes of protecting and restoring the objects identified above, the Secretaries shall jointly prepare a management plan for the monument and shall promulgate such regulations for its management as they deem appropriate. The Secretaries, through the USFS and the BLM, shall consult with other Federal land management agencies in the local area, including the National Park Service, in developing the management plan. In promulgating any management rules and regulations governing the NFS lands within the monument and developing the management plan, the Secretary of Agriculture, through the USFS, shall consult with the Secretary of the Interior through the BLM. The Secretaries shall provide for maximum public involvement in the development of that plan including, but not limited to, consultation with federally recognized tribes and State and local governments. In the development and implementation of the management plan, the Secretaries shall maximize opportunities, pursuant to applicable legal authorities, for shared resources, operational efficiency, and cooperation.

The Secretaries, through the BLM and USFS, shall establish an advisory committee under the Federal Advisory Committee Act (5 U.S.C. App.) to provide information and advice regarding the development of the management plan and, as appropriate, management of the monument. This advisory committee shall consist of a fair and balanced representation of interested stakeholders, including State and local governments, tribes, recreational users, local business owners, and private landowners.

In recognition of the importance of tribal participation to the care and management of the objects identified above, and to ensure that management decisions affecting the monument reflect tribal expertise and traditional and historical knowledge, a **Bears Ears Commission** (Commission) is hereby established to provide guidance and recommendations on the development and implementation of management plans and on management of the monument. The Commission shall consist of one elected officer each from the Hopi Nation, Navajo Nation, Ute Mountain Ute Tribe, Ute Indian Tribe of the Uintah Ouray, and Zuni Tribe, designated by the officers' respective tribes. The Commission may adopt such procedures as it deems necessary to govern its activities, so that it may effectively partner with the Federal agencies by making continuing contributions to inform decisions regarding the management of the monument.

The Secretaries shall meaningfully engage the Commission or, should the Commission no longer exist, the tribal governments through some other entity composed of elected tribal government officers (comparable entity), in the development of the management plan and to inform subsequent management of the monument. To that end, in developing or revising the management plan, the Secretaries shall carefully and fully consider integrating the traditional and historical knowledge and special expertise of the Commission or comparable entity. If the Secretaries decide not to incorporate specific recommendations submitted to them in writing by the Commission or comparable entity, they will provide the Commission or comparable entity with a written explanation of their reasoning. The management plan shall also set forth parameters for continued meaningful engagement with the Commission or comparable entity in implementation of the management plan.

To further the protective purposes of the monument, the Secretary of the Interior shall explore entering into a memorandum of understanding with the State that would set forth terms, pursuant to applicable laws and regulations, for an exchange of land currently owned by the State of Utah and administered by the Utah School and Institutional Trust Lands Administration within the boundary of the monument for land of approximately equal value managed by the BLM outside the boundary of the monument. The Secretary of the Interior shall report to the President by January 19, 2017, regarding the potential for such an exchange.

Nothing in this proclamation shall be construed to interfere with the operation or maintenance, or the replacement or modification within the current authorization boundary, of existing utility, pipeline, or telecommunications facilities located within the monument in a manner consistent with the care and management of the objects identified above.

Nothing in this proclamation shall be deemed to enlarge or diminish the rights or jurisdiction of any Indian tribe. The Secretaries shall, to the maximum extent permitted by law and in consultation with Indian tribes, ensure the protection of Indian sacred sites and traditional cultural properties in the monument and provide access by members of Indian tribes for traditional cultural and customary uses, consistent with the American Indian Religious Freedom Act (42 U.S.C. 1996) and Executive Order 13007 of May 24, 1996 (Indian Sacred Sites), including collection of medicines, berries and other vegetation, forest products, and firewood for personal noncommercial use in a manner consistent with the care and management of the objects identified above.

For purposes of protecting and restoring the objects identified above, the Secretaries shall prepare a transportation plan that designates the roads and trails where motorized and non-motorized mechanized vehicle use will be allowed. Except for emergency or authorized administrative purposes, motorized and non-motorized mechanized vehicle use shall be allowed only on roads and trails designated for such use, consistent with the care and management of such objects. Any additional roads or trails designated for motorized vehicle use must be for the purposes of public safety or protection of such objects.

Laws, regulations, and policies followed by USFS or BLM in issuing and administering grazing permits or leases on lands under their jurisdiction shall continue to apply with regard to the lands in the monument to ensure the ongoing consistency with the care and management of the objects identified above.

Nothing in this proclamation shall be deemed to enlarge or diminish the jurisdiction of the State of Utah, including its jurisdiction and authority with respect to fish and wildlife management. Nothing in this proclamation shall preclude low-level overflights of military aircraft, the designation of new units of special use airspace, or the use or establishment of military flight training routes over the lands reserved by this proclamation consistent with the care and management of the objects identified above.

Nothing in this proclamation shall be construed to alter the authority or responsibility of any party with respect to emergency response activities within the monument, including wildland fire response.

Nothing in this proclamation shall be deemed to revoke any existing withdrawal, reservation, or appropriation; however, the monument shall be the dominant reservation.

Warning is hereby given to all unauthorized persons not to appropriate, injure, destroy, or remove any feature of the monument and not to locate or settle upon any of the lands thereof.

IN WITNESS WHEREOF, I have hereunto set my hand this twenty-eighth day of December, in the year of our Lord two thousand sixteen, and of the Independence of the United States of America the two hundred and forty-first.

BARACK OBAMA

On 28 December 2016, President Obama made the following Statement:

STATEMENT BY THE PRESIDENT ON THE DESIGNATION OF BEARS EARS NATIONAL MONUMENT AND GOLD BUTTE NATIONAL MONUMENT

Today, I am designating two new national monuments in the desert landscapes of south-eastern Utah and southern Nevada to protect some of our country's most important cultural treasures, including abundant rock art, archeological sites, and lands considered sacred by Native American tribes. Today's actions will help protect this cultural legacy and will ensure that future generations are able to enjoy and appreciate these scenic and historic landscapes. Importantly, today I have also established a **Bears Ears Commission** to ensure that tribal expertise and traditional knowledge help inform the management of the Bears Ears National Monument and help us to best care for its remarkable national treasures.

Following years of public input and various proposals to protect both of these areas, including legislation and a proposal from tribal governments in and around Utah, these monuments will protect places that a wide range of stakeholders all agree are **worthy of protection.** We also have worked to ensure that tribes and local communities can continue to access and benefit from these lands for generations to come.

Source:
The White House

For further information about the Bears Ears National Monument see U.S. Forest Service website:

"The Bears Ears National Monument is the 12th national monument managed by the Forest Service; it is the fifth to be managed jointly by the Forest Service and BLM. Monuments generally preserve current uses of the land, including tribal access for traditional plant and firewood gathering and for ceremonial purposes, off-highway recreation on existing routes, grazing, hunting and fishing and water and utility infrastructure."

Source:
https://www.fs.fed.us/visit/bears-ears-national-monument
U.S. Department of Agriculture]

NEWS RELEASE FROM US FOREST SERVICE

Secretaries Jewell, Vilsack Applaud President's Designtion of New National Monuments in Utah and Nevada

President's Action Follows Decades Long Campaigns by Members of Congress, Tribes, Local Conservationists to Protect Areas of Extraordinary Cultural Importance and Natural Beauty

WASHINGTON, D.C., DECEMBER 28, 2016 AT 5:45 PM EST - U.S. Secretary of the Interior Sally Jewell and U.S. Secretary of Agriculture Tom Vilsack today joined tribes, members of Congress, state and local officials, and local business and community leaders in applauding the President's designation of the Bears Ears National Monument in south-eastern Utah and the Gold Butte National Monument in south-eastern Nevada. Representing the best of America's natural wonders, today's designations complete what tribes, members of Congress, state and local officials, and local business and community leaders have sought for decades, but Congress failed to take action.

The new monuments protect approximately 1.64 million acres of existing federal land in two spectacular western landscapes – 1.35 million acres in Utah and nearly 300,000 acres in Nevada. Both areas contain land sacred to Native American tribes, important cultural sites, and fragile wildlife habitat. The monument designations maintain currently authorized uses of the land that do not harm the resources protected by the monument, including tribal access and traditional collection of plants and firewood, off-highway vehicle recreation, hunting and fishing and authorized grazing. The monument designation also does not affect valid existing rights for oil, gas, and mining operations, military training operations, and utility corridors.

"The rock art, ancient dwellings, and ceremonial sites

concealed within these breathtaking landscapes help tell the story of people who have stewarded these lands for hundreds of generations," said Secretary Jewell. "Today's action builds on an extraordinary effort from tribes, local communities, and members of Congress to ensure that these treasures are protected for generations to come, so that tribes may continue to use and care for these lands, and all may have an opportunity to enjoy their beauty and learn from their rich cultural history."

"Utahns of all creeds are rightfully proud of the spectacular Bears Ears landscape, treasuring the opportunity to recreate, hunt, ranch and engage in their traditional cultural and spiritual practices. Rather than closing off opportunities to continue those uses, today's announcement is a recognition that those activities can continue, and the natural and cultural resources the communities prize are worthy of permanent protection to be shared with all Americans," said Secretary Vilsack. "As we move forward with planning for monument implementation, the deep knowledge of the tribal community as well as ranchers, recreationists, archeologists and local community citizens will be heard."

The 1.35 million-acre Bears Ears National Monument protects one of the richest cultural landscapes in the United States, with thousands of archaeological sites and areas of spiritual significance. These lands are sacred to many Native American tribes today who use them for ceremonies, collecting medicinal and edible plants, and gathering materials for crafting baskets and footwear. To ensure that management decisions affecting the monument reflect tribal expertise and traditional and historical knowledge, the Presidential proclamation establishes a Bears Ears Commission, comprised of tribal representatives, to provide guidance and recommendations on management of the monument.

Congressmen Rob Bishop and Jason Chaffetz's Utah Public Lands Initiative (H.R. 5780 (link is external)) proposed to conserve 1.39 million acres (1.28 million Federal acres) in mostly the same area (link is external) as the Bears Ears National Monument by designating two new National Conservation Areas (link is external) and a Wilderness (link is external), which would prohibit future mining and oil and gas activities in these areas. Their legislation also proposed a Tribal Commission to help inform management of the area and created additional opportunities for interested stakeholders to offer input, similar to what today's action has established. These designations build on the framework developed by the Congressmen to both protect and allow for continued use and enjoyment of the area by residents and visitors.

"President Obama has been consistent in his commitment to work with Tribal governments, and this historic designation builds on his legacy," said Navajo Nation President Russell Begaye. "We are particularly pleased that the designation affirms tribal sovereignty and provides a collaborative role for Tribes to work with the federal government in maintaining the land. Because Tribes will help manage this land, it reaffirms President Obama's fundamental commitment to human rights and equity in voice. Furthermore, while the land will be protected, our local Utah-based tribal members will continue to have access to the land for gathering ceremonial herbs. The land has always been a place of sacredness and fortitude for our people. Now it will be preserved for all future generations." Begaye further said, "We appreciate the great effort and everyone involved, including the Utah Congressional delegation who worked very hard on a parallel proposal. It is heartening to know our friends from the Utah delegation care deeply about conserving this irreplaceable land. We look forward to working with them and all our elected representatives in Congress on our constituents' shared priorities."

Abundant rock art, ancient cliff dwellings, ceremonial kivas, and countless other artifacts provide an extraordinary archaeological and cultural record surrounded by a dramatic backdrop of deep sandstone canyons, desert mesas, and forested highlands and the monument's namesake twin buttes. For these reasons, the Bears Ears area has been proposed for protection by members of Congress, Secretaries of the Interior, state and tribal leaders, and local conservationists for at least 80 years(link is external) (link is external). Native American tribes whose ancestral lands include the Bears Ears area advocated for permanent protection, led by the Bears Ears Inter-Tribal Coalition made up of the Hopi Nation, Navajo Nation, Ute Indian Tribe of the Uintah Ouray, Ute Mountain Ute Tribe, and Zuni Tribe. Numerous tribes with ties to the region, including the above tribes, have passed resolutions and sent letters in support of a national monument designation.

The area's tradition of ranching, which dates back to the late 1800s, will continue. Grazing permits and leases will continue to be issued by the BLM and the USFS.

In July (link is external), Interior Secretary Sally Jewell, Agriculture Under Secretary for Natural Resources and Environment Robert Bonnie, and other senior Administration officials visited Bears Ears along with staff from Governor Herbert's office and Utah Congressional delegation staff, and attended a public meeting where the majority of an overflow crowd encouraged permanent protection for this iconic landscape. Input from individuals and groups who raised concerns at the meeting were also considered in the terms outlined in the proclamation. Other national monument supporters (link is external) include elected officials in Utah, national and local conservation groups, archaeologists, and faith-based organizations. Recreationists strongly support the monument, which will protect the area's world-class rock climbing, hunting, backpacking, whitewater rafting, mountain biking, and off-highway vehicle recreation – activities that will continue to be a source of economic growth for south-eastern Utah.

The proclamation also directs the Secretary of the Interior to explore within 30 days a land exchange with the State of Utah, which would transfer Utah School and Institutional Trust Lands Administration land within the Bears Ears boundary in exchange for Bureau of Land Management land outside of the boundary. The Department of the Interior's Bureau of Land Management (BLM) (link is external) and the Department of Agriculture's Forest Service (USFS) will jointly manage Bears Ears National Monument. In doing so, both agencies will jointly prepare a management plan developed with maximum public involvement, including tribal, local and State governments, permit holders, other stakeholders and other federal land management agencies in the local area, including the National Park Service.

"The Bears Ears National Monument is an incredible resource for the people of Utah," said U.S. Forest Service Chief Tom Tidwell. "The Forest Service is honored to work with the local communities and tribes to manage these lands for the public's enjoyment and preserving them for future generations."

A map of Bears Ears National Monument can be found here (link is external).

A fact sheet on Bears Ears National Monument can be found here (link is external).

The Gold Butte National Monument protects nearly 300,000 acres of remote and rugged desert landscape, where dramatically chiseled red sandstone, twisting canyons, and tree-clad mountains punctuate desolate stretches of the Mojave Desert. The brightly hued sandstone provides a stunning canvas for the area's famously beautiful rock art, and the desert provides critical habitat for the threatened Mojave Desert tortoise. Evidence of indigenous communities' remarkable ability to survive in arid conditions here abounds, from ancient rock shelters and hearth remains to agave roasting pits and projectile points.

Today, Gold Butte remains culturally and spiritually important to the Southern Paiute people, particularly the Moapa Band of Paiute Indians, who collect water from the mountain springs, gather traditional sources of paint, harvest pinyon pine nuts and other resources, and access ceremonial sites. The area is popular for outdoor recreation, and visitors to the monument can hike to rock art sites, drive the Gold Butte Backcountry Byway to the area's namesake mining ghost town, hunt desert bighorn sheep, or tour the area's peaks and canyons on horseback.

This presidential designation is the result of Senator Harry Reid's strong leadership along with Representative Dina Titus, as well as support from the Moapa Band of Paiutes and Las Vegas Paiute Tribe. In 2015, Deputy Secretary of the Interior Michael Connor and BLM Director Neil Kornze attended a public meeting (link is external) hosted by Senator Reid and Representative Titus to hear from the public about protection and conservation of Gold Butte and other areas in southern Nevada. Supporters of protecting the area include local elected officials and governments, area businesses, hunters, anglers, recreationists, and local land trusts and conservation groups.

Livestock grazing has not been permitted in the Gold Butte area since 1998, in support of Clark County's Habitat Conservation Plan to conserve critical Mojave Desert tortoise habitat.

The Monument will be managed by the Bureau of Land Management (link is external).

Both the Gold Butte National Monument and the Bears Ears National Monument are comprised exclusively of existing federal lands, and their designations honor valid existing rights. The plans will be developed in an open process with maximum public involvement, building upon the provisions outlined in the proclamations. Both proclamations also establish a local advisory council made up of a diverse array of interested stakeholders including state and local governments, tribes, recreational users, local business owners, and private landowners.

"These monuments will preserve sacred lands and ancient treasures that hold deep meaning for us all, illuminating the history of some of the earliest civilizations on this continent," said Bureau of Land Management director Neil Kornze. "Local collaboration is key to the successful management of these incredible landscapes, and the BLM is committed to continuing and expanding our work with community partners."

The BLM and USFS staff will schedule informal open houses on Bears Ears National Monument in January to answer questions from permittees and other interested stakeholders, and as part of the formal management planning process will announce public sessions later this winter and spring. Details of these listening sessions, including dates and locations, will be shared with local newspapers and posted to the monuments' websites. The BLM will also hold public meetings on Gold Butte National Monument. Planning for both monuments will be done with full public involvement, with special emphasis on understanding the ideas and concerns of the local communities.

The Antiquities Act has been used by 16 presidents starting with President Theodore Roosevelt in 1906 and used to protect treasures such as the Grand Canyon, the Statue of Liberty, and Colorado's Canyons of the Ancients. Altogether, President Obama has protected more than 550

million acres of public lands and waters – more than any
other President – and has preserved sites that help tell
the story of significant people and extraordinary events
in American history.

A map of the Gold Butte National Monument can be
found here (link is external).

A fact sheet and Questions and Answers on Gold Butte
National Monument can be found here (link is external).

~

To extend your research please see the following link, for the external
links mentioned above:

https://www.fs.fed.us/visit/secretaries-jewell-vilsack-applaud-designa-
tion-new-national-monuments-utah-nevada
Source: US Forest Service, U.S. Department of Agriculture

~

For information on the Bears Ears Commission, see:
bearsearscoalition.org

https://bearsearscoalition.org/bears-ears-commissioners-selected-fo-
cus-on-the-future-of-the-national-monument/

~

For information on the Tribal Leaders response, see the following press
release entitled; *Tribal Leaders Extremely Disappointed over Action by
President Trump to Revoke and Replace Bears Ears National Monument.*

https://bearsearscoalition.org/tribal-leaders-extremely-dis-
appointed-over-action-by-president-trump-to-revoke-and-re-
place-bears-ears-national-monument/

A selection of photographs of the places cut from Bears Ears National Monument

Source:
https://bearsearscoalition.org/media-resources/

Location: The Bears Ears Buttes
framed with summer wild flowers
Credit: Tim Peterson

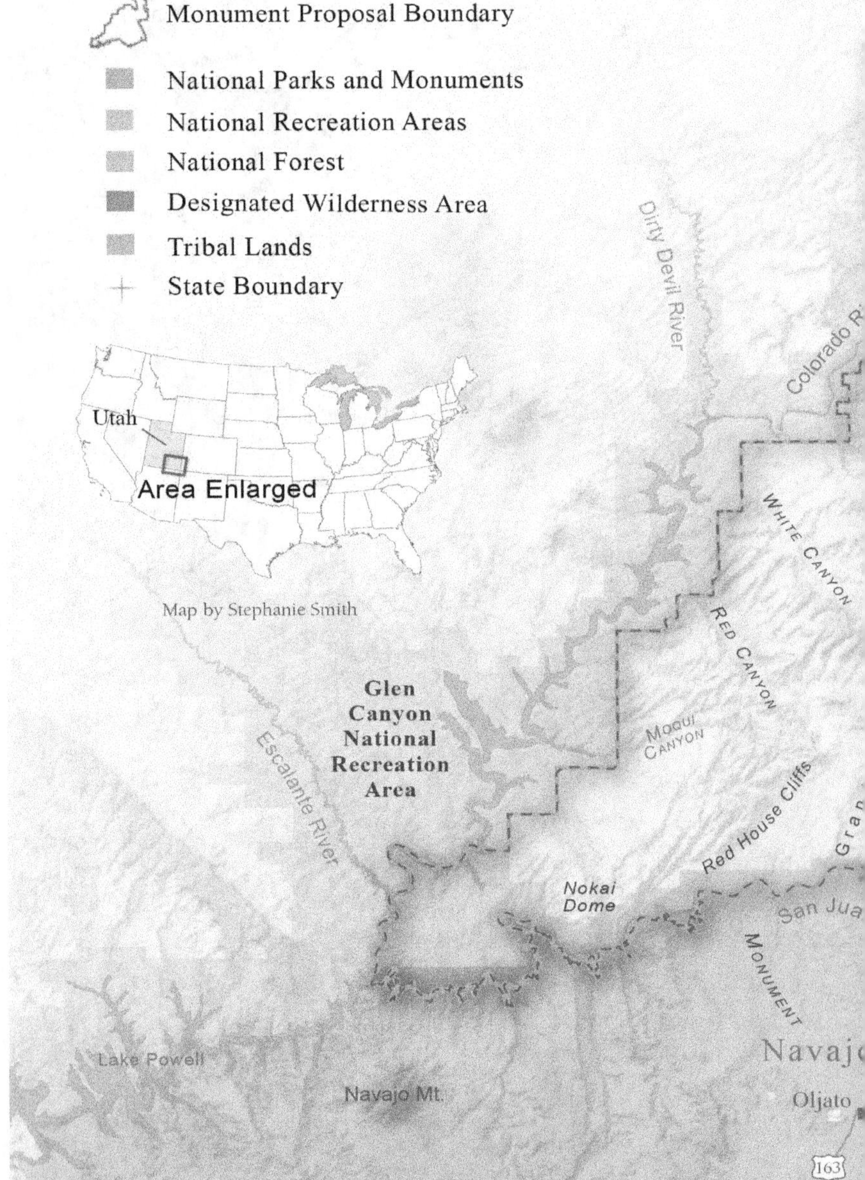

Proposed Bears Ears National Monument
Monument Proposal Boundary
National Parks and Monuments
National Recreation Areas
National Forest
Designated Wilderness Area
Tribal Lands
State Boundary
Utah
Area Enlarged
Map by Stephanie Smith
Dirty Devil River
Colorado R.
White Canyon
Red Canyon
Moqui Canyon
Red House Cliffs
Gran
San Jua
Monument
Glen
Canyon
National
Recreation
Area
Escalante River
Nokai
Dome
Navajo
Lake Powell
Navajo Mt.
Oljato
163

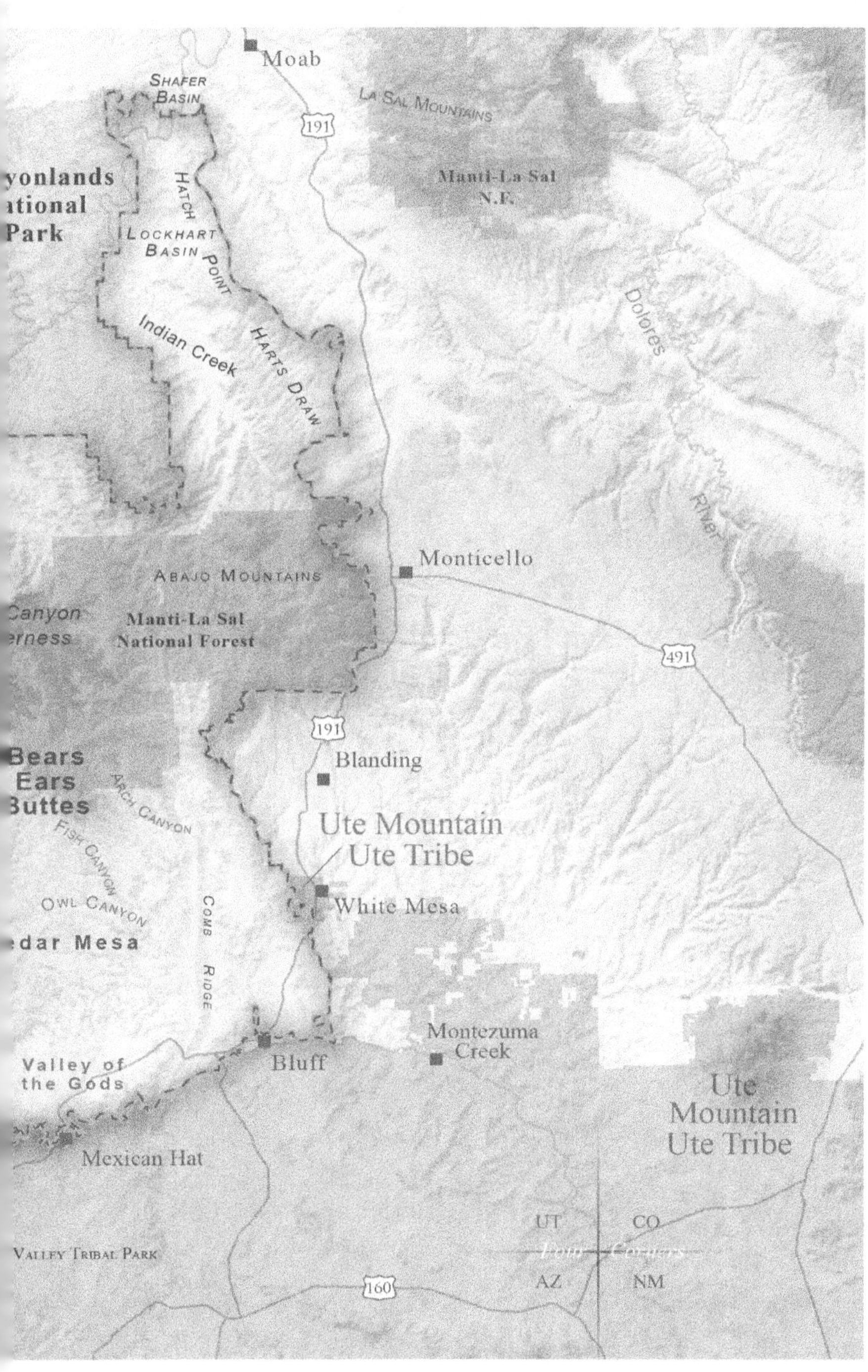

Moab
SHAFER BASIN
LA SAL MOUNTAINS
191
Manti-La Sal N.F.
Canyonlands National Park
HATCH POINT
LOCKHART BASIN
Indian Creek
HARTS DRAW
Dolores River
Monticello
491
ABAJO MOUNTAINS
Canyon erness
Manti-La Sal National Forest
191
Blanding
Bears Ears Buttes
ARCH CANYON
FISH CANYON
OWL CANYON
Cedar Mesa
COMB RIDGE
Ute Mountain Ute Tribe
White Mesa
Montezuma Creek
Valley of the Gods
Bluff
Ute Mountain Ute Tribe
Mexican Hat
VALLEY TRIBAL PARK
UT
CO
Four Corners
AZ
NM
160

Location: Grand Gulch
Credit: Bruce Hucko

Location: The Bears Ears Buttes framed with summer wild flowers
Credit: Tim Peterson

Location: Rock Art Central Cedar Mesa
Credit: Jonathan Bailey

Location: Painted Ruin
Credit: Josh Ewing

Location: Cedar Mesa Granary
Credit: Amanda Podmore

Location: Vandalized Hand Panel - FS lands
Credit: Tim Peterson

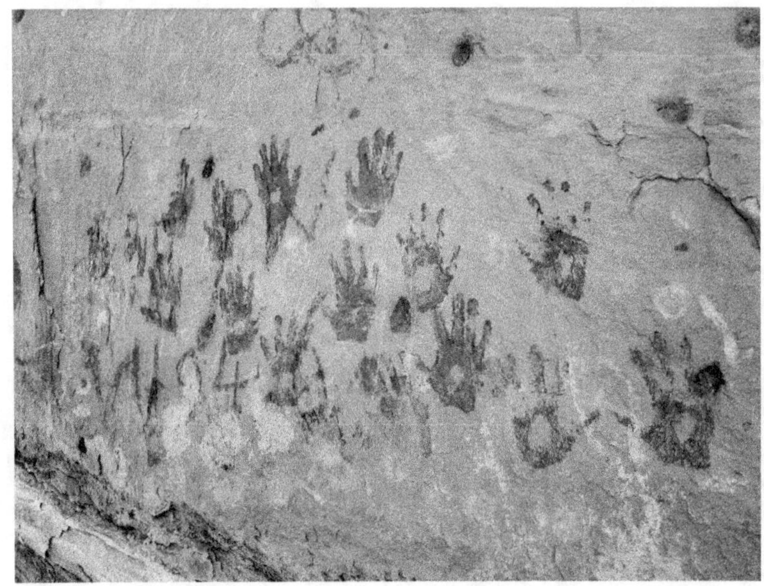

Location: Horse Petroglyphs
Credit: Greg Child

Location: Mancos Mesa 3 - LightHawk
Credit: Tim Peterson

Location: Edge Of Mancos Mesa
Credit: Brant Hart

Location: Moqui Rock Art 3
Credit: Tim Peterson

Location: Mancos Mesa - Broken Pot
Credit: Greg Child

Location: Cedar Mesa Ruin
Credit: Don Rommes

Location: SJR Corridor
Credit: Jonathan Bailey

Location: Spirals and Cactus
Credit: Josh Ewing

Chapter 160

**REMARKS BY PRESIDENT TRUMP AT
SIGNING OF EXECUTIVE ORDER ON
FEDERALISM EDUCATION
ROOSEVELT ROOM**

26 April 2017

2:41 P.M. EDT

THE VICE PRESIDENT: Well, good afternoon. It's my great honor, on behalf of the President and the First Lady, to welcome you all to the White House. This is a distinguished group of American leaders, governors and members of Congress, and members of our Cabinet, and we're grateful to have you all here.

You know, for nearly 100 days, **President Trump has been delivering on the promises that he made to the American people**. The President has been fighting for American jobs every single day since he was elected, putting renewed emphasis on American energy, cutting through a mountain range of red tape from the last administration. And today, the administration outlined the President's vision for tax reform which will include one of the largest tax cuts for individuals and businesses in the history of this country. (Applause.)

Thanks to the President Trump's leadership, more than 500,000 jobs have been created in 2017 alone. Businesses and consumers are more confident than they have been in years, and by some measure, for decades. It is truly extraordinary.

In a word, President Trump has simply been in the **promise-keeping business** since Inauguration Day. He signed 28 bills into law, the most of any President since 1947, and he'll have signed some 30 executive orders in his **first 100 days**, including the action today.

And today the President is actually delivering on one more of his **promise**s to the American people. Since day one, President Trump has been working tirelessly to uphold the Constitution and restore the proper balance between the states and the federal government. And that's been especially true with the President's focus on education.

Now as a former governor myself, I've always believed, as the President does, that education is a state and local function, and that decisions in education are best made by parents and teachers and local administrators. The decisions over our children's school should be made by parents and local administrators, not by politicians or unelected bureaucrats in a far, distant capital.

The President believes the same thing, and the efforts that he will take today through this executive order will continue that process of empowering our families, empowering our states to ensure that every child in America has access to a world-class education.

And so with a grateful heart, I say, on behalf of the 45th President of the United States and on behalf of all those gathered here today, it is my high honor and distinct privilege to introduce to you the President of the United States, President Donald Trump. (Applause.)

THE PRESIDENT: Well, thank you very much, Vice President Pence, who has done an absolutely outstanding job as Vice

President. We very much appreciate it.

And I want to thank also Education Secretary Betsy
DeVos for spearheading out effort to restore state and
local control of our schools. Thank you very much, Betsy. With her help, we are empowering those who know
our students best -- I would say, by far, the best, right,
Betsy? -- their parents and the teachers, so that every child
has the chance to succeed.

In fact, we're proud to have some of those wonderful
teachers here with us today, and we'd like to welcome
all of them to the White House. It's a great honor. (Applause.)

Thank you. Thank you. Thank you very much.

I also want to thank members of Congress, local leaders,
and governors for joining us here today, including Governor Ivey of Alabama, a new and great governor. You will
be fantastic. I've been hearing about you for years in the
positive way, so I'm not surprised that you're governor of
Alabama. Congratulations. Tremendous.

Governor Branstad, who is soon going to be heading out,
I suspect, to a place called China. They love him, I will tell
you. They really love the soon-to-be ambassador, but he
also loves China. So it was a good combination. I was very
happy to put it together. They're looking forward to seeing
you. Very much so. Thank you. Thank you,
Governor. (Applause.)

Governor LePage of Maine, Governor Sandoval of Nevada,
Governor Herbert of Utah, Governor Mead of Wyoming --
we want to thank you all and everyone else for being with

us. It's really an honor to have you in White House.

For too long, the federal government has imposed its
will on state and local governments. The result has been
education that spends more and achieves far, far, far
less. My administration has been working to reverse this
federal power grab and give power back to families, cities,
states. Give power back to localities.

Before this administration, only one time in our nation's
history had a President signed a bill that used the
Congressional Review Act to cancel a federal regulation. In less than *100 days*, I have signed 13 bills such
congressional resolutions to cancel federal regulations
and give power back to the people, and I'm very honored
to have done so. (Applause.)

That's true. As you said, five have come from your committee, that's exactly right. Good job. I think she's done a
good job. (Applause.)

I've also signed over a dozen executive actions that reverse
federal intrusion and empower local communities.

The executive order I'm signing today is another critical
step to restoring local control, which is so important. This
executive order directs Secretary DeVos to review current
federal regulations and ensure that they don't obstruct the
ability of states, local governments, teachers, and most
importantly, parents, to make the best decisions for their
students and, in many cases, for their children.

Previous administrations have wrongfully forced states and
schools to comply with federal whims and dictate what our
kids are taught. But we know that local communities do

it best and know it best. The time has come to empower
parents and teachers to make the decisions that help their
students achieve success. That's what this executive order
is all about. So important.

Thomas Jefferson put it best when he said, "I believe the
states can best govern our home concerns." With this executive order and the many actions, we have taken in less
than *100 days*, we are providing our states and communities with control over the matters that are most important
to them. Together we are going to fight to give our children the bright and beautiful future they deserve. (Applause.)

So I want to thank you all. As you know, I'm heading over
to a Senate meeting. It's a very important meeting. So I'll
be leaving now, but I just wanted to introduce our really
exceptional Education Secretary. She's caught on -- you
wouldn't believe it, all of the great things I'm hearing
about you, Betsy. I'm very proud. So, Secretary Betsy
DeVos. Thank you very much. Thank you. (Applause.)

Q   Mr. President, would you want to see a healthcare vote
by the end of this week? Would you like to see that, sir?

THE PRESIDENT: Always.

SECRETARY DEVOS: So it has been all of our experience,
that those closest to the problem are best equipped to
solve it. That means empowering parents, teachers, state
and local leaders -- not the federal government. Time and
time again, we've seen that one-size-fits-all policies and
mandates from Washington simply don't work. We can't
have a cookie-cutter approach to education. Each state
and each school have different challenges, and each indi-

vidual student has unique needs.

Our solutions should be as varied as the students we serve. *The Every Student Succeeds Act* was a good step in this direction, **giving flexibility to states to best meet the needs of their communities**. We're going to implement this law as Congress intended, not how the previous administration dictated. When we give decision-making power back to states and communities, students benefit. This executive order puts us on that track.

So I thank the President for signing this executive order, and for his commitment to an education policy that puts students first. It's my honor now to introduce the governor of the great state of Nevada, Brian Sandoval. (Applause.)

GOVERNOR SANDOVAL: Thank you Madam Secretary and Mr. President.

THE PRESIDENT: Oh, it's going to be a short speech because I -- I just felt I had to stay here. (Laughter.)

GOVERNOR SANDOVAL: It just got shorter, Mr. President. (Laughter.)

Mr. Vice President, members of Congress, my fellow governors, representatives, teachers, educators, it really is a privilege and honor to be with you all today. You know, in my home state of Nevada, I often say that what happens in our schools today will determine the future of our great state. And Mr. President, I know that your action today will empower every state to improve our delivery of education. Most importantly, it will allow governors across the nation to ensure that all states serve all students from all backgrounds.

Now, as the incoming chair of the *National Governors Association*, I know that the governors will collectively continue to act as the national voice on federalism. And as the leaders of education in our states, we look forward to working with this administration to ensure our role is reflected in federal policy.

Now, over time, the Department of Education's obligations have grown beyond its initial charge, and many well-intended act resulted in states feeling more and more constrained by federal rules. Today, Mr. President, you're signing of this executive order will place the states back in the driver's seat. Thank you, sir. (Applause.)

So, Mr. President, again, I'm going skip a page -- (Laughter.)

THE PRESIDENT: Education for North Korea. (Laughter.)

I like education.

GOVERNOR SANDOVAL: This is even better than I hoped for, Mr. President. The *Every Student Succeeds Act* embodies the vision you have for education and the limited role of the federal government.

Mr. President, you have changed the game for the better in the United States, and for that I thank you for your leadership. (Applause.)

THE PRESIDENT: This is a good one, right -- on federal control of education. Doesn't get better than that, right?

(The President signs the Executive Order.)

Q   Mr. President, can you say to the American people that your tax plan will not blow a hole in the deficit?

THE PRESIDENT: Great plan. It will put people back to work.

END
2:54 P.M. EDT

Chapter 161

**REMARKS BY PRESIDENT TRUMP AT
NATIONAL TEACHER OF THE YEAR EVENT
OVAL OFFICE**

26 April 2017

4:40 P.M. EDT

THE PRESIDENT: Busy day, hasn't it been? Busy, busy day. These are great people. We're with great people right now.

So I want to thank you. It's my pleasure to welcome so many extraordinary teachers to the White House. This is called The People's House. I also want to congratulate the *Council of Chief State School Officers* on their 65th year recognizing America's outstanding teachers. These are the greatest there are -- nobody better. So I want to congratu-late you all. It's amazing.

Each of you has dedicated yourself to inspiring young minds and to putting our children on a path to happiness and success -- lots of success. There are 55 Teachers of the Year who are here with us from every state -- every state in the union, is that right? Every single state.

So let's see, who's from Alabama? Great state.

PARTICIPANT: We would love for you to come and visit us. (Laughter.)

PARTICIPANT: He's coming to Maryland. It's right next

door.

THE PRESIDENT: Who's from Indiana? Oh, wow, that's fantastic. We have our Vice President. We have Karen Pence. So thank you very much.

Today, we honor one teacher in particular. She is the 2017 *National Teacher of the Year*, Sydney Chaffee. (Applause.)

Sydney is a ninth grade humanities teacher at *Codman Academy Charter School* in Dorchester, Massachusetts -- nice place, by the way. Sydney is the first teacher from Massachusetts ever to win the award, and the first from a public charter school. That is really something special. Sydney, I would like to congratulate you on this tremendous achievement. There is nothing more important than being a teacher, and certainly for being a great teacher. You're all great, great teachers, and congratulations to all. (Applause.)

When you go home, I hope you all say that your trip to the White House was something very special. I know Melania has been working with you now for quite a while. She is a tremendous fan of wonderful teachers. But she's worked very hard and we're having some special times here.

This is Melania's birthday and you were very nice to sing *Happy Birthday*, even though we're celebrating you.

So thank you all very much and God bless you all. And you go back and keep teaching those students because, like I said -- oh, look, and you're crying --

PARTICIPANT: Sorry, I'm always crying! (Laughter.)

THE PRESIDENT: I know, the Oval Office can do that. I
have had some of the biggest executives in the world and
they've been here many times. I said, have you ever been
to the Oval Office, and they said no. I mean, I once had
here like the biggest, from the biggest companies. And
they walk into the Oval Office and they start crying. I said,
I promise I won't say to your various stockholders that you
cried. (Laughter.)

But I have seen people cry that you'd never believe. It's a
very special place, and it's a special building. So thank you
all very much. Thank you.

END
4:45 P.M. EDT

Chapter 162

REMARKS BY PRESIDENT TRUMP IN MEETING WITH PRESIDENT MACRI OF ARGENTINA
OVAL OFFICE

27 April 2017

11:32 A.M. EDT

PRESIDENT TRUMP: First time in the Oval Office for the President and Mrs. Macri. And it's a great, great honor to have them here. He's been my friend for many years. We've known each other for long, prior to politics. And who would have thought this was going to happen --

PRESIDENT MACRI: Nobody.

PRESIDENT TRUMP: -- for both of us. But he is a great, wonderful person, and he will be a great President of Argentina, I have absolutely no doubt. Absolutely no doubt.

Q   Mr. Trump, what do you want to achieve with our country, with Argentina?

PRESIDENT TRUMP: We're just going to be great friends, better than ever before. And we're off to a wonderful start, because I've known Mauricio for so many years, and I know the kind of person he is. He's a great person and he's a great leader. He will do a fantastic job for Argentina. And I feel very comfortable backing him, because they need certain things from the United States. I feel very comfortable backing him because I know what I'm back-ing. I'm backing a man who loves his people and loves his country.

Q   If he's such a good President, Mr. President, are you going to let the lemons -- the Argentine lemons in, in your country? They are very good. People will love you if you let them in.

PRESIDENT TRUMP: I know about all the lemons. And believe it or not, the lemon business is a big, big business.

Q   Just say yes! (Laughter.)

PRESIDENT TRUMP: But we are going to give that very se-rious consideration. One of the reasons he's here is about lemons -- (laughter) -- and I'll tell him about North Korea, and he'll tell me about lemons. I think that we're going to be very favorably disposed. We're going to be talking.

Q   What do you think about Venezuela, Mr. President?

THE PRESIDENT: Venezuela is a mess. Venezuela is a mess.

Q   Mr. President, on renegotiating NAFTA, tell me how you came about the decision --

PRESIDENT TRUMP: Well, I was going to terminate NAFTA as of two or three days from now. The President of Mex-ico, who I have a very, very good relationship, called me, and also the Prime Minister of Canada, who I have a very good relationship. And I like both of these gentlemen very much. They called me and they said, rather than terminat-ing NAFTA, could you please renegotiate? I like them very much. I respect their countries very much. The relationship is very special. And I said, I will hold on the termination; let's see if we can make it a fair deal. Because NAFTA has been a horrible deal for the United States. It's been very good for Canada, it's been very good for Mexico, but it's been horrible for the United States.

And **if you check my campaign -- any of my speeches** -- I said, I'll either renegotiate or I'll terminate. So they asked me to renegotiate -- I will. And I think we'll be successful in the renegotiation, which, frankly, would be good because it would be simpler. But we have to make a deal that's fair for the United States. They understand that. And so I decided rather than terminating NAFTA, which would be a pretty big shock to the system, we will renegotiate.

Now, if I'm unable to make a fair deal, if I'm unable to make a fair deal for the United States, meaning a fair deal for our workers and our companies, I will terminate NAFTA. But we're going to give renegotiation a good, strong shot.

Thank you very much, everybody. Thank you very much.

Q   What about Venezuela, Mr. President? Mr. President, about Venezuela, what is your position?

PRESIDENT TRUMP: I'm very sad for Venezuela. I'm very sad to see what's happened in Venezuela. Venezuela is a very sad situation.

END
11:36 A.M. EDT

Chapter 163

REMARKS BY PRESIDENT TRUMP AT SIGNING OF EXECUTIVE ORDER ON IMPROVING ACCOUNTABILITY AND WHISTLEBLOWER PROTECTION DEPARTMENT OF VETERANS AFFAIRS WASHINGTON, D.C.

27 April 2017

4:44 P.M. EDT

THE PRESIDENT: Thank you very much. And, Mike, you've been so magnificent as our Vice President that we very much appreciate it. Thank you very much.

I'm pleased to be here. And we're joined by so many members of Congress. It's been really a fantastic period of time for me. And I'm honored also to be at the Department of Veterans Affairs, because I will tell you this has been something, right from the beginning of the campaign -- does not get any more important for me than making life really great for our phenomenal veterans. That I can say.

So we're sharing the stage with a lot of great people, a lot of great friends. A couple of my friends are out in the audience today -- Ike Perlmutter, Laurie Perlmutter. Where are they? Where are they? Where are they? These are incredible people, incredibly successful people. And they just have an affinity for helping the veterans and for helping David. And I want to thank them. Unbelievable. (Applause.)

Thank you. Dr. Moskowitz, also. (Applause.)

And **we're going to protect those who protect**. And we're
going to protect the people that are protecting us.

First of all, Secretary Shulkin -- and I call him the
100-to-nothing man, because in a totally obstructionist
group of Democrats -- we say that with affection -- (laughter) -- he got not only the Republicans but he got all of the
Democrat votes. And he won at a 100-to-nothing clip.

So I guess -- boy, do they know. I hope they're right, you
know. (Applause.)

But David is doing a phenomenal job. He was voted unanimously out of the United States Senate, and he's worked
ever since then, day and night, to reform and improve the
VA.

I'm also pleased that we're joined by so many members of
Congress. We have with us Senators Ernst -- where's Joni
Ernst? Where is Joni? What a tremendous woman. And
right from the beginning, she has been -- (applause) -- and
she knows more about veterans than anybody. Thanks,
Joni. Really appreciate it.

Senator Isakson -- thank you, Senator. Thank you very
much. (Applause.)

Senator Moran and Senator Tester. Thank you. Thank
you. Thank you, all. (Applause.)

Along with Congressmen Arrington, Bergman, Bridenstine,
Dent, Roe, and Wenstrup. I look forward to serving our
veterans with all of you.

And I can tell you, this group, whether they're Democrat or

Republican, they're here to help. And we're going to help, and we're going to make this so good, it's going to be one of our crown jewels. And it's happening already.

As part of that process, Secretary Shulkin has carried out a really thorough review -- he had some very inside understanding of the VA because he's been here -- but a thorough review of the VA to uncover all of the problems and challenges that we inherited, of which there are so many. Based on those findings, we're putting plans into place to fix those problems and give our veterans the healthcare they need and the healthcare they deserve.

And they were so for me during this recent election, and I can promise them, and they know it's going to happen -- we're not going to let them down. We have a team the likes of which has never, ever been assembled. That includes outside people who are so brilliant and so good -- like Ike and Laurie. And they're helping us. And they don't fail.

Much work lies ahead, but we will not rest until this job is totally done. During these *first 100 days* -- which, as you know, I've been saying there's a very extreme emphasis placed on these *100 days*, Joni. It's not quite as big as they're saying. But we have really laid a foundation -- had a lot of legislation passed, which nobody understands. I think it's 28 bills as of this moment. Somebody said, by the time it ends, it's 32 bills. And tremendous legislation. But we've already made huge strides to improve the VA and the VA services.

We've imposed new standards of accountability and transparency, including a new website that publishes wait times at every VA hospital. This is a website that works. This is not the $5 billion Obamacare website. Do we remember that? Nobody remembers that. Does anybody remember the $5 billion website? No, I don't think so. We don't have to remember it anymore.

We've implemented same-day mental health services at all 168 VA medical centers, so that the veterans in crisis can find help at the VA, without any delay.

Last week, I signed the Veterans Choice Improvement Act -- very proud of that -- so that more veterans can see the doctor of their choice, and don't have to travel long distances or wait forever for VA care. They were waiting on lines for seven days, eight days, nine days, two weeks. Some instances were horrible. They we're waiting so long -- they had a very curable problem and they died before they got to see the doctor. It's not going to happen any longer.

Already this year, using the Choice Program, veterans have received 42 percent more approvals to see the doctor of their choosing. But that's just the very beginning of what we have planned. So much more is coming.

Today, we're taking another bold step forward. I'm signing an executive order to create an Office of Accountability and Whistleblower Protection at the Department of Veterans Affairs. (Applause.)

This executive order makes it clear that we will never, ever tolerate substandard care for our great veterans. With the creation of this office, we are sending a strong message: Those who fail our veterans will be held, for the first time, accountable.

At the same time, we will reward and retain the many
VA employees who do a fantastic job -- of which we have
many. And I will tell you, some of the doctors in the VA,
I've heard it from so many people, they're the finest in
the world. These are great, great people. We have to get
our vets to those doctors. But we have some of the finest
doctors in the world.

We have also some of the most honest employees, and
some of them expose wrongdoing, and we will make sure
that they're protected.

We're also calling on the Senate to pass legislation to
give the Secretary the authority he needs to ensure all VA
employees are held accountable for how they treat our
veterans.

Today's action is historic. But it is only the start of our
reforms. Our veterans have secured this nation with
their blood, sweat and tears, and we will not let them
down. These are our great, great people. We will always
stand with those who stood for freedom and who stood for
us. They protected us. They've made it all possible, and
now we're going to protect and take care of them. (Applause.)

So I'd like to thank David and his family, and all of the people that are working so hard at the VA. They haven't had
enthusiasm -- David was just telling me -- like this for many,
many years. And the veterans see what's happening --
because I'm getting so many different messages through all
forms of communication, of which we now have many. But
they're very, very happy, very pleased with what's going
on.

So, David, we want to God bless you and your family. We
want to wish you a lot of luck, with a lot of talent, because
you have a big job ahead.

I want to wish everybody Godspeed. And we will do
a fantastic job at the VA, rest assured. Thank you very
much. And we're going to sign right now. Thank you very
much. (Applause.)

Thank you.

(The Executive Order is signed.)

END
4:53 P.M. EDT

Chapter 164

28 April 2017

NRA-ILA Executive Director Chris W. Cox addresses the
crowd at the NRA-ILA Leadership Forum:

CHRIS W. COX (NRA-ILA EXECUTIVE DIRECTOR):
How are y'all doing today? Let me ask you a question.
How many of you were with us in Louisville last year?
(Cheering.)

[Photo: screengrab.]

You know, it's almost hard to believe but, back then, the
fate of individual freedom truly hung in the balance. We
didn't know whether our God-given rights would even
be recognized by the time this event came around. All

we knew for sure was that we were ready to fight like hell for the soul of this country and we had a partner in Donald Trump. (Cheering.)

Now he wasn't the establishment's candidate, and he sure wasn't the media's candidate. He was our candidate: the most proudly pro-Second Amendment nominee in American history. So, we made the earliest endorsement for president in the NRA's history. And all of you had his back from that moment on. But the media drew their knives from the very beginning. I've never seen a more vicious, cut-throat and no-holds-barred attempt to destroy a candidate. They didn't just want him to lose. They wanted to leave him utterly disgraced.

As the summer wore on, the fight got ugly. There were times when we were the only group in America with the guts to stand and fight for Donald Trump. You kept your focus where it mattered: protecting and defending the Constitution of the United States. And on Election Day, NRA members and gun owners stormed the polls in an act of sheer defiance of the elites.

And on Inauguration Day, our candidate became our president! (Cheering.)

I spoke to the president shortly after the inauguration. He wanted me to thank all of you. I mentioned how ridiculous it was that the media was lying about the number of people who attended his inauguration. And I told him that the only number that mattered was the number of people who watched Hillary Clinton's inauguration—zero. (Cheering.)

But, we can laugh now. But there was nothing funny

about the threat we faced when we met last year. The Supreme Court was deadlocked, 4-4, and the most basic right to defend yourself with a firearm in your own home was in jeopardy. Imagine the media fawning over President Hillary Clinton's newest Supreme Court Justice, Barack Obama. She said he'd make a wonderful justice and together they would've torn the Second Amendment to shreds in no time.

Last year was a truly dangerous time for our country. After eight years of leading from behind, ISIS was on the rise, the threat from terrorism had never been greater, and our enemies no longer even pretended to take us seriously.

At home, illegal immigration was out of control. Sanctuary cities were allowing illegal criminal aliens unfettered access to destroying families and communities. A coldly calculated failure to enforce the law left the very concept of justice, on the brink of total collapse. Cities like Chicago became safe havens for killers, where nearly 4,000 people were murdered while Obama was president. And law enforcement everywhere—heroes who wake up every day willing to risk their lives for our safety—were left vulnerable by a deliberate and despicable lack of support from their so-called leaders.

And the men and women who sacrificed the most for our freedom— our veterans—were treated with a carelessness and contempt that should forever stain the legacy of Barack Obama. The corruption, dishonesty and elitism in Washington had truly reached a tipping point. Those were the stakes in last year's election. Not hyperbole. Not fake news. The truth. But you know what else is true? The men and women of the National Rifle Association haven't backed down from a fight in 146 years and we sure as hell weren't scared of Hillary Clinton. (Cheering.)

So we made sure every American understood the catastrophic consequences of Hillary in the White House. Take a look.

[VIDEO: COMMERCIAL]

[Photo: screengrab.]

That's the America we could be living in right now: an America where even the most basic, fundamental freedoms are destroyed. But you refused to let that happen. And now, thanks to you, a true defender of constitutional principles, Justice Neil Gorsuch, sits on the US Supreme Court! (Cheering.)

His appointment alone is a monumental victory for American freedom. But you accomplished even more than that. How about Vice President Mike Pence? (Cheering.)

He's committed to his faith, his family and the God-given freedoms that make America great—and thanks to you, he's fighting for us every day!

Thanks to you, Jeff Sessions runs the Justice Department. (Cheering.)

It's going to take a hazmat suit to clean up the poisoned, politicized disgrace of a legacy left by Eric Holder and Loretta Lynch, but if anyone has the passion and the integrity to restore the rule of law, it's Attorney General Jeff Sessions. Thanks to you, our enemies truly fear us once again, because General James "Mad Dog" Mattis runs the Department of Defense! (Roaring and cheering.)

And the list goes on. Across the Trump administration, we have an all-star team of principled leaders. You should be proud, because this organization made the difference and saved the soul of America. But the fight is far from over.

All you have to do is turn on the TV to understand that we didn't win the media with this election. We still don't control Hollywood and Michael Bloomberg is still short, rich and angry. (Laughter.)

And they're such hypocrites. They love their armed security, but they hate the idea of you being able to defend yourself with a firearm. And the truth is, in too many places today, you can't. Folks, it's a sorry state of affairs when 10 states can deny a constitutional freedom to law-abiding American citizens. It's even worse when the media refuses to cover it. They won't report that honest, well-meaning people—nurses, stay-at-home moms, veterans, even a disaster relief worker—have been charged with felonies for simply having a lawfully owned firearm. Each was legally licensed to carry a gun in their home state, but arrested and charged as criminals when safely carrying it through another, less free state. It's an absolute outrage. And it goes unreported day after day. This freedom makes a life-or-death difference in innocent people's lives. It isn't just illegal for states to deny it, it's downright immoral and it needs to change. For that to happen, it will take the same intensity and moral purpose that we brought to last year's election—but we can and we will make Congress pass National Right to Carry Reciprocity! (Roaring and cheering.)

We fight for self-defense because your life is worth fighting for. This is who we are. Please watch.

[VIDEO: COMMERCIAL]

[Photo: screengrab.]

Folks, it's not easy to tell a painful personal story like that, much less on national television. And to do it in the heat of a brutal and violent election takes a special kind of courage. But that's Kristi. She was ready to do everything she could to make sure other women never have to experience the hell that she went through. Kristi endured hateful, vicious attacks on social media just for speaking her mind. They tried to bully and intimidate her into silence. But she stood strong. She weathered the storm. And she didn't back down, not one inch. Kristi is a life member of the NRA, and she will never be alone because she's got 5 million of us watching her back. She's here with us today. Kristi, please stand up and let us thank you.

Friends, you, and I and Kristi, we're part of something special. Something unique, not just in American history, but in world history. Six thousand years of human civilization say we aren't supposed to be able to make a difference. We aren't supposed to pick history's winners and losers. We're not even supposed to have a say.

Because we are nothing more than a gathering of the most common of common people. We're presidents of our dinner tables, kings and queens of the grocery list and emperors of the bleacher seats. And yet, last November, we accomplished what no one thought was possible.

We didn't just swing an election—we altered the course of history. If you take every million-dollar PR firm— every self-important media operation ... all the experts and pollsters and professional know-it-alls ... every pedigree and resume and fancy title from Washington, D.C. to San Francisco and beyond—if you take every last one of 'em and add 'em together, they don't have an ounce of your influence.

That's why they fear you. And that's why they hate you. From the bottom of my heart: there's no one else in the world I'd rather fighting by your side. You are the most committed, most principled, most worthy group of modern-day patriots and I am truly humbled to serve on your behalf. I don't care if we're the only people in the arena. I don't care who we're up against. I don't care how lonely it gets, or how tough it gets. We will never stop fighting for this country and this freedom. If we stick together, there is nothing we can't achieve, no enemy we can't defeat, no battle we can't win.

Let us vow on this day, that November was more than a temporary moment. It was a permanent political redl-line for every would-be holder of power: If you run against the Second Amendment freedom of everyday American citizens, you put your future in direct opposition to the most powerful grassroots force in history.

We are the National Rifle Association of America. And we are, now and forever, 'freedom's safest place'. Thank you. Thank you. (Applause and whistling.)

You know the National Riffle Association is he only organization in the world, that can make a rightful claim to the phrase. **'Freedom's Safest Place,'** above all that's testament to you, the five million men and women of the NRA, thirty-seven years ago that number was not five million, it was barely one million. And the idea that a bunch of everyday average people would have the power to pick the president of the United States was hard to fathom.

There is one man who has seen this monumental change first hand; for nearly the past four decades. In his time as the leader of our organization he has gone toe - toe with governors, senators and yes Presidents. He has called out fake news on behalf of gun owners for his whole career. And when he has been faced with the most intense pressure to give in, to give up the freedom generations of veterans have fought and bleed for, he has never backed down, not one inch.

Under his leadership, this organization has grown into the most powerful grassroots organization on earth. And this freedom has experienced a rebirth when every other freedom has been on decline.

Ladies and gentlemen please welcome the CEO and Executive Vice President of your National Riffle Association, Wayne LaPierre.

WAYNE LAPIERRE: Thank you so much, thank you so much.

Hello America! I tell ya. It's great to be with you today. And I want to welcome ya to this great celebration of our values. I know you're excited to see President Trump. I am too. America's gun owners can already see a real difference since the election—especially now in the Supreme Court - yeah—and I know you join me in saying, "Thank you Mr. President, and keep it up!" (Cheering.)

We must do all we can to support our president because, as you well know, there is an intense war that's being waged by leftist zealots to destroy President Trump and to destroy his administration. They'll seemingly stop at nothing, including tearing apart our country. It's all part of a larger war being waged right now—a war against 'truth' in America.

It's a calculated, orchestrated attack against the values upon which our great nation was founded. Against our uniquely American, true freedom. If we don't stand up to them—and I mean now—an entire generation of Americans could be lost and our nation along with them.

It is up to us to speak up against the three most dangerous voices in America: Academic elites, political elites and the media elites. These are America's greatest domestic threats. Academic elites salt the soil of fertile young minds. Political elites plant lies to take advantage of the under- and misinformed. And leftist media elites deliberately deceive and spin and twist the truth to grow their anti-American agenda. The radical left in this country have hijacked too many of our schools and colleges, and now they're trying to hijack our youth. Young Americans are taught national shame over exceptionalism, socialism and communism over free market capitalism, government control over self-destiny. The collective good over individualism. Scores aren't kept, no winners or losers—it's about "participation" trophies—and young people are left unprepared for the real world.

No longer do young minds study the Constitution, especially not the individual freedom and self-empowerment of the Second Amendment. True American history and even American heroes and real American values—the values and principles that built our nation—are rewritten or omitted altogether. The result is an emerging generation of citizens with warped minds. When their turn comes, how can they possibly lead while lacking any fundamental grounding in American principles and values?

Even now, the political elites feed off this uninformed, self-absorbed, self-minded generation. Free safe spaces. Free college. Free health care. Free jobs … or, if not, free money to get by. Free immigration. Free sanctuary cities. Bernie Sanders was not a movement, as a fawning media called his campaign. Bernie is a political predator of young voters who were lied to by school teachers and college professors… set up for his message of big government socialism. Free, free, free for ME! No one told the truth about how all that free stuff was going to be paid for. It was all one big, fat lie. And the media was in on the lie from the start, because it fit their agenda.

When did the media stop being journalists and start becoming PR flaks for the destruction of our country? Cheering.)

You know It's a question that Americans are asking all our country every-time they turn on their TV or pick up their newspaper. It's all about their own celebrity and ratings and agenda. The truth doesn't matter because truth is no longer a fundamental principle—it's now just a political device. There is no limit to how far truth can be stretched or perverted so long as it suits their political end game.

I've long believed that one of America's greatest threats is a national news media that fails to tell the truth. (Cheering.)

Theirs is a calculated campaign to destroy honest truth, to pervert it, to dictate how we should think, and we should feel or how we should act. It's all drowning truth of America's better voices, its all drowning that out — good voices, all over America, our families, our churches, our neighbors and our co-workers.

Voices that insist on the priorities of math and science and English in our schools. The voices that demand reverence for the constitutional freedoms that have always defined our nation. Voices that demand law and order and justice and liberty for all. America's better voices, right here in this room today, that cry out for the values and freedom we hold dear and demand that left-wing social engineers leave us and our families and our children alone! (Cheering.)

More and more all over this country good, decent, honest Americans are seeing through all the lies of the elites. Amen! And you got it.

For the last quarter century, in poll after poll whether it's Gallup or NBC or the Wall Street Journal, Americans have said they view the NRA more favorably than both chambers of Congress and either national political party. Yeah.

And heck, I like baseball. But the NRA is even more popular than Major League Baseball. It's true check the polls. The majority of Americans admire and trust the NRA because we say out loud what we believe. We speak the truth, even when it may be hard, and we fight like hell to defend it. Our success, our victories, our growth, our strength has always been grounded in truth. Confronted with the three most dangerous voices in America, the NRA has consistently beaten them back. We've kicked hundreds of politicians out of office and sent them into obscurity by speaking truthfully to citizens all over this country. By educating and teaching the value of our Second Amendment to an ever-growing body of

Americans who are reaching for their rights to defend their lives, their homes and their communities—and by giving the media the big, fat black eye it so often richly deserves. Please watch. Watch this:

[VIDEO: FREEDOM'S SAFEST PLACE "TAKING IT TO THE TIMES"]

[Photo: screengrab.]

Dana Loesch stated:
> "They use their media to assassinate real news. They use their schools to teach children that their president is another Hitler. They use their movie stars and singers and award shows to repeat their narrative over and over again. And then they use their ex-president to endorse the resistance. All to make them march, make them protest, make them scream racism and sexism and xenophobia and homophobia and smash windows, burn cars, shut down inter-staes and airports, bully and terrorize the law abiding until the only option left is for the police to do their jobs and stop the madness. And when that happens, they'll use it as an excuse for their outrage. The only way to stop this, the only way we save our country and our freedom is to

fight this violence of lies with the clenched fist of truth.

**"I'm the National Rifle Association of America and
I'm freedom's safest place**."

To defend our Second Amendment freedom, the NRA
has deployed its First Amendment freedom through
innovative, state-of-the-art news and content platforms
to deliver the truth directly to all freedom-loving Americans. We're all over the country and you can see it all on
NRATV.com including the latest on NRA Carry Guard.

You know, back in 1987, the NRA launched the national concealed carry movement. We started it and we
fought for it in states all over the country. The NRA is the
reason that, today, 15 million Americans legally carry a
firearm for personal protection.

That's why we've introduced Carry Guard—the most
comprehensive level of personal protection training, education and insurance for every law-abiding citizen who
carries a firearm. It's the most elite, essential and effective training available, and a Carry Guard card should
be in the wallet and purse of every American. Only, only
with strong voices and new, innovative 21st century
programs— echoing together all over this country—can
the dangerous voices be overcome. And the National
Rifle Association of America is the strongest voice of
freedom on the planet. (Applause.)

Sometimes the elites of the radical left, they suck so
much air out of the atmosphere, there's nothing left to
breathe but their poison. And that's what leads to all the
angst and anxiety and hatred that's dividing this country.

Only our loud and clear and life-changing messages of American values and liberty that can rescue our youth. Only strong voices of truth and good can save our country. The election of our president proof, that's proof of that. The NRA stood with Donald Trump through the darkest days of his campaign. We never wavered, we never flinched, we never lost focus of the true priorities of that election: the Supreme Court, a return and respect for law and order in our country, a strong national defense and an absolute determination to restore the full measure of Second Amendment freedom for all honest law-abiding citizens. (Applause.)

Our victory in that fight has made possible the fights we continue to face, and face them we will. I know that you, all of you are up for the challenge. I know gun owners all over this country are eager to again stand and fight for their freedom and fight for their president. We love our country, we cherish our freedom, we believe in America as the greatest nation on Earth and we are all forever proud to be an American. Thank you very much. Thank you so much. (Applause.)

Ladies and gentlemen, please welcome another proud American ... the great Lee Greenwood!

[Lee Greenwood sings *God Bless the USA*.]

[Photo: screengrab.]

CHRIS COX (PRESIDENT OF THE NRA): Lee Greenwood everybody, let's give him another round of applause.

Anyone here Proud to be an American? Whose proud to be an NRA member? Whose proud of what we accomplished in November?

You know the media won't admit it but President Trump has had a hell of a first 100 days. For starters, he saved the second amendment and individual freedom by putting Neil Gorsuch on the US Supreme Court. (Cheering.)

He restored the rule of law when he put Jeff Sessions in as Attorney General.

Our enemies now fear us again, because he put General Mad Dog Mattis in charge of our military.

Oh I forgot to mention, we now have a Commander in

Chief who isn't afraid to bomb the ever loving hell out of ISIS. (Applause, cheering and whistling.)

I have a message for the New York Times, CNN and MSNBC. Look, look I get it - I know you don't want to be here. You thought you would be covering President Hillary Clinton this year. Well, sorry about that, you're not. So get over it and join the men and women of the National Riffle Association in welcoming the 45th President of the United States of America - Donald Trump. (Applause, roaring and music.)

[Donald Trump on stage approaches Chris Cox and Wayne LaPierre (CEO of the NRA) clapping and he shook their hands.]

Audience: USA! USA! USA!

[Photo: screengrab.]

2:06 P.M. EDT

[Photo: screengrab.]

THE PRESIDENT: Thank you, Chris, for that kind introduction and for your tremendous work on behalf of our
Second Amendment. Thank you very much. (Applause.)

I want to also thank Wayne LaPierre for his unflinching
leadership in the fight for freedom. Wayne, thank you very
much. Great. (Applause.)

I'd also like to congratulate Karen Handel on her incredible
fight in Georgia 6. (Applause.)

The election takes place on June 20th. And, by the way,
on primaries, let's not have 11 Republicans running for the
same position, okay? (Laughter.)

It's too nerve-shattering. She's totally for the NRA and
she's totally for the Second Amendment. So get out and
vote. She's running against someone who's going to raise
your taxes to the sky, destroy your healthcare, and he's

for open borders -- lots of crime, and he's not even able to vote in the district that he's running in. Other than that, I think he's doing a fantastic job, right? (Laughter.)

So get out and vote for Karen.

Also, my friend -- he's become a friend, because there's nobody that does it like Lee Greenwood. Wow. (Applause.)

Lee's anthem is the perfect description of the **renewed Spirit** sweeping across our country. And it really is, indeed, sweeping across our country. So, Lee, I know I speak for everyone in this arena when I say, **we are all very proud indeed to be an American**. Thank you very much, Lee. (Applause.)

No one was more proud to be American than the beloved patriot -- and you know who I'm talking about -- we remember on gatherings like today, your former five-term President, the late Charlton Heston*. How good was Charlton? (Applause.)

And I remember Charlton, he was out there fighting when maybe a lot of people didn't want to be fighting. He was out there for a long time. He was a great guy.

And it's truly wonderful to be back in Atlanta, and back with my friends at the NRA. You are my friends, believe me. (Applause.)

Perhaps some of you remember the last time we were all together. Remember that? We had a big crowd then, too. So we knew something was happening. But it was in the middle of a historic political year, and in the middle of a truly historic election. What fun that was -- November

8. Wasn't that a great evening? Do you remember that evening? (Applause.)

Remember that? (Applause.)

Remember they were saying, "We have breaking news: Donald Trump has won the state of Michigan." They go, "Michigan? How did that" -- "Donald Trump has won the state of Wisconsin, whoa." But earlier in the evening, remember, Florida, North Carolina, South Carolina, Pennsylvania, all the way up -- we ran up the East Coast. And, you know, the Republicans have a tremendous disadvantage in the Electoral College, you know that. Tremendous disadvantage. And to run the whole East Coast, and then you go with Iowa and Ohio, and all of the different states. It was a great evening, one that a lot people will never forget -- a lot of people. (Applause.)

Not going to forget that evening.

And remember they said, "There is no path to 270." For months I was hearing that. You know, they're trying to suppress the vote. So they keep saying it, so people say, you know, I really like Trump, he loves the Second Amendment, he loves the NRA; I love him, but let's go to the movie because he can't win. Because they're trying to suppress the vote.

But they'd say -- I mean, hundreds of times I heard, there is no -- there's no route. They'd say it, "There is no route to 270." And we ended up with 306. So they were right: Not 270, 306. (Applause.)

That was some evening. Big sports fans said that was the single-most exciting event they've ever seen. That includes

Super Bowls and World Series and boxing matches. That
was an exciting evening for all of us, and it meant a lot.
Only one candidate in the General Election came to speak
to you, and that candidate is now the President of the
United States, standing before you again. (Applause.)

I have a feeling that in the next election you're going to
be swamped with candidates, but you're not going to be
wasting your time. You'll have plenty of those Democrats
coming over and you're going to say, no, sir, no thank you
-- no, ma'am. Perhaps ma'am. It may be **Pocahontas**, remember that. (Laughter and applause.)

And she is not big for the NRA, that I can tell you.
But you came through for me, and I am going to come
through for you. (Applause.)

I was proud to receive the NRA's earliest endorsement
in the history of the organization. And today, I am also
proud to be the first sitting President to address the NRA
Leadership Forum since our wonderful Ronald Reagan in
1983. (Applause.)

And I want to thank each and every one of you not only for
your help electing true friends of the Second
Amendment, but for everything you do to defend our flag
and our freedom.

With your activism, you helped to safeguard the freedoms
of our soldiers who have bled and died for us on the battlefields. And I know we have many veterans in the audience
today, and we want to give them a big, big beautiful round
of applause. (Applause.)

And, like I promised, we are doing a really top job already

-- 99 days -- but already with the Veterans Administration, people are seeing a big difference. We are working really hard at the VA, and you're going to see it, and you're already seeing it. And it's my honor. I've been telling you we're going to do it, and we're doing it. (Applause.)

Thank you.

The NRA protects in our capitols and legislative houses the freedoms that our service-members have won for us on those incredible battlefields. And it's been a tough fight against those who would go so far as to ban private gun ownership entirely. But I am here to deliver you good news. And I can tell you that Wayne and Chris have been fighting with me long and hard to make sure that we were with you today, not somebody else with an empty podium. Because believe me, the podium would have been empty. They fought long and hard, and I think you folks cannot thank them enough. They were with us all the way, right from the beginning. (Applause.)

But we have news that you've been waiting for a long time: The eight-year assault on your Second Amendment freedoms has come to a crashing end. (Applause.)

You have a true friend and champion in the White House. No longer will federal agencies be coming after law-abiding gun owners. (Applause.)

No longer will the government be trying to undermine your rights and your freedoms as Americans. Instead, we will work with you, by your side. We will work with the NRA to promote responsible gun ownership, to protect our wonderful hunters and their access to the very beautiful outdoors. You met my son -- I can tell you, both sons, they love the outdoors. Frankly, I think they love the outdoors more than they love, by a long shot, Fifth Avenue. But that's okay. And we want to ensure you of the sacred right of self-defense for all of our citizens. (Applause.)

When I spoke to this forum last year, our nation was still mourning the loss of a giant, a great defender of the Constitution: Justice Antonin Scalia. (Applause.)

I promised that if elected, I would nominate a justice who would be faithful and loyal to the Constitution. I even went one step further and publicly presented a list of 20 judges from which I would make my selection, and that's exactly what we did.

And, by the way, I want to thank, really, Heritage. And I want to thank also all of the people that worked with us. Where's Leo? Is Leo around here? Where is he? He's got to be here. Where is he? He has been so good. And also from Heritage, Jim DeMint. It's been amazing. I mean, those people have been fantastic. They've been real friends. (Applause.)

The Federalist people -- where are they? Are they around here someplace? They really helped us out.

I kept my promise, and now, with your help, our brand-new Justice -- and he is really something very special -- Neil Gorsuch, sits on the bench of the United States Supreme Court. (Applause.)

For the first time in the modern political era, we have con-firmed a new justice in the *first 100 days*. (Applause.)

The last time that happened was 136 years ago, in

1881. Now, we won't get any credit for this, but don't worry about it, the credit is in the audience, right? The credit
is in the audience. (Applause.)

All of those people. They won't give us credit, but it's been
a long time, and we're very honored. We've also taken
action to stand up for America's sportsmen. On their very
last full day in office, the previous administration issued
an 11th-hour rule to restrict the use of lead ammunition
on certain federal lands. Have you heard about that,
folks? I'm shocked to hear that. You've all heard about
that. You've heard about that. On his first day as Secretary
of the Interior, Ryan Zinke eliminated the previous administration's ammunition ban. (Applause.)

He's going to be great. Ryan is going to be great.
We've also moved very quickly to restore something gun
owners care about very, very much. It's called the rule of
law. (Applause.)

We have made clear that our administration will always
stand with the incredible men and women of law enforcement. (Applause.)

In fact, countless members of law enforcement are also
members of the NRA, because our police know that responsible gun ownership saves lives, and that the right of
self-defense is essential to public safety. Do we all agree
with that? (Applause.)

Our police and sheriffs also know that when you ban guns,
only the criminals will be armed. (Applause.)

For too long, Washington has gone after law-abiding gun
owners while making life easier for criminals, drug dealers,

traffickers and gang members. MS-13 -- you know about
MS-13? It's not pleasant for them anymore, folks. It's
not pleasant for them anymore. That's a bad group. (Applause.)

Not pleasant for MS-13. Get them the hell out of here,
right? Get them out. (Applause.)

We are protecting the freedoms of law-abiding Americans,
and we are going after the criminal gangs and cartels that
prey on our innocent citizens. And we are really going
after them. (Applause.)

As members of the NRA know well, some of the most important decisions a President can make are appointments
-- and I've appointed people who believe in law, order, and
justice. (Applause.)

That is why I have selected as your Attorney General,
number one, a really fine person, a really good man, a man
who has spent his career fighting crime, supporting the police, and defending the Second Amendment. For the first
time in a long time, you now have a pro-Second-Amend-
ment, tough-on-crime Attorney General, and his name is
Jeff Sessions. (Applause.)

And Attorney General Sessions is putting our priorities into
action. He's going after the drug dealers who are ped-
dling their poison all over our streets and destroying our
youth. He's going after the gang members who threaten
our children. And he's fully enforcing our immigration laws
in all 50 states. And you know what? It's about time. (Applause.)

Heading up the effort to secure America's borders is a

great military general, a man of action: Homeland Security Director [sic], John Kelly. (Applause.)

Secretary Kelly, who used to be General Kelly, is following through on my pledge to protect the borders, remove criminal aliens, and stop the drugs from pouring into our country. We've already seen -- listen to this; it never happened before, people can't even believe it. And, by the way, we will build the wall no matter how low this number gets or how this goes. Don't even think about it. Don't even think about it. (Applause.)

You know, they're trying to use this number against us because we've done so unbelievably at the borders already. They're trying to use it against us. But you need that wall to stop the human trafficking, to stop the drugs, to stop the wrong people. You need the wall. But listen to this: We've already seen a 73 percent decrease -- never happened before -- in illegal immigration on the southern border since my election -- 73 percent. (Applause.)

You see what they're doing, right? So why do you need a wall? We need a wall.

AUDIENCE MEMBER: Build the wall!

THE PRESIDENT: **We'll build the wall**. Don't even think about it. Don't even think about it. Don't even think about it. That's an easy one. We're going to build the wall. We need the wall.

I said to General Kelly, how important is it? He said, very important. It's that final element. We need the wall. And it's a wall in certain areas. Obviously, where you have these massive physical structures you don't need, and we have certain big rivers and all. But we need a wall, and we're going to get that wall. (Applause.)

And the world is getting the message. They know that our border is no longer open to illegal immigration, and that if you try to break in, you'll be caught and you'll be returned to your home. You're not staying any longer. And if you keep coming back illegally after deportation, you will be arrested, prosecuted, and you will put behind bars. Otherwise it will never end. (Applause.)

Let's also remember that immigration security is national security. We've seen the attacks from 9/11 to Boston to San Bernardino. Hundreds of individuals from other countries have been charged with terrorism-related offenses in the United States.

We spend billions and billions of dollars on security all over the world, but then we allow radical Islamic terrorists to enter right through our front door. That's not going to happen anymore. (Applause.)

It's time to get tough. It's time we finally got smart. And yes, it's also time to put **America First**. (Applause.)

And perhaps -- I see all of those beautiful red and white hats --- but we will never forget our favorite slogan of them all: **Make America Great Again**. All right? (Applause.)

Keeping our communities safe and protecting our freedoms also requires the cooperation of our state leaders. We have some incredible pro-Second Amendment governors here at the NRA conference, including Governor Scott of Florida. Where is Governor Scott? Great guy doing a great job. Governor Bryant of Mississippi. What

a wonderful place. Governor Bryant is here. Thank
you. Governor Deal of Georgia. (Applause.)

And we're also joined by two people that -- well, one I
loved right from the beginning; the other one I really liked,
didn't like, and now like a lot again. (Laughter.)

Does that make sense? Senator David Perdue -- he was
from the beginning -- and Senator Ted Cruz -- like, dislike,
like. (Applause.)

Where are they? Good guys. Good guys. Smart cookies.
Each of these leaders knows that public officials must serve
under the Constitution, not above it. We all took an oath
to preserve, protect, and defend the Constitution of the
United States -- and that means defending the Second
Amendment. (Applause.)

So let me make a simple **promise** to every one of the
freedom-loving Americans in the audience today: As your
President, I will never, ever infringe on the right of the people to keep and bear arms. Never ever. (Applause.)

Freedom is not a gift from government. Freedom is a gift
from God. (Applause.)

It was this conviction that stirred the heart of a great
American patriot on that day, April, 242 years ago. It was
the day that Paul Revere spread his Lexington alarm -- the
famous warning that "the British are coming, the British
are coming." Right? You've all heard that, right? The
British are coming.

Now we have other people trying to come, but believe me,
they're not going to be successful. That I can tell you. (Ap-

plause.)

Nothing changes, right, folks? Nothing changes. They are not going to be successful. There will be serious hurt on them, not on us.

Next, came the shot heard around the world, and then a rag-tag army of God-fearing farmers, frontiersmen, shopkeepers, merchants that stood up to the most powerful army at that time on Earth. The most powerful army on Earth. But we sometimes forget what inspired those everyday farmers and workers in that great war for independence.

Many years after the war, a young man asked Captain Levi Preston, aged 91, why he'd fought alongside his neighbors at Concord. Was it the Stamp Act? Was it the Tea Tax? Was it a work of philosophy? "No," the old veteran replied. "Then why?" he was asked. "Young man," the Captain said, "what we meant in going for those Redcoats was this: We always had governed ourselves, and we always meant to" govern ourselves. (Applause.)

Captain Preston's words are a reminder of what this organization and my administration are all about: the right of a sovereign people to govern their own affairs, and govern them properly. (Applause.)

We don't want any longer to be ruled by the bureaucrats in Washington, or in any other country for that matter. **In America, we are ruled by our citizens**. We are ruled by each and every one of you.

But we can't be complacent. These are dangerous times. These are horrible times for certain obvious reasons. But we're going to **make them great times again**.

Every day, we are up against those who would take away
our freedoms, restrict our liberties, and even those who
want to abolish the Second Amendment. We must be vigilant. And I know you are all up to the task.

Since the first generation of Americans stood strong at
Concord, each generation to follow has answered the call
to **defend freedom** in their time.

That is why we are here today: **To defend freedom for our
children. To defend the liberty of all Americans. And to
defend the right of a free and sovereign people to keep
and bear arms**.

I greatly appreciated your support on November 8th, in
what will hopefully be one of the most important and positive elections for the United States of all time. And to the
NRA, I can proudly say I will never, ever let you down.

Thank you. God Bless you. God Bless our Constitution,
and God bless America.

Thank you very much. Thank you. Thank you. (Applause.)

END
2:35 P.M. EDT

[*Charlton Heston, was the President of the NRA and
spokesman from 1998 to 2003, when he resigned.]

Chapter 165

REMARKS BY PRESIDENT TRUMP AT SIGNING OF
EXECUTIVE ORDER ON
AN AMERICA-FIRST OFFSHORE ENERGY STRATEGY
ROOSEVELT ROOM

28 April 2017

11:04 A.M. EDT

THE PRESIDENT: Thank you, Mike Pence -- a really wonderful guy, and my great friend, and a truly great Vice President. He will go down as a truly great Vice President. Many thanks to Secretaries Wilbur Ross and Ryan Zinke. Very proud of the job they're doing.

We're also pleased to welcome many members of Congress and energy industry leaders to the White House. And I want to get them immediately back over there because I know they're going to be voting on lots of different things, right? So we can't spend too much time talking about drilling in the Arctic, right? But we're opening it up.

This is a great day for American workers and families, and today we're unleashing American energy and clearing the way for thousands and thousands of high-paying American energy jobs. Our country is blessed with incredible natural resources, including abundant offshore oil and natural gas reserves. But the federal government has kept 94 percent of these offshore areas closed for exploration and production. And when they say closed, they mean closed.

This deprives our country of potentially thousands and thousands of jobs and billions of dollars in wealth. I pledged to take action, and today **I am keeping that promise**.

This Executive Order starts the process of opening off-shore areas to job-creating energy exploration. It reverses the previous administration's **Arctic leasing ban**. So hear that: It reverses the previous administration's Arctic leasing ban, and directs Secretary Zinke to allow responsible development of offshore areas that will bring revenue to our Treasury and jobs to our workers. (Applause.)

In addition, Secretary Zinke will be reconsidering burdensome regulations that slow job creation.

Finally, this Order will enable better scientific study of our offshore resources and research that has blocked everything from happening for far too long. You notice it doesn't get blocked for other nations. It only gets blocked for our nation.

Renewed offshore energy production will reduce the cost of energy, create countless good jobs, and **make America more secure and far more energy independent**. This action is another historic step toward future development and future -- with a future -- a real future. And I have to say that's a real future with greater prosperity and security for all Americans, which is what we want.

So I'm very proud of the people standing behind me. I'm far less proud of the people standing in front of me. (Laughter.)

The media. But I have to tell you that this is a very

important day, and I want to congratulate Wilbur and Ryan and all of the people that have worked so hard to get this put together so quickly. And it's going to lead to a lot of great wealth for our country and a lot of great jobs for our country.

So God bless America. Thank you very much. (Applause.)

(The Executive Order is signed.)

Q   Mr. President, what's made this job harder than you thought?

THE PRESIDENT: We're moving awfully well. We're getting a lot of things done. I don't think there's ever been anything like this.

It's a false standard, 100 days, but I have to tell you, I don't think anybody has done what we did over the 100 days.

So we're very happy. (Applause.)

END
11:09 A.M. EDT

Chapter 166

28 April 2017

11:55 A.M. EDT

THE VICE PRESIDENT: On behalf of the President of the United States, it is my honor to welcome you all today to the Office of the Vice President here at the White House complex for a very important moment in the life of this administration and in our national life, as I administer the oath of office to the 27th Secretary of Labor for the United States of America, Alexander Acosta. (Applause.)

We're fortunate to be joined today by his father, Rene, his wife, Jan, and their beautiful and charming daughters, Delia and Rosie. Would you welcome them as well? (Applause.)

I also want to thank all of our distinguished guests who have joined us for this important moment, especially Congresswoman Ileana Ros-Lehtinen, and all the Hispanic business and community leaders who are here with us today. Thank you for being here on this historic day.

This Saturday marks the end of *President Trump's first 100 days in office*, and as this period draws to a close, it's worth reflecting for just a moment on the optimism and the progress that is sweeping across America, thanks to the leadership of President Donald Trump.

For nearly 100 days, President Trump has been **delivering on the promises** that he made to the American people, one after another. He picked a world-class Cabinet, which we're adding to today, which is working around the clock to implement an agenda to **Make America Great Again**. In Justice Neil Gorsuch, President Trump **kept his promise** to nominate a Supreme Court justice in the mold of the late and great Justice Antonin Scalia.

President Trump has been putting **America First -- rebuilding** our military, **restoring the arsenal of democracy**, and he's signing legislation to give our veterans the care that they deserve. In fact, in *now just short of 100 days*, President Trump has signed 28 Bills into law, 30 Executive Orders -- historic numbers that show that not only is President Trump a man of his word, President Trump is a man of action. (Applause.)

And since day one, the President has taken decisive action to get our economy moving again and **restore opportunity** and **prosperity** for every American family. President Trump, I always like to say, has a three-part agenda: Jobs, jobs, and jobs. And to kick-start jobs and growth, the President has been slashing through mountains of red tape. He's **renewed** focus even earlier today on **American energy and American energy independence**. And just a few short days ago, the President put forward a plan for the biggest tax cut for individuals and businesses in American history. (Applause.)

And the result? More than 500,000 **new jobs** have been created so far this year. **Small-business confidence** has sky-rocketed to its highest level in decades, and for manufacturers, the highest level in two decades. And company after company is announcing plans to invest in our country for the benefit of **American workers, American jobs, and America's future**.

The fact is that President Trump's leadership has been making a difference every single day, and we're just getting started. And with our new Secretary of Labor, Alex Acosta, the President and I are confident that we will accomplish even more for working Americans and job creators all across this nation. (Applause.)

Alex Acosta is the right man at the right time to lead the Department of Labor. Born the son of two Cuban refugees, Alex showed his potential from his earliest days, earning both his undergraduate and law degrees from Harvard University. He went on to clerk for Justice Samuel Alito on the Third Circuit Court of Appeals, and after a few years in private practice and as a professor at George Mason University School of Law, he entered into the noble path of public service.

In 2002, President George W. Bush appointed Alex to serve as a member of the National Labor Relations Board. Only one year later, President Bush appointed him to be the Assistant Attorney General for the Civil Rights Division at the Department of Justice, and two years after that, he be-came the U.S. Attorney for the Southern District of Florida.

Alex, I know you've tried to retire from public service more than once. (Laughter.)

In 2009, you did it when you became Dean of Florida International University College of Law. But President Trump has now called you back -- called you back to public service, to bring you character, your intellect, and your ability to serve the country. And we couldn't be more grateful.

Your service, past, present, and future, is truly a testament to the **American Dream** and to your own character and your own abilities. I want to thank you again.

Thank you for stepping up to serve our country and to serve working Americans at such a time as this. Given your long and distinguished record, your integrity and your leadership, the President and I are absolutely confident that as -- with you as our new Secretary of Labor, we will continue to **restore opportunity, prosperity and growth for working Americans** now and for generations to come. (Applause.)

And so, on behalf of President Trump, it is my great privilege to administer to you the oath of office. Step aside and we'll make it official.

(The Oath is administered.) (Applause.)

SECRETARY ACOSTA: I want to thank President Trump, Vice President Pence, and the members of the Senate for the privilege of serving as Secretary of Labor. I want to thank my wife, Jan. Her unyielding support and her heartfelt love means the world to me. It's amazing to be loved, and I love her back more than words can really say. And so, thank you. (Applause.)

My daughters, Delia and Rosalia, are amazing. They have followed this process in their own way. When President Trump nominated me, I had to sit down and explain to them that we were, if confirmed, moving to Washington, and they wanted to know why. And so I sort of took a pause and I tried to explain what being Secretary of Labor means in words that a four- and then six-year-old could understand. And this is what I said. I said, Daddy helps his students find good jobs, and so the President has asked Daddy to help people all over America find good jobs too. (Applause.)

And then it struck me: Explaining the responsibilities of the Secretary of Labor to a four- and a six-year-old really helped me encapsulate so many of the responsibilities of the Department of Labor. Because, as the Vice President said, it is about finding and helping and supporting jobs and job growth.

My parents fled a Cuban dictatorship in search of freedom. They met in high school. They fell in love, and they married young. Neither attended college. What an amazing nation this is that the son of refugees who forwent an education to support a family could be standing here in this room, taking this oath, administered by the Vice President of the United States. **That is what America is about.** (Applause.)

My parents' experience is part of who I am and frames my perspectives that I will bring to the important responsibilities of the Department of Labor. We have a lot of work to do.

Too many Americans have seen jobs go overseas.

Too many Americans have seen jobs filled by foreign workers.

And too many Americans see that jobs are available, but that they don't have the skills or the experience to fill those jobs.

The skills gap is real and needs to be addressed.

Supporting Americans' ability to find good jobs, safe jobs is a priority for President Trump, for Vice President Pence, and for me.

I am honored and I am profoundly humbled to be called in service of this important effort.

Thank you very much. (Applause.)

END
12:08 P.M. EDT

Chapter 167

28 April 2017

Transcript:

My fellow Americans,
I truly believe that the *first 100 days* of my Administration has been just about the **most successful in our country's history**.

Most importantly, we're bringing back jobs. You asked the people of Michigan; you asked the people of Ohio; you can ask the people of Pennsylvania. See what's happening. See the car companies come roaring back in. They don't want to leave. They want to stay here. They want a piece of the action.

Our country is going up and it's going up fast. Our companies are doing better – they just announced fantastic profits – all because of what's happened in this rather short period of time. And that's just the beginning. We're putting in a massive tax cut for the middle class and for business. It's going to have an enormous effect.

The massive Keystone Pipeline, the Dakota Pipeline – tens of thousands of jobs right there. And so many other businesses. We're really proud of what we're doing.

The F-35 fighter jet program – it was way over budget. I've

saved 725 million dollars plus, just by getting involved in the negotiation. We're cutting costs, and we're going to have a truly competitive and great country again.

In just fourteen weeks, my administration has brought profound change to Washington.

The **most fundamental change** can be found in the relationship **between the people and their government**. For too long, politicians cared more about special interests than they did about a very successful future for all Americans. They took our taxpayers' money, and sent their jobs and wealth to other countries.

Not anymore. From the first day of my administration, I have governed by a simple idea: **My only allegiance is to you, our wonderful citizens.**

Together we are seeing that great achievements are possible when we put **American People First**.

That is why I withdrew the United States from the Trans-Pacific Partnership. That day was a turning point for our nation. It put the countries of this world on notice that the sell-out of the American worker was over.

In the following weeks, I took unprecedented actions to reverse Federal overreach and unleash job creation. We have slashed burdensome regulations, and imposed a policy that for each new regulation, two regulations must be erased from the books.

We've done it all while moving quickly to restore the most basic protection for all citizens, the rule of law. A truly great judge, Neil Gorsuch, now sits on the United States

Supreme Court. Justice Gorsuch is deeply devoted to our Constitution. My Administration is the first in the modern political era to confirm a new Supreme Court Justice in the *first 100 days* – the last time it happened was 136 years ago in 1881.

Defending the rule of law is a priority, not just in the courts, but also on the streets and on the border. We've told the incredible police of our nation that they have our full support as they work to bring down violent crime rates. We've taken bold action to go after criminal cartels, and made it a top priority to prosecute anyone who targets law enforcement.

This has been the work of my administration – fighting for the American worker, defending the rule of law, and returning the power to the American people.

Since my inauguration, **economic confidence** has soared— reaching higher than any time in 9 years.

Optimism among manufacturers is at a record high. And small business confidence has seen its largest increase in nearly four decades.

Perhaps the greatest change of all is the **renewal of the American Spirit**. As long as we have faith in each other, and trust in God, then the sun will always shine on our very Glorious Republic.

Thank you, God Bless You, and God Bless America.

Chapter 168

REMARKS BY THE VICE PRESIDENT AT THE CHRISTENING OF THE USS INDIANA NEWPORT NEWS SHIPYARD NEWPORT NEWS, VIRGINIA

29 April 2017

11:59 A.M. EDT

THE VICE PRESIDENT: Acting Secretary Stackley, Mrs. Diane Donald and the Admiral, Admiral Fargo, Vice Admiral Tofalo, Vice Admiral Mulloy, Captain Lemon, Commander Zimbauer, Petty Officer Haugh, the crew members of the USS Indiana -- (applause) -- the present and the past members of the crew of the USS Indiana -- (applause) -- members of the United States Navy, distinguished guests, I bring greetings from your Commander-in-Chief, the President of the United States of America, President Donald Trump. (Applause.)

It is my great privilege on his behalf to join you here today for the christening of what will soon be the best-named boat in the United States Navy -- the USS Indiana. (Applause.)

Senator Donnelly, Congressman Scott, members of the Virginia delegation, members of the Indiana General Assembly who are with us here today, it is a real joy for me to be with you. As I served as governor of the State of Indiana, I learned of this extraordinary boat, but I could not have well imagined that I would be standing before you today in this moment with the great privilege to be at this christening. And I thank you all for being here and for the work that you have done to arrive at this moment. Christening the new USS Indiana just one-day shy of the 75th anniversary of the dedication and christening of the last USS Indiana that feels providential to me. (Applause.)

So to Matt Mulherin, to Jeff Geiger, to Mike Petters, to Samuel Brandon, to the extraordinary craftsmen of Newport News Shipbuilding, let's give these great builders a round of applause. This is impressive work. (Applause.)

Today marks the 100th day since President Donald Trump took his oath of office and I took mine. And he sent me here today on this historic occasion as a sign of his deep commitment to the Armed Forces of the United States of America -- and to his commitment to make the strongest fighting force in the world even stronger still. (Applause.)

It is the greatest privilege of my life to serve as Vice President to a President who is so dedicated to the men and women of our armed forces, to their families, to our veterans, and to the brave Americans who work tirelessly every day to support our military.

And that really includes all the shipbuilders that we just applauded a few moments ago.

For more than 120 years, the men and women gathered here -- many of you second-, and third-, and fourth-generation shipbuilders -- have built from the bottom up the American fleets that have fostered **security and prosperity** on the high seas and between our land and distant others. Know today that you have the gratitude -- all the builders gathered here, you have the gratitude of our Commander-in-Chief for your unwavering commitment to your country, your patriotism, your craftsmanship, and rest assured President Trump will honor your commitment with historic investments in our national defense. (Applause.)

In just his *first 100 days in office*, President Trump has already taken decisive action to end an era of budget cuts to America's military and to America's security.

The President has actually submitted a budget which will rebuild our military, restore the arsenal of democracy. And we will move in the next year one of the largest increases in defense spending since the days of President Ronald Reagan. (Applause.)

And just next week, with President Trump's leadership, and the strong support of the members of Congress gathered here today, Congress will pass a spending bill with long-overdue investments in our military readiness even before this fiscal year ends. That's what leadership looks like.

At a time of mounting threats across the globe, President Trump has made it clear America's national security is this President's highest priority now and always. (Applause.)

Rest assured, President Trump will make the strongest fighting force in the world stronger still. For as history attests, **when America is strong, the world is safe**. And the USS Indiana will bear witness to this truth.

It really is deeply humbling for this son of Indiana to be here today at the christening of this mighty and majestic boat, the Virginia-class nuclear submarine, the USS Indiana. I have to tell you it's more than a little bit emotional to me to be standing here in Newport News, seeing the Indiana flag fluttering just below the American flag behind you all. It makes me feel like I'm back home.

This boat bears the name, I can promise you, of one of the most patriotic states in America. And I truly believe that she reflects the unmatchable courage and the unwavering spirit of those Hoosiers past and present who have stood up and stepped forward to defend the flame of freedom. For generations, stretching back into the mists of American history, the sons and daughters of Indiana have donned the uniform to serve our nation, and they have done so with distinction and with courage.

Our history books are filled with proof.

In the wake of World War Two, no less an authority than the United States Navy declared Indiana's representation in the Navy was "extraordinary in quality," with three of the seven admirals in 1944 hailing from the Hoosier State. The 12 stars they had between them shone bright not just on the Wabash, but on waves all across the world.

And the Navy's recognition of Indiana's service and sacrifice goes back even further.

The boat that sits beside me today is not the first to bear the name of USS Indiana, as we heard many times from this podium. Captain Zimbauer, you and the men and women who you will lead are the heirs of a long and proud tradition that reaches back to the 19th century.

One-hundred and twenty-six years ago, tomorrow, in 1891, the keel of the first USS Indiana was laid down in Philadelphia. Less than two years later, she steamed out of dry dock and into American history.

In the Spanish-American War, the USS Indiana joined the blockade of Santiago, where she helped sink two Spanish vessels and eliminated an entire fleet.

The second ship to bear the name was even more impressive. From 1939 to 1941, this very shipyard built and launched a second battleship emblazoned with USS Indiana on her seal.

From the Solomon Islands to Iwo Jima, she served on the front-lines of freedom and helped establish the foundation of peace and prosperity that reins in the Asia Pacific to this very day.

And I am humbled to say that these 14 members of that very crew are here with us today -- including I'm told two of her plank owners who were there at her commissioning -- Ozen Carrier and John Wright. Would you all mind giving a standing ovation one more time to the extraordinary crew of the USS Indiana and to those two plank holders who are with us today? (Applause.)

Men, I never saw your ship in all her glory, but she still lives on in the hearts and minds of Hoosiers, more than just memory. I can tell you the teak planks from her main deck were actually made into a beautiful desk that every Indiana governor has sat behind since 1964, me included. It was always very humbling for me to come to work every day at the Indiana State House and rest my elbows on the deck of a battleship. (Laughter.)

And now we turn the page to another chapter in the Hoosier history, and it will be just as proud. This USS Indiana -- the third to bear the name, and the first submarine -- is a worthy inheritor of the name and legacy of our state. And already she bears the mark of Indiana -- not just in her name, but from bow to stern.

More than 100 Hoosier businesses have contributed to this boat's creation in one way or another. At least two members of her crew and four of her shipbuilders hail from our great state, and so many of volunteers for the commissioning committee call Indiana home. Would you mind giving all the Hoosiers who are here a big, big round of applause, especially those two on the crew? (Applause.)

I am personally grateful to everyone who has lent their talent, their time, and their treasure to the USS Indiana, and I know that President Trump is thankful as well.

This submarine is the most advanced to ever serve America. The steel within her skeleton -- all 7,600 tons -- and the steel in the hearts of her crew form the unbreakable, unshakeable backbone of American freedom.

When the USS Indiana goes to sea in just a few short weeks, she'll give witness to our country's strength of will and to our strength of arms. And as her sailors begin to fulfil their duty, they'll do so, as the saying goes, "not for self, but for country" -- proving through their service and their sacrifice that those that stand before us in those emblazoned white uniforms, they are from the rest of us -- but they are the best of us. (Applause.)

We know they're ready. We pray that they never feel the heat of battle. But we're grateful that the USS Indiana will be ready, will be there beneath the waves, the hidden chariot of the "Silent Victors," faithfully guarding our freedom, faithfully guarding **our way of life.**

And so, on behalf of the Commander-in-Chief, President Donald Trump, we christen the USS Indiana. Today this humbled son of Indiana is truly grateful to have the opportunity to be with you today to see my beloved state and all of her people so aptly embodied in this extraordinary boat.

From this day forward, the **spirit** and the service of the Hoosier State will find a home on the seven seas in this majestic and mighty submarine, and in the proud crew who walk her decks. And only a few short months from now, when she completes her maiden voyage, the world will take note. For the USS Indiana signifies the enduring strength and leadership of the United States, a beacon of freedom in these stormy and uncertain times.

Know today that under President Donald Trump that beacon will shine bright, brighter than ever before. And **with this President's leadership, the United States I believe is entering a new era of security, prosperity, and strength**. And so I close with a word of confidence that with your help, with God's help, with the USS Indiana at sea, and the great Armed Forces of the United States of America, and the valor and vigilance of all those who serve, that today we go forth to meet a glorious future together.

May God bless and protect the USS Indiana and all who serve aboard her every day beneath our seven seas. My God bless Indiana and may God bless the United States of America. (Applause.)

END
12:12 P.M. EDT

Chapter 169

**REMARKS BY PRESIDENT TRUMP AT SIGNING OF
EXECUTIVE ORDERS ON
TRADE AMES COMPANIES, INC.
HARRISBURG, PENNSYLVANIA**

29 April 2017

7:10 P.M. EDT

THE PRESIDENT: Thank you, everybody, very much. I appreciate you being here today. Great people outside, you can see that. These are great, great Americans and unbelievable workers. Nobody has better than what we have.

And it's wonderful to be at Ames -- an incredible company with a rich, rich history and a long history. Centuries ago, before our country was even founded -- couldn't believe that one -- this company produced the tools that helped to build our nation. Later, *Ames Tools* would be used at the Statue of Liberty, the Empire State Building, the Hoover Dam, just to name a few of the monuments within our country.

We believe in "**Made in the USA**," and it's coming back stronger and better and faster than even I thought. You can see that by our great, great workers throughout the plant, and plenty of other plants. But for a long time, our government has sacrificed American companies and workers to unfair foreign competition.

Today, I'm signing two orders to help keep jobs and wealth in our country. First, in fulfilment of a very, very important and **major campaign promise** I made not far from here last June, I'm directing the Secretary of Commerce, who's with us -- Wilbur, where's Wilbur? --

SECRETARY ROSS: Right here, Mr. President.

THE PRESIDENT: -- Wilbur, a legend -- to identify every violation and abuse of our trade agreements, and to use every available measure under the law to end these abuses against our workers. (Applause.)

And if they don't get cleared up, Wilbur will end the trade agreements. Do you agree with that?

SECRETARY ROSS: Yes, sir.

THE PRESIDENT: Second, I'm establishing the Office of *Trade and Manufacturing Policy* within the White House. Its mission will be to defend American workers and companies from those who would steal our jobs and threaten our manufacturing base. (Applause.)

Peter Navarro, one of the greats trying to protect our jobs. Right, Peter? Thank you, Peter. Appreciate it.

We're only 100 days in. It's been a lot of work, but we've loved it. We've loved doing it. You know, when you love something, it's really easy. And we love it. And we're helping people. We're helping our workers.

And already we've created nearly 150,000 new manufacturing and construction jobs, and over 600,000 jobs have already been created. The *National Manufacturers* survey found the **highest level of optimism in the history** of a very, very old survey. It's been around for a long

time. It just last week hit the highest point it's ever hit in
the history of the survey. That means they're looking for
action. And we love that.

We've taken unprecedented action **to bring back American
jobs, American wealth, and American dreams**. And we
are just getting started. So I want to thank Wilbur. (Applause.)

So this is addressing trade agreement violations and abuses. Very powerful. They're shouting back there because
they know exactly what I'm saying. (Laughter.)

They know better than anybody else, believe me.

(The Executive Order is signed.)

And this is the establishment of the *Office of Trade and
Manufacturing Policy* right out of the White House. And
it's going to have a huge impact on jobs.

(The Executive Order is signed.)

Wilbur, with your permission, I think what I'm going to do
is give this pen to Peter Navarro. Is that okay?

SECRETARY ROSS: Sure. Surely, sir.

THE PRESIDENT: Peter, come on over here. (Applause.)

Peter Navarro has fought against trade abuse for a long
time. And, Peter, this is the first time you're seeing something happen -- all those decades you've been fighting.

MR. NAVARRO: It's been *a great 100 days*, and lots more

to go.

THE PRESIDENT: Thank you, Peter. Great job. Thank you, everybody. (Applause.)

END
7:15 P.M. EDT

Chapter 170

29 April 2017

7:51 P.M. EDT

THE PRESIDENT: Thank you. Ladies and gentlemen, it is truly great to be back in the wonderful, beautiful state of Pennsylvania. (Applause.)

[Photo: screengrab.]

I love this state and I love the people of this state. It's special and it carried us through a big, beautiful victory on November 8th. (Applause.)

I want to recognize some of our friends that have helped us so much. Congressman Scott Perry. (Applause.)

G.T. Thompson. A couple of my originals, Mike Kelly -- who I watched on television. He was great. Where's Mike Kelly? Where is Mike Kelly? He's here someplace. Where is he?

Boy, were you great on television this morning. And, of course, one of our other originals, Congressman Tom Marino. Right? (Applause.)

Thank you. Thank you, Mike. Thank you, Tom.

[Photo: screengrab.]

As you may know, there's another big gathering taking place tonight in Washington, D.C. Did you hear about it?

AUDIENCE: Booo --

THE PRESIDENT: A large group of Hollywood actors and Washington media are consoling each other in a hotel ballroom in our nation's capital right now. (Applause.)

They are gathered together for the *White House Correspondents Dinner* -- without the President. (Ap-

plause.)

And I could not possibly be more thrilled than to be more than 100 miles away from [the] **Washington Swamp** -- (applause) -- spending my evening with all of you, and with a much, much larger crowd and much better people. Right? (Applause.)

Right?

AUDIENCE: U-S-A! U-S-A!

THE PRESIDENT: And look at the media back there. They would actually rather be here, I have to tell you.

AUDIENCE: Booo --

THE PRESIDENT: That's right.

AUDIENCE: CNN Sucks! CNN Sucks!

THE PRESIDENT: Media outlets like *CNN* and *MSNBC* are fake news. Fake news. And they're sitting and they're wishing, in Washington -- they're watching right now, they're watching. And they would love to be with us right here tonight. (Applause.)

But they're trapped at the dinner, which will be very, very boring. (Laughter.)

But next year, maybe we'll make it more exciting for them in Washington, and we'll show up. But we have a good chance of showing up here again next year, too. (Applause.)

The truth is, there is no place I'd rather be than right here in Pennsylvania to celebrate our **100 day milestone** to reflect on an incredible journey together, and to get ready for the great, great battles to come, and that **we will win** in every case, okay? We will win. (Applause.)

Because make no mistake, we are just beginning in our fight to **Make America Great Again**. (Applause.)

Now, before we talk about **my first 100 days**, which has been very exciting and very productive, **let's rate the medias 100 days**.

Should we do that? Should we do it?

Because, as you know, they are a disgrace.

According to a *Morning Consult* poll, more than half of Americans say the media "is out of touch with everyday Americans." And they've proven that.

According to *Media Research Center*, 89 percent of the media's coverage of our administration has been negative -- and purposefully negative --

AUDIENCE: Booo --

THE PRESIDENT: And perhaps that's because, according to the *Center for Public Integrity*, 96 percent of journalists who made donations in the last election gave to our opponent.

Does anybody remember who our opponent was? Huh? That was some opponent.

Finally, according to a poll last year from the *Associated Press*, only 6 percent of Americans have a lot of confidence in America [sic].

That's very bad. That's much lower than Congress, by the way.

But I'll give you an example of something really incredible.

AUDIENCE: Booo --

THE PRESIDENT: That's right, get them out of here. Get them out.

AUDIENCE: U-S-A! U-S-A!

THE PRESIDENT: Thank you. Thank you. Thank you. (Applause.)

Do we love our law enforcement, or what? (Applause.)

And I want to thank the fire marshals. They have a lot of people standing outside. We really maxed out.

We broke the all-time record for this arena. How old is this arena? This is not -- we broke the all-time record. And I don't have a guitar, which is pretty tough.

So just as an example of media, take the totally failing *New York Times*.

AUDIENCE: Booo --

THE PRESIDENT: Pretty soon they'll only be on the Internet. The paper is getting smaller and smaller. You haven't noticed? It's starting to look like a comic book. (Laughter.)

[Photo: screengrab.]

But I will tell you, because I watched, and I used to be in
the real estate business, they sold their beautiful *New York
Times* building in Manhattan -- *A Cathedral to Journalism*;
such a beautiful, beautiful building -- for around $130
million.

And a group that bought it later sold it for approximately
$500 million. And now they live in a very ugly office build-
ing in a crummy location. (Laughter.)

Next, they buy the *Boston Globe* newspaper, with losses,
for $1.3 billion, invest millions and millions and millions of
dollars to get it going. And, in the end, they sell it for zero;
they give it away. And then they write nasty editorials and
op-eds telling me how I should be handling world events
and our country. **Tell me**.

AUDIENCE: Booo --

THE PRESIDENT: But that's what we have. They're incom-

petent, dishonest people, who, after an election, had to
apologize because they covered it, us, me, but all of us
-- they covered it so badly that they felt they were forced
to apologize because their predictions were so bad. You
remember their predictions? They lost a lot of people
because of the way they covered.

So here's the story. If the media's job is to be honest and
tell the truth, then I think we would all agree the media
deserves a very, very, big fat failing grade.

AUDIENCE: Booo -

THE PRESIDENT: Very dishonest people. And not all of
them. You know, we call it the "fake news." Not all of
them. If you notice now, they're using -- everybody is
using the world fake news. Where did you hear it first,
folks? (Applause.)

By contrast, for the **last 100 days**, my administration has
been delivering every single day for the great citizens of
our country -- whether it's putting our coal miners back
to work, **protecting America's steel and aluminium** workers -- we love that steel and aluminium -- or eliminating
job-killing regulations, **we are keeping one promise after
another**. And, **frankly, the people are really happy about
it**. They see what's happening. (Applause.)

But to understand the historic progress that we've made,
we must speak honestly about the situation that we and I
inherited. Because believe me, **the previous administration gave us a mess**!

AUDIENCE: Booo --

THE PRESIDENT: For decades, our country has lived through the greatest jobs theft in the history of the world.

You people know it better than anybody, in Pennsylvania. Our factories were shuttered, our steel mills closed down, and **our jobs were stolen away** and shipped far away to other countries, some of which you've never even heard of.

Politicians sent troops to protect the borders of foreign nations, but left America's borders wide open for all to violate.

We've spent billions and billions of dollars on one global project after another, and yet, as gangs flooded into our country, we couldn't even provide safety for our own people.

Our government rushed to join international agreements where the United States pays the costs and bears the burdens, while other countries get the benefit and pay nothing.

AUDIENCE: Booo --

THE PRESIDENT: This includes deals like the one-sided *Paris Climate Accord,* where the United States pays billions of dollars while China, Russia and India have contributed and will contribute nothing.

AUDIENCE: Booo --

THE PRESIDENT: Does that remind you of the Iran deal? How about that beauty, right?

On top of all of that, it's estimated that full compliance with the agreement could ultimately shrink America's GDP by $2.5 trillion over a 10-year period. That means factories and plants closing all over our country. Here we go again. **Not with me, folks**. (Applause.)

Those are the facts, whether we like them or not. The dishonest media won't print them, won't report them, because the Washington Media is part of the problem: their priorities are not my priorities and they're [sic.] not your priorities, believe me. (Applause.)

Their agenda is not your agenda. And I'll be making a big decision on the *Paris Accord* over the next two weeks. (Applause.)

And we will see what happens.

But they're all part of a broken system that is profited from this **global theft** and plunder of **American wealth** at the expense of the **American worker**.

We are not going to let other countries take advantage of us anymore. Because, from now on, it's going to be **America First**. (Applause.)

And I have to --

AUDIENCE: U-S-A! U-S-A!

THE PRESIDENT: And I have to just interject -- because, as you know, I've been a big critic of China, and I've been talking about currency manipulation for a long time.

But I have to tell you that, during the election, number

one, they stopped. But more importantly, just to show you the dishonesty -- so we have currency manipulation by China, but China is helping us possibly, or probably, with the North Korean situation, okay? (Applause.)

Which is a great thing.

And I met with the President of China at great length in **Florida**, and we had long, long talks -- hours and hours and hours. He's a good man. Now he's representing China.

He's not representing us. But he's a good man. And I believe he wants to get that situation taken care of. They have tremendous power, and we'll see what happens.

But the media said, Donald Trump refuses to name China a currency manipulator. Now, think of this. Think of this. Now, we have to have a little flexibility. So I meet with the President of China, and I say, could you help us out with North Korea?

You know, you give them 93 percent of their different materials that they need and their food. You have a lot of power. We have a great relationship.

And then the media said, why didn't he call Donald Trump, and why didn't Donald Trump at a meeting say you're a currency manipulator?

So here's the story. "Listen, Mr. President, will you help us out with North Korea? But, by the way, you're manipulating your currency."

It doesn't work, right? (Laughter and applause.)

So instead of -- you understand. So instead of saying that,
let's see what happens.

I honestly believe that he's trying very hard. Not an easy
situation for China, believe me. Not an easy situation. But
we have somebody there who's causing a lot of trouble
for the world. We have China, who is really trying to help
us. You've seen they've sent back vast amounts of coal
coming out North Korea. So let's see what happens.

And I think it's not exactly the right time to call China a currency manipulator right now. Do we agree with that? (Applause.)

But they never say that. They say, why didn't he do it.

So **I promised you** in my inaugural address, **100 days ago**,
that now arrives the hour of action. And we've, believe
me, started from day out. And that is what **we've delivered -- 100 days of action**.

In fact, those people and others are exhausted. They've
never seen anything like that. They've never seen anything
like this. (Applause.)

We are ending the off-shoring and **bringing back** our beautiful, wonderful, **great American jobs**. (Applause.)

We are eradicating the criminal gangs and cartels that have
infiltrated our country. You're reading about them all the
time. Some of you have big problems with them.

Thank you for that sign. "Blacks for Trump." I love that
guy. (Applause.)

"Blacks for Trump." Thank you. Thank you. Thank you, man. That's great. That's really cool. I appreciate it.

[Photo: screengrab.]

And we're taking steps to renegotiate or cancel any agreement that fails to protect American interests. Here are just some of our great achievements from the **first 100 days**. And I will tell you, in addition to that, we have built such strong foundations with the leaders of foreign countries. And we're set to rock. But we have great relationships with Germany and Japan and China and so many others, the UK. Such great relationships. That's part of the process.

We've appointed and confirmed a brand new justice of the United States Supreme Court -- (applause) -- Justice Neil Gorsuch, who will uphold the Constitution and the right of Americans to govern their own affairs.

And the last time a new Supreme Court justice was confirmed in the **first 100 days** was 136 years ago, in 1881. And **I was devastated to hear that, because I**

thought I'd be the only to have done that. (Applause.)

A long time ago.

To protect our jobs and our economic freedom, I immediately withdrew the United States from the horrible, disastrous, would have been another but worse, *Trans-Pacific Partnership*. (Applause.)

That would have taken your jobs in Pennsylvania, that I can tell you. That was a total hoax. The *TPP* would have been a tremendous disaster for our country, and we are **not going to surrender Pennsylvania jobs ever again**. We've done that once before. It's not going to happen. (Applause.)

We've just launched an investigation into foreign steel dumping and aluminium dumping throughout our country.

We are reviewing every single trade deal, and **wherever there is cheating**, we will take immediate action and there will be penalties. (Applause.)

And we have with us tonight, Secretary of Commerce Wilbur Ross, and one of the great, great people on fair trade and good trade, Mr. Peter Navarro. (Applause.)

Thank you. Thank you.

And we will renegotiate *NAFTA*. And if we don't get a good deal and a fair deal for our country -- and I've been saying for a long time, we'll either renegotiate or we'll terminate. I announced the other day, we were going to terminate. Everybody said we'll terminate.

Two people that I like very much -- the President of
Mexico, the Prime Minister of Canada -- they called up;
they said, could we negotiate? I said, yes, we can renegotiate. So we'll start a renegotiation, and hopefully it will be
fair for everybody. (Applause.)

And if it's not a fair deal for our country -- because you
have to understand, we have been on the wrong side of
the *NAFTA* deal with Canada and with Mexico for many,
many years, many decades. We can't allow it to happen. So we're going to renegotiate. And if we can't make
a fair deal for our companies and our workers, we will
terminate *NAFTA*, okay? (Applause.)

Our directives will put brand new Pennsylvania steel into
the Spine of America. (Applause.)

We've ordered billions and billions of dollars in unpaid
duties to be collected at the border from countries that
break the rules. And that just started. It's going to be a lot
coming in. (Applause.)

We just want fairness. And **I've followed through on my
promise** and issued a new government directive to **Buy
American and Hire American**. (Applause.)

In just these first few months, we've created 99,000 new
construction jobs, 49,000 new manufacturing jobs, and
27,000 new mining jobs. Who are the miners here? The
miners -- finally, we're taking care of our miners. (Applause.)

We love our miners. And we have over 600,000 new
jobs. And, by the way, the stock market, since our election -- (applause) -- is through the roof. I believe, from the

point of the election, isn't it too bad that the Obama administration gets a lot of credit for those couple of months, but --

AUDIENCE: Booo --

THE PRESIDENT: It's all right. Because we're doing fine, but they get credit for that because people started going wild with the stock. But I believe we have a record, from the time we got elected -- **from November 8th -- we have a record, an all-time record, for the biggest increase in the stock market**. So I'm very happy about that. (Applause.)

We've removed the shackles on energy exploration imposed by the last administration, lifting the restrictions on the production of oil, shale, and natural gas. And, very importantly for Pennsylvania, we have ended the war on beautiful, clean coal, and we are putting our great coal miners back to work. (Applause.)

We love our miners.

I am also very pleased to say that we have finally cleared the way for the construction of the Keystone XL and Dakota Access Pipelines. (Applause.)

48,000 new jobs. They couldn't get their approvals. **We got them their approvals in 24 hours -- one day**. And I want to tell you, the heads of those two companies, they didn't know what the hell happened. They said, how did this happen? They should go to bed and say their prayers. But that's going to be approximately 48,000 jobs.

My administration has also scrapped a job-killing regulation that was threatening our auto workers. We want

More Cars Made in the USA. And that's going to happen. (Applause.)

We've created a new rule which requires that for every
one new regulation, two old regulations must be eliminated. (Applause.)

And we have signed massive executive orders, clearing up
the environmental bureaucracy. We're going to have jobs,
and you're seeing them already.

**We've also been very busy on the legislative front,
which we have gotten no credit for, and yet I am signing
away. I've signed 29 new bills -- a record not surpassed
since the Truman administration.** (Applause.)

This includes 13 resolutions to eliminate intrusive federal
regulations -- the most ever signed in our history.

In **keeping our promise** to our veterans, I've signed legislation to extend *Veterans Choice*. And David, the head of
the *Veterans Administration*, is here with us tonight. David
Shulkin. (Applause.)

He's done an incredible job. And we've increased by 42
percent the approvals for veterans using the *Choice
Program*. (Applause.)

I've also created an *Office of Accountability* at the VA. Our
message to federal workers is clear: If you fail our veterans, you will be held accountable. **First time**. (Applause.)

To create accountability across government, I've issued a
five-year ban on federal officials becoming lobbyists after
they leave government service. Good? (Applause.)

I've got a lot of people in my staff who are not exactly happy with that one, but that's okay. And I've issued a lifetime ban on federal officials becoming lobbyists for a foreign government. (Applause.)

I've imposed these bans for a simple reason: It is time to **Drain the Swamp**. (Applause.)

[Photo: screengrab.]

And that's what we're doing in Washington, D.C.

Perhaps in no area have past governments sold out to special interests and foreign lobbyists more than on the issue of immigration. Year after year, you pleaded for Washington to enforce our laws as illegal immigration surged, refugees flooded in, and lax vetting threatened your family's **safety and security**.

Your pleas have finally been --

AUDIENCE MEMBER: Build the wall!

THE PRESIDENT: Oh, don't worry, we're going to have the wall. Don't worry about it. (Applause.)

AUDIENCE: Build the wall! Build the wall!

THE PRESIDENT: You know, we've done so well at the border, a lot of people are saying, oh, wow, maybe the
President doesn't need the wall. We need the wall to stop
the drugs and the human trafficking. We need the wall.

In just **100 days**, we have taken historic steps to secure our
border, impose needed immigration control like you've
never seen before -- is that true? -- and properly screen
and vet those seeking admission into our country. They
are going to come in because they love our country. We're
not taking them otherwise.

We are operating on a very simple principle: **that our
immigration system should put the needs of American
workers, American families, American companies, and
American citizens First**. (Applause.)

I appointed a great military general, John Kelly, to lead the
Department of Homeland Security. (Applause.)

Since my election, we've already achieved an unprecedented 73 percent reduction in illegal crossings on our southern border. (Applause.)

The greatest reduction in the history of our country. And
we just started.

The world is getting the message: If you try to illegally enter the United States, you will be caught, detained, deport-
ed, or put in prison, and it will happen. (Applause.)

As I campaigned across the nation, I met with the grieving
mothers and fathers of children who had been killed --

viciously killed, violently killed -- by illegal immigrants. And **I made them a promise**: We will **protect American lives**. Your family member will not have died in vain. (Applause.)

Last week, we opened an office to support the *Victims of Immigration Crime*, called *VOICE,* to make sure that no American victim is ever **Again** ignored by their government. Not going to happen anymore. (Applause.)

And many people are now talking, as I just said, and using this tremendous early progress on the border to say we don't need the kind of safety that we will do need, including the wall. **We need safety.** We need cameras. We need all of the things that we're going to be putting in, and we need the wall. And we will build a wall as you are standing there tonight. We need the wall. (Applause.)

AUDIENCE: Build the wall! Build the wall!

THE PRESIDENT: We'll build the wall, folks. Don't even worry about it. Go to sleep. Go home, go to sleep. Rest assured. That's the final thing -- we need it. We need it. And if the Democrats knew what the hell they were doing, they'd approve it so easy, because we want to stop crime in our country. Obviously, they don't mind illegals coming in. They don't mind drugs pouring in. They don't mind, excuse me, MS-13 coming in. We're getting them all out of here.

Members of Congress who will be voting on border security have a simple choice: They can either vote to help drug cartels and criminal aliens trying to enter the United States, like, frankly, the Democrats are doing. **Or they can vote to help American citizens and American families be**

safe. That's the choice. Who do you want to represent you? (Applause.)

Unfortunately, Democrats in Congress have no leadership. They're rudderless. Senator Schumer is a bad leader.

AUDIENCE: Booo --

THE PRESIDENT: I've known him a long time. Senator Schumer is a bad leader, not a natural leader at all. He works hard to study leadership. When you have to study leadership, you got problems. And his policies are hurting innocent Americans and making it easier for drug dealers to enter our country. Schumer is weak on crime and wants to raise your taxes through the roof.

AUDIENCE: Booo --

THE PRESIDENT: He is a poor leader -- known him a long time -- and he's leading the Democrats to doom. It's sad to see for our country what's happening to the Democrat Party.

At the heart of my administration's efforts to restore the rule of law has been a nationwide crackdown on criminal gangs. And that means taking the fight to the *sanctuary cities* that shield these dangerous criminals from removal. (Applause.)

The last Administration allowed thousands of gang members to cross our borders and enter into our communities.

The last, very weak administration allowed thousands and thousands of gang members to cross our borders and enter into our communities where they wreaked havoc on our citizens.

As you know, the bloodthirsty cartel, known as MS-13, has infiltrated our schools, threatening innocent children. We've seen the horrible assaults and many killings all over Long Island, where I grew up.

We have seen the vicious spread of transnational gangs into all 50 states, and the human suffering they bring with them. I've been with the parents; I've seen the parents. It's devastation.

A very respected general recently told me that MS-13 are the equivalent in their meanness to al Qaeda.

My administration will not rest until we have dismantled these violent gangs, and we're doing it rapidly, and we're sending them the hell out of our country. We're sending them back home where they belong. (Applause.)

One by one, we're finding the illegal immigrant drug dealers, gang members, and killers, and removing them from our country. And, once they are gone, folks -- you see what we're doing -- they will not let them back in. They're not coming back. (Applause.)

In this effort to **restore safety to our country**, we are going to strongly support the incredible men and women of law enforcement. (Applause.)

I just signed an executive order directing Attorney General Jeff Sessions **to combat crimes of violence against our police, and the Department of Justice is now prioritizing the prosecution of criminals who attack officers of the law**. (Applause.)

And we are also working around the clock to keep our nation safe from terrorism. (Applause.)

My administration has taken historic steps to improve screening and vetting for those seeking visas to enter the United States. We have seen the attacks, from 9/11 to Boston to San Bernardino.

We have seen the bloodshed overseas. You look at what's happening in other countries.

We already have enough problems to worry about in the United States, which we love so much. We don't need to be admitting people who want to oppress, hurt or kill innocent Americans. They're not coming in. (Applause.)

So let me state this as clearly as I possibly can: We are going to keep radical Islamic terrorists the hell out of our country. (Applause.)

AUDIENCE: U-S-A! U-S-A!

THE PRESIDENT: So I have a question for you. You've been to a lot of countries; you've seen a lot of rallies. First of all, **is there any place like a Trump rally**? In all fairness. Right? (Applause.)

So I did this a little bit during the rally. Haven't done it in a long time. Who has heard the poem called *"The Snake"*? So I have it.

Does anybody want to hear it again? (Applause.)

You sure? Are you sure? Okay.

So let's dedicate this to General Kelly, the Border Patrol, and the ICE agents for doing such an incredible job. (Applause.)

This was written by Al Wilson a long time ago. And I thought of it having to do with our borders and people coming in. And we know that we're going to have; we're going to have problems. We have to very, very carefully vet. We have to be smart. We have to be vigilant.
So here it is, "The Snake." It's called "The Snake":

"On her way to work one morning, down the path along the lake, a tender-hearted woman saw a poor, half-frozen snake. His pretty colored skin had been all frosted with the dew. "Poor thing!" she cried. "I'll take you in and I'll stake care of you." The border. (Laughter.)

> "Take me in, oh, tender woman. Take me in for Heaven's sake. Take me in, oh, tender woman," sighed the vicious snake. "She wrapped him up all cozy in a comforter of silk, and laid him by her fireside with some honey and some milk. She hurried home from work that night, and as soon as she arrived, she found that pretty snake she'd taken in had been revived. Take me in, oh, tender woman. Take me in for Heaven's sake. Take me in, oh, tender woman, sighed that vicious snake. She clutched him to her bosom, 'You're so beautiful,' she cried. 'But if I hadn't brought you in by now, oh, heavens you would have died.' She stroked his pretty skin again and kissed him and held him tight. But instead of saying, 'thank you,' that snake gave her a vicious bite! Take me in, oh, tender woman. Take me in for Heaven's sake. Take me in, oh, tender woman, sighed the vicious sake. 'I have saved you,' cried the woman. 'And you've bitten me, heavens why? You know your bite is poisonous, and now I'm going to die.' 'Oh, shut up, silly woman,' said the reptile with a grin. 'You knew damn well I was a snake before you took me in.'" (Applause.)

Does that explain it, folks? Does that explain it?

Keeping America safe also means rebuilding our defenses. Under the leadership of General "Mad Dog" Mattis --
(applause) -- and he is doing great; he is doing great. And,
by the way, he's the man that recommended General
Kelly. I said, Mad Dog, you got to give me a great general
for the border. He gave me a great general, General
Kelly. We have begun the process of rebuilding our military and restoring full readiness.

We are also protecting taxpayer dollars. I've already saved
more than $725 million on a simple order of F-35 planes. I
got involved in the negotiation. (Applause.)

And there's billions of dollars to be saved on that and many
other things.

We've also stepped up the fight against ISIS, and we will
not stop until ISIS has been destroyed. (Applause.)

At the same time, we've strengthened our friendships and
alliances around the world. For instance, we were very
proud to quietly work with the Egyptian government last
week to ensure that an American citizen, a beautiful young
woman named Aya, came home after being in an Egyptian
prison for the past three years. (Applause.)

She was going to be there for another 28 years.

President Obama worked diligently for three years and
didn't get them out. I met with President el-Sisi and it
worked out quickly, and he was great. (Applause.)

He was great about it. And not only did the court system
in Egypt and President el-Sisi let her out, but they let out
her husband, and they let out a total of eight people that

were innocent.

And they're all back here right now. (Applause.)

Now, they won't include that in **the 100 days**, but I'm very proud to have done it. And she's a happy young woman, believe me.

She's very happy.

I said, "How tough, Aya, was it in that prison?" She said, you don't want to know. That was a tough prison.

We're also getting *NATO* countries to finally step up and contribute their fair share. They've begun to increase their contributions by billions of dollars, but we are not going to be satisfied until everyone pays what they owe. And I've been complaining about that for a long time. And it's a lot different now, but they still a lot of money.

Over the last eight years, America's average military and defense spending was double what all other *NATO* countries spent, combined. Not fair. As we work to get other countries to pay their fair share abroad, we will continue our rebuilding at home. We're rebuilding everything, including, by the way, our great military. We will have the finest military that we've ever had at any time in the history of our country. (Applause.)

Last week, **my economic team outlined one of the biggest tax cuts in American history** -- even bigger than that of Ronald Reagan. We are proposing major tax relief for the middle class, and lowering the business tax from 35 percent all the way down to 15 percent. (Applause.)

Now, you will see companies expand, companies come back into our country, companies not leave our country anymore because taxes and regulations are so onerous. You will see what happens.

Let me also be very clear in saying that we are going to save **Americans' healthcare, and repeal and replace** that disaster known as *Obamacare*, which is dying, dying, dying. (Applause.)

Obamacare is dead anyway, folks. You know, they always like to compare -- well, what about *Obama* -- *Obamacare* is dead. It's gone.

The increases were massive last year, and they're going to be bigger this year. And the insurance companies are fleeing. One of the top people in the insurance industry said, *Obamacare* is in a death spiral, there's nothing they can do. So they can't compare something to it because it won't be there very long, believe me. Can't be there very long. It's not working. It's been a failure.

Under *Obamacare*, we have seen double- and triple-digit hikes in premiums, and many Americans left with only a single insurer to choose from. And now, many of those insurers are fleeing also. You have places like the great state of Tennessee, where I left two weeks ago, where half of the state already has no insurance carrier. And many others.

So *Obamacare* is a catastrophe created exclusively by the Democrats in Congress. And they know it's no good. They know it's not working. And, by the way, we're going to get something great.

We're going to get the premiums down. We're going to get the deductibles way down. We're going to take care of every single need you're going to want to have taken care of. But it's not going to cost that kind of money. We're going to bring it down. You're going to see it. Premiums down.

We will repeal and replace *Obamacare*. You watch. (Applause.)

We're going to give Americans the freedom to purchase the healthcare plans they want, not the healthcare forced on them by the government. (Applause.)

And I'll be so angry at Congressman Kelly and Congressman Marino and all of our congressmen in this room if we don't get that damn thing passed quickly. (Applause.)

They'll get it done. We know them. They'll get it done. In all things, we are returning power to the people where it belongs.

We're going to defend the Second Amendment -- (applause) -- and **your right to keep and bear arms**. We are going to bring education local, and we are going to end Common Core. (Applause.)

We are going to stop federal overreach, and defend the God-given rights of every American family.

Just imagine what we could accomplish if we all started working together to **rebuild this nation**, the nation that we so dearly love. (Applause.)

Our jobs will come back home, our dying factories will

come roaring back to life. It will be a beautiful thing to watch. And this is what's going to happen in the United States of America, and it's going to happen soon. And it's actually already happening. (Applause.)

**Cities small and large will see a rebirth
of hope, safety and opportunity.
America's children will be taught to love their country
and take pride in our great American flag**. (Applause.)

And other countries -- and you see that happening -- will finally treat America, and our citizens, with the respect that our country and our citizens deserve. (Applause.)

**It's time for us all to remember that
we are one people,
with one great American destiny, and that
whether we are black or brown or white, we all bleed the
same red blood of patriots**. (Applause.)

**And we all share the same glorious freedoms of our
magnificent country.
We are all made by the same Almighty God.** (Applause.)

As long as we remember these truths, we will not fail.

*We will never fail.
We are Americans, and the future belongs to us.
The future belongs to all of you.*

So with hope in our souls, and patriotism in our hearts, I say these words to you tonight, **on 100 days of devotion, hard work, and love for our great country:**

Together, we will **Make America Strong Again**.
We will **Make America Wealthy Again**.
We will **Make America Prosper Again**.
We will **Make America Proud Again**.
We will **Make America Safe Again**.
And we will **Make America Great Again!**

[Photo: screengrab.]

Thank you. God bless you. (Applause.)

END
8:49 P.M. EDT

Sources

THE WHITE HOUSE
THE STATE DEPARTMENT (UNITED STATES)
DEPARTMENT OF DEFENSE (UNITED STATES) WEBSITE
YOUTUBE
THE INTERNET
ABC2NEWS
SCREENGRABS - VARIOUS GOVERNMENT + INTERNET

Sources

HTTPS://BEARSEARSCOALITION.ORG

HTTPS://BEARSEARSCOALITION.ORG/MEDIA-RESOURCES/
MAP OF THE PROPOSED SITE FROM THE
BEARS EARS COALITION

FULL CREDIT TO ALL PHOTOGRAPHERS FOR THEIR WORK IN
RELATION TO THE BEARS EARS CAMPAIGN
THEIR WORK IS ONLY
REPRODUCED FOR JOURNALISTIC AND EDUCATIONAL PURPOSES, AND
IN SUPPORT OF THE BEARS EARS CAMPAIGN

JOSH EWING - HORSECOLLAR GRANARY
BRUCE HUCKO - GRAND GULCH
TIM PETERSON - THE BEARS EARS BUTTES FRAMED WITH
SUMMER WILD FLOWERS
JONATHAN BAILEY - ROCK ART CEDAR MESA
JOSH EWING - PAINTED RUIN
AMANDA PODMORE - CEDAR MESA GRANARY
TIM PETERSON - VANDALIZED HAND PANEL - FS LANDS
GREG CHILD - HORSE PETROGLYPHS
TIM PETERSON - MANCOS MESA 3 - LIGHTHAWK
BRANT HART - EDGE OF MANCOS MESA
TIM PETERSON - MOQUI ROCK ART3
GREG CHILD - MANCOS MESA BROKEN POT
DON ROMMES - CEDAR MESA RUIN
JONATHAN BAILEY - SJR CORRIDOR
JOSH EWING - SPIRALS AND CACTUS